Imagining Adoption

Imagining Adoption
Essays on Literature and Culture

Edited by
Marianne Novy

Ann Arbor
THE UNIVERSITY OF MICHIGAN PRESS

First paperback edition 2004
Copyright © by the University of Michigan 2001
All rights reserved
Published in the United States of America by
The University of Michigan Press
Manufactured in the United States of America
♾ Printed on acid-free paper

2007   2006   2005   2004   5   4   3   2

A CIP catalog record for this book is available from the British Library.

Library of Congress Cataloging-in-Publication Data applied for

ISBN 0-472-11181-7 (cloth : alk. paper)

ISBN 0-472-03002-7 (pbk : alk. paper)

Contents

Acknowledgments   vii

Introduction
Imagining Adoption   1
Marianne Novy

Adoption and the "Improvement of the Estate" in
Trollope and Craik   17
Tess O'Toole

Adoption in *Silas Marner* and *Daniel Deronda*   35
Marianne Novy

Outlaws, Outcasts, and Orphans
The Historical Imagination and *Anne of Green Gables*   57
Beverly Crockett

Redefining "Real" Motherhood
Representations of Adoptive Mothers, 1900–1950   83
Julie Berebitsky

From Charlotte to the Outposts of Empire
Troping Adoption   97
Beverly Lyon Clark

The Immaculate Deception
Adoption in Albee's Plays   111
Garry Leonard

"I Am Your Mother; She Was a Carrying Case"
Adoption, Class, and Sexual Orientation in Jeanette
Winterson's *Oranges Are Not the Only Fruit*   133
Margot Gayle Backus

A Junction of Amends
Sandra McPherson's Poetics of Adoption   151
Jan VanStavern

Adoption, Identity, and Voice
Jackie Kay's Inventions of Self   171
Nancy K. Gish

Genealogy Revised in *Secrets and Lies*   193
Paris De Soto

Natural Bonds, Legal Boundaries
Modes of Persuasion in Adoption Rhetoric   207
Judith Modell

"File It under "L" for Love Child"
Adoptive Policies and Practices in the Erdrich Tetralogy   231
Jill R. Deans

Adoption as National Fantasy in Barbara Kingsolver's
Pigs in Heaven and Margaret Laurence's *The Diviners*   251
Kristina Fagan

Should Whites Adopt African American Children?
One Family's Phenomenological Response   267
Martha Satz

Incorporating the Transnational Adoptee   277
Claudia Castañeda

Select Bibliography   301

Contributors   305

Index   309

Acknowledgments

Although the contributors to this book vary greatly in their relationship to the adoptee search movement, this book would never have happened without that movement. Before discussing adoption in literature and culture could become a collective enterprise, adoption itself had to enter into public discussion. Two of the people who contributed most to that discussion, in both their books and their activism, are Jean Paton and Betty Jean Lifton. They both also took the time to give me individual advice in my search for birth parents, as I broke my own silence about adoption. Years later, Jean Paton made available to me the resources of her Museum of Orphanhood—her collection of books about adoptees and orphans, then in Colorado. More recently, Betty Jean Lifton read and commented on an earlier version of the introduction to this volume. Penny Partridge and Katie Lee Crane welcomed me to the 1993 American Adoption Congress meeting, my first, and shared their own writings and literary interests. Other adoptee activists who encouraged me and shared information, literary and otherwise, are Amy Jane Cheney, Janine Baer, William Gage (who maintains an on-line bibliography on adoption), Anne Steytler, and Jean Vincent (who has kept Pittsburgh Adoption Lifeline going for more than twenty years). Two other friends who helped by sharing memories of their own experiences with adoptive and foster families are Suzanne Polen and Jim Simmonds.

At the Modern Language Association Convention in Toronto, also in 1993, I met, for the first time, other literary academics interested in writing about adoption: Margot Backus, Jill Roberts (now Jill Deans), Eric Goodheart, Tanya Gardiner-Scott, and Giavanna Munafo. The support of Margot and Jill, especially, has been very important in the development of this volume. I came into contact with them, and with most of my contributors, because the MLA published in its newsletter my calls for papers on adoption in literature. The MLA also sponsored events that contributed to the essays here by Garry Leonard and Nancy Gish. I would like to thank the Three Rivers Adoption Council for the use of their library; Elizabeth Bartholet for sending me her book and other information; Wayne Carp, Judith Modell, and Maureen Molloy for copies of their articles; Meredith Skura and Heather Dubrow for their encouragement and letters (and Heather for a prepublication copy of her book chapter); Tess O'Toole for her comments on my introduction; and Carol Singley, founding cochair with me of the Alliance for the Study of Adoption, Identity, and Kinship, for much advice and help. Judith introduced me to LeAnn Fields, whose editorial support and advice have been crucial.

Acknowledgments are also due to Fred Small, Jackie Kay, and Sandra McPherson for permission to reprint their lyrics, interview, and poetry; to *Nineteenth-Century Literature* for permission to reprint Tess O'Toole's essay; and to the Center for Instructional Design and Distance Education of the University of Pittsburgh for help with photography.

Last, I would like to thank my husband and daughter, David and Liz Carrier, for their support in this project, and my two mothers, Dorothy Kern (1904–88) and Geraldine Govier, for their love.

Introduction

Imagining Adoption

Marianne Novy

In one of the most famous works of literature dealing with adoption, Oedipus remembers a strange event of his youth: "At a feast, a drunken man maundering in his cups / Cries out that I am not my father's son."[1] How can any man not be the son of his father? This memory sets forth a basic paradox of adoption: it establishes, whether legally or informally, a parental relationship that is not genetic, and thus it forces either a redefinition of parenthood or the definition of adoption as a pretense or fiction.[2] As the adoptee and poet Jackie Kay says, interviewed by Nancy Gish in this anthology, "It is different to grow up knowing that your mother is not actually your mother, and that your father is not actually your father, but nonetheless they are your mother and father."

Is an adoptive parent a real parent? If so, is a biological parent who does not nurture after birth really a parent? How does the biological mother's experience of pregnancy and birth—enforced nurturance—make her situation different from that of the biological father? Adoption makes ambiguous the definition of parenthood and of such other important terms as *family, kinship,* and *identity,* as well as *father* and *mother.*

Many well-known works of literature have plots that turn on the definition of parenthood. After discovering birth parents, Oedipus thinks of them as his parents, and, less tragically, so does Perdita in Shakespeare's *Winter's Tale.*[3] But in such novels as *Silas Marner, Oliver Twist, Anne of Green Gables,* and, more recently, *The Bean Trees,* the ending is the confirmation of adoptive parenthood. These examples suggest three mythic stories that European and American cultures have typically used to imagine adoption: the disastrous adoption and discovery, as in *Oedipus,* the happy discovery, as in *Winter's Tale,* and the happy adoption, as in the novels mentioned.[4]

These stories are myths because of the way they act as paradigms (though they conflict) to shape feelings, thoughts, language, and even laws about adoption. In the two versions of the search story, the birth parents are clearly the "real parents." In the happy adoption story, the birth parents may exist in memory, but no matter how important this memory is, as in *Oliver Twist,* it does not constitute a living complication to the reconstructed family. All three myths assume that a child has, in effect, only one set of parents. To many readers, this will seem like an inevitable axiom. But for others—including many adoptees—it is not necessarily so obvious.

Although these are the dominant paradigms through which our culture has traditionally tried to imagine adoption, much literature complicates them considerably, as essays in this book will show. Even the works I mention have more dimensions to their analyses of adoption. Some of the literature and media representations discussed in this anthology follow these dominant plots; others, however, look at them obliquely, examine their cost, follow their characters after their supposed end, or play off against readers' expectations, explicitly dramatizing deviation from them. One of the purposes of the book, indeed, is to emphasize how much variety is possible in ways of imagining adoption, even though many of the same conflicts recur in different contexts.

Why has adoption figured so importantly in literature? First, as I have been suggesting, adoption plots dramatize cultural tensions about definitions of family and the importance of heredity.[5] These tensions, which also appear in recent controversies over such books as *The Bell Curve* and *The Nurture Assumption,* have special relevance for adoptees.[6] Questions about whether adoptees need knowledge of their ancestry, about whether it is healthy or possible for a birth mother to put the memory of a relinquished child behind her and what her privacy rights are, and about whether birth or nurture is more important in cases of disputed custody, all now being debated in legislative sessions and in courts, are also at issue in such novels as *Silas Marner, Great Expectations,* and *Bleak House.*

Furthermore, representing adoption is a way of thinking about the family, exploring what a family is, that is at the same time a way of thinking about the self, exploring distance from the family. While both of the happy-ending stories celebrate the family, that celebration is ambivalent. As Freud discussed in his theory of the family romance, for most people—nonadopted people—the fantasy of discovering that they were adopted and can be reunited with a different family elsewhere is a way of dealing with negative feelings about their parents.[7] The same could be said, even more emphatically, about the fantasy of being an orphan who is then happily adopted. And the more interesting the outsider in literature that follows the disastrous adoption plot, the more that plot too deals with ambivalence about the family—as in *Oedipus,* where the hero is determined to find the truth about his parents and discovers that he has destroyed them. In each story, one set of parents is erased—either the biological parents, whose death generates the need for adoptive parents, or the adoptive parents, who are superseded when the biological parents return.

In literature about adoption particularly close to these fantasies, the superseded parents are often stereotyped—in one version of polarities the birth parents are irrational and irresponsible, in another the birth parents are warm while the adoptive parents are cold. These stereotypes, closely related to images of fertility and infertility as well as to class, weigh more heavily on female characters—the ready-made dichotomy (biology vs. culture) that adoption plots provide is particularly useful for dealing with ambivalence about women. Another stereotype found in some literature related to the disastrous adoption story, such as *Wuthering Heights* or P. D. James's *Innocent Blood,* is the pathological, antisocial adoptee. This stereotype, as Katarina Wegar discusses, emphasizes the importance of blood ties and the disruptive influence of alien heredity, and it assumes "that the adoptee is doomed to stand outside the natural order of things."[8]

Adoption involves many other social issues. Novels in which the happy ending is an adoption, such as *Oliver Twist,* often attack the stigma of illegitimacy and the treatment of the poor. Adoption often implicates in each other's lives people from groups usually widely separated—frequently by economics, sometimes by ethnicity, and increasingly by nation of birth. Its use in fiction can structure an exploration of their contrasting lifestyles and can protest against their split and/or against the victimization of one group by the other. *Silas Marner* uses adoption in part to protest the class divide in England; this issue is at the center of the recent British musical *Blood Brothers,* in which a rich family adopts one of a pair of poor twins. The utopian ending of the American musical *Ragtime* involves adoption of the black orphan Coalhouse Junior by the WASP Mother and the Jewish Tateh. In the film *Secrets and Lies,* a black adoptee's meeting with her white birth mother helps a whole family bridge gaps of race and economic position. In *Daniel Deronda,* the search for a birth parent involves the search for a cultural history, for a usable past, for the imagined community of a nation.

Surprisingly few literary critics have previously considered literary representations of adoption. More have written about the orphan or the bastard, but such discussions miss the adoptee's specific condition—the relation to two different kinds of parents.[9] And precisely because adoption is so useful a plot device for dramatizing issues like familial ambivalence or class or race relations, previous literary critics have been more apt to look *through* adoption in literature, rather than *at* it.[10] Only a handful have considered literary images in relation to the institution of adoption itself.[11] The writers whose books thus far contain the most wide-ranging references to adoption in literature are not literary critics but pioneering adoptee activists for open records, Betty Jean Lifton and Jean Paton. This anthology is the first extended attempt to look at a group of portrayals of adoption together, along with other examples of adoption discourse. Thus, it begins to identify a group of writings that could be called the literature of adoption and to explore what concerns and motifs these writings share and what issues they debate.[12] To begin this project of analyzing representations of adoption, we must briefly survey some of the changes in how adoption has functioned in history.

Recent historical work has shown how much adoption itself has differed in different times and cultures. John Boswell's *The Kindness of Strangers*, examining a vast quantity of documentary material, concludes that in ancient Rome, as well as medieval Europe, an enormous number of children were exposed with the expectation that strangers would adopt them informally, usually raising them without informing them of their birth.[13] In another Roman mode of adoption discussed by Boswell, the relation of "alumnus" to foster parent was idealized—hence universities today use the term *alumnus* to emphasize continuing relationships with their graduates. (Imagine how different a "Yale Adoptee Association" would sound from the "Yale Alumni Association"!) Roman adults could also be legally adopted as a way of continuing a family line. Although legal adoption disappeared, other forms of surrogacy continued or developed. Renaissance England's child raising involved not only wet-nursing but also what has been called "a mass exchange of adolescent children," including fostering out, apprenticeship, service, and wardship.[14] Kristin Gager's *Blood Ties and Fictive Ties* explores notarized adoption contracts in sixteenth-century France, a time and place when adoption was long believed by historians not to exist.[15] Two centuries later, the French revolutionary government, during its most radical period, encouraged adoption to eradicate class differences. As Wayne Carp notes, in a number of islands in the South Pacific today, "adoption is common, public, casual, and characterized by partial transfer of the adopted child to the new family and dual parental rights and obligations. . . . it is common for adopted children to maintain a relationship with their biological parents."[16] Similar characteristics occur in informal adoptions among many indigenous people in the United States and New Zealand, as well as among some African Americans.

In the United States, adoption was first formalized as a legal procedure with concern for children's welfare in the nineteenth century, in Massachusetts in 1851.[17] During the second half of the century, almost every state legalized civil adoption—by contrast, Britain did not legalize it until 1926. Informal adoptions existed in both England and America before and during the time that adoption was legally formalized, but the delay in its legalization in England did reflect a difference in national values: in Dinah Craik's English novel *King Arthur: Not a Love Story* (1886), an American doctor says, "In my country, where every man stands on his own feet, where we have neither the curse of primogeniture, nor the burthen of hereditary rank, any respectable person, or any married couple, agreeing together, can legally adopt a child."[18] Carp shows that most of the twentieth century adoption laws in America assumed that adoptees would eventually be allowed to learn the names of their birth family, although this policy gradually changed. Rickie Solinger's *Wake Up Little Susie: Single Pregnancy and Race before Roe v. Wade* discusses how interest in adoption increased after World War II and how it was structured by race, being seen as appropriate for white unwed mothers but not for black ones (although black families frequently practiced informal adoption).[19]

In the kind of adoption dominant in the mid–twentieth century in both America and England, the background of the plays of Albee (as discussed by Garry Leonard in this anthology), and the novels of Winterson (as discussed here by Margot Backus), adoptees could learn little or nothing about their heredity. Closed adoption—its symbol the birth certificates that replaced the original names with the adoptive parents' names—went virtually unchallenged. Often, adoptees and their parents were expected to be silent about the very fact that they were an adoptive family. If adoption agencies succeeded in their ideal of matching the appearance of new parents and children, the adoption might well be invisible.

This history of silence and invisibility has made it difficult for members of the adoption triangle to form a community or communities. Unlike many minority groups, neither adoptees nor adoptive parents necessarily grow up among, raise children with, or wish to socialize with others in their category. Birth parents have been brought together in unwed mothers' homes, and adoptive parents in preadoption classes, but these experiences have, until recently, not formed continuing groups. Because their relation to adoption has been associated with loss and even with stigma, adoptees and adoptive and birth parents have generally been, for the most part, isolated and fragmented in this aspect of their identity. (Thus, the versions of adoption that they have seen in literature may have been particularly important to them.)

In the 1950s, since adoptees were isolated and generally silent about their feelings and even about their adoptive status, for an American adoptee to be curious about heredity seemed an individual idiosyncrasy; in subsequent decades, it was to be part of the adoptees' rights movement, related to a greater interest in minority history, racial identity, and ethnicity around the world.[20] In the 1970s, when for the first time a number of adoptees began to write publicly about their search for their biological ancestors, the models of decolonization and the black search for a heritage had prepared the way for some understanding in a wider audience.[21] As a result of international activism, adoptees in many countries have a regular procedure for learning the names of their birth parents, at a specified age (for example, eighteen in England, according to a law established in 1975); in the United States, as I write, only six states (Alabama, Oregon, Tennessee, Alaska, Delaware, and Kansas) officially have open records, but a number of adoptees from other states have managed to find out more about or meet their birth parents. In another significant change, in "open adoption" some adoptees are brought up with knowledge of their birth parents from the beginning.[22]

In the past thirty years, because of both the adoptees' rights movement and the increased number of international and transracial adoptions, adoption has become much more visible.[23] Changes in language have marked some of its changing status. Betty Jean Lifton wrote, at the beginning of her influential autobiography *Twice Born:* "The adopted child can never grow up. Who ever heard of an *adopted adult?*"[24] Now new words and phrases have come into use. *Adoptee* can refer to either a child or an adult. *Birth parents* and especially *birth mother* provide a way to avoid such terms as *real parents* or *natural parents* (with their apparent assumptions that adoptive parents are unreal or unnatural), while sounding less detached than *biological parents* or *genetic parents.* This anthology's discussions of the poetry of Sandra McPherson and Jackie Kay, the film *Secrets and Lies,* the rhetoric of the search movement, Barbara Kingsolver's novel *Pigs in Heaven,* and interracial adoption deal with this new world of adoption. Now, not only have adoptees organized to open records, but also birth mothers have formed continuing groups, and adoptive parents sometimes meet together to provide mutual support. Many local groups include members from different parts of the triad; the American Adoption Congress, which according to its mission statement seeks to promote "honesty, openness and respect for family connections," is an umbrella organization for those affected by adoption and for adoption professionals.

Yet adoptees vary in their attitudes toward open records (as do birth parents and adoptive parents), and at least one organization, the National Committee for Adoption, opposes such openness. Adoption today exists at the intersection of many contested issues. I have already mentioned the meaning of heredity, the meaning of family, the structure of identity. Let me add the role of culture as distinct from heredity, the rights of children, the rights of parents, the relation of the individual to group membership, the rights of minorities, the rights of poor people, the role of the state in social engineering. We can expand the central questions: Are one's identity and real family determined primarily by heredity, primarily by nurture, by both, by an idiosyncratic mix that differs for each person, or by neither? Is parenthood determined by genetics? By pregnancy and childbirth? By the work of child care? By fighting to have, keep, or reclaim a child? By not fighting, if it might hurt the child, as in the judgment of Solomon? By the child's best interest, as determined by a court? By the meaning those involved give to their biological link or child care? By the child's preference? What criteria of a good family are relevant in custody battles? Should disabled and gay people have the right to adopt? Should more effort be given to finding adoptive homes for children in troubled homes or to preserving the biological family? How important is the right to privacy of a birth parent or adoptive parent in comparison with the adoptee's right to acknowledgment, information about their heredity, or medical information? What if it's the birth parent who wants a meeting? If the adoptee is entitled to information and a meeting when adult enough, what is the age? What is the relation of an adoptee to adoptive parents' ethnicity? Are there some races or ethnicities that, because of their social oppression, cultural history, and physical identifiability, should always prevail in an adoptee's self-definition? Which should have precedence, the need to keep children with their racial/ethnic group or the need to find them a stable adoptive home? Are international adoptions exploitative or helpful? Answering these questions is far beyond the scope of this anthology. I list them here to indicate the range and significance of the issues that the representations of adoption discussed here raise. How adoption is represented in the literature and media people see affects how they will answer these questions; even if they experience adoption in their own lives, the way they experience it—and the ways they imagine the experience of those at other positions in the adoption triad—may be shaped in part by the cultural images of adoption they know.

It is part of the general ambiguity surrounding adoption that no one knows how many people are personally affected by the institution. For 1992, the most current information available at this writing, the National Adoption Information Clearinghouse cited a figure of 127,441 children adopted in the United States (42 percent of them by biologically related family members or by stepparents) and estimates that between 2 and 4 percent of American families include an adopted child.[25] Such figures, of course, would not include people who were informally adopted. Unlike many other kinds of minority groups, adoptees, adoptive parents, and birth parents still maintain enough confidentiality that the results of questions about these issues on the 2000 census long form may well be highly unreliable, and though the Department of Health, Education, and Welfare kept annual statistics on adoptions between 1951 and 1975, this practice has ended. The peak rate of unrelated domestic adoptions involved eighty to ninety thousand every year in the late 1960s and early 1970s.

The most obvious causes of the recent decline are the 1973 *Roe v. Wade* decision legalizing abortion, the relative destigmatization of bearing children out of wedlock, and the development of new reproductive technologies, such as artificial insemination and surrogate motherhood (to which many of the controversies around adoption are also relevant). By contrast to the number of whites seeking to adopt, relatively few healthy white infants are available for adoption now in the United States—a relatively larger number of adopters now look either for international adoption or for older children, often "special needs" children with serious emotional and/or physical problems. In the United States, more pregnant women who plan to relinquish their children are able to choose among several potential adoptive families. The availability of children for international adoption, which is much more expensive, often varies according to fluctuations or surges in countries' nationalistic interest in keeping their own.

The recent increase in international adoption makes it especially obvious that the adoptive relation evokes the quintessentially North American issue of communicating culture across bloodlines, which these days is also a European issue. Immigrants have often been referred to as America's adopted children;

their teachers and their government deal with some of the same issues about accepting otherness that face adoptive parents. Optimism about how well adoption can work, as about Americanization, can be based on a belief in the universal similarity of human nature and in its infinite malleability, as suggested by Castañeda, but it need not be. The attempt to define America as a culture of pluralism and diversity, in Henry Louis Gates's phrase "a conversation among different voices," parallels the attempts by many transcultural adopters today to learn from and celebrate the culture of their child's birth parents.[26] Several contributors to this volume trace the historical development of attitudes toward adoption and acculturation: Julie Berebitsky quotes a 1916 physician's wife praising adoption as a way to Americanize children; Jill Deans shows how Erdrich can present adoption as a way for U.S. policy to erase tribal identity; Kristina Fagan and Claudia Castañeda examine more thoroughly the colonizing dimensions of adoption. These essays make it clear that adoption is not simply a metaphor for intercultural relations; it is a process in which they are often very much implicated.

The essays included here and the writers discussed in them take widely different perspectives on the contested issues involved in adoption. The anthology has greater range not just because of its historical and cultural scope but also because some of the essays are more concerned with adoptees, some with adoptive parents, some with the institution. That the representation of birth parents is not the dominant concern of any essay here is symptomatic of a problem in the field—birth parents are invisible when adoption works as it was long expected to work.[27] However, the essays on Eliot, Winterson, Erdrich, Kay, McPherson, and *Secrets and Lies* deal in part with how birth parents are imagined. Tensions within the anthology, between essays prioritizing these different concerns, enact some of the tensions that constitute adoption as a field of study.

Identity is a repeated concern of the anthology: identity issues for the adoptee are the subject, for example, of Leonard's essay on Albee, Jan VanStavern's on McPherson, Paris De Soto's on *Secrets and Lies,* Nancy Gish's on Kay, my own on Eliot, and Modell's on the rhetoric of adoptee rights activists. In some essays identity is seen as primarily biological (or primarily affected by a cultural stress on heredity) and therefore especially problematic for the adoptee because it is unknown in a time of closed records. This is the context for the identity confusion of the adoptee in Albee's works. If heredity is known and/or if nurture is seen as at least equally important, a different set of questions about identity confront the adoptee, as in *Secrets and Lies,* Eliot, McPherson, Kingsolver, Laurence, and Kay. Sometimes the adoptee finds birth parents similar to her, as in McPherson's poetry; sometimes heredity reveals mainly difference, as in *Secrets and Lies.* In all cases identity is complex. Several of the contributors included here suggest that adoptees may respond to their awareness of another possible family by developing an especially vivid imagination; this theme occurs in discussing both adoptee writers (McPherson, Kay, and Winterson) and fictional adoptees created by others (Anne of Green Gables and Daniel Deronda).

However, all members of the adoption triangle can be seen as deviating from norms in some way. A question touched on in many essays is how much to emphasize the difference between adoptive and biological families and how much to emphasize their similarities.[28] Identity can be an issue for all positions. Berebitsky's essay deals with how adoptive mothers between 1900 and 1950 wrote about themselves; Martha Satz's analyzes how members of a (transracial) adoptive family negotiate their identities today. Closely linked with these identity concerns are the essays that deal with representations of the conflicting claims of biological and adoptive parenthood, such as those of Backus and Modell.

Some essayists, such as Tess O'Toole, Beverly Clark, and Julie Berebitsky, discuss texts in which adoption is seen as a personal and social good. Others, such as Castañeda, Backus on Winterson, Leonard on Albee, and Kristina Fagan on Kingsolver and Laurence, discuss adoption as psychologically and/or culturally repressive through commodification, use of the adoptee as a fantasy space, and international/interracial power structures. Beverly Crockett discusses adoption as sometimes commodifying and sometimes beneficial; Deans finds it sometimes subversive and sometimes restrictive in Erdrich. Backus and Castañeda analyze situations in which adoptive parents are represented as feeling the same way as do some of the adoptive parents discussed by Berebitsky and Clark, yet Backus and Castañeda look critically at the consequences for the adoptee. Castañeda criticizes a utopian image of transracial adoption in Elizabeth Bartholet rather similar to the one Fagan criticizes in Kingsolver.

Though this collection treats male adoptees in Albee and George Eliot, adoptive fathers in Eliot and Trollope, and a birth father in Eliot, and although some authors discuss both birth or adoptive parents, most of the essays deal primarily not only with female authors but also with female adoptees, birth mothers, and/or adoptive mothers. This is probably not just an arbitrary emphasis or an accidental result of my interest in feminist criticism. Adoption is a more salient issue for women since family membership is in general more salient for women. Birth (inevitably) and relinquishing for adoption and choosing to adopt (in our culture) have been issues more for women than for men.[29] When a girl thinks about her birth mother or about her adoptive mother, it is much more likely to be with the thought that she could be in their situation than when a boy does. Many more female than male adoptees seek changes in the current American system by joining such groups as the American Adoption Congress or the Adoptees' Liberty Movement Association and/or seeking their birth parents.[30] Insofar as it is possible to collect statistics about this, it seems that many more birth mothers than birth fathers seek to meet their adopted-away children as adults and welcome meetings when they are sought.[31] Thus, the emphasis on representations of women in the anthology may reflect both demography and the cultural associations that in part create that demography.

The insight that these essayists give us into the complex history of how adoption has been imagined comes in part from many other issues they bring into play. The essayists pay attention to issues of racial/ethnic difference (see Clark, Deans, Gish, Satz, De Soto, Novy, Fagan, and Castañeda) as well as to structures of gender and sexuality, with special reference to constructions of infertility and of maternal instinct (see especially Berebitsky and Backus). They concern themselves with different kinds of adoption (informal/formal; infant/older child; open records/closed records; domestic/transnational). They show the implications of laws about who is allowed to adopt (see Berebitsky, Backus, Satz, and Castañeda). They show adoption working to reinforce traditional heterosexual and gender images in the adoptee and the adopter (see Backus), though they also suggest that it can deconstruct compulsory reproductive heterosexuality (see Castañeda). They trace varying manifestations of cultural stigma on adoption and illegitimacy (see Crockett and Leonard). They show different and even opposing images of reunion with birth relatives (VanStavern, De Soto, Modell, Novy). In essays on Albee, Kay, and McPherson, they analyze how treatment of many other issues can be seen as transformations of writers' experiences as adoptees.

We can see a hint of the ambiguity of the institution in the recurring images for adoption that some of the essays present. Deans and Clark emphasize that in the works they discuss, adoption is a way of connecting—an image made most vivid in the web spun by the spider found both as White's Charlotte and in Erdrich's Indian mythology; O'Toole repeats the theme of adoption as connection with regard to some of the novels she discusses. But one of O'Toole's other themes closely relates to the emphasis of those writers more critical of adoption. She compares adoption to "the remaking of the world in which fiction engages." For Backus and Castañeda, however, the image of adoption as a rewriting of history (the adopters', the adoptee's, and the birth parents') has more negative implications than in the novels O'Toole examines. The concealment of one part of their past and its replacement by another is indeed the basis of the complaints against the closed-record system that are made by the adoptees whose rhetoric Modell studies. In this system, adoption is a making of one set of connections and the denial of another set. In a few of the works discussed in this anthology, that concealment is undone and the adoptee regains knowledge of the apparently erased story; the process of making connections returns, but this time it is the birth relatives with whom connections are made.

To rephrase the question posed at the beginning of this essay, does adoption make a real family or a fictive one? Perhaps it does both. Perhaps there is a way to discuss family that breaks down this dichotomy. Relations of adoption are constructed relationships—at least in that sense, they are fictions. But there is a sense in which the relationship of a parent and child who have always been together, as well as of a reunited birth parent and child, is also a constructed relationship—one built up out of many small interactions. We are used to the idea that mothering is a continuous activity of nurturance—not just childbearing. In her book *Kinship with Strangers,* Modell argues that openness in adoption is forming the basis for a new American system, "in which the significance of *work* in kinship will increase" and "genealogy is only one way of constructing parenthood."[32] Sara Ruddick, developing the concept of "maternal work," goes so far as to say, "all mothers are 'adoptive.' . . . Even the most passionately loving birthgiver engages in a social, adoptive act when she commits herself to sustain an infant in the world."[33] If Modell is right, then Ruddick's claim may become more widely accepted.

For many adoptees, connections with their birth family are fictional in a different sense; they have little or no information and so they make up fantasies about their birth parents. Arguably, adoptees ultimately construct a different kind of genealogy for themselves in determining what is meaningful to them in both their families as they know and imagine them, somewhat as writers construct their genealogies by their use of literary traditions.[34] Perhaps we can lessen the contrast between adoptees and others here too. The enterprise of imagining and claiming a lost familial past is not unique to adoptees; anyone who thinks about her (or his) family's earlier life and ancestry eventually asks questions that have no clear answers and must decide what meaning she gives her connection to family.[35] Indeed, for many orphans, refugees, and others whose loss of familial past is accompanied by much more material loss than most adoptees experience, adoptees' consciousness of difference may seem like a luxury. And the fictions that adoptive and birth parents may make about their adopted child's heredity or their birth child's life have some parallels in the fictions that other parents make about their children, whose lives they can never entirely know.

Still, a family connected by love, effort, habit, and adoption papers (or an informal agreement) *is* different in some ways from one connected by love, effort, habit, and heredity. Knowing that you share an interest with a parent who raised you is different from hypothesizing something shared with a birth parent about whom you have little or no information. Meeting a birth parent for the first time since infancy is different from reuniting with a parent after an alienation during adulthood. And yet the range of variations within adoptive families, and within adoptee–birth parent relations, is probably as great as the range of variations within any other kind of kinship. I hope that this anthology will begin to give a sense of how these differences and these variations have been imagined.

Proposals by the 1996 Congress to remove children from "unfit" mothers and to increase the stigma on illegitimacy show how much adoption practices are interwoven with other aspects of our culture. To some, adoption may seem a simple solution for social problems; but however much the contributors to this book and the authors discussed in this book represent varying views on adoption, none of them thinks it is simple. The techniques of literature and of literary and cultural analysis facilitate exploring its complexity.

NOTES

1. Sophocles, *Oedipus Rex*, in *The Oedipus Cycle*, trans. Dudley Fitts and Robert Fitzgerald (New York: Harcourt, Brace, and World, 1939), 40. David Grene's translation (1954; reprint, New York: Washington Square, 1967) has, instead, "accused me in his drink / Of being bastard" (45). The key word in the original is *plastos*, which is translated as "invented, fabricated, supposititious" by R. D. Dawe in the notes to line 780 on p. 171 in his edition (Cambridge: Cambridge University Press, 1982). See Pietro Pucci, *Oedipus and the Fabrication of the Father* (Baltimore: Johns Hopkins University Press, 1992), 99–100.

2. *Fiction* is the word chosen to describe adoption by J. S. Maine in *Ancient Law* (London: J. Murray, 1861), 239, and, following him, Judith Modell in *Kinship with Strangers: Adoption and Interpretations of Kinship in American Culture* (Berkeley: University of California Press, 1994), 2. The informed adoptions dealt with in this anthology can also be, and sometimes are, discussed as "foster parenting."

3. I discuss adoption in Shakespeare in "Multiple Parenting in Shakespeare's Romances," in *Domestic Arrangements*, ed. Kari McBride (Pittsburgh: Duquesne University Press, 2001); and in "Multiple Parenting in *Pericles*," in *Pericles: Critical Essays*, ed. David Skeele (New York: Garland, 2000). See also Heather Dubrow, *Shakespeare and Domestic Loss: Forms of Deprivation, Mourning, and Recuperation* (Cambridge: Cambridge University Press, 1999).

4. The happy and disastrous adoption stories correspond approximately to the two kinds of adoption novels identified by Patricia Howe in "Fontane's 'Ellernklipp' and the Theme of Adoption," *Modern Language Review* 79 (1984): 121, and developed further by Tess O'Toole in "Adoption and the 'Improvement of the Estate' in Trollope and Craik," in this collection. Howe suggests that disastrous adoption plots are more frequent in German literature than in English.

5. Katarina Wegar (*Adoption, Identity, and Kinship* [New Haven: Yale University Press, 1997], 99) views images of adoption in literature and popular culture "in terms of a deep-rooted ambivalence regarding the nature of family bonds." However, Elizabeth Bartholet (*Family Bonds: Adoption and the Politics of Parenting* [Boston: Houghton Mifflin, 1993], 164–86) sees our culture as stigmatizing adoption.

6. In *The Nurture Assumption* (New York: Simon and Schuster, 1998), Judith Rich Harris argues for the importance of heredity and peer environment as opposed to parental environment. She frequently refers to her adopted daughter and to adoption studies. In *The Bell Curve* (New York: Free, 1994), Richard J. Herrnstein and Charles Murray argue, overall, the importance of heredity but refer to adoption studies to support their argument that illegitimate children should be moved to better home environments. For a critique, see Valerie Hartouni, *Cultural Conceptions: On Reproductive Technologies*

and the Remaking of Life (Minneapolis: University of Minnesota Press, 1997). See also Barbara Katz Rothman, *Genetic Maps and Human Imaginations: The Limits of Science in Understanding Who We Are* (New York: Norton, 1998). Rothman, a medical sociologist, also discusses her experience as a mother by adoption and birth.

7. Sigmund Freud, "Family Romances," in *Complete Psychological Works*, trans. James Strachey (London: Hogarth, 1959), 9:237–41. Freud argues that these fantasies are also disguised ways of manifesting the child's affection for original parents, who can be seen as appearing in them exalted in rank.

8. Wegar, *Adoption, Identity, and Kinship*, 103. Use of the term *blood* with regard to biological kinship comes from the ancient (false) tradition that semen (once thought to be produced by both women and men) is refined blood. See Elise V. Lemire, "From Blood to DNA: The Failed Narratives of Interracial Kinship," paper delivered at MLA convention, Chicago, December 28, 1999; also Clara Pinto-Correia, *The Ovary of Eve: Egg and Sperm and Preformation* (Chicago: University of Chicago Press, 1997), 85–86. Rothman (*Genetic Maps*, 16), while pointing out the inaccuracy of this use of "blood ties" to refer to "genetic ties," emphasizes that pregnancy is a literal blood tie.

9. Some of the critics who have discussed related motifs in literature are Northrop Frye, in *The Secular Scripture: A Study of the Structure of Romance* (Cambridge: Harvard University Press, 1976) (mysterious birth); Edward Said, in *Beginnings: Intention and Method* (New York: Basic Books, 1975) (orphanhood); Peter Brooks, in *Reading for the Plot: Design and Intention in Narrative* (1984; reprint, Cambridge: Harvard University Press, 1992) (orphanhood and surrogacy); Marthe Robert, in *Origins of the Novel*, trans. Sacha Rabinovitch (Bloomington: Indiana University Press, 1980) (the bastard and the foundling); Marie Maclean, in *The Name of the Mother: Writing Illegitimacy* (London: Routledge, 1994); Alison Findlay, in *Illegitimate Power: Bastards in Renaissance Drama* (Manchester: Manchester University Press, 1994); and Michael Ragussis, in *Acts of Naming: The Family Plot in Fiction* (Oxford: Oxford University Press, 1988). Some adoptees self-identify as orphan or bastard; two adoptee organizations are named Orphan Voyage and Bastard Nation, and as Garry Leonard writes in his essay in this volume, attitudes toward bastardy are crucial to the history of adoption. However, the position of a person born to and raised by the same single mother is quite different from the position of one born outside of marriage and adopted by someone else.

10. For this distinction, I am indebted to Marjorie Garber. In *Vested Interests: Cross-Dressing and Cultural Anxiety* (New York: HarperPerennial, 1993), 389, she comments on how frequently cross-dressing is looked *through* rather than *at* in critical and cultural analysis.

11. One of the few books of literary criticism to include a historically informed study of literary representations of adoption is Marc Shell's *Children of the Earth: Literature, Politics, and Nationhood* (New York: Oxford University Press, 1993).

12. Two recent anthologies that collect—but do not analyze at length—the literature of adoption are *The Adoption Reader: Birth Mothers, Adoptive Mothers, and Adopted Daughters Tell Their Stories*, ed. Susan Wadia-Ellis (Seattle: Seal, 1995), and *A Ghost at Heart's Edge*, ed. Susan Ito and Tina Cervin (Berkeley: North Atlantic, 1999).

13. John Boswell, *The Kindness of Strangers: The Abandonment of Children in Western Europe from Late Antiquity to the Renaissance* (New York: Pantheon, 1988).

14. Lawrence Stone, *The Family, Sex, and Marriage in England, 1500–1800* (New York: Harper and Row), 107; see also Ilana Krausman Ben-Amos, *Adolescence and Youth in Early Modern England* (New Haven: Yale University Press, 1994), 54–64, and Paul Grif-

fith, *Youth and Authority: Formative Experiences in England, 1560–1640* (Oxford: Clarendon, 1996), 33.

15. Kristin Gager, *Blood Ties and Fictive Ties: Adoption and Family Life in Early Modern France* (Princeton: Princeton University Press, 1996).

16. E. Wayne Carp, *Family Matters: Secrecy and Disclosure in the History of Adoption* (Cambridge: Harvard University Press, 1998), 4.

17. Michael Grossberg, *Governing the Hearth* (Chapel Hill: University of North Carolina Press, 1985), 271–72.

18. Dinah Craik, *King Arthur: Not a Love Story* (London: MacMillan, 1886), 40, quoted by Tess O'Toole in her essay in this collection. See George Behlmer, *Friends of the Family: The English Home and Its Guardians* (Stanford: Stanford University Press, 1998), 272–300, on de facto adoption in England before 1926 and its abuses.

19. Rickie Solinger, *Wake Up Little Susie: Single Pregnancy and Race before Roe v. Wade* (New York: Routledge, 1992).

20. The first nonfiction book about adoptees' interest in their heredity was Jean Paton's *The Adopted Break Silence*, privately published in 1954. As she says in *Orphan Voyage* (1968; reprint, Cedaredge, Colo.: Country, 1980), after a few favorable reviews, "a great silence fell" (41).

21. When *Roots*, Alex Haley's book about finding his African ancestors, was televised, the article "Everybody's Search for Roots," *Newsweek* (July 4, 1977, 25–38), described it as expressing a widespread interest in family genealogy beyond the black community, with a sidebar about the developing adoptee search movement. See Carp, *Family Matters*, 164; the article is also part of my own file of clippings. See also Judith Modell's essay in this volume.

22. According to the National Adoption Information Clearinghouse (NAIC), a service of the Children's Bureau of the U.S. Department of Health and Human Services, 69 percent of public and private agency adoptions in recent years are open by their definition: the birth parents have met the adoptive couple. Modell's *Kinship with Strangers* describes a type of adoption much further on the spectrum of openness: "The exchange of a child by people who know one another, expect to have an ongoing relationship and to share a child" (16).

23. According to the NAIC, quoting figures from the U.S. State Department, between 1989 and 1998, intercountry adoptions to the United States per year increased from 8,102 to 15,774. For an overall picture of adoption in the United States today, see Adam Pertman, *Adoption Nation: How the Adoption Revolution is Transforming America* (New York: Basic, 2000).

24. Betty Jean Lifton, *Twice Born: Memoirs of an Adopted Daughter* (1975; reprint, New York: Penguin, 1977), 3. Jean Paton (*The Adopted Break Silence*) similarly made a point of using the phrases *adopted people* and *the adopted* instead of *adopted children*.

25. The NAIC cites K. S. Stolley, "Statistics on Adoption in the United States," *The Future of Children: Adoption* 3 (1993): 26–42. Carp (*Family Matters*, 1, 239) quotes an estimate that 2 to 4 percent of the population (5 to 10 million people) are adoptees and cites a figure for 1990 of 118,779 domestic adoptions, of which he implies about half are between biologically related family members. His most specific figures come from the National Committee for Adoption.

26. Henry Louis Gates, *Loose Canons: Notes on the Culture Wars* (New York: Oxford University Press, 1992), 175. On transcultural adoption, see Drucilla Cornell, "Reimag-

ining Adoption and Family Law," in *Mother Troubles: Rethinking Contemporary Maternal Dilemmas,* ed. Julia E. Hanigsberg and Sara Ruddick (Boston: Beacon, 1999), 213–15. Imagery of adoption is also used of immigrants in Victorian England. See Edward Augustus Freeman, "Race and Language," *Contemporary Review* 29 (1877):711–41, reprinted in *Images of Race,* ed. Michael D. Biddiss (New York: Holmes and Meier, 1979), 214–35.

27. Many people currently writing about adoption in literature have identified themselves as adoptees or adoptive parents; some have identified themselves as not personally involved. No scholar on this topic has identified herself (or himself) as a birth parent. Perhaps the stigma is still greater for birth parents; perhaps their socioeconomic position (especially if they are women) is lower on the average and they are less likely to be in a position to do academic writing; perhaps the topic is either too distant from them or too painful to be dealt with academically. Experiences of birth parents are represented in *A Ghost at Heart's Edge* and *The Adoption Reader* and analyzed in Modell, *Kinship with Strangers;* Solinger, *Wake Up Little Susie;* and Anne Else, *A Question of Adoption* (Wellington, N.Z.: Bridget Williams, 1991). See also recent personal narratives such as Carol Schaefer, *The Other Mother: A Woman's Love for the Child She Gave Up for Adoption* (New York: Soho, 1991); Jan Waldron, *Giving Away Simone* (New York: Times, 1995); *Out of the Shadows: Birthfather Stories,* ed. Mary Martin Mason (Edina, Minn.: O. J. Howard, 1995); and Margaret Moorman, *Waiting to Forget* (New York: Norton, 1996).

28. This issue is discussed by H. David Kirk in *Shared Fate: A Theory of Adoption and Mental Health* (New York: Free, 1964), as well as by Wegar (*Adoption, Identity, and Kinship*), who uses the theories of Kirk and those Martha Minow develops in *Making All the Difference: Inclusion, Exclusion, and American Law* (Ithaca: Cornell University Press, 1990).

29. However, in classical Greece, where legal adoption was usually of adults, only men could adopt, and Shakespeare's plays focus more on men's feelings about lost and found children than on women's. Perhaps one of the reasons that George Eliot entered the literary canon earlier than most women writers is that she dealt with such issues as adoption with regard to men as much as with regard to women.

30. The newer Bastard Nation (founded in 1997) has attracted more male adoptees.

31. Wegar notes (*Adoption, Identity, and Kinship,* 63): "Adoptees who do search are predominantly white, middle-class females in early adulthood. . . . the overwhelming majority initiate the search for the biological mother." Wegar also emphasizes the overwhelming predominance of women among the biological parents who search. It is possible that there are more female adoptees than male in the United States, since adoptive parents often express preference for girls, and since in some of the cultures from which parents adopt, girls are more likely to be relinquished than boys.

32. Modell, *Kinship with Strangers,* 229 (emphasis Modell's), 238.

33. Sara Ruddick, *Maternal Thinking* (1989; reprint, New York: Ballantine, 1990), 51. Ruddick defines a mother as "a person who takes on responsibility for children's lives and for whom providing child care is a significant part of her or his working life" (40). Among the factors that contribute to her distinction of mothers from "birthgivers" (the term she uses instead of *birth mothers,* perhaps partly to emphasize that giving birth is a phase of experience also for those who will keep their children) is a desire to "empower birthing women while not detracting from the work of adoptive mothers" (49). Ruddick admits (40) that her definition, which includes males who are primary caretakers, is "somewhat

eccentric;" it is aimed at identifying a "distinctive thinking" involved in mothering. See also Mary Lyndon Shanley, "De-essentializing Family Ties: Feminist Reflections on Transracial and Open Adoption," paper delivered at NOMOS, Sept. 2, 1999. Thanks to Iris Young for a copy of this paper.

34. See my anthology *Women's Re-Visions of Shakespeare* (Urbana: University of Illinois Press, 1990) and my *Engaging with Shakespeare* (1994; reprint, Iowa: University of Iowa Press, 1998) for discussion of many women writers' claiming of Shakespeare as a literary ancestor.

35. See, for example, Stuart Hall, "Ethnicity, Identity, and Difference," *Radical America* 23, no. 4 (1989): 19. I thank Margot Backus for pointing me to this essay. Gates's interpretation in *Loose Canons* of black tradition and community as a story of "elective affinities, unburdened by an ideology of descent" (151) or "blood" (127) or "ancestral purity" (xvi) could provide another analogy for adoptees' connections with either their hereditary or their adoptive line. See also Mary Waters, *Ethnic Options* (Berkeley: University of California Press, 1990).

Adoption and the "Improvement of the Estate" in Trollope and Craik

Tess O'Toole

Adoption strives with nature and choice breeds
A native slip to us from foreign seeds.
   —Shakespeare, *All's Well That Ends Well*

Despite the Victorian novel's well-documented preoccupation with the tracing of origin and descent, a surprising number of family plots in novels of this period pivot on a disruption or alteration in the genealogical line, in the person of the adopted child. Heathcliff, the most notorious adoptee of the Victorian novel, illustrates a recurrent paradox: the family saga depends on the importation of the nonfamiliar to set in motion its own plot.[1] Nineteenth-century fiction engages in an affirmation of the family that is inseparable from the reconfiguration of the family it displays. The family's confrontation with or absorption of outside forces serves both narratological and ideological imperatives; while the introduction of an element of difference is a catalyst to plot, the family's reconstitution also allows the novelist to represent the broader social reconfigurations transforming Victorian society. Though the marriage plot is the novel's most familiar vehicle for reshaping the family, the adoption plot is a prominent alternative (and sometimes intersecting) paradigm.[2] The growing cultural currency of discourses of the family in the nineteenth century invested the traditional foundling plot with new potential.

In the family plots of Victorian fiction, orphans are taken in or children are removed from one family to another according to a wide variety of arrangements: in *Bleak House* (1852–53) Jarndyce becomes guardian to Esther Summerson; in *Great Expectations* (1860–61) Miss Havisham rears Magwitch's daughter, Estella, to enact her own revenge plot; in *Daniel Deronda* (1876) Sir Hugo Mallinger keeps his promise to Alcharisi to raise her son as an English gentleman in his own household; in *Doctor Thorne* (1858) the eponymous hero swears on the Bible that his brother's illegitimate daughter will be to him as his own child; in *Felix Holt* (1866) Reverend Lyon raises his French wife's child, Esther, as his daughter. The various natures of these "adoptions" reflect the fact that legal adoptions did not exist in England (until the passage of the Adoption Act in 1926), despite the fact that de facto adoption was not an uncommon prac-

17

tice in the nineteenth century.[3] The lack of a legal framework with which to legitimize an adoption made such reconfigurations of the family both more flexible and more tenuous than modern adoptions and, thus, arguably more closely aligned with fiction than would otherwise be the case. As a "jural fiction,"[4] moreover, even a legal adoption act shares some of the affinities to the fictive that Tony Tanner locates in marriage as a contractual rather than a sanguinally based form of kinship.[5] The reconfiguration of natural arrangements that adoption effects parallels the remaking of the world in which fiction engages; as Susan R. Cohen notes in an essay on *Silas Marner* (1861): "Adoption [is] a model for creative human action, for the power of human fictions to displace and reshape reality."[6] This description suggests why adoption, like marriage, is a privileged event in fiction.

The particular importance of adoption to the Victorian novel lies in adoption's relationship to the rather antithetical impulses that the Victorian family plot displays. The drive to preserve and defend the family and to safeguard its integrity is balanced by the need to revitalize the family, the need for blood regeneration. The adoption act is critically placed in relation to both of these imperatives. The adoptee can inject needed new material and vitality into the family; thus, in Dinah Craik's *King Arthur: Not a Love Story* (1866), the narrator comments on the adopted child: "Perhaps both his adopted parents loved him all the better for being so unlike themselves—for bringing into their quiet household new elements which otherwise would have been unknown there."[7] Alternatively, the adoptee can be the entirely unassimilable other whose difference threatens to destroy the family. These two possibilities accord with the comic and tragic paradigms that Patricia Howe identifies in the novel of adoption.

> Literary adoptions fall into two groups, those in which the adopted child not only flourishes in the care of its new parents, or more often parent, but consoles and redeems these parents, forging lost links with a wider world, with the world of nature and the community of men; and those [in which adoptees] bring chaos and disaster not only to themselves, indeed they may be least touched by them, but to those who take them into their families.[8]

In both kinds of adoption novels, however, the repercussions of the adoption act frequently extend beyond the family. Adoption can serve as a model—either metaphoric or prescriptive—for the regrouping of society. In Trollope's *Doctor Thorne*, adoption is the key to a social mobility that benefits not just the individual but the community at large.

While the many instances of adoption in the Victorian novel are no doubt symptomatic of the culture's faith in the family unit as the framework in which an individual might best develop, I am less interested in the child's experience of the remolding of his or her identity under adoption than I am in the re-molding of the family's character through the adoption act. I focus on the in-tersection of the comic adoption plot with the theme that Alistair M. Duck-worth, in his study of Austen, terms "the improvement of the estate."[9] The view of adoption as a means to restore the family and the estate recalls the fact that in the Roman empire, where legal adoption first flourished, the practice was motivated not by a concern with child welfare but by the imperative to control heirship: "Adoption was made use of for the purpose of handing on honours and estates to adopted children deemed more fitted to make good use of them than the natural children."[10] One of Seneca the Elder's *Controversiae* addresses the desire of a wealthy citizen to adopt a poor man's child after disinheriting his own sons; his position is explained thus: "That is how the nobility of the patri-cians has survived to this day from the founding of the city. Adoption is the rem-edy for Chance."[11] Likewise, in the Victorian adoption plots that I discuss here, the diversion of the genetic line serves a conservative agenda; the process of adoption safeguards the estate and, by extension, the nation.

Property issues loom large in Victorian adoption plots. In *Felix Holt,* for ex-ample, the most significant repercussion of the exposure of Esther Lyon's adop-tion is the fact that the Transomes might lose their estate. Heathcliff's scheme to take over family estates in *Wuthering Heights* (1847) reflects contemporary fears about the potential of adoption to disturb traditional inheritance patterns. Charlotte Yonge's 1859 adoption novel, *Hopes and Fears,* directly addresses this concern with adoption's impact on the transmission of property. The spinster heroine, who inherits adoptive children from one suitor and an estate from an-other (her cousin), feels that it would be unethical to leave the property to the adopted son she adores, because she received it in trust from someone unrelated to him. The potential of adoption to disrupt property transmission, "the fun-damental problem associated with the concept of legal adoption in [En-gland],"[12] contributed to the late advent of legal adoption there. (The first Adoption Act, passed in 1926, specified both that the adoptee would not lose rights of succession within the natal family and that the adoption would not au-tomatically accord the adoptee rights of inheritance in the adoptive family.) In a number of Victorian adoption plots, countermodels to *Wuthering Heights,* this concern over adoptees' potential to encroach on property is overridden by the fact that they turn out to be the most worthy stewards available for the fam-ily estate; these novels tend to demonstrate as well that it is the adoptions that have made them so. In the adoption plots I discuss below, the reconfiguration of the family through adoption ultimately serves the estate and the traditional values for which it stands.

In 1886, the popular novelist and conduct-book writer Dinah Mulock Craik, herself an adoptive mother, published a *roman à these* illustrating the advantages of wise adoption, a novel that, Sally Mitchell notes in her study of the author, is devised for the purpose of "reveal[ing] the problems caused by lack of an adoption law."[13] *King Arthur: Not a Love Story* tells the story of the Trevenas, a childless, middle-aged couple who adopt the unwanted infant son of a woman they encounter in a Swiss resort. A pitch for the institution of legal adoption is made through the character of the American doctor who delivers the baby and who negotiates his transfer from the negligent birth mother to the eminently maternal Susannah Trevena. Discussing the process by which she and her husband might take the child, the doctor informs them:

> In my country, where every man stands on his own feet, where we have neither the curse of primogeniture, nor the burthen of hereditary rank, any respectable person, or any married couple, agreeing together, can legally adopt a child . . . by presenting a petition to one of our courts of law, and after due examination of the parents, if alive and deserving, and of the child, if old enough, obtaining a decree of adoption which . . . makes it the adopting parents' lawful heir, and the real parents have no more right over it. (40)

Craik's novel addresses the widely held fears that fed the resistance to institutionalizing adoption. One of Austin Trevena's neighboring clergymen, for instance, castigates his colleague for "bringing a nameless child, possibly the offspring of sin and shame, into a respectable and above all a clergyman's household" and asks, "what would the Trevenas say?" (82). Trevena's profligate brother perceives the adopted child as a competitor, scolding his brother for taking in someone else's child when he has a blood relative who could use any money he has to spare.[14] On the part of the adoptive parents, too, there is an assumption that an adopted child's relationship to his parents' property is problematic. Arthur is expected to make his own way, through scholarships; though his adoptive mother dotes on him, she concedes: "Her husband in his old age would need all his own money; he must not be stinted in anything for the sake of a son—who was not his son. Passionately as she loved her boy, Susannah held the balance of justice even" (142). Even the doctor who advocated adoption tells the boy that his adoptive father's money should go to educating his niece rather than him, "because, you see, she is his own flesh and blood, and you—" (224). Fears about the potential of adoption to disrupt both bloodlines and property transmission are assuaged, however, by the success story of Arthur's adoption, which ultimately serves to revitalize both the families and the property.

Arthur is not illegitimate; rather, he is the legitimate son of a wealthy woman who bore him in secret and gave him away because she despised her husband and had no maternal feelings.[15] That husband, physically and morally weak, afraid of his devious wife but unaware of her deception, inherits the large estate in the Trevenas' neighborhood. When the truth about Arthur's parentage is made public on his natal father's death, Arthur becomes heir to the estate. His healthy body, sound mind, and virtuous character, all cultivated by the middle-class upbringing his adoption has secured him and all contrasting sharply with the characteristics of his father and of his aristocratic relatives, make him the best possible steward for the Damerel estate. When Arthur was a toddler, his true parentage still unknown, his adoptive mother compared him to the present Damerel heir: "Her boy, . . . , blossoming day by day into rosy infancy . . . , was happier than the heir of all the Damerels—a poor idiot, report said, never seen or heard of, whose family home was let, and the property put into Chancery, until his fortunate death cleared the way for some distant cousins, ready to fight over the title and estate like dogs over a bone" (89). The Damerel estate is restored by Arthur, who "conscientiously spen[ds] every forenoon in his study with his steward, repairing much evil that had come about in his father's days, and planning no end of good that was to be done in his own" (325). His qualifications are attributed to his adoptive upbringing; after Susannah Trevena has died, the narrator comments: "She had lived long enough to make her boy all that he was; to form his mind and character, heart and soul: to fit him for the aims and duties of life; high aims and serious duties, for Sir Arthur Damerel is not the sort of man to hide himself, or submit to be hidden under a bushel" (335). The adoption of Arthur has benefited not only the Damerel family but society at large. That Susannah named him after King Arthur, another foundling, drives home the point that Arthur's estate (located in Cornwall!) is to serve as a metonym for the nation. The nation will be healthier, Craik suggests, if adoption is institutionalized.

Arthur improves the Trevena family as well as the Damerels. Susannah is the last surviving member of her family, and her husband's family is in danger of dying out as well after the death of their infant son; his one brother's only child is a daughter. Arthur compares favorably not only with "the last of the Damerels" but with "the last of the Trevenas" as well—their mousy niece, Nanny, whom they take in after her mother dies.[16] Living in close proximity, Arthur and Nanny fall in love and marry; as in a number of adoption plots, the adopted child marries a member of the household, thus legalizing his or her place in the family. The understated Nanny blossoms when united to Arthur's brilliance, while her dutiful, self-effacing nature "give[s] the neighbourhood an entirely new and revised edition of the Lady Damerels of Tawton Abbas" (335). As a result of this match, Arthur's descendants are sanguinally linked to the Trevenas. A family relation that could not be ratified by law will now be ratified by blood. Still, the adoption is seen as essential in the process of generational transmission; as Susannah lies dying, our attention is called to the fact that her "influence" (rather than her husband's blood) "will descend" to Arthur's grandchildren (337).

While Sally Mitchell concludes that the revelation of Arthur's good birth and his inheritance of a handsome property have "the unfortunate effect of virtually destroying the story's point by making it seem that legitimate birth and inherited rank do matter a great deal after all" (*Dinah Mulock Craik,* 77–78), Arthur's inheritance in fact reinforces Craik's polemic in favor of adoption: it is Arthur's adoption that has made him a worthy heir to the estate. This equation between adoption and the improvement of the estate is enacted as well in a number of more complex nineteenth-century adoption novels. When Arthur's adoptive mother compares him to a trodden piece of sweet william that she rescued and planted and that flourished, Craik draws on a familiar trope linking two types of "cultivation"; as Patricia Howe notes: "Adoption is frequently seen as a process of domestication, running parallel to activities such as building and gardening. Successful adoptions become associated with civilized places, landscapes subtly ordered by man, whether they be great parks and houses . . . or tiny cottages and gardens" ("Fontane's 'Ellernklipp,'" 124). The metaphoric link between adoption and estate ordering works in harmony with the metonymic link between them that is forged when the adopted child becomes the key to the improvement of the estate.

While in *King Arthur: Not a Love Story* the heir to an estate must be adopted by another family to equip him to fulfill his birthright, in other adoption plots, such as *Mansfield Park* (1814) and *Doctor Thorne,* an estate is redeemed by an adopted child rather than by a member of the natal family. The difference in these cases is related to the gender of the protagonists. In *King Arthur* the mother frets over the fact that an adopted status is much more problematic for her son than it would have been for a daughter; she reflects that while "many a King Cophetua lives to bless the day he wooed his 'beggar-maid,' and especially if she has no blood relations" (146), a male's value cannot inhere to as great a degree in his individual self. The adoptive father in Trollope's novel shares Susannah Trevena's assumption about the difference gender makes; in an argument that recalls Mr. B.'s defense of his marriage to Pamela, Doctor Thorne comforts the illegitimate niece he has adopted by asserting: "A man raises a woman to his own standard, but a woman must take that of the man she marries."[17] It would appear, then, that due to the greater malleability of the female's class identity, female adoption plots are particularly fitted to serve the improvement of the estate theme. In *Doctor Thorne* the ideas of adoption as a civilizing process and of the female as a civilizing agent become intertwined. Civilization works both ways in the adoption in Trollope's novel; it is reflected not only in the nurturing and education the adopted child receives but also in the fact that the process of adopting a female child recivilizes her bachelor uncle, leading him literally to put his house in order.

> Mary was thirteen when she came to take up her permanent abode as mistress of the establishment. . . . This advent greatly changed the tenor of the

doctor's ways. He had been before pure bachelor; not a room in his house had been comfortably furnished. . . . He had had no fixed hour for his meals. . . . But when Mary came . . . things were altogether changed at the doctor's. People had hitherto wondered . . . how a gentleman like Dr. Thorne could continue to live in so slovenly a manner. . . . [But] the doctor made a thorough revolution in his household, and furnished his house from the ground to the roof completely. He painted . . . he papered, he carpeted, and curtained, and mirrored, and linened. . . . [W]hen Mary Thorne came home from her school at Bath . . . she found herself called upon to be the presiding genius of a perfect paradise. (38–39)

The achievement of domestic order in the doctor's household that is occasioned by the arrival of Mary, "the angel who gave to that home in Greshamsbury so many of the joys of Paradise" (175), is complemented by the greater social integration to which the adoption leads Thorne. He is a fitting adopter of the illegitimate child, for he is himself disenfranchised. It is not only his bachelorhood that reveals the doctor as a solitary figure. A member of his family's junior branch, "only a second cousin" to the Thornes of Ullathorne (20), he is estranged from his own relatives over a family quarrel. As a doctor, he occupies an ambiguous and marginal position within the social hierarchy of Barchester. He is in danger of misanthropic withdrawal from society at the point when the adoption of Mary gives him a domestic role and an incentive to participate in the community. The integration of Mary into the Thorne family via her adoption, then, also produces the social reintegration of the doctor. At another level, the adoption itself becomes the means to a renewed social cohesiveness; the twists in the inheritance plot serve this larger goal as much as they do Mary's individual happiness. Even the language Mary uses to articulate the nature of her relationship to the doctor—"people must be bound together" (153, 177)—refers as well to the connections on which social order rests.

Doctor Thorne pivots on the adoption of the illegitimate Mary, daughter of a wellborn but dissolute father and a working-class mother, by her uncle, the novel's eponymous hero. The narrative begins, however, not with an account of the child's genesis but rather with an account of a region's development. The region is agricultural Barsetshire, an area "no[t] so widely spoken of as some of its manufacturing leviathan brethren in the north, but . . . , nevertheless, very dear to those who know it well" (1), where "the town population of the county reckons for nothing" (2). The narrator's description becomes an occasion to extoll what he perceives as the traditional English way of life.

England is not yet a commercial country in the sense in which that epithet is used for her; and let us still hope that she will not soon become so. She might surely as well be called feudal England, or chivalrous England. If in western civilized Europe there does exist a nation among whom there are high signors, and with whom the owners of the land are the true aristocracy, the aristocracy that is trusted as being best and fittest to rule, that nation is the English. (12)

Signs of social change and division are present, however: the Reform Bill has divided Barsetshire into east and west, Tory and Whig, and one of the first families of East Barsetshire, the Greshams, can no longer feel themselves so secure in their stronghold as formerly; the old family motto, "Gardez Gresham" (11), no longer suggests "Beware of Gresham" so much as its alternate interpretation: "Beware, Gresham." This threat of decline is reflected in an instance of generational decline, for the current Squire Gresham has not been able to live up to the standard set by his father; assuming he would be a member of Parliament for Barsetshire all his life as his father before him was, he yet "failed to take any of the steps which had secured his father's seat" (5). His failure of stewardship is reflected in the fact that expenses relative to a rapidly expanding family, an extravagant wife, repeated lost elections for Parliament, and a stint as master of the hounds for the county have forced him to sell off part of the estate. The first episode in the novel is the coming-of-age of the squire's son; the celebration is notably smaller in scale than was his father's before him, and the villagers are no longer proud of their squire as they were at his twenty-first birthday. It is against this backdrop of a traditional order at risk and a failure of customary patterns of generational succession to secure it that the adoption plot featuring Mary Thorne is set.[18] Her adoption becomes intertwined with the recovery of the Greshamsbury estate; it is through the anomalies characterizing Mary's birth and nurture as well as the inheritance that is attendant on them that the family will be able to "gardez Gresham."[19]

The preservation of the Gresham's estate and name is inseparable from the preservation of a nameless child. Pitying both the "poor bastard whose father was already dead, and whose mother's family was such as the Scatcherds!" (29), and the betrayed mother whose only chance of social salvation hinges on her leaving her child to marry and emigrate with a worthy suitor of her own class, Doctor Thorne initially takes charge of the baby out of compassion and a sense of duty. That act of rescue ultimately becomes the means to complete another rescue in which Thorne is engaged—that of Greshamsbury. Thorne acts as the go-between in the financial negotiations in which Mary's uncle Roger Scatcherd (who has amassed a fortune as a railway contractor) buys a piece of the property that Gresham is forced to sell and advances Gresham money, with the estate as security. Purportedly a neutral mediator, Thorne has Gresham's best interests at heart; for instance, he convinces Scatcherd to advance further money without demanding the title deeds to Greshamsbury by saying, "I thought you would have done as much to oblige me" (170). When Scatcherd decides to leave his fortune, in the event of his son's death, to his sister's eldest child, Thorne insists on the more specific designation of that heir. While his ostensible motive is to ensure that Scatcherd does not unwittingly leave it to his illegitimate niece over his sister's eldest legitimate child, his intervention does ensure that Mary will incontestably inherit the fortune. When he arranges for the marriage of Mary and Frank Gresham (a betrothal accompanied by the return to the Greshams of the title deeds to Boxhall Hall as well as all of Scatcherd's claims on the rest of the estate, whose value cancels out the liability of Mary's illegitimacy), Thorne completes the act of preserving Greshamsbury for the Greshams. Thus, in Trollope's plot the salvation of the bastard baby and the salvaging of the estate are intertwined. Of course, Thorne's nurture of "his adopted bairn" (148) and the intimacy with the family circle at Greshamsbury that it has secured her have served to make that child into a suitable bride for Frank Gresham. Her eligibility for the role is ensured by one uncle's fortune and the other's adoption.

Mary's adoption not only makes upward mobility possible for her but also equips her for it. In his study of Trollope's novels, James Kincaid writes that *Doctor Thorne*, like *Framley Parsonage* (1861), involves "recruitment, bolstering the ranks of the good" (*Anthony Trollope,* 95). Specifically, the marriage of the younger Frank Gresham to the illegitimate Mary Thorne illustrates the self-preserving flexibility of the class system: "The outside world must in a limited way be incorporated in order to avoid contamination. The principle is that of vaccination, and Mary is the perfect vaccine" (ibid., 117). However, a prior act of "incorporation" and "vaccination," Mary's adoption, makes this one not only possible but desirable.[20] While Jane Nardin views marriage as the key to upward mobility in Trollope's novel,[21] mobility hinges more on the adoption than on the marriage; Mary's adoption secures her access to polite society and the breeding necessary to fulfill her role as mistress of Greshamsbury. Through his intervention in her history, Thorne ensures that Mary is raised with proper middle-class values and that she is kept quarantined from her working-class relatives: "Dr. Thorne, in undertaking to bring up the baby, did not choose to encounter any tie with persons who might hereafter claim to be the girl's relations on the other side" (*Doctor Thorne,* 28). While Thorne's adoption of Mary is ratified as a pact with the mother whom his brother had duped (Thorne urges her to emigrate with her loyal working-class suitor, promising her, "If you will go with this man I will be father . . . and mother to [your baby]" [27]), his adoption is contingent on the exile of the mother, who, like her daughter, is in a sense reborn at this juncture through Thorne's offices, marrying and starting a new family in America. Because of Thorne's intervention, Mary never meets her discredited mother. "Recruited" for the Thorne side of the family—and, ultimately, for the Greshams—Mary becomes the vehicle for the restoration of the estate in both a literal way, through her property, and a figurative way, through her qualities.[22]

That an adopted child should be the key to the preservation of Greshamsbury recalls Austen's *Mansfield Park*. Duckworth introduced the term "the improvement of the estate" in a study of Austen's oeuvre in which *Mansfield Park*
serves as the paradigmatic novel. It is not coincidental that Austen's novel features a heroine who, like Mary Thorne, is informally adopted by a relative who
is financially and socially better placed than her immediate family. Duckworth
writes of Austen's Fanny: "That the initially deracinated individual, the adopted
daughter of the house, should be the true trustee of its traditions is the instructive irony of the novel, an irony whose meaning requires careful interpretation"
(*Improvement of the Estate*, 72).[23] The same irony informs *Doctor Thorne*, for
Mary, more than any of its members, embodies the values that Greshamsbury
should seek to uphold (she is far better suited to be mistress of the estate than
is the querulous Lady Arabella),[24] and her inheritance becomes crucial to the
preservation of Greshamsbury only because the older Gresham has been guilty
of a failure of stewardship that has led to a literal loss of control over much of
the estate. Duckworth argues that Fanny's adopted status is meant to suggest
that personal commitment must animate inherited forms; the displacement of
Julia and Maria, daughters by birth, by Fanny, daughter by adoption, suggests
"the imperative need for the social order to be informed by individual worth"
(79). Trollope, who shares with Austen an interest in the negotiation between
tradition and individualism, figures that dilemma through Mary, whose adoption gives her an ambiguous class status. Illegitimate but raised a gentlewoman,
with distinguished blood in her veins but the corresponding name hers only by
sufferance, Mary is led to ponder the extent to which good birth should qualify
and low birth should disqualify the individual.

> Was it not within her capacity to do as nobly, to love as truly, to worship her
> God in heaven with as perfect a faith, and her god on earth with as leal a
> troth, as though blood had descended to her purely through scores of purely
> born progenitors? So to herself she spoke; and yet, as she said it, she knew
> that were she a man, such a man as the heir of Greshamsbury should be,
> nothing should tempt her to sully her children's blood by mating herself
> with any one that was base born. (*Doctor Thorne*, 107).

Mary is led to these contradictory reflections in part by her surprise that Augusta Gresham consents to marry the son of a wealthy tailor. But the instructive
subplot concerning Augusta Gresham, who is willing to marry a man she does
not love or respect (or indeed even know) as a sacrifice to what she perceives as
the family's needs, reveals the erasure of the individual that can occur when
there is too great an identification with family name. The adoptive family identity, in contrast to a hereditary one, is to a greater extent an "earned" identity
and is one where personal choice and personal commitment are given greater

prominence. The adoptive relation of Mary and the doctor is itself a model of this ratification through individual commitment. When Mary takes up permanent residence in the doctor's house at age twelve, the narrator comments:

> It must not be supposed that [Thorne] had lost sight of his charge during her earlier years. He was much too well aware of the nature of the promise which he had made to the departing mother to do that. He had constantly visited his little niece, and long before the first twelve years of her life were over had lost all consciousness of his promise, and of his duty to the mother, in the stronger ties of downright personal love for the only creature that belonged to him. (44)

If Trollope's and Austen's adoption plots have in common a concern with individual merit, they are divided by an important difference as well. In marked contrast to Fanny, aspects of Mary's natal background play an important role in the social function she is to fulfill. From her working-class mother, "a model of female beauty of the strong and robuster cast, and [with] a better reputation as being a girl of good character and honest, womanly conduct" (21), Mary inherits the vitality badly needed in the static Gresham/De Courcy household: "sober and demure as was her usual settled appearance, she could talk, when the fit came on her, with an energy which in truth surprised those who did not know her. . . . Energy! nay, it was occasionally a concentration of passion" (46). From her mother's brother, of course, she inherits a fortune that includes all the outstanding claims on Greshamsbury. Kincaid notes of *Doctor Thorne:*

> The informing myth is one of blood restoration, almost blood-sucking. . . . The Greshams are preserved by the energy (and money) they absorb from the lower class. The message is finally clear—and grim—enough. . . .
> That the novel seems far warmer and less disturbed than all this suggests is due to the wonderful rhetorical control Trollope establishes over us and never loses for more than a moment throughout. He disguises the violence of the primitive myth of blood transfusion and reintegration . . . by a variety of means, among which are a style more than ordinarily relaxed and a narrator of supreme serenity. (*Anthony Trollope,* 114–15)

Just as the narration proceeds at a leisurely pace, so does the process of adoption itself, which allows for gradual assimilation. Thanks to her adoption, Mary becomes so thoroughly one of those whose interests she will be made to serve that the idea of appropriation is suppressed. Thus, Mary's adoption, which participates in the process of blood restoration, itself serves to mask the latent violence inherent in that process. Mary's rescue of the Greshams is presented as an extension of her rescue by Doctor Thorne; given the alliance between Gresham and Thorne, this suggests a structure of reciprocity. Moreover, Trollope ingenuously presents Mary's heirship as a solution not only for the Greshams but for the Scatcherds as well. Scatcherd speaks to Thorne of his and his wife's inability to be happy after their dramatic change in fortune; neither by nature nor by experience are they equipped to play the roles that their new fortune suddenly assigns them. The next generation of their own family is no more capable than they of living up to the new position. Louis Philippe is even less qualified than his father; he lacks his father's drive, which he had no impetus to develop, and he could not hope to acquire from his father a compensating gain in refinement. Thanks to her adoption by Thorne (and thanks perhaps to her Thorne blood as well), Mary, unlike Scatcherd's own child, is a suitable heir; when Scatcherd discovers that the doctor's niece is also his own niece, he delights in the thought of her probable accomplishments and writes her into his will forthwith.

In the case of the Scatcherds, property transmission does not follow the line of direct descent, because of a failure in the genetic project; their son, Louis Philippe, is a sickly, dissolute, and spineless youth, "strong neither in mind nor body" (*Doctor Thorne*, 142), "a poor, puny creature, without physical strength . . . [and] killing himself with alcohol" (147). His father has passed onto him his alcoholism but not the strong constitution that in his own case ensured survival.[25] The successful adoption of Mary contrasts with the genetic failures the novel displays. While many of Louis Philipe's problems stem from the anomalies of his parents' situation, the genetic project of the upper classes is not entirely successful either. As background to the story, the narrator recounts the rapid and uneconomical accumulation of ten children in the Gresham family (all daughters save one), a process that contributes to the financial woes of Gresham. Moreover, a number of the daughters are sickly and die while still children, so that of the last birth the narrator says, "Then came the youngest of the flock, she whose birth . . . was not heralded with loud joy; for when she came into the world, four others, with pale temples, wan, worn cheeks, and skeleton, white arms, were awaiting permission to leave it" (8). The affective links between the generations are under strain as well. The unfortunate Louis Philippe is again at extreme case in point: he becomes an object of distaste to his father and of fear for his mother, who actually prefers Frank Gresham, her former nursling, to her own child and tries to convince her husband to make Frank an heir. (It is interesting that this situation stems from the fact that the doomed Scatcherd progeny, in an unsettlingly literal application of Kincaid's metaphor, "had been dismissed from his mother's breast in order that the mother's milk might nourish the young heir of Greshamsbury" [142].) The elder Scatcherd acknowledges, "what could he do for his boy except die?" (327). This question echoes a note sounded at the other end of the social scale: in the aristocratic De Courcy family, where the dictates of self-interest prevail, the sons speak of losing a father as a stroke of good fortune, since it enables a man to come into his inheritance.

While both Frank Greshams, father and son, are genuinely fond of each other, the Gresham household is rendered unhappy by the factionalism that characterizes it. In fact, the only successful family the novel shows is the adoptive one constituted by Doctor Thorne and Mary.

The "single-parent household" of Doctor and Mary Thorne avoids the factionalism that characterizes the Gresham family. Because Thorne virtually suppresses one-half of Mary's genetic equation by segregating her from her maternal inheritance as she is raised, he avoids the conflict of values that can inform a household combining two family lines. At the beginning of *Doctor Thorne*, the history of the union between the Tory Francis Gresham and the Whig Lady Arabella De Courcy illustrates the difficulty of integrating contrasting bloodlines and contrasting family traditions through marriage. Divided by politics and by priorities (she wants to refurnish the London house; he wants to bring the county hounds to Greshamsbury), their incompatibility seems irresolvable.[26] There is no affection between them, and the failures of their marriage have a direct impact on the events leading to the mortgaging of the estate. So antithetical are the two lines of Gresham and De Courcy that their children must be either one or the other and must serve either one or the other interest. While "young Frank was every inch a Gresham, and was the darling of his father's heart[,] . . . the Misses Gresham were made in the De Courcy mould, and were not on this account the less dear to their mother" (8). In the doctor's household, there is no such factionalism; Mary is so thoroughly a daughter of her single parent/uncle that there is a complete unanimity of interests. The novel's emphasis on the factionalism produced by a marriage of opposites suggests that adoption is a better method of blood restoration than marriage, since it allows for a more gradual—and hence more successful—process of integration. In this novel, adoption, rather than marriage, becomes the key to a greater social cohesiveness.

If *Doctor Thorne* follows the example of *Mansfield Park* in yoking a female adoption plot to an "improvement of the estate" theme, a later novel that flirts with the same possibility but ultimately rejects it is George Eliot's *Felix Holt*. The initial histories of Mary Thorne and of Esther Lyon have a number of features in common: both are adoptees of mixed lineage who are informed of their true origins as they reach marriageable age, and both are revealed to be the unexpected heirs to large estates. Just as Mary does, Esther becomes the vehicle for restoring that estate to longtime owners she might have dispossessed. As an attractive, single young woman who can be courted by Harold Transome, Esther is initially viewed by Harold and his mother as a tool through whom they can literally save Transome Court. Ultimately, however, they see her as the potential savior of their home in a deeper sense, perceiving qualities in her that could restore hope and happiness to their household were she to join it. This possibility is rejected, however, as Esther allies herself instead with an associate of her adoptive father whose goal is to help bring the working class to man's estate. The adoption plots of Trollope and George Eliot work in opposite directions: rather than the adopted woman serving as the estate's redeemer, the adoption in *Felix Holt* redeems the woman by allowing her to escape the corrupting influence of the estate.

The different ends that adoption serves in *Doctor Thorne* and *Felix Holt* are linked to the respective treatments of the heroines' identities in the novels. In each case, the adoptive milieu dramatically differs from that associated with the daughter's natal origin, creating the potential for alternative identities. Mary's mother is working-class and sexually fallen, while Esther's French mother is suspect on racial grounds. Thus, both Mary and Esther must disidentify with their maternal heritages to qualify themselves as proper English wives and mothers. This is an easier process for Mary than it is for Esther. There is never any threat of Mary repeating her mother's fall; the class identification her affiliation with Thorne secures her is apparently proof against any such eventuality. By contrast, Esther Lyon is in danger of reproducing her mother's features; her finicky taste and her sentimental weakness for such authors as Byron—characteristics associated with her French mother and her aristocratic father—are tendencies that flourish even in a dissenting preacher's household. Throughout the novel, Esther appears to everyone who encounters her to be an anomaly in what turns out to be an adoptive household. In contrast to Mary Thorne, Esther (like George Eliot's other adopted heroine, Eppie Marner) must actively choose between her adoptive class and her natal class. (Eppie must choose directly between her two fathers; Esther must choose between two suitors, Harold Transome and Felix Holt, who are linked, respectively, to her natal and adoptive fathers.) While Mary Thorne will inevitably belong to the upper class, George Eliot has both of her adopted heroines choose to align themselves with a respectable working class.

The importance of the adoptive, freely chosen identity in *Felix Holt* is linked to the concern in that novel with the oppressiveness of the past—whether it is the individual's past, as in the case of Mrs. Transome, or the family's past, as in the case of her son. A number of the characters are engaged in projects that involve the rejection of inherited traditions. Felix refuses to continue the family business; Harold Transome leaves what has historically been his family's and his class's political party to stand as a Radical; the dissenting sect of Reverend Lyon eschews the inherited form of worship in favor of a religion that emphasizes individual selection. Esther's choice of her adoptive class over her natal class might be viewed in the same light, especially as this choice leads her to join Felix in a way of life whose goal is to contribute to a process of social evolution. The connection of the adoption plot to this project is suggested by the implicit metaphor in Felix's description of his philosophy: "It is held reasonable enough to toil for the fortunes of a family, though it may turn to imbecility in the third generation. I choose a family with more chances in it."[27]

NOTES

An earlier version of this essay appeared in *Nineteenth-Century Literature* 52 (1997): 58–79. Permission to reprint is gratefully acknowledged.

1. D. H. Lawrence's *The Rainbow* (1915) illustrates the same maxim. The child through whom the family line and the narrative line are transmitted is an adopted daughter; Anna Brangwen is the product of her mother's first marriage, to Paul Lensky.

2. The similar novelistic potential of the two events is reflected in the frequent intertwining of adoption plots with marriage plots, in the manner of Austen's *Mansfield Park*, where the adopted cousin, Fanny, marries her "brother" Edmund.

3. See T. E. James, "The Illegitimate and Deprived Child: Legitimation and Adoption," in *A Century of Family Law, 1857–1957*, ed. R. H. Graveson and F. R. Crane (London: Sweet and Maxwell, 1957), 46.

4. The term is from Julian Pitt-Rivers, "The Kith and the Kin," in *The Character of Kinship*, ed. Jack Goody (Cambridge: Cambridge University Press, 1973), 95: "Adoption involves a jural fiction which is accompanied by a social fiction to a greater or lesser extent."

5. See Tony Tanner, *Adultery in the Novel: Contract and Transgression* (Baltimore: Johns Hopkins University Press, 1979), 16.

6. Susan R. Cohen, "'A History and a Metamorphosis': Continuity and Discontinuity in *Silas Marner*," *Texas Studies in Literature and Language* 25 (1983): 416.

7. Dinah Maria Mulock Craik, *King Arthur: Not a Love Story* (London: Macmillan, 1886), 137. All subsequent references to this text refer to this edition and are indicated parenthetically.

8. Patricia Howe, "Fontane's 'Ellernklipp' and the Theme of Adoption," *Modern Language Review* 79 (1984): 121.

9. Alistair M. Duckworth, *The Improvement of the Estate: A Study of Jane Austen's Novels* (Baltimore: Johns Hopkins University Press, 1971).

10. William Clarke Hall and Justin Clarke Hall, introduction to *The Law of Adoption and Guardianship of Infants, with Special Reference to Courts of Summary Jurisdiction* (London: Butterworth, 1928), 4.

11. Seneca the Elder, *Controversiae*, in *Declamations*, ed. and trans. M. Winterbottom, 2 vols. (Cambridge: Harvard University Press, 1974), I. 223.

12. Alan Teague, *Social Change, Social Work, and the Adoption of Children* (Aldershot: Avebury, 1989), 65.

13. Sally Mitchell, *Dinah Mulock Craik* (Boston: Twayne, 1983), 77.

14. In Trollope's *Ralph the Heir* (1871; ed. John Sutherland, 2 vols. in 1, New York: Oxford University Press, 1990), this issue preys on the conscience of a father of two daughters who decides to adopt his orphaned niece: "That question of adopting is very difficult. If a man have no children of his own . . . he can give all, and there is an end of his trouble. But a man feels that he owes his property to his children; and, so feeling, may he take it from them and give it to others? Had she been in truth his daughter, he would have felt that there was enough for three; but she was not his daughter, and yet he was telling her that she should be to him the same as a child of his house" (I, p. 84).

15. The depiction of Arthur's biological and adoptive mothers is class inflected: an unmaternal upper-class woman is contrasted with a maternal middle-class one. As I suggest below, it is Susannah Trevena's middle-class virtue that equips her to instill strong morals in Arthur.

16. The subplot involving Nanny, who is fostered rather than adopted, reflects on the novel's main theme. Fosterage of a relative was a traditional practice, while Arthur's case resembles the modern form of adoption. Interestingly, the arrangement regarding Nanny is effected by Susannah and her sister-in-law rather than by Trevena and his brother. Nanny's mother, a victim of domestic abuse, is reluctant to have her child involved with her husband's relatives. Susannah reminds her that she is not a Trevena by birth and promises her, woman to woman, to protect her child. This scenario reinforces the notion that adoption is grounded in the claims of maternity, an idea introduced early in the novel when the narrator states that men are less drawn than women to children who are not their biological offspring and suggests that Arthur's adopted status cannot be as irrelevant to Susannah's husband as it is to her.

17. Anthony Trollope, *Doctor Thorne,* ed. David Skilton (New York: Oxford University Press, 1980), 100. All subsequent references to this work refer to this edition and are indicated parenthetically.

18. A number of critics have commented on Trollope's depiction of social change in *Doctor Thorne;* see especially Robert M. Polhemus, *The Changing World of Anthony Trollope* (Berkeley and Los Angeles: University of California Press, 1968), and James R. Kincaid, *The Novels of Anthony Trollope* (Oxford: Clarendon, 1977). I am stressing the importance of the heroine's adoption in figuring and controlling that change and how this element makes Trollope's novel exemplary of a certain kind of Victorian adoption plot.

19. On the significance of the estate motif in a range of Trollope's fiction, see Juliet McMaster, "Trollope's Country Estates," in *Trollope Centenary Essays,* ed. John Halperin (London: Macmillan, 1982), 70–85.

20. The metaphor of vaccination is a resonant one in the context of adoption plots, for unassimilable adoptees like Heathcliff are sometimes figured as agents who infect or poison the family. In William Thackeray's *Henry Esmond* (1852), the supposedly illegitimate Harry, who has been taken into the Castlewood family, infects the woman who calls herself his mother with the smallpox he has contracted by consorting with a working-class girl. That the disfigurement that results from this disease is credited with the husband's alienation of affection from his wife suggests the way that the adopted child may be seen as poisoning the family and its patterns of affection.

21. Jane Nardin, *He Knew She Was Right: The Independent Woman in the Novels of Anthony Trollope* (Carbondale: Southern Illinois University Press, 1989).

22. Kincaid's use of the term *recruitment* is apt, for the novel displays a number of attempts to recruit individuals. The De Courcys recruit the elder Gresham as a son-in-law and in so doing hope to recruit him for the Whig Party; a generation later, the De Courcy women attempt to recruit the younger Frank for the maternal side of his family. Miss Dunstable is recruited by the Barsetshire set for wealth. I am suggesting that the adoption of Mary, because it involves claiming her for the group whose interests the novel champions, can be seen as another instance of recruitment. Recruitment in the adoption plot is also visible in *Daniel Deronda,* where the protagonist must turn away from his adopted world when he is recruited to serve in the Zionist project associated with his natal heritage.

23. The trajectory followed by the two adopted heroines is also similar. Duckworth notes Fanny's odyssey from periphery to center of *Mansfield Park,* followed first by full expulsion after she refuses the offer from Crawford and finally by a return to the center. Like Fanny, Mary is allowed to exist on the margin of the Greshamsbury family circle, but she is banished from it when Frank's declaration of love for her lands her in disgrace, only to be ultimately let back in, this time to the very center.

24. Mary's qualification to be the mistress of Greshamsbury is foreshadowed by an incident from her childhood. When a nursery maid who is a daughter of one of the tenants is falsely accused of stealing jewelry actually taken by the French governess imported from De Courcy Castle, Mary staunchly defends the local girl and is the only person to do so. This incident, we are told, initially wins her the senior Gresham's affection. Importantly, it also wins her the support of the tenants, who are in sympathy with her during her period of exile from the Hall after Frank's proposal. This ratification by the tenants is also found in Trollope's *Cousin Henry* (1879), where Indifer Jones agonizes over a choice between leaving his unentailed estate to the heir presumptive—the course his own investment in tradition dictates—and leaving it to the beloved niece he has raised. His lawyer explains that in this case, violating the letter of the law of primogeniture is necessary to preserve its spirit, since Isabel is the more worthy steward of the estate. She has demonstrated this in part through her engagement with the tenants, an engagement the heir presumptive is never able to achieve. As in the case of *Doctor Thorne*'s illegitimate heroine, in *Cousin Henry* a customary pattern of succession is diverted to achieve a conservative end.

25. Kincaid notes a similarity between Louis Philippe Scatcherd and Linton Heathcliff as scapegoats who "drain off the bad blood" (*Anthony Trollope,* 120).

26. Frank and Mary will be more compatible spouses than his parents in part because they have been raised largely together and thus have shared values; like Fanny Price, who is educated with the Bertram sisters at *Mansfield Park,* Mary takes her lessons with the Gresham daughters, to the extent that the squire "accustom[s] himself to look at Mary Thorne running about the house with his own children as though she were one of the same brood" (*Doctor Thorne,* 104). Thus, another advantage secured by her adoption is an almost sanguinal affinity with her future husband.

27. George Eliot, *Felix Holt, the Radical,* ed. Fred C. Thomson (Oxford: Clarendon, 1980), 225.

Adoption in *Silas Marner* and *Daniel Deronda*

Marianne Novy

Adoption as a theme appears significantly again and again in George Eliot's novels. Very often, in the plot of those novels, an adoptee must choose between a biological heritage and an adoptive one. Eppie in *Silas Marner* and Esther in *Felix Holt* both, at the crucial moment, choose their adoptive father. However, in two works written near the end of Eliot's career, the pattern seems to be reversed: the adoptee in her poetic drama *The Spanish Gypsy* chooses her gypsy ancestry, and the adoptee in *Daniel Deronda* chooses to identify with his hereditary Jewishness.

Why was Eliot so interested in adoption? And why is there such a reversal in the choices her adoptees make? Eliot's representations of adoption and adoptees are plot devices and, as Bernard Semmel points out in *George Eliot and the Politics of National Inheritance,* ways of dealing with the nation's cultural past and recent social change.[1] But I want to analyze them as well in terms of their specificity precisely as analyses of adoption, as I compare the best known of these four works—*Silas Marner* and *Daniel Deronda.*

The number of adoptions in Eliot's and other nineteenth-century English novels is particularly striking because the institution was not legally formalized in England at that time. Figures on the frequency of informal adoptions are impossible to obtain (partly because of the difficulty of determining what counts as adoption, if it is informal), and historians differ significantly in their guesses.[2] But George Eliot was not adopted in any of the usual senses. Nor were most of her readers. We are dealing to a large extent with adoption as the precondition for the family romance plot, adoption in its mythic dimension—the fantasy that people develop to deal with uncongenial parents by imagining better parents elsewhere. Indeed, this fantasy—related to Eliot's experience of alienation in her own family of origin—enters into her most directly autobiographical novel, *The Mill on the Floss,* when Maggie imagines the gypsies as her "unknown kindred."[3]

Nevertheless, the most immediate variety of adoption in George Eliot's horizon was her own relation to G. H. Lewes's sons. In 1859, when she and Lewes made their own mutual commitment that would have been marriage except for the law forbidding Lewes to divorce his unfaithful wife, Lewes's oldest son Charles, then sixteen, wrote her a letter in which he addressed her as "Mother."[4]

Rosemarie Bodenheimer has traced in detail George Eliot's relation to her three stepsons and has noted, "her focus on children brought up by substitute parents, and her privileging of fostering over kinship, was a dominant feature of her imagination from 1860 to the end of her career; the experience of her stepsons gave her the authority for those imagined lives."[5]

When Charles began to call her "mother," Eliot was forty, the same age Silas is when little Eppie wanders into his home. When Charles came to live with them, she and Lewes moved to a home in town (although she preferred the country), because Charles needed to live near his work. These biographical details are surely among the reasons why *Silas Marner*, as Eliot put it, "thrust itself" on her to interrupt her work on *Romola* at this time.[6] She was thinking about child rearing, in particular about the rearing of a child not born to her.

Silas Marner rewrites the plot of many earlier novels and plays in which a character is reunited with biological parents. Godfrey Cass refuses to acknowledge the wife he has secretly married. When she dies, their daughter, Eppie, wanders into the home of the poor, isolated weaver Silas. Silas raises her with much love; she flourishes, and through his concern for Eppie, Silas develops ties with many other people. After many years, childless by his acknowledged wife, Nancy, Godfrey reveals himself to Silas and Eppie as her father and asks her to return to him. He says, "I have a natural claim on her that must stand before every other" (169),[7] but she does not agree.

In one sense, this conflict is a dramatized custody case. But instead of the legal system, Eppie herself—and the readers—must decide which family she should choose. Nancy's father believes that "breed [is] stronger than pasture" (98),[8] but *Silas Marner* challenges this belief—unless breed is redefined. How does Eppie's rejection of heredity in favor of nurture become the inevitable choice in a novel full of descriptions and imagery of natural growth?

At stake is the definition of two key words—*father* and *nature*. As these words and their variants sound repeatedly in the dialogue and narration, it is clear that the novel portrays child rearing as defining both. The novel challenges the opposition between adoption and nature and presents adoptive relationships as natural in themselves.[9] Indeed, in a letter to her publisher as she is completing *Silas*, Eliot describes as its intended emphasis "the remedial influences of pure, natural human relations" (*GEL*, 3:382).

Long before the novel explicitly engages with prejudices against adoption, its language, like the plot, encourages the reader to see parenthood as not only genetic and to see the nurture of adoption as natural. Dolly, the book's authority in child rearing, says to Silas, "you'll have a right to her if you're a father to her, and bring her up according" (123). Dolly predicts that with Silas, "The child 'ull grow like grass i' May" (121). Silas's raising of Eppie is compared to the way "some man who has a precious plant to which he would give a nurturing home in a new soil, thinks of the rain and sunshine, and all influences, in relation to his nursling, and asks industriously for all knowledge that will help him to satisfy the wants of the searching roots" (131). He acts like a parental bird: "the stone hut was made a soft nest for her, lined with downy patience" (129). Silas goes out to the meadows with Eppie; she plucks flowers; they listen for birds: nurturing his adoptee, Silas puts them both in close contact with nature. At sixteen, Eppie is "the freshest blossom of youth" (138), with a suitor, Aaron, who woos her partly by promising to bring her flowers from the gardens where he works—they will be doing more transplanting and nurturing, as, metaphorically, Silas did.

In the crucial confrontation scene, from Nancy's point of view, Godfrey is the "real father" and "father by blood" (171) and Silas is "foster-father" (171); she thinks "there's a duty you owe to your lawful father" (173). On the other hand, from Eppie's point of view, in the same scene, Silas is the "long-loved father" and Godfrey is the "unfamiliar father"—note the pun on family in "unfamiliar" (171). Pointing up the irony in the term *real,* Eppie thinks of Silas as "a father very close to her, who loved her better than any real fathers in the village seemed to love their daughters" (147). As Silas says to Godfrey, "It's me she's been calling her father ever since she could say the word" (170).

Though Godfrey maintains, "I have a natural claim on her that must stand before every other" (169), the novel contests this argument. When he finally acknowledges that he cannot reclaim Eppie, his language invokes nature; he says, "While I've been putting off and putting off, the trees have been growing—it's too late now" (174).

The novel treats its community's valorization of heredity and its ideas of what is natural critically. In a comic exaggeration of restrictive views, the town of Raveloe welcomes Doctor Kimble "as a doctor by hereditary right" and believes that "Kimble was inherently a doctor's name." Since he has no son, the practice may "one day be handed over to a successor, with the incongruous name of Taylor or Johnson. But in that case the wiser people in Raveloe would employ Dr. Blick of Flitton—as less unnatural" (98).

More centrally, in Nancy's early rejection of the idea of adopting Eppie, whose heredity she does not know, the novel engages explicitly with prejudices against adoption. According to Nancy, "to adopt a child, because children of your own had been denied you, was to try and choose your lot in spite of Providence; the adopted child . . . would be a curse to those who had wilfully and rebelliously sought what it was clear that, for some high reason, they were better without" (156). She recalls an acquaintance's story about an adopted child who became a criminal: "That was the only adopting I ever heard of: and the child was transported when it was twenty-three" (157). Notice of her reference to the twenty-three year old as a child and her pronoun "it," used of human beings only when they are children or for some other reason denied full humanity. In giving Nancy this language, Eliot anticipates adoptees' criticism of their treatment as children in some popular writing and legal discourse today.

Eliot encourages the reader to criticize Nancy's prejudice, associating it with the past: "Adoption was more remote from the ideas and habits of that time than of our own" (155–56). She links it with other examples of Nancy's "unalterable little code": "she insisted on dressing like Priscilla, because 'it was right for sisters to dress alike'" (156). Then she suggests that Nancy's thinking is "nearly akin to that of many devout people, whose beliefs are held in the shape of a system quite remote from her knowledge" (157). Prejudice against adoption is thus associated with system—and the narrator comments that "human beliefs, like all natural growths, elude the barriers of system," which suggests that a too rigid system like Nancy's or that of the more educated "devout people" is unnatural. Furthermore, Eliot criticizes Nancy's prejudices by the implied contrast between Eppie and the transported twenty-three year old, as well as by the sadness and guilt that both Nancy and Godfrey feel when they find out the truth.

Heredity does, of course, have some effect in this novel. Eppie's hair and eyes are like Godfrey's—so much so that her birth mother plans to use her similarity to him as proof of their relationship when she confronts old Squire Cass, his father. However, throughout the novel, among the many characters who have some acquaintance with both Eppie and Godfrey, no one else thinks of this resemblance. As Eppie grows up, we are told that she "cannot help being rather vexed about her hair, for there is no other girl in Raveloe who has hair at all like it, and she thinks hair ought to be smooth" (138). What she sees as unruliness is also associated with nature: "the hair ripples as obstinately as a brooklet under the March breeze." With Eppie's limited perception, she does not understand that her curly auburn hair would, by many people, be regarded as more beautiful; in this detail, the novel includes a remnant of the traditional romance of separated family members, which emphasizes their physical similarity by contrast to others—even perhaps a trace of the ugly duckling story, in which the cygnet must find the swans to avoid being judged by ducks' standards. However, only after Godfrey's acknowledgment does anyone remark on this visible heredity: Nancy says, "with just your hair and eyes: I wondered it had never struck me before" (175). The great social gap between the two figures has prevented anyone not already aware from thinking about whether the two auburn heads might have some connection.

In *Silas Marner,* the bond of child-father kinship, in its most significant sense, is a matter of responsible action, more than of biology. Even Nancy, despite her prejudice against adoption, eventually concedes, "It's natural you should cling to those who've brought you up" (173). She then falls back on duty to define Godfrey's tie to Eppie, but his own behavior has discredited this appeal. Although Eliot uses the tradition of showing the adopted child as different from the other children in her environment, she makes a point of attributing as much of this difference to Silas's loving care as to Eppie's upper-class heredity.

The tender and peculiar love with which Silas had reared her in almost inseparable companionship with himself, aided by the seclusion of their dwelling, had prevented her from the lowering influences of the village talk and habits. (146)

While Eppie's "delicate prettiness" must to some extent come from her heredity, Eliot emphasizes the influence of Silas's "perfect love" and its "breath of poetry" on her "refinement and fervour" (146). Nevertheless, Eppie presents her choice of Silas not just as a choice of an individual family, but also as a choice of class—"I wasn't brought up to be a lady, and I can't turn my mind to it. I like the working-folks, and their houses, and their ways. And . . . I'm promised to marry a working-man" (173).

As Rosemarie Bodenheimer has noted, Silas's rearing of Eppie is idealized in many ways that can be seen as transmutations of Eliot's own experience as a stepmother—and of anyone's experiences of child rearing. There is no problem when Eppie interrupts Silas's work; there is no problem when Silas does not discipline Eppie. The novel is in many ways a fantasy—a fantasy particularly appealing to someone who values parenting beyond genetic lines. The transfer of Eppie from her mother to Silas is, as Bodenheimer writes, "performed when both adults are unconscious," thus eliminating conflict; and both birth parents are, in different ways, clearly unworthy and out of the picture for most of the novel.[10] Silas is completely open with Eppie about her history: "It would have been impossible for him to hide from Eppie that she was not his own child" (146). Though he is modest here in thinking about his claim on her, she thinks hardly at all about any other father; she wants to know more about her mother, but does not know enough to worry about her mother's addiction to drink or opium and about what of this she might have inherited. It is, however, very important that the parents were married—her mother's wedding ring is very precious to her. This ring is necessary to the plot because Godfrey's relationship to her mother must be serious enough to be an obstacle to the higher-status marriage he wants, but it also saves Eppie from some stigma.

Molly Farren, Eppie's mother, is almost as absent from the novel as she can possibly be. Godfrey's secret marriage to her is described as coming from "a movement of compunction . . . on a pliant nature . . . an ugly story of low passion, delusion, and waking from delusion" (30). Eliot devotes two pages of chapter 12 to Molly's point of view, which is no prettier. As she walks through the snow to confront the Cass family, "Molly knew that the cause of her dingy rags was not her husband's neglect, but the demon Opium to which she was enslaved, body and soul" (107). When portraying any good impulse in Molly, however, the narrator explicitly phrases it both as maternal and as in conflict with the rest of herself. The sentence just quoted, for example, continues, "except in the lingering mother's tenderness that refused to give him her hungry child." Cold and tired, Molly thinks of getting comfort from "the familiar demon in her bosom," but "the mother's love pleaded for painful consciousness rather than oblivion—pleaded to be left in aching weariness, rather than to have the encircling arms benumbed so that they could not feel the dear burden" (108). Nancy Paxton says that Eliot here, as in *Adam Bede*, is emphasizing the idea that maternal altruism is a capacity that must be cultivated, not an instinct that takes over automatically.[11] But in effect Eliot sacrifices the birth mother to save the reader's sympathies for Godfrey and, much more, for Silas. Considering how often this book has been required school reading, how many adoptees have formed pictures of their birth mothers based on it? How many birth mothers who came back to school with the assurance that no one would ever know where they had been could tell no one why they hated this book?

The family romance, discussed by Freud, analyzed by Frye and others, and repeated in many tales, novels, and plays, including *The Winter's Tale*, casts the birth parents as rich nobility and the adoptive parents as poor commoners.[12] In real life, the situation is more likely to be the opposite. Molly's poverty is the detail of this novel that resonates most with the actual circumstances of most historical and recent birth mothers. And in its insistence that even Molly knows that Godfrey is not really the cause of her problems, the novel is class-biased and conservative.

Nevertheless, in other ways, the novel uses the adoption plot to protest against the split of classes. This point is made very subtly by the fact that no one thinks about the similarity between Godfrey's and Eppie's hair, despite the fact that they live very close together (Godfrey is eventually revealed as Silas's landlord). The protest is made more explicitly at one point in the words of Aaron: discussing the excess of flowers owned by the Casses, he says, "there need nobody run short o' victuals if the land was made the most on" (140).

Eliot's last novel, *Daniel Deronda*, published in 1876, likewise gives the adoptee a choice of identities, but this time heredity, rather than nurture is compelling. Daniel has been raised as the nephew of an English gentleman; in the process of helping a poor Jewish girl, Mirah, he discovers that he is himself Jewish by ancestry. His mother, a former opera singer who felt stifled by Judaism and by his birth, had placed him with his guardian with the aim that he would be free from Judaism and she would be free to sing; thwarted in her career anyway, she tells him the story out of guilt but does not want a continuing relationship with him. Though disappointed in his mother, Daniel is so committed to his newfound identity that, at the novel's end, he leaves England to help begin a Jewish nation in Palestine.

Though Daniel's choice is opposite to Eppie's, it seems similarly inevitable, since the novel emphasizes his questions about his origin from an early point.[13] Reading Renaissance history with his tutor, the thirteen-year-old Daniel discovers that the word *nephew* could be a euphemism for illegitimate son. He at once applies this to himself, with a sudden sense of loss, disillusionment with his beloved guardian Sir Hugo, and "the idea that others probably knew things concerning him which they did not choose to mention, and which he would not have had them mention."[14] He notices that no one looks like him in the gallery of family pictures, but he never asks his uncle about his heredity, both because he thinks his uncle wants the issue kept silent and because he does not want to "bring himself near even a silent admission of the sore that had opened in him" (145). As a consequence, Daniel seems reserved when other boys talk about their families. His speculations about his heredity are turned into persistent silent questions about who he looks like and into sympathy for his unknown mother (who he feels was wronged) and by extension for all women.

The novel also prepares for Daniel's choice by showing Sir Hugo's lapses of sensitivity. Earlier in Daniel's life, Sir Hugo tells him, "You lost your father and mother when you were quite a little one" (139), but after that he never discusses the matter; the most he says to Daniel before he is, late in the book, forced to, is, "The best horse will win in spite of pedigree" (138), which, though intended as encouragement, presumably reinforces Daniel's sense that his own pedigree is bad. Hugo is pleased that Daniel is generally thought of as his son: "his imagination had never once been troubled with the way in which the boy himself might be affected, either then or in the future, by the enigmatic aspect of his circumstances. . . . what could be more natural [that word again] . . . than that he should have a beautiful boy like the little Deronda to take care of?" (148).

Unlike Silas's child rearing, however, Hugo's care for Daniel is rarely associated with natural growth. Instead, the narrator often suggests that Hugo regards Daniel as a possession—at best a pet, at worst an object: "a convenience in the family . . . , this substitute for a son" (192–93). Most devastatingly, Daniel himself realizes that Hugo treated children as "a product intended to make life more agreeable to the full-grown, whose convenience alone was to be consulted in the disposal of them." Daniel half-excuses Hugo by thinking that this attitude "was massively acted on at that date of the world's history" (612), but this observation adds to Eliot's social critique.

Although he always has much affection for Hugo, Daniel has an "early-rooted feeling [one of the few instances of nature imagery with regard to their relationship] that his birth had been attended with injury for which his father [Hugo, as he thinks] was to blame" (237). It is true that when Daniel is beginning to think that his ancestry might be Jewish, he acknowledges more positive ties to his nurture: "Feelings which have struck root through half my life may still hinder me from doing what I have never yet been able to do" (430). However, nature imagery enters the novel most intensely in the language used by Mordecai, who turns out to be Mirah's brother, about the restored Jewish nation he envisions: "Is it rational to drain away the sap of special kindred that makes the families of man rich in interchanged wealth, and various as the forests are various with the glory of the cedar and the palm?" (451). Daniel longs to be part of an organic social unit, and Mordecai, convinced they are related, offers him one: "Have we not quivered together like the leaves from a common stem with stirrings from a common root?" (489). When he discovers his Jewish birth, Daniel picks up this imagery in telling his mother, "Your will was strong, but my grandfather's trust which you accepted and did not fulfil—what you call his yoke—is the expression of something stronger, with deeper, farther-spreading roots" (568).

The nature imagery of roots in this novel, unlike the nature imagery of *Silas Marner*, does not emphasize the conscious choice of the nurturer. At the few key places where imagery of active nurturing occurs, Deronda is clearly dealing with a different issue than the child rearing of *Silas*: he speaks of "the men who had the visions which, as Mordecai said, were the creators and feeders of the world— moulding and feeding the more passive life which without them would dwindle and shrivel into the narrow tenacity of insects" (586).

The imagery suggests, furthermore, that while Daniel's mother provided "natural parentage," she herself is associated not with nature but with the mythic and preternatural. Sick of a disease that in her description sounds both terminal and caused by guilt, she is described as "a Melusina, who had ties with some world which is independent of ours . . . a mysterious Fate rather than . . . the longed-for mother" (536); "a sorceress who would stretch forth her wonderful hand and arm to mix youth-potions for others, but scorned to mix them for herself, having had enough of youth" (565); "a dreamed visitant from some region of departed mortals" (571). These are very different from the descriptions given of Godfrey, who is in some ways comparable as a birth parent reunited with a child late in life. This difference, I think, results partly from the different emotional weight carried by birth mothers as opposed to birth fathers. Godfrey has behaved in a relatively ordinary, if coldhearted way, juxtaposing the novel suggests, while Leonora, most often referred to as "the Princess," has behaved in an extraordinary way. Godfrey is punished in having no children in his marriage, but Leonora, though she has children, sounds emotionally removed from them as well as Daniel, as if she had been cast out of the world of human connection.

But could anyone live up to the image of the lost mother that this novel evokes? Before Daniel's early life is revealed, several characters in its other main plot participate in staging a scene from *The Winter's Tale*, in which a lost mother appears to come to life out of a statue. In this play, she speaks in a way that fulfils all needs of her now grown child. In the scene as it appears in *Deronda*, however, the child is missing, and Gwendolen, who is playing the role of Hermione, shrieks in terror at the sudden appearance of a dead face at the moment when she should act out her return to life. This, like the other roles Gwendolen plays in the novel, is more difficult than she expects. The nightmarish transformation of *The Winter's Tale*'s happy ending foreshadows the way Leonora too finds the role of the returning mother too difficult.

Our culture is full of plots in which successful reunions occur. Daniel has made up similar plots in his own daydreams; at the beginning of his first meeting with his mother, he thinks, "He had lived through so many ideal meetings with his mother, and they had seemed more real than this!" (535). His fantasies have presented her as sacred: "To Daniel the words Father and Mother had the altar-fire in them; and the thought of all closest relations of our nature held still something of the mystic power which had made his neck and ears burn in boyhood" (402).

At the same time, his idea of his mother has also been associated with fear, since the age of thirteen, when he first thought of himself as Sir Hugo's son born out of wedlock. Seeing a "forsaken" girl about to attempt suicide, he thinks "perhaps my mother was like this one" (162). Furthermore, as he learns that this girl, Mirah, is searching for *her* mother, the fear spreads: "The desire to know his own mother, or to know about her, was constantly haunted with dread; and in imagining what might befall Mirah it quickly occurred to him that finding the mother and brother from whom she has been parted . . . might turn out to be a calamity" (176). Daniel lives with a "threatening possibility of painful revelation about his mother" (429). He assumes she is a fallen woman and fears she is a prostitute. Closely related to these fears is the element in Daniel's characterization that can be described either as extreme caution about sex or as asexuality.

When he finally meets Leonora, he learns that both his pictures of the fallen woman and his pictures of the "ideal meetings" are false. Instead, Leonora is a respectable woman whose passions have all been devoted to her art—in which she was once a true star. She speaks with convincing passion of "the slavery of being a girl":

> To have a pattern cut out—'this is the Jewish woman; this is what you must be; this is what you are wanted for; a woman's heart must be of such a size and no larger, else it must be pressed small, like Chinese feet; her happiness is to be made as cakes are, by a fixed receipt.' (541)

This scene suddenly introduces a different world into the book, for previously women's complaints about restrictions come chiefly from the rather frivolous Gwendolen. Leonora had the discipline and musical talent Gwendolen lacked. Yet after the fascination with which the book has depicted Jewish culture, Leonora too can sound shallow when she complains:

> I was to love the long prayers in the ugly synagogue, and the howling, and the gabbling, and the dreadful fasts, and the tiresome feasts, and my father's

endless discoursing about Our People, which was a thunder without meaning in my ears. . . . I wanted to live a large life, with freedom to do what every
one else did, and be carried along in a great current [note the self-contra-
diction in the desire for freedom and conformity both; they are presumably
linked in her mind because she equates freedom with assimilation to gen-
tile England], not obliged to care. (540)

Eliot, so often interested in the physical similarities among relatives, points
them out in this scene; Daniel, whose face in the mirror had for him long been
associated with the thought of someone else he resembled and had never seen,
now finds that similar face. But physical resemblance is combined with opposition of values, in an irony Eliot also uses in novels where the related characters
have always lived as a family and articulates in *Adam Bede* where she calls Nature the "great tragic dramatist" who "knits us together by bone and muscle, and
divides us by the subtler web of our brains . . . and ties us by our heart strings
to the beings that jar us at every movement."[15] Daniel has longed for familial
and communal identity and a sense of duty—Leonora felt oppressed by her father and her inherited Judaism and was happy only as an opera star in a life she
describes as "a myriad lives in one" (537) with "no bonds" (547). Among the
many images she uses to explain her rejection of Judaism is one associating it
with an animal nature that she scorns: "I was not, like a brute, obliged to go with
my own herd" (544).

At his most dispassionate, Daniel can make "room for that effort at just allowance and that admiration of a forcible nature whose errors lay along high
pathways, which he would have felt if, instead of being his mother, she had been
a stranger who had appealed to his sympathy" (542). Part of the pain of their
two scenes together is that he does feel sympathy for her and offers her more
help, but she can accept little from him and can give him no unblocked emotion in return. "Is it not possible that I could be near you often and comfort
you?" he asks, and she responds: "No, not possible. . . . I have a husband and five
children. None of them know of your existence" (547). So this formerly brave
and unconventional woman keeps on maintaining secrets and lies.

Yet as their dialogue continues and then proceeds again in their second and
last meeting, it is clear that Leonora feels deeply troubled. She is preoccupied by
the thought of her dead father, who wanted a grandson and who, she feels, is
now getting his revenge in Daniel's love of Judaism. She hopes that in giving
Daniel his family history, recorded in the papers in the chest her father's friend
Joseph Kalonymos has kept, she will lose her obsession with her father's judgment against her. Though she wants to keep her emotional distance, her "agitation" and "trembling" are clear when she says: "You shall let me think of you as
happy. I shall have done you no harm. . . . And I shall see you instead of always
seeing your grandfather" (569). After all her hatred of Judaism, she invokes its

ritual prayer for the dead; after her double rejection of Daniel, she imagines a tableau in which their relationship is forever memorialized as loving: "if you think *Kaddish* will help me—say it, say it. You will come between me and the dead. When I am in your mind, you will look as you do now—always as if you were a tender son,—always—as if I had been a tender mother" (569). The formulation of this last phrase recalls the fact that her behavior has been described as "sincere acting" (539). This seems the most intense moment of their interview; after this point, she asks about the woman he loves, imagines what her life would have been like if they had stayed together—"you would have hampered my life with your young growth from the old root" (571)—and acknowledges, with regard to her other children, "I am not a loving woman" (571). Daniel is "saddened more and more" and has "a grave, sad sense of his mother's privation" (571) in the unhappiness that her lack of love seems to produce: "All his boyish yearnings and anxieties about his mother had vanished. He had gone through a tragic experience which must forever solemnize his life, and deepen the significance of the acts by which he bound himself to others" (571). His choice of binding acts reverses her glorification of "escaping from bondage" (541) by being a singer.

What a nemesis George Eliot places on the birth mother, one might say. But what power some of her lines have. Leonora has the eloquence of the determined female artist/individualist, and even a minimal knowledge of Eliot's life might suggest that she was drawing on some of her own feelings in writing this dialogue. Her ability to project herself into both Daniel and Leonora is part of what contributes to this scene. Rosemarie Bodenheimer has suggested a more specific biographical resonance, returning to Eliot's relationship with her stepchildren. By the time Eliot wrote *Daniel Deronda,* her two younger stepsons, Thornie and Bertie, had both died. These were the stepsons who, unlike Charles, had lived with her only briefly—except in that Thornie came home to die while she was writing *Middlemarch.* Thornie had been, according to Lewes's journal, "shipped off to Natal, well equipped with funds, outfit, and letters, to seek a career for himself there."[16] Bertie had followed him to the Transvaal. Bodenheimer shows that Eliot and Lewes occasionally wondered about their behavior with regard to these stepsons and concluded that they had done the best they could have. Bodenheimer's conjecture that Eliot was emotionally somewhat removed from these stepsons puts a different light on Leonora's withdrawal.[17]

But the significance of this portion of the book is not limited to its connection to Eliot's biography. It provides, among other things, one of the most detailed pictures in literature of a confrontation between adoptee and birth mother. Many issues potentially involved in these confrontations—issues of guilt, forgiveness, family history, and secrecy, as well as the question of alternative pasts—are raised here in depth provided by no other work of literature that I know. In *Oedipus,* Jocasta kills herself before she and her son can have this conversation. Literature does not provide such talks with birth fathers, either. In *The Winter's Tale*, Perdita and her mother have lines of happiness at being reconciled to each other, but once the family is miraculously restored, neither confronts Leontes about his earlier decision to get rid of his daughter. Even in Eliot's own *Silas Marner*, when Eppie discovers that Godfrey is her birth father, the scene ends without an extended dialogue between the two of them.

It may seem ironic that a work where the adoptee chooses hereditary identity is the one that has the most explicit confrontation with a birth parent—but perhaps it is not ironic but logical. If this were a reunion that reconstituted a family, the novel might end there and, in the let-bygones-be bygones spirit of Shakespearean conclusions, save the explanations for later. But since Leonora does not want any continuing relationship with him, the more important heredity is to Daniel, the more she must account for her behavior. Two aspects of hereditary identity are at stake for Daniel—being a Jew and being a son. Although his mother will not acknowledge him publicly, he can still regain his heredity by identifying as a Jew.

In *Silas Marner* and *Felix Holt*, the adoptee chooses her adoptive father over biological ancestry. In *Deronda*, the adoptee chooses biological ancestry, even though his biological mother in effect rejects him again. Did Eliot simply change her mind about what aspect of identity was more important for the adoptee?

In each case, turning from a rich but in some ways cold world, the adoptee chooses the group that is more oppressed, whether because of class or poverty (in *Silas Marner* and *Holt*) or race/ethnicity (in *Deronda*). The adoptee also always chooses the group or person that is more associated with religion or religious imagery or language. Silas, in spite of his disillusionment with the religious sect of his youth, returns to religion, largely under Dolly's influence, wanting to do what is best for Eppie. Daniel chooses a Judaism associated strongly with religious mysticism and ritual; though he speaks of having gained Christian sympathies, and though there are references to historical situations where minority Catholic or Protestant devotion is heartfelt ("Gwendolen kept her faith [in Deronda] with a more anxious tenacity, as a Protestant of old kept his Bible hidden or a Catholic his crucifix, according to the side favoured by the civil arm" [507]), the novel's picture of institutional Christianity in its own day is dismal. The Reverend Mr. Gascoyne, for example, urges Gwendolen to the financially advantageous but loveless and ultimately disastrous marriage to Grandcourt. In spite of Eliot's own dissent from any organized religion, in these novels she presents the heritage with spiritual value and the heritage with material value as opposed to each other. The successful adoptions are into households that have or develop a religious sense of community with others. Daniel finds this value in Judaism instead.

Each novel is in part a rejection of the dominant upper-class English culture and a critique of certain kinds of family dynamics, especially secrecy and treating children as possessions and conveniences. In *Silas Marner*, the biological father is secretive, while Silas is completely open. In *Deronda*, the adoptive father, Sir Hugo, becomes open only when forced, after Daniel has for a long time lived with a completely false picture of his heredity. The adoptive father Silas provides hands-on care; Sir Hugo enjoys being with Dan but does not expend much thought or effort on child rearing, as far as we can see. On one level, the adoptee's choice in *Silas* and *Deronda* is a consequence of deficiencies in parenting—in one case by Godfrey, in the other by Sir Hugo. In *Silas Marner*, it is clearly a reward for Silas.

But Hugo's deficiency in parenting does not completely account for Daniel's choice, since his biological mother does even less for him as a parent than Sir Hugo does. The most significant contrast among the novels—closely related to the increasing importance of the ideas of nationalism and blood in nineteenth-century Europe—is that in each one the emphasis on the difference of the adoptee increases.[18] The greater the emphasis on ethnic and cultural difference, the more the adoptee is likely to choose genetic identity. Eppie notices her physical difference from Silas and the other girls of her town, but no one else does, and it is clearly much less important to her than her love of Silas and Aaron and her related feeling that she likes "the working-folks, and their houses, and their ways" (173). In *Felix Holt*, Esther's differences from her adoptive father, Rufus, are associated in part with national differences between French and English (which come in Esther's case from environment as well as from heredity) as well as with her genetic father's aristocratic ancestry. But in *Deronda*, the issue of racial difference, as Eliot considered it, is central; in a letter to Harriet Beecher Stowe, Eliot describes the novel as an effort to counter "the usual attitude of Christians toward Jews" and "to treat Jews with such sympathy and understanding as my nature and knowledge could attain to." She writes, "There is nothing I should care more to do, if it were possible, than to rouse the imagination of men and women to a vision of human claims in those races of their fellow-men who most differ from them in customs and beliefs" (*GEL* 6:301–2).

Eliot uses Daniel's search to find out about Judaism before he knows he is Jewish as a way to inform her readers about it, using this apparently ideal English gentleman as a surrogate to disarm any prejudice.[19] One of her points is that Daniel benefits from learning not only about his birth parents but also about his connection to a valuable cultural tradition and community. Indeed, when Eliot used the word *race*, the meaning was partly cultural, because of her belief in the inheritance of acquired characteristics—experience transmitted by heredity.[20] The most important part of Jewishness for Daniel is not simply biology but the Jewish culture that his mother has rejected. And it is Mordecai and Mirah, whom he marries at the end of the novel, who consolidate this part of his identity. Daniel says, "I am finding the clue of my life in the recognition of my natural parentage" (643), but in some ways the "spiritual parentage" (his term) that he finds in Mordecai is at least as important.[21] The biblical Mordechai's status as an adoptive parent (in the Book of Esther) may well be relevant here: perhaps reinforcing the affinity that the characters have in the novel is the fact that both the biblical Daniel and the biblical Mordechai are dreamers and interpreters of prophetic dreams. So, in some ways, *Daniel Deronda* too can fit Bodenheimer's generalization about Eliot's privileging of fostering over kinship. Sir Hugo is an inadequate foster parent for Daniel, but Mordecai is the spiritual parent he really needs. As Gillian Beer says, Eliot recognizes, in herself and her culture, the "drive back toward origins, the Oedipus story," and counters it "with an equally intense movement toward differentiation, expansion, lateral kinning, fostering and foster parenting, and sympathetic generalisation, which all create new and multiple relationships."[22] Yet Mordecai's kind of fostering—focusing on Daniel's need for vocation, tradition, and identity—is crucially different from Silas's child-nurturing.

With the combination of his heredity and Mordecai's "spiritual parentage," Daniel is able to enter into a Jewish culture that is enough of an "imagined community," in Benedict Anderson's term, to become a nation. The novel includes explicit suggestions of parallelism between Jewish nationalism and Italian nationalism—Mirah sings "O Patria Mia," Leopardi's grand ode to Italy (414), and Daniel uses Mazzini's struggle for a united Italy as a model for the possible rebirth of a Jewish nation (457). But other kinds of nationalism are evoked too, Scottish—suggesting a parallel between the situation of Scotland and the Jews in England developed by Sir Walter Scott—and American.[23] Early in his life, Daniel "easily forgot his own existence in that of Robert Bruce" (143), a hero of Scottish nationalism, and tells his tutor that he would like to be a "leader, like Pericles or Washington" (147).

Daniel's desire to be such a leader—and his eventual commitment to political leadership at the end of the novel—had a special meaning at the time of the novel's writing, when Benjamin Disraeli, a Jew converted at a young age to Christianity but still maintaining a strong identification with Judaism, was prime minister. As Michael Ragussis has shown, Daniel is a kind of fantasy transformation of Disraeli, whose emphasis on what Jewishness and Christianity have in common is echoed in some of the dialogue in Eliot's novel. Eliot's early letters show that in her youth she had strong criticisms to make of the "fellowship of race" (*GEL*, 1:246)—referring to Judaism—in Disraeli's novels, but Eliot's views about Judaism and race changed later in her career. Deronda and Disraeli "both are descended not only from English and Italian Jews but from those Iberian Jews persecuted and banished in the late fifteenth century," Ragussis points out.[24] The preparation for leadership Deronda receives from his double identity—Jewish ancestry, Christian English education—rewrites a frequently hostile comparison often made between Disraeli and the prototypical adoptee Moses. Ragussis argues convincingly that the plot of *Daniel Deronda* "functions symbolically to liberate Disraeli to do what his critics accused him of doing, under cover of being the leader of Protestant England—to represent his own ancestral people, to seek their best interest."[25]

Nevertheless, in each of these novels there is at least one gesture toward the identity—biological or adoptive—that is not chosen. Eppie allows Godfrey to pay for her wedding, though no one knows why. Esther keeps her natural curls and can improve Felix's French accent. In *Deronda,* Daniel says to his mother:

> The effect of my education can never be done away with. . . . The Christian sympathies in which my mind was reared can never die out of me. . . . I will admit that there may come some benefit from the education you chose for me. I prefer cherishing the benefit with gratitude, to dwelling with resentment on the injury. I think it would have been right that I should have been brought up with the consciousness that I was a Jew, but it must always have been a good to me to have as wide an instruction and sympathy as possible. (566–67)

To use a modern phrase, Daniel is a cultural hybrid.[26] As Gillian Beer says, he is "enriched by the multiple past, both genetic and cultural."[27] Though he wants to found a Jewish nation, he knows that he cannot return to a pure Judaism from the past: "I shall call myself a Jew. . . . But I will not say that I shall profess to believe exactly as my fathers have believed. Our fathers themselves changed the horizon of their belief and learned of other races" (620). In Daniel's words, the narrator's, and even Mordecai's, the novel values both nation building and diversity. "We English are a miscellaneous people" (85), says the narrator, invoking the late Victorian commonplace that English people came from a variety of ethnic traditions—even if not as various as today.[28] Mrs. Meyrick, the best mother in the novel, possesses a "happy mixture of Scottish caution with her Scottish fervour and Gallic liveliness" (484). Klesmer, similarly, is a "felicitous combination of the German, the Sclave, and the Semite" (37). When Mordecai describes his vision of a Jewish nation, he imagines it as carrying "the culture and the sympathies of every great nation in its bosom" (456), not only as "purified," but also as "enriched by the experience our greatest sons have gathered from the life of the ages . . . Only two centuries since a vessel carried over the ocean the beginning of the great North American nation. The people grew like meeting waters—they were various in habit and sect. . . . What had they to form a polity with but memories of Europe, corrected by the vision of a better?" (458).

Much as I—a hybrid myself—would like to stress Daniel's hybridity, however, his final discussions of his identity seem more unified than this term suggests. His upbringing outside Judaism is placed in a very Jewish context—he has been prepared, "as Moses was prepared, to serve [his] people the better" (641).

He identifies himself to Mordecai, without qualification, as a Jew, "enjoying one of those rare moments when our yearnings and our acts can be completely one, and the real we behold is our ideal good" (640). He compares himself to

> the stolen offspring of some mountain tribe brought up in a city of the plain, or one with an inherited genius for painting, and born blind—the ancestral life would lie within them as a dim longing for unknown objects and sensations, and the spell-bound habit of their inherited frames would be like a cunningly-wrought musical instrument, never played on, but quivering throughout in uneasy mysterious moanings of its intricate structure that, under the right touch, gives music. (642)

The attitude toward Daniel's identity in this novel is split. This corresponds to the ideological currents in conflict at the time, in which racial and biological concepts of nationhood were beginning to become more widespread. Eliot uses imagery of biological ancestry, as in the preceding passage and in the plot, for which the revelation of Daniel's original parentage is crucial. But Daniel's choice of Judaism, like the choices of Eliot's earlier adoptees, can also be seen as an act of sympathy, though in David Marshall's phrase it is more obviously "far-reaching" than theirs.[29] As Eliot emphasizes, this sympathy is partial, not universal, but the same is true of Eppie's choice of Silas and the poor instead of Godfrey and the rich. In *Deronda,* however, we see more of Eliot's interest in the way that sympathy brings what is distant close, as well as the special paradox that the strangers to whom sympathy brings Daniel close are in some ways already close to him without his knowledge.

As Beer points out, there are links between Eliot's interest in sympathy and her interest in fostering—and, I might add, in good and bad conditions for adoption.[30] With both sympathy and adoption, Eliot is interested in relationships that are not confined to the biological family. Using adoption permits her to explore two kinds of what Judith Modell has called "kinship with strangers"—both adoptive kinship and the kinship of the adoptee with unknown relatives.[31] Arguably, adoption can be seen as a kind of paradigmatic gesture of sympathy—taking on responsibility for another—which often then presents the adult adoptee with the further challenge of deciding where sympathy makes the strongest claim. But Eliot's portrayal of some adoptive parents enacts what could be called either a critique of sympathy or a critique of apparent sympathy unaware of its object's real needs. While Silas and Rufus show sympathy, Sir Hugo's wish to raise Daniel does not bring an understanding of Daniel's feelings.

While sympathy has often been gendered as feminine, none of Eliot's fictional portrayals of an adoptee's choice includes a living adoptive mother. Eliot does not exclude women from an interest in nurturing outside the family. Dolly helps Silas bring up Eppie, and Mrs. Meyrick provides a temporary home for Mirah. But Eliot does not focus on the relationship of a woman and her adopted child over time from infancy to adolescence or older. In all three novels, *Silas Marner, Felix Holt,* and *Daniel Deronda,* the focus on an adopting father dramatizes more emphatically the continued loss of the birth mother. Raised by men, Eppie, Esther, and Daniel all wonder about the woman who bore them in a way they might not if they had adoptive mothers. Furthermore, because Silas and Rufus do not have wives and are less social than Sir Hugo (who marries late in the novel), their relationship with their daughters involves more emotional need and dependence on the fathers' part. The maternal absence raises more emphatically the question of how much the fathers will take on maternal nurturing, and the novels show clearly that Silas, at one extreme, does, and Hugo, at another extreme, does not.

In focusing on parental relationships that are complicated, in one way or another, by adoption, Eliot is, among other things, moving away from the celebration of maternal instinct common in her society. The women who nurture outside their family, the men who adopt, and the unmaternal mothers such as Leonora, all provide implicit arguments against seeing nurturing as an instinctive capacity determined by women's biology alone.[32] This seems parallel to the critique in *Silas Marner* and *Felix Holt* of the belief that loyalty should be determined by heredity alone.

Daniel is the only one of Eliot's adoptees in these novels with a living birth mother and a dead birth father; he is also the only one whose dead grandfather is a strong presence. This gender distribution is inextricably involved with the novel's complex consideration of Judaism and of women's experiences versus cultural ideas about women. Daniel must have a Jewish mother to be unquestionably Jewish by blood, and his mythic image of what his birth mother will be like is rather like the traditional Jewish image of woman—Leonora cannot fit into either. The grandfather's love of Jewish traditions and, especially, his longing for a grandson are presented in the novel as at the same time oppressive to Leonora and appealing to Daniel.

Daniel is also the only male adoptee Eliot represents as choosing between birth and adoptive families—after she has considered that choice in Eppie and Esther.[33] He is, however, repeatedly identified, by both Eliot and her critics, as having many qualities conventionally considered feminine. This "femininity" is partly related to a tradition of analogy between Jews and women, as oppressed groups and cultural others. The analogy has its positive dimension as well as its negative one; Daniel values Judaism for its transmission of emotion rather as Eliot values cultural femininity ("gentleness, tenderness, possible maternity suffusing a woman's being with affectionateness, which makes what we mean by the feminine character" [*GEL*, 4:469]).

As an adoptee, Daniel is a member of another group in some ways outside the dominant culture; this is dramatized in his inability to inherit his uncle's estate, an inability he shares with his uncle's daughters.[34] The novel closely links exclusion related to birth status—seen in the condition of Mrs. Glasher's illegitimate children as well as in Daniel's assumed bastardy—with exclusion related to gender. Arguably the novel thus suggests that Daniel as an adoptee is in a feminine position. The very situation of being transferred from one family to another, of having their name changed, gives adoptees early in their life an experience of forced adaptability similar to what is expected of women when they are married; Daniel's too diffuse sympathy and his passivity continue this adaptability until his final commitment to build a Jewish nation.[35]

More obviously, the novel encourages thought about analogies between prejudices and restrictions against women (from which Gwendolen suffers) and prejudices against Jews (from which Daniel is apparently protected by his upbringing, but which occur in many characters' casual statements).[36] In her own earlier life, Eliot had dealt with restrictions against women, but her late letters emphasize her solidarity with women as a group in a way that could be compared to Deronda's attitude toward being a Jew. One might say that her novels had become the woman's homeland she could create, except that Eliot's solidarity with women was not of the kind that wanted, either literally or metaphorically, a separate land for women. Eliot could not have the kind of heroic nation-founding life that Daniel could have, and the novel reminds us that no woman in her time could. Yet history since Eliot's time has shown that such nation building as Daniel's has problems when it is ethnically based as well, so it is possible that some of the difficulties of a hypothetical feminist nation—the problems of exclusion—have a message for everyone.

The relation between these two novels by Eliot is amazingly similar to the relation between two novels written by Barbara Kingsolver in the United States more than a hundred years later—when adoption apparently has quite a different national status. In Kingsolver's *The Bean Trees* (1988), Taylor's adoption of the abused child she calls Turtle is seen as an unproblematic good for Turtle; in *Pigs in Heaven* (1993), discussed by Kristina Fagan in this collection, Turtle's Cherokee relatives, her hereditary milk intolerance, and how she will deal with anti-Indian prejudice must all be reckoned with. Furthermore, *Pigs in Heaven*, like *Daniel Deronda*, emphasizes the importance to the adoptee of having an identity as part of a community, not just as an individual, and gives a vivid picture of the culture that has been maintained by the group to which the adoptee is linked by birth. Both novels have as one aim educating their readers about the history of an oppressed minority group and criticizing some aspects of the dominant culture. Both novels can be seen as very much in dialogue with ethnic/racial controversies of their day.

From the shift in Eliot's and Kingsolver's emphases, we can see that the construction of identity in novels dealing with adoption depends on many other cultural and historical issues. While Eliot finally shows Deronda as a Jew who must leave England to struggle for a Jewish nation, Kingsolver's adoptee, living in the United States at a time of contested multiculturalism, can have loving homes in both the Cherokee Nation and Tucson.

Pigs in Heaven follows a road not taken in *Daniel Deronda,* an alternative to Daniel's clear choice not only of a minority identity but of a new nation. As Fagan argues, Kingsolver's ending is a fantasy; as other critics have written, *Deronda*'s ending is a fantasy as well, though its prophetic dimension shows one of the more obvious ways in which novelistic fantasies can have real historical effects.[37] But the multicultural quality of Mordecai's fantasy nation, modeled on a diversity associated with the United States, is seldom remembered.

Silas Marner and *Daniel Deronda* are unusual among Victorian novels in the extent to which their plots turn on an adoptee's choice between two families. Did Eliot change her mind about adoption in the years between them? There are many continuities in her treatment of adoption in the two novels, but clearly in *Daniel Deronda* she was interested in making the adoption/discovery plot intersect with more concerns. The first book redefines the terms *father* and *nature.* The second, written in a time of increasing nationalism, shows how adoption narratives can deal not only with individual identity and kinship constructions but also with how these are related to ethnicity, nationhood, and cultural traditions. Its exploration of the pain possible in a cross-cultural adoption—together with the joy possible in reaffirming one's newly discovered culture, even without a continuing relationship to a close biological family—could resonate with many adoptees and with those who have lost and found traditions for other reasons. In focusing on the loss and recovery of Jewishness, the novel deals with an identity particularly targeted by prejudice—and particularly ambiguous about whether it is ethnic or religious—and therefore hidden in many more families than adoptive ones. Yet despite the novel's emphasis on culture as well as heredity, its move from finding a parent to founding a nation may well seem dangerously close to the biological nationalism that we have seen leading to too much bloodshed at the end of the twentieth century.

NOTES

For helpful comments on earlier versions of this essay, I would especially like to thank Rachel Brownstein, Nancy Glazener, Suzanne Juhasz, David Moldstad, Tess O'Toole, and Carol Singley.

1. Bernard Semmel, *George Eliot and the Politics of National Inheritance* (New York: Oxford University Press, 1994).

2. See George K. Behlmer, *Friends of the Family: The English Home and Its Guardians* (Stanford: Stanford University Press, 1998), 272–300, on what he calls de facto adoption and its abuses. See also Penny Martin, *Victorian Families in Fact and Fiction* (New York:

St. Martin's, 1995), 135: "anybody could give or sell a child to somebody else and any-body could take on a child—without it acquiring any legal rights within a new family."

3. George Eliot, *The Mill on the Floss*, ed. Carol T. Christ (New York: Norton, 1994), 90. Rosemarie Bodenheimer, in *The Real Life of Mary Ann Evans: George Eliot, Her Letters and Fiction* (Ithaca: Cornell University Press, 1994), 32, notes that in her youth, Eliot "never had a family member who understood or shared anything about her intellectual ambition or her emotional volatility," and, of course, during her adulthood most of her relatives rejected her because of her relationship with Lewes. Semmel (*George Eliot*, 16) also discusses this issue.

4. Bodenheimer, *Real Life*, 188.

5. Ibid., 230. Around 1855, during the time that she had committed herself to Lewes but they had not revealed this to his sons, she took notes on a story in which "a man of wealth in Rome adopted a poor boy he had found in the street" who turned out to be a great villain (George Eliot, *A Writer's Notebook, 1854–1879, and Uncollected Writings*, ed. Joseph Wiesenfarth [Charlottesville: University Press of Virginia, 1981], 23). This dysphoric adoption plot is the germ of the Tito/Baldassare plot in *Romola*, and it is also tempting to see her interest in this story at this time as a suggestion of some anxiety about her prospective relation to Lewes's sons.

6. *The George Eliot Letters*, ed. Gordon S. Haight, 9 vols. (New Haven: Yale University Press, 1954–78), 3:360. Subsequent references to this collection (hereafter cited as *GEL*) appear parenthetically in text. The adoption at issue for most of *Romola* is the disastrous one of Tito, though Romola herself becomes an adoptive mother near the end.

7. George Eliot, *Silas Marner* (London: Everyman, 1993), 169. Subsequent references to this work are given parenthetically in text.

8. This saying is introduced while discussing Lammeter's difference in appearance from Squire Cass and the Raveloe farmers generally. Introducing such differences, like Silas's difference from the other villagers, is one of the ways the novel breaks up the effect of the class/physical contrast between Silas and Godfrey.

9. As Susan R. Cohen says in "'A History and a Metamorphosis': Continuity and Discontinuity in *Silas Marner*," *Texas Studies in Literature and Language* 25 (1983): 416, "the true bond is creative human affection."

10. Bodenheimer, *Real Life*, 206.

11. Nancy Paxton, *George Eliot and Herbert Spencer* (Princeton: Princeton University Press, 1991), 110.

12. See Northrop Frye, *The Secular Scripture* (Cambridge: Harvard University Press, 1976), 101–2, 161.

13. For a detailed discussion of this theme in *Deronda*, see Carolyn Dever, *Death and the Mother from Dickens to Freud: Victorian Fiction and the Anxiety of Origins* (Cambridge: Cambridge University Press, 1998), 143–75.

14. George Eliot, *Daniel Deronda*, ed. Graham Handley (New York: Oxford University Press, 1988), 142. Subsequent references to this work are given parenthetically in text.

15. George Eliot, *Adam Bede*, ed. Valentine Cunningham (New York: Oxford University Press, 1996), 39–40.

16. Quoted in Bodenheimer, *Real Life*, 214.

17. Bodenheimer, *Real Life*, 227–30.

18. On changing modes of nationalism in the nineteenth century, see Benjamin Barber, *Jihad vs. McWorld* (New York: Ballantine, 1996), 159–60, and Eric Hobsbawm, *Na-*

tions and Nationalism since 1780 (Cambridge: Cambridge University Press, 1992), 101–23. On the greater biological emphasis in late nineteenth-century racial theory, see Robert J. C. Young, *Colonial Desire: Hybridity in Theory, Culture, and Race* (London: Routledge, 1995), 118–41. In a notebook that includes material on Jewish history relevant to *Deronda*, Eliot also records evidence of hereditary gestures found in Darwin and Galton: see *Some George Eliot Notebooks: An Edition of the Carl H. Pforzheimer Library's George Eliot Holograph Notebooks,* ed. William Baker, vol. 3: Ms. 711 (Salzburg: Institut für Anglistik und Amerikanistik, 1980), 13.

19. Rachel Brownstein discusses this strategy in *Becoming a Heroine: Thinking about Women in Novels* (New York: Viking, 1982), 208.

20. See William Baker, *George Eliot and Judaism* (Salzburg: Institut für Englische Sprache und Literatur, 1975), 64–66. Eliot's views on this were not unusual.

21. Dever (*Death and the Mother,* 157) shows how Mordecai "represents, more than anyone else in the novel, the potential fulfillment of [Daniel's] eroticized phantasy of maternal reunion."

22. Gillian Beer, *George Eliot* (Bloomington: Indiana University Press, 1986), 54.

23. Michael Ragussis, *Figures of Conversion: "The Jewish Question" and English National Identity* (Durham: Duke University Press, 1995), 97.

24. Ibid., 263ff.; quote is from 281.

25. Ibid., 289.

26. Young (*Colonial Desire,* 6) writes that in the nineteenth century the term *hybrid* "was used to refer to a physiological phenomenon; in the twentieth century it has been reactivated to describe a cultural one." I am not using the word in the nineteenth-century sense involving a crossing between species or races.

27. Gillian Beer, *Darwin's Plots: Evolutionary Narrative in Darwin, George Eliot, and Nineteenth-Century Fiction* (London: Routledge and Kegan Paul, 1983), 201.

28. See Young, *Colonial Desire,* 17, and Hobsbawm, *Nations and Nationalism,* 33, 108.

29. David Marshall, *The Figure of Theater* (New York: Columbia, 1986), 219.

30. Beer, *George Eliot,* 109.

31. Judith Modell, *Kinship with Strangers: Adoption and Interpretations of Kinship in American Culture* (Berkeley: University of California Press, 1994).

32. Paxton, *George Eliot and Herbert Spencer,* 110, 215.

33. Tito in *Romola* is a very different kind of male adoptee.

34. See Tess O'Toole's chapter on Eliot in her book in progress on adoption in the Victorian novel.

35. Elements of Daniel's characterization that some critics have found implausible—his failure to question Sir Hugo about his heredity, his apparent asexuality, his extended sense of responsibility—correspond to behavior found by psychologists in someone who has taken on the role of the "good adoptee." See Betty Jean Lifton, *Lost and Found: The Adoption Experience* (1979; rev. ed. New York: Harper & Row, 1988), 54–57.

36. This theme in *Daniel Deronda* is treated by Susan Meyer in *Imperialism at Home: Race and Victorian Women's Fiction* (Ithaca: Cornell University Press, 1996), 157–94. However, I disagree with her argument that gender issues are displaced onto racial issues. As she indeed observes, there are many moments of protest against women's subordination in the novel. For more discussion of these, see Marianne Novy, *Engaging with Shakespeare: Responses of George Eliot and Other Women Novelists* (Athens: University of Georgia Press, 1994; rpt. Iowa City: University of Iowa Press, 1998), 123–24, 130, 132.

37. On fantasy elements in the presentation of Deronda's work for Judaism, see, for example, Susan Morgan, *Sisters in Time* (New York: Oxford, 1989), and Christina Crosby, *The Ends of History: Victorians and the Woman Question* (New York: Routledge, 1981). For the appeal of the "new nation" concept to other adoptees interested in their biological ancestry, note the name of an organization formed in 1997 to promote open records, Bastard Nation.

Outlaws, Outcasts, and Orphans

The Historical Imagination and *Anne of Green Gables*

Beverly Crockett

Discussions of L. M. Montgomery's popular girls' novel *Anne of Green Gables* (1908) have emphasized the "sunny" personality of the protagonist, literary allusions, and the presentation of romance and gender roles.[1] Those few scholars who have considered the historical circumstances of late nineteenth- and early twentieth-century Canada have focused primarily on autobiographical details, using Montgomery's diaries and letters to make connections between her writings and her life—her losing (at twenty-one months) her mother, spending little time with her father, living for many years with her grandparents, and eventually having to care for her grandmother.[2] The element that inspired the Anne story has been noted: in her journal, Montgomery recorded reading in 1895 a newspaper clipping about a couple who requested a child to work on their farm and were sent a girl, instead of the boy they wanted.[3] But the historical circumstances that would make such a request possible, events examined by historians during the past twenty years, have not been fully integrated into a comprehensive critical reading of Montgomery's most popular novel.[4]

Readers, especially younger ones, of *Anne of Green Gables* are carried along on the main current of the story by Anne's references to and acting out of the "hidden hero" myth, represented by such figures as Joseph and King Arthur.[5] The surface of the novel chiefly presents the bright, optimistic, and often comic view of an adopted girl's surviving her difficult past, overcoming obstacles, and growing up in a new family and environment.[6]

Nevertheless, a neglected subtext or underground current runs through the novel; it appears as well in popular culture, legal documents, and public records and represents children—particularly unsupervised children and orphans—as dangerous, alien, even monstrous creatures. Although the opposite view of children as the most vulnerable and helpless of victims, facing threats, exploitation, and abuse, gained ground during the nineteenth century, reforms in the legal and social structures and changes in popular ideology seldom kept pace. Thus, conflicting and ambivalent views of children appear in *Anne of Green Gables*, with negative attitudes usually articulated by unsympathetic and eventually discredited characters.

The first chapters of *Anne of Green Gables* might suggest that Montgomery is simply contrasting the imaginative protagonist, who responds to those places that nurture her aesthetic sense and provide "scope for the imagination,"[7] with the practical, unimaginative Prince Edward Island inhabitants, including Marilla and Matthew, Anne's adoptive parents. Anne's imagination draws on the dark romanticism of tragedies and melodramas, stories emphasizing danger and suffering,[8] but it also allows her to interpret and construct her life story, casting herself as a hero and transforming adversity into opportunity.[9]

Other characters in the novel also possess active, but malevolent, imaginations that spur their fears and reflect their ethnocentrism and prejudice; consequently, they view children of unknown parentage and other "alien," foreign creatures as potential threats. Even Marilla can be mistrustful, prompted by gossip and fear of the stranger. And because Anne is "literary" and less constrained by certain gender roles, she inadvertently exacerbates the Islanders' fears.

Central to the novel is the historical phenomenon of "placing out." Adult readers of Montgomery's generation would have known about children sent from institutions to "foster homes," and this knowledge would have affected their interpretation of *Anne of Green Gables;* perhaps, like Marilla, they initially might have been suspicious of Anne and would even need to be "educated" to see placing out from the orphan's perspective. But Marilla possesses enough of a sympathetic imagination to understand the contexts and subtexts that run through the girl's "autobiography" and thus can pity her.[10] The turning point occurs early in the novel, when Marilla, who had wanted a boy to help on the farm, decides that she will instead keep, raise, and educate Anne. The narrator's comment that Marilla is "shrewd enough to read between the lines" (*AGG* 41) can be seen as instructing all readers to be aware of social and historical contexts, especially the attitudes toward and treatment of orphans, foundlings, and other poor children.[11]

Even though Montgomery shows her protagonist winning over not only Marilla and Matthew but also neighbors, the author indicates lingering suspicions and prejudices against children who were placed out. Other realistic elements are the epithets flung at Anne (though milder than those endured by real home children) and the rumors associated with her coming to Prince Edward Island as an orphan; these recapture the negative social responses that actual children encountered when they were placed out during the late nineteenth and early twentieth century in America and Canada.

Historical Treatment of Orphans and Other Children

At least you don't know what it is to feel no one cares if you live or die—and wants you only if you can work hard.[12]

Children who are not under the direct control of adults—orphans, foundlings, runaways, others who must make their own way in the adult world and whose parentage and background is lower-class or unknown—have frequently been the objects of speculation and suspicion; they have often been represented in myth, literature, and popular ideology as threatening members of the "dangerous classes." These myths and popular beliefs encode the anxieties of many and may also shape the expectations of the children themselves.

Turn-of-the-century attitudes toward poor children and the processes of institutionalized care, apprenticing and indenturing, placing out, and adoption in Canada and the United States must be considered within the larger context of the history of the family and the presumed value of work, topics that have been explored by scholars during the last forty years.[13] Asylums, Foucault contends, were first established to control the poor, the insane, and the criminal.[14] For centuries, significant distinctions among groups of institutionalized children—vagrants, delinquents, bastards, foundlings, orphans, half-orphans, and other poor children who were temporary residents—have been overlooked by the public.

All these children might be stereotyped as bastards, troublemakers, or even congenitally corrupt young criminals. Because foundlings in hospitals were assumed to be bastards, a status that to the English, Canadian, and American middle class was opprobrious, attempts were made to set up institutions that dealt *only* with orphans and not with foundlings.[15] Although in nineteenth-century America, most of the institutions that cared for dependent children were popularly called "orphan asylums," Timothy Hacsi notes that "many children in the homes were not orphans but returned" to their families eventually.[16] Similarly, scholars surveying Canadian institutions have discovered that most "homes" or "asylums" for children "rarely included a majority of orphans—much less foundlings."[17] Children who had families were institutionalized as a result of parental behaviors or conditions—disease, presumed mental defects, sexual promiscuity, alcoholism, drug addiction, antisocial characteristics, or other conditions that resulted in poverty. Because the public believed these were genetic traits, they often assumed the children in institutions would develop the same afflictions. When the fear of immigrants intensified, the phrases "home children" (from Homes of Industry, i.e., institutions where children were supposedly trained to work), "orphans," or "Barnardo boys" (after one of the more famous reformers) might be cast as insults at children placed out by any institution, whether they were native-born Canadian orphans or street children from London or New York. Perceived as illegitimate, degenerate children and adolescents of unknown parentage and inferior genetic stock who had survived as "street Arabs" by criminal habits learned in the gutters in some city, they were now sent to rural areas in Canada and America, where they were thought to threaten the healthy and pure native stock.

Demographics and economics, historians note, could significantly affect the value accorded children.[18] Children who were a burden in cities might be welcome in rural areas;[19] for example, during the early and middle years of the nineteenth century in Canada, more workers were needed, and demand for children to work on farms outstripped the supply.[20] But when prosperity declined and inflation and a surplus of workers plagued urban areas, immigrants, "foreigners," and their children were accused of immorality, degeneracy, and spreading diseases, thus threatening "native" Canadians—rhetoric that disguised the underlying economic issue.[21]

The traditional discourse on the poor has invariably divided them into those who were "worthy" of help and those who were not. Even children's advocates in the nineteenth century distinguished between the "redeemable" poor children and the "corrupt" or "incorrigible" children, those seen as so degenerate and dangerous they might contaminate other, recoverable children, male or female.[22] Reformers, like politicians, believed that fixed "character" governed behavior.[23] But as historians have frequently noted, boundaries between categories of the poor were not permanently established: under the pressure of changes in the economy or personal circumstances, members of the honest "perishing" class might turn to crime or vice.[24]

Similarly, reformers employed rhetorical patterns that articulated social problems so that the victims themselves seemed to be the cause, as in the phrase "the problem of street children." Whether expressed by ordinary urban dwellers who feared theft and fraud or by reformers who worried that "dangerous" children would corrupt the "redeemable" ones, the language presented unsupervised children as threatening elements that must be controlled, not just for their own good, but for the protection of society. In Toronto at the turn of the twentieth century, adolescent girls, some fourteen and younger, who came to the city were viewed ambivalently: at first, there was worry that they were "potential victims" of sexual predators, but because they were without male supervision, freer than their rural or married sisters, and lacked adequate income, they were later seen as a "potential source of moral danger."[25] Instead of the public recognizing that these vulnerable workers were exploited by the capitalist system, the young women ultimately were thought to be the *cause* of the "girl problem."[26]

Pauper Apprenticeships, Indenturing, and Placing Out

From the middle of the sixteenth century, under the Poor Laws, English children could be arrested and sent to poorhouses (workhouses) if they were vagrants or beggars; they might then be bound out as "pauper apprentices," usually as agricultural laborers or domestics.[27] Considerably different from apprenticeships that were sought out and paid for by children's parents, pauper apprenticeships filled some of the same needs for adults, providing labor for tradesmen and control of the potentially unruly young, especially young men, a continual source of public anxiety.[28]

By the nineteenth century, various plans for pauper apprenticing placed children out in English factories and then in areas far removed from their homes. Placing out and other schemes were supported by most so-called social reformers, including the "child savers," who believed in the myth of the idyllic, healthful, pure, rural retreat and were inspired to send drunkards, former prostitutes, and children into the countryside as laborers, away from the urban environment (including the poor family), the presumed source of corruption.[29] The social reformers had middle-class values and an abiding concern with economics; exploitation was concealed by the mask of charity. Poor children, it was claimed, should expect nothing, be grateful for anything, and learn the work ethic and moral values by "earning their keep," an outlook suited to the class of working poor. But reformers' discourse ignores the obvious—children's labor benefited the institutions and foster families.[30]

Because overseers and governors of the English parish poorhouses were primarily concerned with economics, not pauper apprentices' training or welfare, they took little care in choosing households or in checking on the children. Since apprenticeships were established to control the young, "reasonable" corporeal correction—beating or whipping—was permitted by the master or mistress, as it would be by parents. Legal records indicate that many apprentices, most often boys, risked whipping, imprisonment, and branding by running away from their masters, which suggests intolerable conditions. Governors of institutions eagerly sought out official guardianships and power over these vulnerable children, a potential resource. But through the early twentieth century, sufficient care was not always taken to examine the foster homes or monitor the children.

In contrast to the regular English apprentice, who worked under a formal written contract that described the duties of the apprentice and master or mistress, a child placed out in North America—as a temporary worker or as a prospective adoptee—had few guarantees; his or her legal situation, and that of the foster family, was often nebulous. Even when written agreements existed, children's foster families did not always understand them, sometimes thinking that indenture papers were articles of adoption. Other children had no formal paperwork granting them legal protection at all.[31] In England and most of Canada, adoption was not codified until the 1920s.[32] Children had been taken in as family members before then in England and North America, but their legal situations under the common law seems to have been handled on an ad hoc basis.[33]

Many poor children in English, American, and Canadian cities around the turn of the century were described by observers and journalists as facing a struggle for survival.[34] But even well-intentioned reformers failed to distinguish between two groups: those children who were truly alone, such as orphans, the abandoned, and runaways; and those with impoverished families who used the asylum as a *temporary* refuge, intending to reclaim the children when circumstances improved.[35] Reformers often believed that having poor parents or relatives was worse than having none at all, and poor families were pressured to give up guardianship of children to institutions.[36]

Annie McPherson, Maria Rye, and Thomas Barnardo were among the better-known nineteenth-century reformers who gathered children from the slums in urban areas of the British Isles and fed them to Canadian farmers hungry for agricultural laborers (Bagnell, *Little Immigrants,* 19–36, 91–176). Andrew Doyle, appointed in 1874 by British legislators to investigate the practice, described deplorable negligence in the distribution of children; for example, Maria Rye handed out children who just disappeared (ibid., 33–57).

Despite Doyle's report, pauper apprenticing continued until the 1930s, because it benefited nearly all adults who had any political power: it eased the anxieties of urban dwellers who were frightened by the hordes of street children, offering the middle class a promise of supervision and control of latent criminals; and it provided farmers with cheap help (ibid., 61). Estimates vary, but at least eighty thousand children from Great Britain were placed out in Canada alone.[37] Changes in nineteenth-century indenturing did children little good and much harm; children were literally sold to factory owners or sent overseas to work on farms.[38] When, in November 1895, the body of fifteen-year-old George Green, pauper apprentice to Helen R. Findlay in Ontario, was found by a local doctor who testified the boy had been beaten, starved, and left lying in filth when he was too weak to move, the response of newspapers and public opinion was extraordinary—they blamed the dead child, labeling him a defective foreign creature. During these hard economic times when cities were overrun with children of immigrants and competition for jobs was keen, George Green became an emblem of the feared alien. Despite extensive evidence against Findlay, the jury could not reach a verdict and she went free (ibid., 63–69).

The trial after George Green's death, Kenneth Bagnell argues, marks the turning of the tide in Canada's use of children from institutions as cheap labor; from the 1870s onward, there were more complaints about the foreign threat and the evil influence of such children and other immigrants—reactions to an oversupply of workers in urban areas (ibid., 68–73, 81–84). Yet investigations by J. J. Kelso proved that some home children accused of assaults with fists and knives on their masters, sexual misbehavior, arson, poisonings, and a multitude of other crimes, were neither orphans nor foreigners (ibid., 73–74, 88–90, 177–80). Nevertheless, hysteria escalated while rumors and reports of the misdeeds of dangerous children circulated widely (ibid., 69–83). Editorials attacked those who sent to Canada "defective" children with "tainted blood" or genetic deformities, the results of parental syphilis.[39] Attitudes had changed dramatically from welcoming immigrant children as workers to blaming them for all manner of problems.[40]

Meanwhile, in America during the nineteenth century, similar placing-out schemes had been established, prompted by the same motives; most famous was

Charles Loring Brace's plan, which gathered children from eastern cities, loaded them onto trains, and distributed them in the Midwest.[41] But placing out was not just a phenomenon involving Canadian immigrant children from the British Isles or urban American children shipped to the Midwest. Children were also bound out locally from American, British, and Canadian asylums, sometimes for adoption, sometimes with formal indentures, sometimes with few formal agreements at all.[42] For example, children from Halifax and other nearby cities as well as emigrants from Great Britain were placed out in Nova Scotia, including Prince Edward Island.[43]

In Ontario as in England, children as young as six might be placed out as workers; usually permission was required only when the apprentice was fifteen or sixteen.[44] Runaway apprentices could be imprisoned: one boy was reportedly forced to spend the night "in the cell for condemned prisoners" when he threatened to run away from the Canadian farmer for whom he worked; the Barnardo inspector, however, subsequently removed the boy from the farmer's custody (Matthew Clarke, *HC*, 98–99).

Home Children's Own Stories

Though incomplete, the available records relating to children who were placed out suggest they had only a slim chance of truly becoming part of a family. Retrospective personal narratives, relating the subjective experiences of some former home children, have been collected.[45] Phyllis Harrison, for example, has gathered narratives of Canadian home children, and several World Wide Web pages call for more responses.[46] At least one award-winning children's book has been based on the experiences of a child placed out in America.[47] Many of the children's stories are melancholy; some are horrifying. Only a few indicate that home children were fully incorporated into a loving family that provided nurturing and an education as well as material necessities. The majority were not.

Certain themes run through memoirs submitted by former home children and their relatives.[48] Notable is the reluctance—indeed, the refusal—by some to talk about their histories at all.

> Here in Canada there are still people who would look down their noses at anyone raised in a Home. That is why I concoct nice stories to inquisitive friends who wonder how I came out here. I have wept some tears writing this. Much of it I have never told my husband. (Name withheld, *HC*, 197)

Readers can usually only speculate on whether avoidance of shame, painful memories, or other motives account for the silences.[49]

Children from institutions were distributed with some or virtually no checking on the adults who took them, and they were tracked carefully or completely lost track of, depending very much on the agency or institution that placed them out (Bagnell, *Little Immigrants*, 33–57). Those children who first spent weeks, months, or years in institutions report varying conditions. Some were very happy and especially appreciated the chance to obtain an education (Mrs. Lloyd Dorland, nee Vera A. Coote, *HC*, 207), while others were merely "waiting" to find foster homes (name withheld, *HC*, 196). All children were reportedly disciplined strictly and expected to work. Some institutions provided children with education, religious instruction, and training in domestic skills; in others, children might perform tasks requiring little training, such as cleaning. Boys in some institutions reportedly were "thrashed" in public or whipped until they bled (William Tonkin, *HC*, 99–100; W. R. Elliot, *HC*, 251–52). But physical punishment was supposedly against the policy of other institutions (William McFadden, *HC*, 149).

Many children from the British Isles or from cities apparently looked forward to going abroad with great hope and anticipation, eagerly accepting the myth of the New Land, even persuading stepparents or guardians to let them leave (J. L. Churcher, *HC*, 37; Jim Eccleston, *HC*, 113; and John T. Atkinson, *HC*, 119). But others were frightened or very reluctantly left relatives or even a foster family behind and would long to return to England (Gladys Jessie Simm, nee Hunt Harrison, *HC*, 188).

Families that wanted children sometimes advertised in newspapers for apprentices or "applied" in advance, specifying gender, age, and other attributes, with few or no checks at all of the adults' background—children and even infants of two might be shipped across the ocean to them. Children might start their journeys supervised by adults but later be put on trains and instructed to make the rest of the long trip alone.[50] Sometimes children were simply taken to train stations and displayed, like livestock, and then chosen or rejected; they might resent being assessed like horses or cattle and even physically resist selection, if they did not like the adult choosing them.[51] Or they might fear they would not be chosen and seek to make themselves desirable.

Although theoretically only true orphans could be adopted out, parents were pressured—or even deceived—into giving institutions guardianship, and sometimes children who were not orphans but temporarily residents of institutions were sent out, not tracked, and lost forever to their families.[52] Siblings might be kept together, but many were separated, so that years later adults would still be seeking brothers and sisters; others tried, frequently without success, to find remaining family members in England.[53]

Once they were taken home by a foster family, many children would be deeply disappointed.

My first farm home was dreadful. I was young and inexperienced, hardly knew how to wash a dish. The whole family ridiculed my accent and jeered at my clothes. The woman of the farm made no effort to help me and the old grandfather tried to make advances. (Name withheld, *HC*, 196)

This passage touches on several themes that appear frequently in the stories told by former home children. Most children quickly recognized that the so-called foster family saw them primarily as workers. If they seemed too small or fragile or did not work as skillfully or as hard as the family expected, they might be abused, verbally or physically, or returned to the institution.

Almost all of the former home children describe working extremely long hours on farms, even when quite young, doing jobs that would be difficult, exhausting, and even dangerous for larger and stronger adults. A number complained they were cheated of wages or required to pay for everything, including necessities like winter clothing, out of their meager earnings (Emma Magahay, *HC*, 28; daughter of Margaret Cleaves, nee Johnson, *HC*, 57). Foster families were described as impatient, having unrealistic expectations that the children already would be trained in agricultural and domestic work. Instead of being instructed, some former home children who did not known how to cook, take care of animals, or do farm work were returned to institutions (name withheld, *HC*, 196).

Because they were overworked and unable to walk the long distances to schools, especially in the cold Canadian winters, most of the children did not obtain the education promised to them, which they regretted (James Rooke, *HC*, 222; George Penfield, *HC*, 52). And although children were supposed to be placed with foster families that shared the religious beliefs of the children's parents, religious instruction of any kind was rare or, if required, seemed hypocritical (name withheld, *HC*, 155).

In addition to the hard physical labor and deprivation of education, many home children reported frequent, harsh—even brutal and life-threatening—physical abuse (daughter of Emma Magahay, nee Kennett, *HC*, 30–31; Harry Jeffery, *HC*, 62; the wife of William Wood, *HC*, 86; Charles W. Carver, *HC*, 90–91; Florence Horne, *HC*, 148; Michael Driscoll, *HC*, 162; name withheld, *HC*, 180; Charles R. Morris, *HC*, 203; Walter G. Always, *HC*, 227; E. Marshall, *HC*, 234). Some also complained of inadequate food, shelter, and clothing; several were crippled or even lost limbs after working or standing in the cold and damp (Charles W. Carver, *HC*, 91; Anna Hollamby, *HC*, 109–10). Women also reported sexual abuse—one was raped when a teenager; several were sexually molested as children; a number were subjected to sexual aggression or "indecent" male behavior; another suffered because of obliquely described "sex problems" (name withheld, *HC*, 206; Winnifred Titus, nee Jordan, *HC*, 184; Lillian McFadden, *HC*, 151; name withheld, *HC*, 196; Mrs. Selina M. Barker, *HC*, 140). Documents recount sexual molestation of girls at the institutions that were supposed to protect them; when one head of an asylum sexually abused a girl, his "defense" was the degeneracy of this class of children.[54] Because of direct threats, intimidation, a sense of shame, or a lack of anyone sympathetic to confide in, abused children might not reveal the disturbing events (Winnifred Titus, nee Jordan, *HC*, 184). At the turn of the century, when single "working girls" might be suspect because they were unsupervised and when the age of consent for sexual activity was as low as ten in the United States,[55] those who exploited girls sexually could escape legal as well as moral responsibility and cast blame on the victims. Not only did Canadians assume that home children were illegitimate, but they also believed the tendency was "hereditary."[56] However, the much higher rate of illegitimate births among Barnardo girls, Joy Parr asserts, was because apprentice contracts forbad marriage, and "many of the home girls' pregnancies resulted from *involuntary* liaisons with masters or hired men" (emphasis mine).[57] One former home girl explains, "I worked hard for everything I received, and it wasn't easy because people had the idea that Home girls couldn't be much good" (Mrs. Norah Gray, *HC*, 199).

The theme of loneliness also runs through many of the narratives, sometimes because of the differences in ages or status between the foster family's blood relatives and the child worker. Even among home children who expressed gratitude for being treated well, there were sometimes qualifications. Although Walter Baker worked for a young couple for years, he reported, "[a]t social gatherings I was 'our boy from the Barnardo Homes'" (*HC*, 106; see also James H. Atkinson, *HC*, 120–22; Colin Taylor, *HC*, 131).

However, a few children were incorporated into a foster family or were officially adopted (James J. Crookes, *HC*, 248). Mrs. Pollie Jones was "left everything" by an elderly spinster for whom she'd cared for years (*HC*, 122–23). Theodora Brown was adopted at the age of five by a wealthy Methodist couple; she later went on to attend McGill University (Bagnell, *Little Immigrants*, 192–96).

But sadly, even the bright childhood memories of Theodora Brown could be shadowed by her recollection of children shouting at her, "You're a home girl" (ibid., 194). The prejudices and suspicions of the foster families and neighbors, spurred by malicious newspaper accounts and gossip about orphans and immigrants, left impressions that the adults did not forget: often they were falsely accused of stealing, not trusted, believed to be juvenile delinquents, looked at (they felt) as "scum" or "freaks," and ridiculed for everything from their inexperience in doing farm chores to their accents and their clothes (George Sears, *HC*, 64; Jack Saunders, *HC*, 92; Clinton Webb, Sr., *HC*, 112; [first name withheld] Miller, *HC*, 136; Jack W. [full surname withheld], *HC*, 142; Michael Driscoll, *HC*, 161; name withheld, *HC*, 180–81; William Tonkin, *HC*, 102; Mrs. Lloyd Dorland, nee Vera A. Coote, *HC*, 208).

Although agencies claimed they would check on children placed in foster families, some children apparently never saw an inspector. Others reported semiannual visits, and inspectors often did remove children if problems were detected (Frances Burchett, *HC*, 190; James Wilde, *HC*, 153; Michael Driscoll, *HC*, 162). However, if the numerous complaints of mistreatment are true, either some children were not monitored, visits were too infrequent to prevent months of suffering, or the abuse was never noticed.

Many children were moved several times. Older ones were fortunate if they could settle as workers with a family until they turned sixteen or eighteen. Frequently only the youngest children—foundlings, true orphans, or children relinquished by their parents—were eligible for actual adoption. And those who were perceived as having "defects," physical, mental, or moral, were often shuffled from household to household and returned to institutions;[58] some immigrants were considered so "unfit" or "undesirable" that they were deported.[59]

Yet Canada truly became "home" for some former home children who never wished to return or renew relationships with anyone in England (Mary Wallace Blake, *HC*, 119; J. L. Churcher, *HC*, 39). Others were sorely disappointed and distressed by the lack of care, education, or affection; others who still had relatives living felt torn away from their homeland. Not a few of the adolescent young men ran away from their foster families and sought work elsewhere or joined the armed forces, many serving in World War I.

Certain nineteenth-century attitudes help explain some former home children's acceptance of long days of hard work (provided they were paid fairly or treated well in other ways) and their gratitude for the chance to start anew in Canada. As the pragmatic James Rook said: "These people I lived with were kind enough to me. I really had no complaints except that they were childless and I had no one my own age to fraternize with. But after all I was sent there to work and not to play" (*HC*, 222). All members of most families were expected to work; children could go to school only when there was no necessary work to be done. Thus, attempts to educate servants or street children in Canadian cities were often ineffectual.[60] Legal restrictions on child labor during the nineteenth century in England and the United States focused at first on regulating the conditions, hours, and type of work performed by child laborers, though the permitted age for factory work also was gradually raised.[61] Laws passed in late nineteenth-century Canada limited hours for teenage workers and outlawed only factory, not farm, work for boys under twelve and girls under fourteen.[62]

Many children placed with unsatisfactory foster families probably believed that they had few options. At thirteen, one girl endured stays with several violent persons and sexual aggressors but did not request removal because she feared she "might get into a worse place" (Lillian McFadden, *HC*, 151). Fearful, vulnerable, and insecure because of the uncertainty and precariousness of their situations, these children may have clung to what was difficult but stable so long as the situation was not intolerable.

Anne of Green Gables

"Were those women—Mrs. Thomas and Mrs. Hammond—good to you?" asked Marilla, looking at Anne out of the corner of her eye.

"O-o-o-h," faltered Anne. Her sensitive little face suddenly flushed scarlet and embarrassment sat on her brow. "Oh they *meant* to be—I know they meant to be just as good and kind as possible. And when people mean to be good to you, you don't mind very much when they're not quite—always. They had a good deal to worry them, you know. It's very trying to have a drunken husband, you see; and it must be very trying to have twins three times in succession, don't you think? But I feel sure they meant to be good to me."

Marilla asked no more questions. . . . Pity was suddenly stirring in her heart for the child. What a starved, unloved life she had had—a life of drudgery and poverty and neglect; for Marilla was shrewd enough to read between the lines of Anne's history and divine the truth. No wonder she had been so delighted at the prospect of a real home. (*AGG*, 41)

Anne Shirley's life before coming to Green Gables is presented in the harsh terms of the historic use and abuse of children, especially the exploitation of orphans, reminding us that Matthew and Marilla Cuthbert's original motive for requesting a child was to get help on the farm. Montgomery grew up in a household abundantly supplied with newspapers and magazines and later worked as a reporter in Toronto; she must have read and heard much about the attitudes toward and treatment of orphans in Canada.[63] While Montgomery keeps these historical circumstances in the background and discredits the fear of orphans, the alert reader will attend to these articulations of attitudes toward children.

Montgomery's choice of an omniscient narrator allows her to present various points of view, although clearly the narrative voice is sympathetic to Anne and helps shape our responses.[64] The novel opens with a humorous description of how nature, specifically the stream, becomes "a quiet, well-conducted little stream, for not even a brook could run past Mrs. Rachel Lynd's door without due regard for decency and decorum" (*AGG*, 1). Tamed are "brooks and children" alike once they come within range of Rachel's "all-seeing eye" (1–2)—this phrase initiates a recurring theme of the islanders watching out for strangers, alien invaders, or other potentially wild, unsupervised phenomenon, like unruly children. If watching fails, corporal punishment will be advocated.[65]

This passage indicates that Rachel will be the spokesperson for many conventional views; Rachel's discourse also introduces, though humorously, themes of disaster and criminality: she entertains and dismisses the notion that Matthew's unusual departure at midday suggests a medical emergency; later she thinks, "A body can get used to anything, even to being hanged, as the Irishman said" (3), a curious proverb linking the ubiquitous Celtic aliens/foreigners/outsiders to rogues and criminals.

Rachel also thinks Matthew and Marilla are "a little odd" (3): Matthew is shy and taciturn; Marilla, the narrator says, "looked like a woman of narrow experience and rigid conscience, which she was," but she has a latent sense of humor that Anne will appeal to (4). Marilla startles Rachel by explaining that since Mrs. Spencer had gone over to get a little girl from the "orphan asylum in Nova Scotia" (5), Marilla and Matthew requested she also fetch them a boy. This is an eminently practical decision, because Matthew has heart trouble and farm workers are in short supply. But Marilla declares she will take into their home no foreigners, no "stupid, half-grown French boys," no "Barnardo boys." She concedes that they "may be all right," but she adds: "no London street Arabs for me. . . . Give me a native born at least" (6). A child born in Nova Scotia, she believes, "can't be much different from ourselves" (7). Though ethnocentric, Marilla at least assumes that "native-born" Canadian children have certain universal human qualities, and she recognizes that raising any child, even one's own, is taking a chance. The xenophobic Rachel, however, is shocked and relates to Marilla all the stories about home children that had been circulating in newspapers and by word of mouth in Canadian communities for twenty years—from absurdly trivial ones that make children sound like animals, foxes or dogs that cannot be trained not to suck eggs, to those that blame orphans for violent and murderous acts, including poisoning wells and arson.

Eventually, Anne, the "imported orphan" (8), wins Rachel over completely, but these same themes recur later. Away at school, Anne is described by Josie Pye as an orphan "living on charity," whose past is totally unknown and, by implication, shady (280, 244). In *Anne of the Island* (1915), Anne is doubly suspicious to the anti-intellectual and parochial community because she is both a daughter of unknown parentage and a writer—worse yet, a female writer.[66] In that novel, Aunt Atossa believes this embarrassing and shocking situation is what "comes of adopting orphans from goodness knew where, with goodness knew what kind of parents" (*AI*, 118); and Jane Andrews angrily dismisses Anne as "merely an adopted orphan, without kith or kin" (60), when Anne rejects Billy Andrews's proposal (tendered by his sister, Jane). While suspicion and snobbery are not dispelled, these slights and insults come primarily from characters whose persistent xenophobia, smugness, or jealousy make them the object of the narrator's humor.

Readers today may be surprised by another event in the first chapter of *Anne of Green Gables:* the casualness of a spinster sister and bachelor brother requesting that an acquaintance select a child, as though it were a fruit or vegetable (preferably a domestic, not an exotic, type) at the grocery, and drop it off at the train station to be picked up later. Yet Montgomery's contemporaries would have been familiar with the practice, since it was quite in keeping with the actual circumstances of placing out until the "import" of orphans ended in the 1930s. Also familiar would be the emphasis on "usefulness," a theme reiterated in Matthew and Marilla's discourse, and the informality of the process of adoption. Official legal adoption for orphaned children was not instituted in most Canadian provinces until the 1920s; before then, only the decision to keep the child permanently was required. There's no mention of an assessment of the Cuthberts' qualifications for raising a child or of possible legal problems of inheritance. Whenever Anne gets into trouble, she melodramatically declares that Marilla should just send her back to the orphanage. This exaggerated statement reflects a historical reality—these relationships frequently were contingent only on adults and children agreeing to stay together; nothing required the adults to keep or support the child who had been placed with them. Montgomery, of course, never lets us doubt that Anne is now a part of the family, whatever she might do. Readers now, however, may wonder at the lack of formal adoption agreements, a celebration of the signing of a legal document, or another official marking of this important event.

Although requesting a child is an "innovation" (*AGG*, 5) neither Matthew nor Marilla is adventurous; Matthew, completely contained within the masculine sphere of activity and experience, fears those "mysterious creatures," women and girls (*AGG*, 5, 15); Marilla is suspicious of anything she cannot understand. Yet Matthew immediately takes to Anne, whose loquacity, aesthetic responses, openness, and imagination are perfect contrasts and complements to his taciturnity and practicality. For him, this is love at first conversation; for her, this is an immediate rapport with what she had longed for without previously knowing, more important even than a blood relative—a true "kindred spirit" (33), the good father who understands intuitively what she wants and obtains it for her, whether it be a permanent home or a dress with puffed sleeves. Not for nothing does Anne announce to Marilla that she wishes to be called "Cordelia" (24); she has the desire and capacity to be a loving and faithful daughter, if the opportunity is presented to her. Given her loquacity and Matthew's taciturnity, however, the choice is also humorous.

When Matthew first arrives at the train station to pick up this boy who will help on the farm, we get several views of Anne: the station master's sarcastic "She's a case, I should say" (10), suggesting how odd this child seems; the sympathetic narrator's introduction of "this stray woman-child" first to "the ordinary observer," who will note her thinness and her peculiar clothing, and then, with a wink, to "the extraordinary" and perceptive interpreter, the ideal reader (11). Given these different views, readers can more easily understand how children who were placed out felt when teased about their pitiful attire; or shipped from Canadian or English cities, handed tickets, and put on trains to travel alone to remote places; or taken from station to station and displayed, hoping and fearing that they would be chosen. When Anne speaks, Matthew and the reader know immediately what this experience means to her: "Oh, it seems so wonderful that I'm going to live with you and belong to you. I've never belonged to anyone—not really. But the asylum was the worst" (12).

Montgomery indicates in this scene how an intelligent child might survive in miserable circumstances, which included much criticism by adults—using her imagination. For example, Anne imagines that the children in the institution are abandoned or lost offspring of the great and mighty (13). The "hidden hero" is a favorite character type in Western literature, and Anne herself meets several of the criteria for these "leaders of the people," who range from Moses, Joseph, Sargon, Arthur, Lancelot, and Snow White to Superman. Orphans or abandoned infants, they are often sent out on water to escape death (or condemned to exposure or death but spared by a compassionate executioner), display extraordinary abilities, gain recognition, and then set out to rediscover their original identity and parentage.[67] This myth guides Anne, helping her cope with the verbal abuse she encounters, and it provides links throughout the series of *Anne* books. Drowning or near drowning is a recurring theme; and a mark of the hidden hero is a near-death experience, or a symbolic death, often by water. Even in these first speeches, Anne jokes that Mrs. Spencer feared that the girl would "fall overboard" (14). This passage also presents the belief that suffering or discomfort can have good uses, a view that allows Anne to deal with pain and deprivation.

When Anne is finally introduced to Marilla, the spinster at first simply sees the girl as a mistake that must be remedied, as if a friend had fetched the wrong thing from a store. Rachel and others express the same idea—take it back. These articulations of a consumer attitude toward the child (as just a commodity) emphasize the precariousness of Anne's situation. Comments also remind us of the pervasive fear of the mysterious and the unknown, which members of this community are quick to classify as supernatural and threatening. Marilla's ambivalence toward strangers causes her to associate Anne's verbal ability with the original and negative idea of charm: Marilla fears the girl will "be casting a spell over me too," and she thinks Anne has "bewitched" Matthew and Green Gables (35, 29, 102). Neighbors in the novel at first express similar views, a depiction that reflects Montgomery's knowledge of the contemporary suspicions surrounding orphans and children as well as her reading about literary witches and changelings. However, Marilla's and Matthew's terms for Anne, like the narrator's repeated "freckled witch" (15, 51), ultimately become fond nicknames.[68]

An important turning point in the plot occurs in chapter 3, when Marilla, driving Anne back to Mrs. Spencer's, listens to the girl's narrative. Here we must follow Marilla's example and attend to historical subtexts. Anne's history, as she relates it, is a dreary tale of drudgery, much work, and little time for education or play. Forced to take on adult responsibilities but not given respect for her work, never wanted or appreciated, lonely and frequently criticized, Anne would prefer to tell Marilla of an imagined life, those fictions she has read or created to sustain herself.

Unlike many other children who were placed out, Anne truly is an orphan, yet she does know something about her poor but educated and thoroughly respectable parents—just enough to idealize and romanticize both. Both died when Anne was only three months old. Then the infant became a "problem." Anne explains:

> You see, nobody wanted me even then. It seems to be my fate. Mother and father had both come from places far away and it was well known they hadn't any relatives living. Finally Mrs. Thomas said she'd take me, though she was poor and had a drunken husband. (39)

Anne's earliest memories are of verbal abuse and insults that degrade her: Mrs. Thomas, the scrubwoman who took her in, said she was "the homeliest baby" and a "bad girl" (39). Mr. Thomas, the drunkard, eventually got killed, and the grandmother would not accept Anne because she was not *really* family. When Anne was taken in by Mrs. Hammond, who lived in this "very lonesome place," again it was because the girl could be a useful worker, "handy with children" (40). Anne declares that she got "so dreadfully tired carrying [the twins] about" when she was only eight or nine (40). Later, Marilla is shocked to discover that Anne never says her prayers, and Anne explains, "I'd always be too tired at night to bother saying prayers" (50)—a statement that rings true to the circumstances she describes. Exhausted, lonely, Anne made up companions, Katie and Violetta, to talk to, since she never had a friend her own age. When Mr. Hammond died, Anne had to go to the overcrowded asylum in Hopetown, where she spent four unhappy months.

Anne's narrative would sound familiar to the reader who knows the history of children placed out in Canada and America: the child's (and adult's) reluctance to discuss previous experiences, to avoid pain or embarrassment; the suspicions about children of immigrants (Anne's parents are "from places far away"); the view of the infant as a burden; the verbal abuse and the exploitation of the child along with reminders that she should be grateful; the use of corporal punishment to control "unruly" children; the self-righteous and self-serving emphasis, by masters/mistresses/surrogate parents and institutions, on the morality of hard work; the casualness with which a child was given to whomever could use another worker, passed around from family to family, with less concern for the child's welfare than for a stray puppy's; the absence of religious training, formal education, love, or a sense of belonging; the isolation and loneliness of the older child worker, not treated like the biological children, surrounded by adults making demands and babies requiring care, with no real companions her age to talk to; the ridicule of the child by neighbors, even by the surrogate family; the effects on the child of living with working-poor, surrogate families in an environment that included drunkenness, instability, domestic violence, and early death.

Elsewhere in *Anne of Green Gables*, we learn more about the environment she was raised in. Anne shouts, in the middle of a temper tantrum, that Rachel "hurt my feelings worse than they ever were by Mrs. Thomas' intoxicated husband," indicating much verbal abuse by both Mrs. and Mr. Thomas, the alcoholic (65). Anne suggests a low level of domestic violence in describing how "Mr. Thomas smashed [a glass door in a bookcase] one night when he was slightly intoxicated" (58). Nothing here, however, suggests frightening sexual aggression, such as some actual home girls encountered. Nevertheless, we are aware of the dangers to Anne, the "stray woman-child," now approaching adolescence; and Marilla, sheltered spinster though she might be, would perceive the threat as well.

By the time she reaches Mrs. Spencer's house and the end of Anne's narrative, Marilla no longer sees home children only as useful workers, nor does she wish to be rid of this girl; she has accepted Matthew's view that "[w]e might be some good to her" (41). Marilla's change of heart represents the historically older, practical attitude toward children as workers giving way to the newer one—viewing childhood as a special time for nurturing, growth, education, and play. Now Marilla wants to protect Anne from Mrs. Blewett, who assesses the girl as though she were livestock and whose statements echo those of institutions and individuals who exploited children in the guise of charity: "I'll expect you to earn your keep. Yes, I suppose I might as well take her off your hands, Miss Cuthbert. The baby's awful fractious and I'm clean worn out attending to him" (45). Although Marilla later tells Matthew that keeping Anne is an "experiment" and a "duty" (47–48), she actually is moved by Anne's history of deprivation and wants to protect and provide for the vulnerable child.

However, Marilla's assessment of Anne is based on the girl's behavior and on her presumed biological heritage, both of which suggest her potential for development. Anne displays the right qualities and obviously fits into the category of the "worthy" and redeemable poor. Although Marilla thinks Anne talks too much, "there's nothing rude or slangy in what she does say" (41); she seems malleable, "a teachable little thing" who is "[s]mart and obedient, willing to work and quick to learn" (41, 53). But while Marilla takes nurture as well as nature into consideration, making excuses for Anne's lack of training, Anne's personal traits are not all that recommend her; to be content and reassure itself against warnings from Rachel and others about Anne's unknown biological heritage, Marilla must also infer, "It's likely her people were nice folks" (41). Marilla has not entirely escaped the narrow cultural views of her community.

Marilla also falls prey to suspicion when Anne, who lacks conventional religious views and training, is thought to have been the last to touch a family heirloom (96–99). Described by the narrator as Marilla's "most treasured posses-sion," almost a sacred item or relic, the amethyst brooch itself represents what Marilla cherishes and Anne lacks—family history, a physical link to the past, a maternal heritage. It is a gift that literally embodies the mother, since a lock of Marilla's mother's hair is incorporated into the braid around the brooch (94). Thus, it symbolizes the biological and emotional mother-daughter or parent-child link, and Anne has neither a parent nor a gift from a parent to mark her heritage. Marilla's suspicions are so strong, her conviction of Anne's guilt so cer-tain, and Anne's desire to go to an outing so intense that Marilla forces Anne into "confessing." Marilla is furious at both the loss of the brooch and the "lie" Anne told at first when she claimed she'd returned the brooch to the dressing table. All the rumors, Rachel's warnings, and the fears of the unknown child surface in Marilla's thinking: Anne is unrepentant, untrustworthy, totally "wicked," either "crazy" or "utterly bad"; she has done a "dreadful thing" and shown her "[s]lyness and untruthfulness" (97–102). Only the discovery of the brooch caught in the lace of her own shawl makes Marilla realize that the child told the truth at first and merely created a fantasy in attempt to go to the ice-cream social.

Misprision is corrected, and the truth is revealed. What Marilla learns about herself is that she does harbor doubts and fears about this unknown and, to her, strange child and that she did "hear," even as she discounted, some of Rachel's stories about criminal orphans. If the reader in an earlier period also harbored such suspicions, created by urban legends and gossip, she too might have found herself questioning her own prejudices and reconsidering events from the or-phaned child's point of view.

The inhabitants of Prince Edward Island at first view Anne, like the real chil-dren who were placed out in Canada, with distrust, and the imaginative and melodramatic Anne sometimes unwittingly plays into the fears and doubts of neighbors. When Anne accidentally serves alcohol, thinking it is raspberry cor-dial, to Diana Barry, her "bosom friend," who goes home sick and drunk, all of the neighbors' fears of the alien who would try to poison or corrupt the good Christian, native-born Canadian children are brought forth. Though treated lightly, this incident should be seen against the historical backdrop of a vocal temperance movement that believed alcohol was a source of numerous evils, a false first step leading to worse vices, such as lewdness and violence, down a path to perdition.[69] Mrs. Barry had apparently already heard gossip, for Diana says, when she first meets Anne, "I heard before you were queer" (86). Apologizing for the mistake with the cordial, Anne just calls up the protective mother's sus-picions. Mrs. Barry thinks in the languages of those Canadians who feared cor-ruption by degenerate, "unfit" street children: "she really believed that Anne had made Diana drunk out of sheer malice prepense, and she was honestly anxious to preserve her little daughter from the contamination of further intimacy with such a child" (129). She declares to Anne, "I don't think you are a fit little girl for Diana to associate with" (130).

Only Anne's saving a younger Barry child by using the knowledge gained from taking care of multiple sets of twins wins back Mrs. Barry's trust and the coveted permission to again be friends with Diana (141–46). Certainly, this sequence of events has literary precursors as well as historical contexts, and the "drunkenness" incident is treated humorously, like Anne's other mistakes and accidents. The serious themes and problems stay in the background or provide opportunities for Anne to display her sterling qualities. Like Joseph, who urges his brothers not to blame themselves but instead to see all of their actions as God's plan (Genesis 45:1–15), Anne acts out the role of a hidden hero who uses the knowledge gained through years of labor and suffering to overcome prejudices and prove herself worthy in the eyes of the conventional Canadians.

The temperamental, precocious, dreamy orphan, once seen as outlandish, finally is accepted and appreciated: the outcast becomes the hero, acknowledged as exceptionally gifted.[70] When Anne graduates and wins a scholarship, Matthew's comment shows that the Cuthberts have come full circle: "I'd rather have you than a dozen boys, Anne" (292). Marilla's motives are frequently couched in terms of pity or Christian duty, but after Matthew's death, she finally pays the girl the highest compliment a woman of her conventional background can offer: "I love you as dear as if you were my own flesh and blood" (296). Though darkened by the death of her adopted father, the last chapters of *Anne of Green Gables* show Anne making a romantic "sacrifice"—giving up her scholarship to perform, out of love, her filial duty to her (adopted) mother and to maintain her (adopted) home, Green Gables.

Thus, elements of wish fulfillment, myth, and romance predominate: dangers are muted, overcome, or elided. The harsh realities are there as a backdrop, contrasts that provide chiaroscuro to heighten the brightness of the more noble characters. Anne survives the abuse of children that historically marked the placing out movement; overcomes the social prejudices against orphans and girls; endures Marilla's suspicions that she is, as neighbors warn, a dangerous outsider (until Marilla is forced to recognize her own prejudices); and wins over nearly all critics, save those who are envious of her success. Admittedly, this dominant structure presents a "romance" of individual achievement against the odds, a view compatible with many turn-of-the-century, middle-class beliefs ranging from Divine Providence to Social Darwinism; it also diverges from some historically "realistic" elements in the novel.[71] But rather than complain pointlessly that Montgomery did not produce a more radical critique of society or a sociological study of orphans, I would suggest that this "romance" be seen as psychologically important and empowering for adolescent readers, both male and female, but especially for active and unconventional girls who feel like "outsiders": it offers both reassurance of their value and hope that ultimately they will be appreciated for their particular qualities, recognized as "heroes in disguise," and successful in creating a satisfying life for themselves.

Finally, in the impact of *Anne of Green Gables* on some of its readers, we can see the sad mixture of hope and desire that motivated real-life children from poor families or institutions to choose placing out. Kenneth Bagnell tells the melancholy story of a fourteen-year-old girl from Birmingham named Annie Smith, who, because she had read *Anne of Green Gables*, was eager to be placed out with a couple in New Brunswick. Annie worked very hard for three years on their farm, although she was unable to continue her schooling, cheated of her rightful pay, and forced to listen while neighbors and the woman she worked for heaped insults on her (Bagnell, *Little Immigrants*, 219–22). Eventually, as an adult, she built a happier life for herself, but for this real-life Anne, childhood and adolescence offered only the wretched sort of experiences Montgomery's protagonist describes in chapter 3—never the rescue by loving adults who would take her to a beautiful and comfortable home like Green Gables. What Annie Smith could not have known was that the fictional experiences of the loved and happy orphan in *Anne of Green Gables* represented the lives of only some—indeed, not many—of the home children. Annie Smith's life history might have been far more typical of the experiences of most of the children who were placed out in America and Canada.

NOTES

I would like to thank Paul and Mary Voss for their support, David H. Cohen for his advice on style, and Marianne Novy for her encouragement and patience.

1. Recent criticism includes Elizabeth Rollins Epperly, *The Fragrance of Sweet-Grass: L. M. Montgomery's Heroines and the Pursuit of Romance* (Toronto: Toronto University Press, 1992); Shirley Foster and Judy Simons, "L. M. Montgomery: *Anne of Green Gables*," in *What Katy Read: Feminist Re-Readings of "Classic" Stories for Girls* (Iowa City: University of Iowa Press, 1995), 149–71; Elizabeth Waterston, *Kindling Spirits* (Toronto: ECW Press, 1993).

2. For biographies, see Francis W. P. Bolger, *The Years before "Anne"* (Halifax, Nova Scotia; Nimbus, 1991); Mollie Gillen, *The Wheel of Things: A Biography of L. M. Montgomery* (London: Harrap, 1976); and the chronology in Margaret Anne Doody's introduction to *The Annotated Anne of Green Gables*, ed. Wendy E. Barry, Margaret Anne Doody, and Mary E. Doody Jones (New York: Oxford University Press, 1997), 3–34.

3. L. M. Montgomery, *The Selected Journals of L. M. Montgomery*, ed. Mary Rubio and Elizabeth Waterston (Toronto: Oxford University Press, 1985), 1:330.

4. Historical *background* is discussed by Mary E. Doody Jones in "The Exceptional Orphan Anne: Child Care, Orphan Asylums, Farming Out, Indenturing, and Adoption," in Barry, Doody, and Jones, *Annotated Anne of Green Gables*, 422–29; see also in that collection the occasional editorial notes on the novel.

5. On American fictional orphans, see Louie Attebery, "The American West and the Archetypal Orphan," *Western American Literature* 5 (1970); 205–17, and Hana Wirth-

Nesher, "The Literary Orphan as National Hero: Huck and Pip," *Dickens Studies Annual* 15 (1986): 259–73. On the orphan protagonist's desire in British novels to belong and advance socially and financially, see Nina Auerbach, "Incarnations of the Orphan," *ELH* 42 (1975): 395–419. Barbara Estrin, in *The Raven and the Lark: Lost Children in the Literature of the English Renaissance* (London and Toronto: Bucknell University Press, 1985), contrasts Greco-Roman and Hebrew narratives. Anthropological and psychological approaches are Brian Lewis's very thorough study *The Sargon Legend: A Study of the Akkadian Text and the Tale of the Hero Who Was Exposed at Birth* (Cambridge, Mass.: American Schools of Oriental Research, 1980); Vladimir Propp, "Oedipus in the Light of Folklore," in *Oedipus: A Folklore Casebook,* ed. Lowell Edwards and Alan Dundes (1983; reprint, Madison: University of Wisconsin Press, 1995), 76–121; and Otto Rank, "The Myth of the Birth of the Hero," trans. F. Robbins and Smith Ely Jelliffe, in *The Quest of the Hero* (Princeton: Princeton University Press, 1990), 3–86.

6. Demographics cannot completely explain why many authors choose orphans as protagonists; representation in fiction is not necessarily proportional to actual historical instances. Consider also that the orphan can serve as a lightning rod for larger social and philosophical issues and can be available for mythologizing. See Eileen Simpson, *Orphans: Real and Imaginary* (New York: Weidenfeld and Nicolson, 1987). William Veeder, in "The Feminine Orphan and the Emergent Master: Self-Realization in Henry James," *Henry James Review* 12 (winter 1991): 20–54, presents a Freudian interpretation and points out James's explicit statements that he wanted to divest himself of family.

7. A variation on this, in reported speech, is the first thing we "hear" Anne say. See L. M. Montgomery, *Anne of Green Gables* (New York: Bantam, 1992), 10 (hereafter cited parenthetically in text as *AGG*).

8. On allusions and literary predecessors, see Epperly, *Fragrance of Sweet-Grass,* 18–36; Margaret Anne Doody and Wendy Barry, "Literary Allusion and Quotation in *Anne of Green Gables,*" in Barry, Doody, and Jones, *Annotated Anne of Green Gables,* 457–62; and editorial notes on the novel in ibid.

9. The main structure, I would argue, is not a "fantasy," but fits Henry James's description of "romance": "the ways things don't happen [which] may be artfully made to pass for the way things do" ("Preface to the New York Edition (1907)," in *The American,* ed. James W. Tuttleton [New York: W. W. Norton, 1978], 11; see further 1–15). Epperly discusses her concepts of "romance" in the novel in *Fragrance of Sweet-Grass,* 18–38.

10. Echoes of events from Montgomery's life in this passage are pointed out by Doody, in introduction to *Annotated Anne of Green Gables,* 17–18.

11. For another discussion of how adults read "children's novels" differently, see Larry Wolff, "The Boys are Pickpockets and the Girl Is a Prostitute: Gender and Juvenile Criminality in Early Victorian England from *Oliver Twist* to London," *New Literary History* 27, no. 2 (spring 1996): 227–49.

12. The daughter of Agnes McFadden, nee Short, quoted in Phyllis Harrison, *The Home Children: Their Personal Stories* (Winnipeg, Manitoba: Watson and Dwyer, 1979), 35–36 (hereafter cited as *HC*).

13. Philippe Ariès's *Centuries of Childhood,* translated by Robert Baldick (New York: Vintage, 1962), has been highly influential but is contested by more recent scholarship. See Tamara K. Hareven, "The History of the Family and the Complexity of Social Change," *American Historical Review* 96 (February 1991): 95–124.

14. Michel Foucault, *Discipline and Punish,* trans. Alan Sheridan (1977; reprint, New

York: Vintage, 1995), 135–94; *Mental Illness and Psychology,* trans. Alan Sheridan (1976; reprint, Berkeley: University of California Press, 1987), 64–75.

15. Ruth K. McClure, *Coram's Children: The London Foundling Hospital in the Eighteenth Century* (New Haven and London: Yale University Press, 1981), 9–15; Patricia T. Rooke and R. L. Schnell, *Discarding the Asylum: From Child Rescue to the Welfare State in English-Canada (1800–1950)* (Lanham, N.Y., and London: University Press of America, 1993), 115. For various attitudes toward illegitimacy, see *Bastardy and Its Comparative History,* ed. Peter Laslett, Karen Oosterveen, and Richard M. Smith (London: Edward Arnold, 1980).

16. Timothy A. Hacsi, *Second Home: Orphan Asylums and Poor Families in America* (Cambridge: Harvard University Press, 1997), 4.

17. Rooke and Schnell, *Discarding the Asylum,* 139. See also Bettina Bradbury, "The Fragmented Family: Family Strategies in the Face of Death, Illness, and Poverty, Montreal, 1860–1885," in *Childhood and the Family in Canadian History,* ed. Joy Parr (Toronto: McClelland and Stewart, 1982), 109–28.

18. Economics was only one factor. I am not endorsing Lawrence Stone's widely quoted view that parents lacked affection for their offspring: see Stone, *The Family, Sex, and Marriage in England, 1500–1800* (London: Weidenfeld and Nicolson, 1977), 105–14. For one critique of Stone, see Linda A. Pollock, *Forgotten Children: Parent-Child Relations from 1500 to 1900* (London and New York: Cambridge University Press, 1983). See also Valerie Fildes, *Wet Nursing: A History from Antiquity to the Present* (New York: Basil Blackwell, 1988), 186; motivated by affection—not desire for economic gain—wet nurses sometimes sought to adopt infants they had cared for previously.

19. John Boswell, *The Kindness of Strangers* (New York: Pantheon, 1988), claims that children who were abandoned in ancient and medieval Europe were frequently taken in by those who needed workers in rural areas. Evidence for this pattern is more plentiful in later periods.

20. Charlotte Neff, "Pauper Apprenticeship in Early Nineteenth-Century Ontario," *Journal of Family History* 21 (April 1996): 144–71, available on-line from *FirstSearch,* June 28, 1998.

21. Neff, "Pauper Apprenticeship"; Kenneth Bagnell, *The Little Immigrants: The Orphans Who Came to Canada* (Toronto: MacMillan of Canada, 1980), 70–71. Rooke and Schnell argue (*Discarding the Asylum,* 239) that "the bitterness of the response that rejected the young Britons can be understood in light of the new and powerfully seductive eugenic theories of the nineteenth century and the first half of the twentieth." Only the motives for vilifying children and foreigners are debated—whether they were psychological, intellectual, pseudoscientific, cultural, economic, or a combination of these.

22. For example, see Charles Loring Brace, *The Dangerous Classes of New York and Twenty Years' Work among Them* (New York: Wynkoop and Hallenbeck, 1880), 114–18, 300–326. The rhetoric of reformers has been discussed frequently; see Bagnell, *Little Immigrants,* 38–39 (Andrew Doyle) and Judith Fingard, *The Dark Side of Victorian Halifax* (Porters Lake, Nova Scotia: Pottersfield, 1989), 28, 193.

23. For example, Rev. Charles Loring Brace writes of "'professional' streetwalkers" (*Dangerous Classes,* 306), failing to realize that prostitution could be an exigency temporarily resorted to when other means of support were not available.

24. See Fingard, *Dark Side,* 190.

25. Carolyn Strange, *Toronto's Girl Problem: The Perils and Pleasure of the City, 1880–1930* (Toronto: University of Toronto Press, 1995), 3–13.

26. Rebecca Coulter, "The Working Young of Edmonton, 1921–1931," in Parr, *Childhood*, 143–59, relates stories of young women who turned to prostitution when they could not survive as low-wage workers.

27. Joan Lane, *Apprenticeships in England, 1600–1914* (Boulder, Colo.: Westview, 1996), 118–19.

28. On apprentices in crowd disturbances, see ibid., 188–209.

29. Brace, *Dangerous Classes*, 43–45, 225–33; Fingard, *Dark Side*, 130, 192–95.

30. Hacsi, *Second Home*, 133–41.

31. Marilyn Irvin Holt, *The Orphan Trains: Placing Out in America* (Lincoln and London: University of Nebraska Press, 1992), 141–42.

32. Nova Scotia's first adoption laws were passed in 1921 and 1923. Katrysha Bracco reports in "Patriarchy and the Law of Adoption: Beneath the Interests of the Child," *Alberta Law Review* 35 (1997): 1039–40: "The first Canadian adoption law was passed in New Brunswick in 1873. There was no requirement for the petitioning adoptive parent to be married." Bracco notes that Ontario's 1921 and 1927 statutes contain much that is associated with modern legal adoption practice. Neff ("Pauper Apprenticeship," n.7) also cites "The Adoption Act, 1921, Ontario, Statutes, 1921, 11 Geo 5, c. 55." Neil Sutherland dates the beginning of Canadian legal adoption, as contrasted with indenturing, from British Columbia's 1920 statute; see his *Children in English Canadian Society* (Toronto: University of Toronto Press, 1976), 240, 131n. Holt (*Orphan Trains*, 165–66) indicates that Massachusetts, Kansas, and Illinois had adoption laws in the 1850s and 1860s.

33. De facto adoption and England's Adoption Acts of 1920, 1926, and 1939 are discussed by Ivy Pinchbeck and Margaret Hewitt in *Children in English Society* (London: Routledge and Kegan Paul, 1973), 2:581, 603–10. On "informal" adoption, see also Joseph Ben-Or, "The Law of Adoption in the United States: Its Massachusetts Origins and the Statute of 1851," *New England Historical and Genealogical Register* 130 (October 1976): 259–72.

34. See Brace, *Dangerous Classes;* Jacob Riis, *How the Other Half Lives,* ed. Sam Bass Warner, Jr. (Cambridge: Harvard University Press, 1970), 118–38; Jane Addams, *Twenty Years at Hull-House* (New York: Signet Classics, 1961), 169–85; William T. Stead, *If Christ Came to Chicago* (1894; reprint, Evanston, Ill.: Chicago Historical Bookworks, 1990), 164, 243–60, 385–87.

35. Hacsi, *Second Home,* 4.

36. Brace (*Dangerous Classes,* 225, 234–35) saw poor parents as annoying obstacles to his placing children out with wholesome farm families.

37. Bagnell, *Little Immigrants,* 9; Joy Parr, *Labouring Children: British Immigrant Apprentices to Canada, 1869–1924* (London: Croom Helm, 1980), 11.

38. Lane, *Apprenticeships in England,* 1–2; Neff, "Pauper Apprenticeship." See also Janet L. Dolgin, "Transforming Childhood: Apprenticeship in American Law," *New England Law Review* 31 (summer 1997): 1113–80.

39. Bagnell, *Little Immigrants,* 63–83; Sutherland, *Children in English Canadian Society,* 30–35; Rooke and Schnell, *Discarding the Asylum,* 239–51; on American attitudes, see Holt, *Orphan Trains,* 120–28.

40. Whether or not there was an actual increase in serious crime in late nineteenth-

century Canadian cities, citizens were more anxious and fearful, especially about foreigners and juveniles. See Strange, *Toronto's Girl Problem*, 152–56; Susan E. Houston, "The 'Waifs and Strays' of a Late Victorian City: Juvenile Delinquents in Toronto," in Parr, *Childhood*, 129–42; Fingard, *Dark Side*, 21.

41. Holt alone is quite sanguine, citing several governors and other civic leaders who were grateful that placing out gave them a new start (*Orphan Trains*, 60, 125–27.)

42. Hacsi, *Second Home*, 1–4; Dolgin, "Transforming Childhood"; Neff, "Pauper Apprenticeship"; Fingard, *Dark Side*, 130, 192–95.

43. Fingard, *Dark Side*, 130, 192–95. Jones ("The Exceptional Orphan Anne," 424) argues, "Anne's 'Hopetown' orphanage refers to the Halifax asylum founded in 1857 by Reverend Mr. Uniake and Miss Cogswell."

44. Neff, "Pauper Apprenticeship"; Lane gives preferred ages for English apprentices in various occupations in *Apprenticeships in England*, 117–18.

45. The difficulties inherent in using autobiographies are well known. Most basic facts about the results of placing out—though not, of course, all the details in individual narratives—have been independently confirmed and supported by other documents.

46. *HC; The American Experience/The Orphan Trains/Abouttheprogram*, <http://www.pbs.org/wgbh/pages/amex/orphan/index.html> (June 13, 1998); *Orphan Trains of Kansas*, <http://kuhttp.cc.edu/carrie/kancoll/articles/orphans/index.html> (June 13, 1998).

47. Andrea Warren, *Orphan Train Rider: One Boy's True Story* (Boston: Houghton Mifflin, 1996).

48. The summary that follows is based on *HC*; Bagnell, *Little Immigrants*; Rooke and Schnell, *Discarding the Asylum*; Holt, *Orphan Trains*; Hacsi, *Second Home*; and Parr, *Labouring Children*.

49. See comments by the daughters of William Jeffrey Baldwin and of Emma Magahay, nee Kennett, in *HC*, 31, 28.

50. See Holt, *Orphan Trains*, 48–57.

51. *The American Experience/The Orphan Trains*.

52. Rooke and Schnell, *Discarding the Asylum*, 141–43; Holt, *Orphan Trains*, 128–33.

53. A relative reported, "All of his life my father-in-law, Frederick John Bubb, has been searching for some member of his family, but all efforts to locate them have been useless" (*HC*, 156); see also Joseph D. Betts, *HC*, 238.

54. Rooke and Schnell, *Discarding the Asylum*, 235–36.

55. Stead, *If Christ Came*, 244. From the 1880s through the 1920s, various laws raising the age of consent were debated, passed, rescinded, and then reinstated in England, Canada, and the United States; by 1920, Britain and most U.S. states had set sixteen as the age below which carnal knowledge of a child was statutory rape. Excellent discussions of this controversial topic are Deborah Gorham, "The 'Maiden Tribute of Modern Babylon' Re-examined," *Victorian Studies* 21 (1978): 353–79, and Mary E. Odem, *Delinquent Daughters: Protecting and Policing Adolescent Female Sexuality in the United States, 1885–1920* (Chapel Hill: University of North Carolina Press, 1986). The age of consent for heterosexual intercourse is now fourteen in Canada, with some qualifications.

56. Parr, *Labouring Children*, 114.

57. Ibid., 116–17.

58. Hacsi, *Second Home,* 113–41; Rooke and Schnell (*Discarding the Asylum,* 241–50) note that "feeble-minded" children or those with habits such as masturbation were thought to be morally degenerate and were frequently returned to institutions.

59. Rooke and Schnell, *Discarding the Asylum,* 241–50.

60. Houston, "The 'Waifs and Strays'"; Parr, *Childhood,* 137–38.

61. Not until 1938 were children under sixteen legally prohibited, except in very limited circumstances, from working in the United States. See Walter Trattner, "The First Federal Child Labor Law (1916)," *Social Science Quarterly* 50, no. 3 (1969): 507–24. Despite present U.S. laws (5 *CFR* 551.601), plentiful evidence shows that the problem still exists, especially in agriculture.

62. Houston, "The 'Waifs and Strays'"; Parr, *Childhood,* 139.

63. See Montgomery, *Selected Journals,* 1:374–76.

64. In *Fragrance of Sweet-Grass,* 18–20, Epperly offers a fine discussion of point of view and rhetoric in the novel's first paragraphs.

65. Rachel Lynd is treated humorously, of course, as a human substitute for the all-seeing eye of God, but this description is not unlike Michel Foucault's use of Bentham in "Panopticism," in *Discipline and Punish,* 195–28.

66. L. M. Montgomery, *Anne of the Island* (New York: Bantam Classic, 1987).

67. See Estrin, *The Raven and the Lark;* Lewis, *Sargon Legend;* Propp, "Oedipus"; and Rank, "Birth of the Hero."

68. Anne's physical appearance, such as her red hair, lends itself to these interpretations. See Prospero's description of Caliban, bastard child of the witch Sycorax, as "[a] freckled whelp" in Shakespeare's *The Tempest,* ed. Robert Langbaum (New York: New American Library, Signet Classic, 1964), 1.2.258–84.

69. Fingard discusses the temperance movement in Halifax in *Dark Side,* 20, 121–24.

70. Because of her desire to belong socially, Anne partly fits into the pattern of the English orphan protagonist as described by Auerbach in "Incarnations of the Orphan."

71. I am here following James's distinction ("Preface," 1–15) of drawing a fine line between "realism" and "romance," both of which *seem* plausible.

Redefining "Real" Motherhood
Representations of Adoptive Mothers, 1900–1950

Julie Berebitsky

In 1920, a woman who had been adopted as a child wrote an article for a popular magazine in which she tried to dispel many of the misconceptions about adoption. She devoted much of her account to proving that adoptive mothers were in fact "real" mothers. To make the point, she recounted the story of a friend who also had been adopted as a young child. When grown, this woman, now a mother of two, met her birth mother for the first time. "'She kissed me; and I kissed her,' my friend told me. 'Then I sat down in a chair and stared at her. I could see that my features resembled hers. But, in all truth, I could not feel that she was my mother. My mother was the 'mother' of my baby days, just as real as anything can be, despite the fact of my birth. *She* was my children's grandmother—not this stranger! I tell you, I couldn't feel it any other way. It's the love and the care which make a mother a mother, more than the child-bearing does.'"[1]

It is impossible to know how many readers would have agreed with this view, but given the focus of the article and the vehemence with which the author asserted this claim, it seems clear that she felt most Americans believed "real" mothers were biological ones. Throughout the period covered in this study, it has been assumed (to a greater or lesser degree at various moments) that all "normal" women were or wanted to be mothers. Motherhood and maternal sacrifice generally were glorified and romanticized and described as a woman's highest and truest calling and as the key to her female identity. Many people looked askance at married women (especially middle-class and elite women) who were not mothers, often labeling them selfish or immature and questioning their womanhood. These beliefs encouraged—indeed compelled—women to derive their identity from relationships to their children. Aside from any individual maternal desire that a woman may have felt, women lived their lives within a culture filled with social incentives, encouragements, and pressures to mother. In short, motherhood conferred status, nonmotherhood only stigma.[2]

However, the dominant culture's idealization of mothers generally equated motherhood with biology, not nurturance. Because they had not given birth, adoptive mothers found themselves on the edges of the culture's ideal. Commentators often portrayed adoptive motherhood as different from and inferior to biological motherhood. In response, adoptive mothers (and their advocates) argued for a definition of motherhood that would legitimate their identity as "real" mothers. Adoptive mothers never completely rejected the prevailing ideology of motherhood. Rather, they made their claim by showing how their motherhood especially fit with certain tenets of the ideal that were not dependent on a blood tie or physical maternity. Because they defined their motherhood in relation to the ideal, representations of adoptive motherhood shifted as the dominant understanding of motherhood changed.

Before 1920, prescriptive literature emphasized the power of adoption to protect and save society and presented adoptive mothers both as "rescuers" of society's cast-off children and as women with strong, even exceptional, maternal instincts. In this construction, many believed that single women had as much right to adopt as married women. During this period, adoptive mothers had few chances publicly to name their own experience. When they did have the chance, many used the rhetoric of redemption, but they also insisted that motherhood was a spiritual, not a physical, state. After 1920, responding to a changed social climate and an altered understanding of motherhood and family life, the portrayal of adoption and adoptive mothers shifted. Although representations highlighted the everyday similarities between adoptive and biological families, they also emphasized what now could be seen as the positive difference of adoption. Authors used the vocabulary of choice to underscore adoptive mothers' conscious decision to mother and their unique preparedness for motherhood. Adoptive mothers often reiterated and even celebrated the idealized construction of motherhood, yet they also posed a challenge to the narrow definition of motherhood and offered an alternative to the biological family. The united voices of adoptive mothers helped expand the ideal beyond blood to include ties of care and commitment.

Although women have always borne and cared for children, both women's actual experience as mothers and the culture's understanding of the institution of motherhood have changed dramatically over the last three centuries. In the colonial period, women were valued as mothers, but they also were regarded for their roles as wives, neighbors, and Christians. However, in the early nineteenth century, the attention focused on women's role as mothers for a number of reasons. The new American republic's need for virtuous future citizens highlighted the important task of mothers. In addition, the removal of the father's place of work from the middle-class home reconfigured that space as a female place of nurture. Sheltered from the sins of the world, women became society's moral guardians, most especially through their influence over husbands and children. Finally, religious leaders believed that a child's ultimate salvation depended on its mother's wholesome influence during its early years, when character was formed. Together, these factors emphasized the importance of motherhood to society at large, an importance that commanded respect and that would ultimately justify women's movement beyond the confines of their homes. By the

1830s, motherhood was enthroned as women's most important role. In addition, this model of womanhood held that all women, simply because they were women, possessed a maternal and moral sensibility.[3]

Yet even as Americans respected the motherliness of all women, they held the biological mother-child bond apart in special reverence. In 1839, for example, Rev. John Todd wrote that "God planted this *deep*, this *unquenchable* love for her offspring, in the mother's heart." Many commentators believed that only through bearing children could a woman realize true happiness. In 1891, a physician asserted the primacy of maternity when he noted that a woman's "inmost nature yearns to spend its treasures of love and service upon her own offspring. . . . the heart which hears no echo of love from its own child is inexpressibly sad." Even the love between husband and wife, according to nineteenth-century advice givers, paled in comparison to the intensity and purity of a mother's feelings for her child. Marital literature from this period continued the theme: "The mission of woman is childbearing. Women who have not married, or who have married and not borne children, do not know what happiness is. There is a void in their lives which no other experience fills."[4]

Adoptive mothers in the late nineteenth and early twentieth centuries experienced their motherhood in a culture that held these somewhat contradictory understandings of women's nature. On the one hand, given the widespread belief in women's maternal essence, many Americans could accept a woman's decision to adopt as natural or at least understandable. On the other hand, because of the cultural veneration of the physical process of birth and exaltation of the blood tie, most people saw adoptive motherhood as a lesser imitation of biological motherhood.

As late as 1924, for example, S. Josephine Baker, a well-respected physician and consultant to the U.S. Children's Bureau, wrote an article on adoption for the *Ladies' Home Journal*, in which she clearly stated that she believed the adoptive relationship was inferior to one based in biology. Baker told readers: "Of course you cannot at first love just any child as well as you do your own, and I am inclined to believe that the adopted child must show a higher standard of character and 'make good' in a far better way than a natural child to be accepted on anything like the same basis by any father or mother. It is very easy to forgive your own child . . . ; but, try as you will, there is not the same readiness to understand the behavior of the boy or girl who does not belong to you by right of birth." This assessment applied not only to adoptive families in which a birth child was present but also to those families that only had adopted children. As Baker's opinion suggests, many Americans clearly distinguished between women who had given birth and those who expressed their maternal potential in other ways. Although many people understood an adoptive mother's desire and might even respect her decision, they also believed her motherhood was different. Adoption provided a woman with a child to love, but it did not necessarily provide her with a completely recognized claim to "real" motherhood.[5]

In addition, other factors cast doubt and suspicion on childless married women in the early years of the twentieth century. This period saw a drastic decline in the birth rate among white, middle-class women, and many commentators ominously warned that America's "superior stock" was committing "race suicide." Meanwhile, the "new" immigrants from eastern and southern Europe were reproducing at double the rate of their native-born counterparts. Social critics prophesied that the progeny of these "lusty sexual . . . foreign breeders" would soon overrun the nation, and they urged native-born women to do their "duty" and procreate. Much of the pressure to reproduce came in the form of popular articles that represented childless women as selfish and unpatriotic. Doctors often blamed women for their fertility problems, arguing that they had brought on their childlessness by too much education or a stubborn unwillingness to accept their womanly role. Childless marriages were also thought to be especially at risk for divorce. (In this essay, I am focusing especially on the experience of women in infertile marriages. It is important to note, however, that before World War II, adoptions by older couples with grown biological children or by couples who wanted a sibling for their only child were not uncommon. Single women also adopted during this period.)[6]

The problem, many people believed, was not only the relatively high birth rate of the new immigrants but also the large number of homeless, often immigrant children, who might pose a threat to social stability and the American way of life. Most articles on adoption before 1920 presented adoption as a potential solution to this dilemma and encouraged women—especially childless middle-class women—to see adoption as part of their civic duty to society. Adoptive mothers could redeem the masses of dependent children and turn them into solid Americans.

In this regard, if adoptive mothers could not claim status as real mothers, they could at least receive credit as superior citizens. Mrs. Charles Judson, for example, a physician's wife who privately placed children out of her home in Philadelphia, stressed that adoption was a means to Americanize children and maintain Anglo-Saxon values. Judson believed that adoption gave "to our country more of the best class of American citizens." She maintained: "Our forebears, through toil and struggle, often gained ideals, culture, refinement, and beliefs which have built up this nation. So many families where such inheritance obtains are childless. If a child is adopted and these ideas and beliefs passed down to it, we create another American citizen guided by the same uplifting faiths as held and helped our forefathers."[7]

The construction of adoption as rescue helped legitimate adoption, but for adoptive mothers who wanted an identity as real mothers, it also created a critical distinction between their experience and that of a biological mother. The popular understanding of a mother's love encompassed feelings that went well beyond fulfilling civic obligations. The belief that women had a duty to civilize society propelled them into careers as reformers, educators, and health professionals. If adoption was regarded as a woman's duty, adoptive mothers merely occupied a place on the continuum of ways nonmothers expressed their maternal feelings. As rescuers of children, adoptive mothers deserved respect and admiration, but this construction still portrayed their experience as different, as "other" to that of women who achieved motherhood through giving birth.

Saving society was not always enough to save adoptive mothers from an unflattering public portrayal. Most articles about adoption in popular magazines from the early twentieth century spoke positively about adoption in a general way, but even so, some did not portray those who sought children in the most positive light. Sometimes prospective adoptive mothers were portrayed as desperate, conniving, and mentally unstable. A number of articles told of women who approached child-placing agencies looking for a child they could pass off as their own to cement the affections of their wandering (and unsuspecting) husbands. An article in the *New York Times* in 1910 stated that in Chicago alone, over three thousand men had been the victims of this kind of deception. One author told of how adoption transformed "hysterical and nervous women," who, with a child to take care of, forgot "their more or less imaginary ills." Another told the story of a woman who "was on the verge of insanity" from brooding over her childlessness. Her tragedy was complete when she was declared insane only hours before an adoptable infant was located for her. Even though adoptive mothers had actively chosen motherhood, they could not completely escape the stigma that because they had failed to give birth, they were failures as women and not really mothers.[8]

Before 1920, the views of adoptive mothers rarely appeared in print. When they did, however, they challenged the idea that adoptive motherhood was a mere imitation of biological motherhood. Some adoptive mothers presented their experience in a way that blended the concepts of duty and motherly love. An article entitled "A Plea for Adoption," which appeared in 1911 in *Good Housekeeping,* sheds light on the way adoptive mothers, as opposed to social commentators, understood adoption. The article, which actually was a lengthy letter to the editor, was written by a Kentucky woman who described her motivation to adopt as grounded in a desire to mother, not a duty to save. This woman's only biological child had died and she was unable to have any others. When she no longer could suffer her "loneliness" and "sorrow," she adopted a child to whom she could give a mother's love. This mother was devoted to her adopted son and emphatically stated that she could not give him up, even if doing so would bring back her dead son. Only toward the end of the letter, as she attempted to convince readers who might be hesitant, did the woman mention the social aspect of adoption. "The chance that one may make a splendid man of a boy who otherwise would remain a charge upon charity," the author maintained, "is surely sufficient incentive to induce one to brave the responsibility." *Good Housekeeping*, however, chose to emphasize this point by headlining the letter, "The Large Opportunity, Not to Say Duty, Which Confronts Childless Couples."[9]

Other women, however, completely avoided the issue of civic obligation in their descriptions of adoptive motherhood. As one adoptive mother stated, "They say that I can never know the feeling of a real mother, of the woman whose mortal frame has endured the martyrdom of a physical maternity, but nevertheless he is my son, the son of my spiritual self, of all that is best in me." By drawing an explicit comparison between her experience and the experience of birth, this adoptive mother asserted that true motherhood was not an event of the flesh but the essence of womanhood.[10]

In 1909, Zona Gale, a popular writer who later adopted a child, published a short story, "Adoption," which presented a similar understanding of motherhood and challenged those who made a distinction between an adoptive and a birth mother's love. In the story, a childless married woman searches for a child to adopt, not to serve any "social need," but because she is "simply hungering for a child." She sacrifices for the unknown child, scrimping and saving and making do so that she can purchase clothing and furniture. The woman finally locates an infant in a nearby town and eagerly shows his photo to all of her women neighbors. But before she can bring the child home, he dies. The story concludes with a touching portrait of this mother's grief and the response of the neighbors to her. These women try to comfort her, but, as the narrator points out, "many of them had lost little children of their own, and could not regard her loss as at all akin to theirs." The narrator, however, asserting that her loss is just as real, offers a definition of motherhood based not on a physical relationship to a child but on a woman's spiritual acceptance of maternal responsibility. In this story, the motherly emotions society prizes—self-sacrifice and eternal, inexhaustible love—have nothing to do with a blood tie but arise out of a woman's "natural" desire to mother.[11]

In the 1920s, firsthand accounts by adoptive mothers began to appear in popular magazines. These articles took advantage of a changed social climate to present adoption in a new way. This decade witnessed a return to private life and a preoccupation with pursuing individual pleasures, not solving social problems. The popular understanding of womanhood, marriage, and motherhood also underwent a profound transformation. Although sexual behaviors among some groups had changed long before, the 1920s, according to historians John D'Emilio and Estelle Freedman, marked the acceptance of modern sexual practices and values by the culture at large. Suddenly women were erotic beings and a successful marriage demanded both partners' sexual satisfaction. Although children were as necessary as ever for a complete and happy marriage, they were to be consciously and carefully planned for so that all members of the family could reach their "highest personal happiness." To this end, by the 1920s many middle-class women used some form of contraception to limit family size. In addition, as the twentieth century progressed, the sufficiency of maternal instinct was called into question as experts argued that women needed to supplement intuition with professional advice. Courses in parent education flourished as middle-class women (and some men) tried to absorb the latest in child-rearing techniques. Scientific information, not instinct, became the new sine qua non of ideal motherhood. Stories about adoption during the 1920s and 1930s reflect these changes, presenting adoption not as benevolent rescue but as modern American family life.[12]

Stories by adoptive mothers, filled with the minutiae of the adoption process, were realistic, not overly sentimental. These stories tried to demystify and normalize adoption by showing adoptive families experiencing the same trials, tribulations, and joys as nonadoptive families. Adoptive mothers argued that their families were just ordinary families that wanted to be treated as such. One woman lamented that it was "an almost impossible task to raise an adopted child in a normal manner," since neighbors continually brought up the fact that her children were adopted, berated her with "much unsought advice," and zealously scrutinized the way she cared for her children. These portrayals also showed the difficulties of adoption, such as the initial troubles of adjusting to a child. When authors of stories about adoption did acknowledge a difference between their families and biological families, it was a positive difference. After all, their families were consciously planned. As one adoptive father explained: "We took the boy because we wanted him. This cannot always be said of own parents." In the few stories in which the "rescue" theme appeared, it was minimized or an afterthought. The message was clear: adoptive parents benefited as much from adoption as did the adopted child.[13]

A few of these stories were written by women who were both adoptive and biological mothers. That they had given birth gave these women the authority to speak on the subject of motherhood and to be taken seriously. These women were also in a unique position to challenge those who believed adoptive mothers could not love their child as much as biological parents. In doing so, they posed a direct—if unconscious—challenge to the faith in the strength and inimitability of blood ties. In 1935, one woman confided to the readers of *Scribner's Magazine* that she "examined her heart closely" to determine if she loved her biological daughter more than her adopted children. She concluded that she loved each of her children differently, in a way that respected their individuality and had nothing to do with the blood that flowed in their veins. The popular novelist Kathleen Norris, also an adoptive and biological mother, wrote an article for the *Ladies' Home Journal* in which she expressed her belief that "[t]he miracle of bearing a living baby is no more astonishing than the companion miracle of finding a small person adrift in the world without a mother, and bringing him triumphantly home to his silver bowl and spoon." Norris "state[d] from experience" that an adoptive child rewarded a mother's love "just as richly as does the baby Mother Nature sends haphazard."[14]

These women also sought to establish a definition of motherhood and family that would provide them with cultural legitimacy. As one eloquent adoptive mother who also had biological children stated, "love-lines, not blood-lines, make motherhood. . . . true parenthood is a stewardship which has no necessary relation to physical parenthood." As she told her adoptive son (and the world), "I did not give you physical birth; but that doesn't matter. Whoever did, wouldn't have been your real mother until she worked and cared for you and learned to love you as I do. For some reason that neither of us will ever know, she brought you into the world but left motherhood for me. You're my son because I wanted you and took you and raised you and loved you." In this construction of motherhood, conscious choice and conscientious care replaced instinct and intuition.[15]

Articles that appeared in popular magazines used the language of choice to underscore the planning and persistence of adoptive parents in creating their families. When the word *choice* appeared in articles about adoption before 1920, it usually referred to the large selection of available children from which adoptive parents could pick their favorite (although many articles suggested that there was an abundance of children, there was actually a shortage of adoptable infants and young children from as early as 1900). After about 1920, however, *choice* was used in in its modern connotation to show adoptive parents' thoughtful decision to undertake parenthood. For example, the 1937 article "We Wanted Children" details a childless couple's careful preparation and committed determination in each of their three adoptions to get just the family they desired. The author referred to her adopted children as "wanted children." The phrase placed this adoptive family squarely in the middle of the new companionate family ideal and may well have reminded readers of Margaret Sanger's favorite slogan in favor of the modern family and birth control, "Every child a wanted child." A few years later, an editorial in the *Ladies' Home Journal* made the connection even more explicit by noting that "the most truly 'planned families' anywhere are the families with adopted children." This planning, the editor believed, gave legally adopted children "a *better* than normal child's chance. For they go to homes that desperately and genuinely *want* children."[16]

At the same time that some women were using the concept of choice to move the understanding of motherhood toward a definition based on a conscious desire to mother and the reality of day-to-day care, the faith in the infallibility of maternal instinct was being challenged—at least in the scientific community. Although advice books for mothers existed before, reformers began to argue during the Progressive Era that instinct needed to be supplemented with education to ensure the healthy development of children. By the 1920s, a full-fledged campaign had developed to educate parents and replace mothers' "common sense" with scientific knowledge. "Mothercraft classes" and "mother training courses" appeared everywhere. Throughout the 1920s, 1930s, and 1940s, experts bombarded mothers with literature on every aspect of childhood from physiology to psychology. While many child-welfare experts questioned the reliability of maternal instinct, some went so far as to suggest that unchecked intuition could actually harm a child. As numerous scholars have pointed out, this advice made mothers both insecure and dependent on expert, mostly male guidance. Yet from the perspective of some adoptive mothers, if women needed to be educated to motherhood, physical birth no longer gave biological mothers an automatic edge.[17]

In 1929, for example, an adoptive mother used the growing emphasis on maternal education to show the readers of the *Woman's Journal* the similarities between adoptive and birth mothers: "Once people believed in the existence of 'a mother's instinct' and supposed it to be an infallible guide to the proper care of a baby. We know better now. The young mothers among my friends use the months of their pregnancy for a rather intensive study of baby culture. . . . I read as much during those seven months [the period of time she was on an agency's waiting list] as my friends have, and I flatter myself was no more flurried by the first bath than they were."[18]

Some women used the principle of scientific motherhood not only to minimize the difference but to celebrate adoption in its own right. In 1922, Honore Willsie, an adoptive mother and editor of a successful women's magazine, claimed that the unique circumstances of adoption made her a better mother. As she told the readers of *Century Magazine*, "I am undoubtedly stricter with my children than any own mother I know, because I see my children more clearly than own mothers do." She continued: "I saw these children physically as their physician saw them, mentally and spiritually as their psychiatrist saw them. . . . And herein lay my vast advantage over own mothers. I saw my children as they were. And because my responsibility was voluntarily taken, I dare not allow my growing love for them to becloud my vision." On first glance, Willsie's appraisal of her children sounds rather clinical and cold. On closer examination, however, it simply embraces the modern ideals of science and choice and uses them to cast adoptive families' difference from blood families in a positive light. Here, finally, was a climate in which an adoptive mother could challenge the widespread belief that her motherhood was inferior and base that assertion on something "objective."[19]

Although adoption was still seen as a lesser form of family by many Americans, adoption advocates could represent it more positively in the context of this new family ideal, with its emphasis on planning and educated parenthood. Within the framework of the modern family, the differences between adoptive and biological families could be minimized and, paradoxically, acknowledged or, as we saw with Willsie, even embraced. Since the late nineteenth-century debates over the declining native-born birth rate, Americans had made a distinction between women who actively chose to be mothers and those who passively accepted (or even consciously avoided) motherhood. The distinction further solidified in the discussion of family life in the early twentieth century, which established an ideal of thoughtfully and consciously planned families. The growing acceptance of choice as a fundamental principle in family formation helped to normalize adoption, and many adoptive mothers used this to legitimate their motherhood. One adoptive mother recounted how she used the "chosen child" story to tell her child of her adoption: "There are two kinds of mothers; one is a mother because she has to be, and the other is a mother because she wants to be . . . . I am your mother because I wanted to be."[20]

In 1917, the *Living Age,* a weekly periodical published in Boston, reprinted a British article on adoption in England. The anonymous author urged people to set aside their fears that adoption was "flying in the face of Providence." The "deep-rooted notion" that "if Almighty God had intended that a particular woman should be a mother, He would have seen to it; and if, in disregard of His purpose, she adopts a child, He will see that she regrets it" was, in the author's view, a "piece of superstition." Nevertheless, the author wrote: "it must be admitted that . . . no adopted relation is likely to be as good as a natural one. A stepmother is not a mother even when she is a very good stepmother."[21]

Although adoption in America was far more accepted than it was in England, it still seems safe to assume that many Americans would have agreed that anything but a blood tie to a child was second best. Even so, attitudes about the family were in the process of changing—in ways that would make it easier for adoptive mothers to represent their motherhood as the real thing. With the growing focus on planned families and thoughtful parenthood, adoptive mothers could claim adoption's difference as a positive good. In 1947, for example, one woman confidently asserted to the readers of *Woman's Day* that she "knew" that her "chosen son" belonged to her "far more than I ever belonged to my own parents, whom I amazed and chagrined by my advent which disarranged, but only temporarily, their plans for divorce." She argued: "Adopted children are among the very few who can be absolutely sure that their parents definitely desired and planned long for their coming. My son David can be numbered among these happy few—the luckiest children in the world, the children who truly belong."

To speak of a positive change in Americans' perception of adoption is not to say that the stigma completely disappeared. Indeed, in the early 1960s, a large study showed that virtually all adoptive mothers had experienced comments or actions that marked their motherhood as different. Whether a seemingly innocuous remark from an acquaintance ("Isn't it wonderful of you to have taken this child!") or the thoughtless observation of a neighbor "How well you care for your child, just like a real mother"), adoptive mothers could not escape the view that biological motherhood was superior to theirs. Moreover, the issue of difference and how (or whether) to address it continues to occupy adoptive parents. Still, for a moment, changes in the understanding of family life gave some adoptive mothers a way to lay claim publicly to being "real" mothers.[22]

NOTES

This chapter was adapted from *Like Our Very Own: Adoption and the Changing Culture of Motherhood, 1851–1950*, by Julie Berebitsky, copyright © 2000 by the University Press of Kansas. Used by permission of the publisher.

1. "How It Feels to Have Been an Adopted Child," *American Magazine*, August 1920, 72.

2. Gayle Letherby, "Mother or Not, Mother or What? Problems of Definition and Identity," *Women's Studies International Forum* 17 (1994): 525–32. Adoption has only recently been seen as a parenthood, rather than motherhood, issue. After 1920, men occasionally appear in stories about adoption, for example, Ruth Garver Gagliardo's "We Wanted Children" (*Parents*, May 1937, 28–29), which reflected new standards of companionate marriage. Before 1920 (and still somewhat after 1920) articles emphasized that men generally only consented to adoption because their wives really wanted children.

Two recent books provide detail on how women have felt pressure to mother in our pronatalist society and how infertile women especially have felt as though they were failures as women. See Margaret Marsh and Wanda Ronner, *The Empty Cradle: Infertility in America from Colonial Times to the Present* (Baltimore: Johns Hopkins University Press, 1996); Elaine Tyler May, *Barren in the Promised Land* (New York: Basic, 1995).

3. Linda Kerber, *Women of the Republic: Intellect and Ideology in Revolutionary America* (Chapel Hill: University of North Carolina Press, 1980); Jan Lewis, "The Republican Wife: Virtue and Seduction in the Early Republic," *William and Mary Quarterly* 44 (October 1987): 689–721; Laurel Thatcher Ulrich, *Good Wives: Image and Reality in the Lives of Women in Northern New England, 1650–1750* (New York: Vintage, 1991); Nancy Cott, *The Bonds of Womanhood* (New Haven: Yale University Press, 1977); Mary Ryan, *Cradle of the Middle Class* (New York: Cambridge University Press, 1981; Barbara Welter, "The Cult of True Womanhood, 1820–1860," *American Quarterly* 18 (1966): 151–74.

4. Rev. John Todd, "Address to Mothers," *Mother's Magazine*, November 1839, 249, as quoted in Jan Lewis, "Mother's Love: The Construction of an Emotion in Nineteenth-Century America," in *Social History and Issues in Human Consciousness*, ed. Andrew E. Barnes and Peter N. Stearns (New York: New York University Press, 1989), 209; Eli Brown, *Sex and Life: The Physiology and Hygiene of the Sexual Organization* (Chicago: F. J. Schulte, 1891), 103, 106; E. Marea, *The Wife's Manual* (Cortland, N.Y.: n.p., 1896), 18.

5. S. Josephine Baker, M.D., "Choosing a Child," *Ladies' Home Journal*, February 1924, 81.

6. Since national statistics on adoption were not kept in the late nineteenth or early twentieth centuries, it is impossible to assemble a demographic profile of adoptive par-

ents. Although a variety of people adopted, including couples with biological children and single women, evidence suggests that even at this point childlessness was the general rule. As the twentieth century progressed, infertility became more and more the primary reason for adoption. After World War II, virtually everyone who adopted did so because of infertility. See Jamil Zainaldin, "The Origins of Modern Legal Adoption: Child Exchange in Boston, 1851–1893" (Ph.D. diss., University of Chicago, 1976), chap. 5, especially p. 152; Elaine Tyler May, *Barren in the Promised Land* (New York: Basic, 1995), 62–63, 72, 141–49.

7. "Training Babies for the 'Golden Spoon,'" *Literary Digest*, April 8, 1916, 1020.

8. "Adopt Babies, Do Not Tell," *New York Times*, January 29, 1910, 3; Henry Dwight Chapin, M.D., "Finding Babies for Folks to Adopt," *American Magazine*, November 1919, 239; Ewing Galloway, "He Likes Babies," *Collier's*, June 20, 1914, 24.

9. "A Plea for Adoption," *Good Housekeeping Magazine*, July 1911, 132.

10. Most of the articles written by adoptive mothers appear after 1920. Before that, the position and voices of adoptive mothers appear in articles about adoption that use quotes from interviews with or letters from adoptive mothers. Consequently, it must be considered that the quotes represent the author's views on adoptive motherhood more than the views of adoptive mothers. See "Child-Rescue Series," *Delineator*, August 1908, 263.

11. Zona Gale, "Adoption," in *Friendship Village Love Stories* (New York: Macmillan, 1909).

12. John D'Emilio and Estelle Freedman, *Intimate Matters: A History of Sexuality in America* (New York: Harper and Row, 1988), 233, 240–50; Steven Mintz and Susan Kellogg, *Domestic Revolutions* (New York: Free Press, 1988), especially pages 114–16; Sheila Rothman, *Woman's Proper Place: A History of Changing Ideals and Practices, 1870 to the Present* (New York: Basic, 1978), chaps. 3 and 5; Molly Ladd Taylor, *Raising a Baby the Government Way: Mothers' Letters to the Children's Bureau, 1915–1932* (New Brunswick: Rutgers University Press, 1986), 22–23; Ronald L. Howard, *A Social History of American Family Sociology, 1865–1940* (Westport, Conn.: Greenwood, 1981), 63–70.

13. "An Adopted Mother Speaks," *Survey*, March 18, 1922, 962–63; "Foster Parents Speak for Themselves," *Child Welfare League of America Bulletin* 9 (April 1930); 4.

14. "Adopted Mother by Herself," *Scribner's Magazine*, January 1935, 57; Kathleen Norris, "Adopt That Baby," *Ladies' Home Journal*, April 1930, 8.

15. "Adopted Mother by Herself," 57.

16. Gagliardo, "We Wanted Children," 28–29; Dorothy Thompson, "Fit for Adoption," *Ladies' Home Journal*, May 1939, 4; Rothman, *Woman's Proper Place*, 194.

17. Julia Grant, *Raising Baby by the Book: The Education of American Mothers* (New Haven: Yale University Press, 1998), introduction, 60; Rothman, *Woman's Proper Place*, chap. 3; Robert Griswold, *Fatherhood in America* (New York: Basic, 1993), 126–32, 301–2; Barbara Ehrenreich and Deirdre English, *For Her Own Good: 150 Years of the Experts' Advice to Women* (New York: Anchor, 1979), 189; Steven Schlossman, "Before Home Start: Notes toward a History of Parent Education in America, 1897–1929," *Harvard Educational Review* 46 (August 1976): 436–67.

18. "Adopting a Baby," *Woman's Journal* 14 (July 1929), 9.

19. Honore Willsie, "The Adopted Mother," *Century Magazine*, September 1922, 666.

20. Bertha Van Hoosen, M.D., "The Adopted Mother," *Medical Woman's Journal* 34 (December 1927): 1.

21. "The Epidemic of Adoption," *Living Age* 294 (September 8, 1917), 632.

22. Mary Havor, "And after Adoption—What Then?" *Woman's Day*, November 1947, 35; H. David Kirk, *Shared Fate: A Theory of Adoption and Mental Health* (New York: Free Press, 1964), chap. 2.

From Charlotte to the Outposts of Empire

Troping Adoption

Beverly Lyon Clark

Zoos and endangered-species organizations urge us to adopt an animal. Teachers and school officials urge our children to adopt a tree or perhaps a fire hydrant. State transportation officials urge us to adopt a highway or occasionally, more truthfully, a "visibility spot." A magazine advertisement urges us to adopt an acre of rain forest (only $35, plus $2.50 shipping and handling—for the shipping and handling of "a personalized honorary land deed suitable for framing"). In the past six years, in a progressive lab school for the elementary grades, my children and I have been urged to adopt a tree outside a classroom window, to adopt traveling dolls that may never return, to adopt an elderly classroom visitor as a grandmother, to adopt books for the school library, and even to adopt a family by providing them with sweaters and mittens (this last sponsored by our state's Department of Children, Youth, and Families, whose employees should, of all people, know better). All of these endeavors reinforce any tendencies of children who are still thinking concretely to consider adoption only second best, or a simple financial transaction, or merely a temporary convenience—or at the very least as confusing.[1] All too often publicists trope adoption to evoke fuzzy feelings of family connection without the serious obligations of literal adoption. All too often the culture at large trivializes adoption.

Let me give another example and implicate myself in this cultural discourse a bit more. I can easily imagine saying the following with respect to choosing a course text: "I thought I'd adopt this text this year, but that doesn't mean I'm married to it." Note the curious pairing of metaphors—adoption for the temporary arrangement, marriage for the permanent one—when in fact, in our society, marriages dissolve far more frequently than adoptions do. Despite the current realities of adoption, and even when we participate in those realities, we are all spoken by cultural discourses that image adoption as transient and second best.

Yet there are moments when that discourse is interrupted. I turn in this essay to two cultural moments that offer more complex and potentially more empowering portraits of adoption. One is a recent moment in literary criticism: criticism has not generally been kind when it turns to a metaphorics of adoption, but recent cultural and postcolonial criticism reveals some signs of change. The other moment, focused several decades earlier, is an intriguingly proleptic moment in children's literature.

In its earliest recorded appearances, starting in 1387 according to the *Oxford English Dictionary,* the term *adoption* referred to voluntary entry into a familial relationship. Yet its extension to the notion of adopting, say, a stance or policy is so old, dating to at least 1598, that the metaphor has become almost transparent, almost invisible. The familial connection is almost severed yet not quite. My thinking here parallels that of George Lakoff and Mark Johnson, who argue that presumably dead metaphors are in fact systematic—that our values "form a coherent system with the metaphorical concepts we live by."[2] Dead metaphors are never altogether dead. It does not take much to revivify the metaphor of adoption, to evoke the root meaning.

Literary theorists, especially those working across the social constructions of race, frequently deploy the language of adoption, whether they talk of adopting a stance, a language, a literary form, or a strategy. It is not coincidental that when scholars in Lawrence Grossberg, Cary Nelson, and Paula Treichler's collection *Cultural Studies* adopt the language of adoption, they generally do so in the context of discussing not parent-child relationships but cross-racial or even cross-species ones. Sometimes they casually use the term to describe a relationship whose artificiality they want to foreground. Yet sometimes the term refers to a fruitful relationship of choice and commitment. Kobena Mercer distinguishes between "imitative fantasies," such as the short-lived, quasi-parodic White Panther Party of 1969, and "alliances that created new forms of political solidarity": he describes Jean Genet's participation in the work of the Black Panther Party, defending Bobby Seale, in terms of his being "adopted" into the community.[3] Helena Michie writes tellingly, in another context, of the dangers of the metaphor of sisterhood to feminists, how it tempts feminists to subsume otherness;[4] what she is groping for but fails to find is a metaphor for the socially constructed family, such a metaphor as adoption.

It is hardly coincidental that figurative adoption appears with unusual frequency—with greater frequency than in any other work of criticism that I have read in the past five years—in Bill Ashcroft, Gareth Griffiths, and Helen Tiffin's *The Empire Writes Back.* These critics theorize postcolonialism and cultural hybridity and the importance of disrupting "history" and "ancestry." The postcolonial theory that the critics celebrate "has drawn on European theoretical systems . . . cautiously and eclectically."[5] It uses such systems but often disrupts them. At the same time, it goes beyond simple critiques of hegemony and disavowals of imperialism to scrutinize the mutual workings of influence without privileging any of the differentiated terms. For these authors, "hybridity in the present is constantly struggling to free itself from a past which stressed ancestry, and which valued the 'pure' over its threatening opposite, the 'composite.' It replaces a temporal linearity with a spatial plurality" (36).

Drawing from the past without being determined by ancestry: adoption, in short. Some form of the term *adoption* recurs in *The Empire Writes Back* with considerable frequency, on average once every tenth page, but with particular frequency in the chapters that foreground theoretical matters. Often the term is used with seeming transparency—the adopt-a-stance usage that makes familial connotations all but invisible. Yet the term recurs so frequently and the content of the book is so apropos, so resonant with the social constructedness of familial adoption, that the term regains its evocative metaphoricity.

Some of the writers that Ashcroft, Griffiths, and Tiffin cite, writers resisting European imperialism, use the term *adoption* disparagingly, in connection with misguided attempts to subjugate the alien, as when Wole Soyinka describes Négritude as "a foundling deserving to be drawn into, nay, even considered a case for benign adoption by European ideological interests" (21). More often, however, the critics use the term positively, especially in connection with language. Language, they argue, may be "adopted as a tool and utilized in various ways to express widely differing cultural experiences" (39). What Ashcroft and his colleagues call "english"—to distinguish it from the more privileged "received English," which is associated with "metropolitan power over the means of communication" (38)—may be consciously "adopted as the language of government and commerce" and literature (39). "Rastafarians," the critics argue, "have adopted various strategies by which language might be 'liberated' from within" (48), and even silence may be "adopted as the fruitful basis for an indigenizing literature" (141).

Ashcroft, Griffiths, and Tiffin succeed in revaluing the cultural construction of adoption, often in curious tandem with some revaluation of the childish— that immaturity that colonized peoples were often described by colonials as possessing. Figurations of adoption often appear in contexts where childishness is figured too, one figure coupled to the other in a linguistic train of associations. These critics argue that the New Criticism, for instance, itself at root postcolonial,

> in certain ways . . . served to allow the passage of post-colonial writers, whose traditions were by European definitions "childish," "immature," or "tributary" (to adopt the most favoured metaphors of the period), into the English canon, which by the 1960s was in dire need of fresh fodder. William Walsh's books on Commonwealth writers are an example of the way in which New Criticism facilitated the "adoption" of individual post-colonial authors by the "parent" tradition. (161)

But Ashcroft and colleagues do not entirely succeed in revaluing juvenility, in overcoming what I have elsewhere termed "the anxiety of immaturity."[6] By placing the words *childish* and *immature* in quotation marks, they are critiquing the attribution of childishness more than revaluing it. *Adopt* appears in the first sen-

tence parenthetically and unmarked, but *adoption* appears in the second in quotation marks, as if the concept has now been accreted to the filial metaphor, to
that which must be critiqued. The effect is to retreat a little from the positive hybridizing that has previously been associated with the term. Vestigial hints of the
revalued associations, together with hints of a revaluing of what it means to be
a parent or a child, remain—but only briefly. What I see as the beginnings of a
cultural revaluation of the trope of adoption in *The Empire Writes Back* is fragile and precarious, and after the passage just cited, it is as if adoption can no
longer perform its hybridizing function. For in the next few pages, in the final
figurations of adoption in the main text of the book, it takes on a more dysfunctional cast. The authors lament that "theories such as poststructuralism are
adopted more readily than similar views derived from the conditions of postcolonial experience"; they refer to a "critique of the inappropriate adoption of
recent European critical models in Nigeria" (164). The trope of adoption has
great potential for any theorist grappling with the intricacies of social construction, or with "disrupt[ing] the very familial metaphor that Harold Bloom
suggests is the basis of all re(mis)-reading,"[7] as such cultural and postcolonial
critics as Ashcroft and his colleagues are only beginning to recognize.

I turn now to my second moment, to the realm of children's literature. I turn
from deployments of the term *adoption* that at least sometimes evoke the root
familial relationship to an adoptive familial relationship that never speaks its
name. I turn from contemporary postcolonial criticism to children's literature
of the past few decades, focusing especially on a work from the middle of the
century. Such a work of children's literature can anticipate some of what current high theory is groping toward. As Juliet Dusinberre pointed out in *Alice in
the Lighthouse*, juvenile literature can provide an arena for experimenting with
concerns that surface only later in writing for adults.[8]

In the case of adoption, children's literature provides a cultural space for
playing out both the potential dysfunctions and diminutions of adoption and
also its benefits—the way adoption enables both independence and what postcolonial theorists call hybridization, the way it enables connections among
races, species, kingdoms (animal, vegetable, mineral). Such connections are especially evident in cross-species adoption, a powerful figure for all adoption, the
biological difference of adoption figured as difference in species.

Children's literature has long troped adoption. As French critic Isabelle Jan
suggests, "adoption, taken in its widest connotation, is probably the basic psychological theme in children's literature."[9] Jerry Griswold has argued, in *Audacious Kids*, that the classic American children's literature of the nineteenth and
early twentieth centuries always includes a desirable move to a second family
(well, almost always—his thesis works least well for *Little Women*).[10] In fact, I
suspect that the reason I was relatively open to the possibility of adopting chil-

dren (two, from Korea) was that the Pollyannas, Rebeccas, and Annes of my childhood had bathed adoption in a romantic glow. Even—to stray beyond North America—such adventure stories as *Treasure Island*, by troping the adventurers as family, endorse a kind of adoption.

Rarely in this literature for older children, though, are the adoptions cross-racial. True, an emerging literature—comprised of such stories as Linda Walvoord Girard's *We Adopted You, Benjamin Koo*—targets families that have experienced transracial adoption. At times, as in *Benjamin Koo*, these works transcend their origins as bibliotherapy, as fictionalized self-help manuals for children. Yet in other juvenile fiction, fiction that is not self-consciously addressing the "problem" of transracial adoption—such as Virginia Hamilton's *The Planet of Junior Brown*—the families the protagonists cobble together are likely to be all of one race.

Cross-racial adoption seems to pose problems for writers of children's literature, perhaps especially when such adoption is not the problem that the book sets out to solve. Consider the metaphoric cross-racial adoption in *Adventures of Huckleberry Finn* (a crossover book claimed by critics of literature for children as well as by those of literature for adults). The nature of the relationship, the nature of the simultaneous crossing of race and age, is highly problematic: Is Huck the child or is Jim? Is the black man paternal or childish?

Instead of addressing cross-racial adoption directly, a number of works, works especially for younger children, feature cross-species adoption. Before the 1990s many authors seem to have taken care not to stress any parallels between species and race. The West has a long history whereby the racialized other has been bestialized, and it can be very hard to avoid stereotypes if there is even a whiff of a particular animal species being associated with a particular race. In the past few years, though, a number of writers have consciously used cross-species adoption as a trope for cross-racial adoption. These tend to be bibliotherapeutic stories: the point of Holly Keller's *Horace* or Molly Bangs's *Goose* or Keiko Kasza's *A Mother for Choco* is to learn how to come to terms with looking different from one's parents. The best such story is probably *The Surprise Family*, in which a boy hatches—or is present at the hatching of—a chick who later hatches ducklings.[11] Lynn Reiser, the book's author, suggests that adoption functions as a metaphor for the social construction of all families when she notes on the back flap: "All families are surprise families. Parents and children meet as strangers and grow up together, surprising one another with interests and talents that are not exactly what had been expected. And they continue to love one another anyway."[12]

Even before the 1990s most of the works that have troped cross-species adoption have been animal stories. Sometimes it just "happens" that the parental figure Ernest is a bear and the child Celestine a mouse. Sometimes an author may stress resemblances between parent and child, as when Wilma the miniature elephant finds a suitable home with the river pigs or when the egg that Horton the elephant has sat on for so many weeks hatches as an elephant-bird. Sometimes the author stresses the child achieving independence from the adoptive family and its norms, as when the Ugly Duckling discovers that it is not in fact a duck or when the mouse Stuart Little, born to a human family, sets off on independent adventures (and, contrary to the recent film version, does not return). Sometimes the trope of adoption is worked out with considerable complexity. Randall Jarrell's *The Animal Family* problematizes difference by building a family across difference: a hunter woos a mermaid, and the two subsequently adopt a bear, a lynx, and eventually a boy—though since the hunter and mermaid seem to find the greatest emotional resonance not with the animals but with the boy, the novel retreats a little from its celebration of difference. In the film *Free Willy*, a white foster child, aided by a nonwhite adult helper, fosters and then frees the whale Willy; the home-video version opens with a trailer inviting the viewer to adopt an orca—to free it, in effect. In this unusually complex working out of the metaphorics of adoption, adoption means, for the human, finding a modicum of freedom within certain social constraints and for the nonhuman, freeing the individual from all human constraints.

I want to focus here on another resonant working out of the metaphorics of adoption, in *Charlotte's Web*. E. B. White's rendering of the trope is particularly complex because not only is adoption metaphoric but so is the parent-child relationship. As with the famous duck-rabbit figure, now you see them, now you don't. Through his complex indirectness, White brings to the surface many attitudes buried in other children's books.

White overtly celebrates neither adoption nor the parent-child relationship but friendship, especially the friendship between Charlotte and Wilbur. Feeling friendless and dejected, Wilbur early on laments, "I have no real friend here in the barn."[13] "Do you want a friend, Wilbur?" a voice that turns out to be Charlotte's says; "I'll be a friend to you" (31). "You're my best friend," she later tells him as she embarks on weaving the word *terrific* in her web (91). "No pig ever had truer friends," the narrator tells us in one of his more didactic moments, "and [Wilbur] realized that friendship is one of the most satisfying things in the world" (115). In the last paragraph of the book, when we are told that "Wilbur never forgot Charlotte," the narrator adds: "She was in a class by herself. It is not often that someone comes along who is a true friend and a good writer. Charlotte was both" (184).

Calling Charlotte a "good writer" is likely to evoke a smile. For what indeed has she written? "Some pig," "terrific," "radiant," "humble"—her entire opus consists of five words. They are, to be sure, five well-chosen and utterly efficacious words: they change Wilbur's life—indeed save his life. Still, applying the term *good writer* to Charlotte has been called "a playful, ironic, *New Yorker*-ish touch that has the effect . . . of deflating, just a little, the sentimental mood in which the story ends."[14] Or maybe it forces us to dismantle the usual referents of the term and rethink its meaning.[15] Maybe a good writer, to echo White's advice in *The Elements of Style*, is one who uses the fewest words to the greatest effect.

I think a similar dismantling happens with the term *true friend*. When I teach *Charlotte's Web* to undergraduates, I like to address matters of technique. I ask students to think of the challenges White confronted in writing the book. How does one overcome the cultural stereotypes associated with spiders (the "Little Miss Muffett" spider, the *Hobbit* spiders) to create an admirable, maybe even lovable, creature? Perhaps more interestingly—if only because White succeeds less well—how does one create a believable friendship between a pig and a spider?

It is easy to understand why Wilbur would be so appreciative of Charlotte: she befriends him when he is lonely; she saves his life. But why should Charlotte care so much for Wilbur that she repeatedly—even overcoming mortal exhaustion—weaves the words that save his life? In very abstract terms, of course, Wilbur's slops and manure attract the flies that sustain Charlotte: as the narrator notes, "Like Fern, she was truly fond of Wilbur, whose smelly pen and stale food attracted the flies that she needed" (57). Maybe, too, the cuteness and cuddliness that had attracted the young girl Fern when Wilbur was a baby are also attractive to Charlotte—though White never gives any such indication. Certainly Charlotte herself is neither cuddly nor cuddling. White does stress Charlotte's admiration for Wilbur's efforts to imitate her, to spin a web: the fact that Wilbur tries not just once but twice makes him, for Charlotte, "not a quitter" (58). But somehow I do not find this one trait completely convincing as a primary justification for her friendship. Wilbur may eventually rescue Charlotte's egg sac from the fairgrounds and bring it safely back to the barn. But that is after the fact of Charlotte's friendship—after she has died. Besides, what difference does it make to the unhatched spiders that they be born in the born? It makes a difference only to Wilbur, who would otherwise be lonely. White brilliantly shows, rather than tells, throughout most of the novel, but in the matter of Charlotte's friendship for Wilbur, in terms of what is in it for her, he keeps telling us but does not really show us.

Still, beginning with Eudora Welty, who reviewed *Charlotte's Web* in the *New York Times Book Review* in 1952, most critics have taken White at his word and either describe the relationship between Charlotte and Wilbur as one of friendship or claim friendship as a key—even the key—theme in the book.[16] In a 1980 essay, for instance, John Griffith refers to Charlotte as "the perfect friend, at once confidante, instructor, protector, and mother."[17] Yet by 1993 he seems to recognize that these last words may be somewhat odd synonyms for *friend:* he suggests that Charlotte's and Wilbur's friendship is in fact "very peculiar," for "the only substantial interest that Charlotte and Wilbur share are those directly related to Wilbur's well-being." Furthermore, "she is resourceful and self-reliant while he is helpless and dependent; she is generous and self-sacrificing while he is gratefully receptive." Griffith adds, "Affection is mutual between them, but in every other respect their friendship is all give on Charlotte's side, all take on Wilbur's." Such a relationship is a far cry from twentieth-century ideas of the mutuality of friendship.[18]

Consider, too, Peter Neumeyer's commentary in a note in *The Annotated Charlotte's Web*: "White repeats the theme of friendship with sufficient frequency for there to be no question as to its centrality in the book. . . . But we will look in vain for sustained evidence of [White's] emotional involvement in the lives of others, except those of his immediate family." Perhaps White was simply reticent, Neumeyer adds, or perhaps White's marriage was so "fully absorbing and all-encompassing" that "there was neither time nor inclination for sustained engagement in the life of others."[19] Or perhaps in *Charlotte's Web*, I am tempted to say, White used the term *friendship* to describe a relationship that could more aptly be characterized as something else.[20]

The relationship between Wilbur and Charlotte in many ways echoes Wilbur's relationship with Fern.[21] In saving the runt of the litter at the beginning of the novel, Fern agrees to nurse it with a bottle, "like a baby," "her infant between her knees" (3, 6–7). She watches him burrow in the straw to sleep and is "enchanted": "It relieved her to know that her baby would sleep covered up, and would stay warm" (9). She walks him in her doll carriage, next to her baby doll, sometimes "wheel[ing] the carriage very slowly and smoothly so as not to wake her infants" (10). Her relationship is, in short, maternal, a performance of the maternal that the narrator watches with bemusement. It is a performance that in part problematizes the difference between pigs and humans—not least when Fern protests against the killing of the runt of the litter by asking, "If *I* had been very small at birth, would you have killed *me*?" (3).[22]

Charlotte, too, has a maternal relationship with Wilbur,[23] and like Fern's relationship, it too problematizes difference—though White neither reflects on the relationship with bemusement nor uses such words as *mother* or *maternal* or *baby* or *infant* in connection with it. Charlotte tells Wilbur a story on demand and sings him a lullaby to help him sleep. She advises him: "get plenty of sleep, and stop worrying"; "chew your food thoroughly and eat every bit of it"; "gain weight and stay well" (64). When Wilbur invites her to attend the County Fair with him as she is preparing to lay her eggs, she complains, "I can't arrange my family duties to suit the management of the County Fair" (117)—though of course she does, effectively expanding her family duties to encompass not just the laying of eggs but also the saving of Wilbur. She leads Zuckerman to think he has some terrific pig, attracting celebrity for miles around and winning "this radiant, this terrific, this humble pig" a special medal at the County Fair (158)—so, of course, Fern's uncle would never consider slaughtering Wilbur. In her influential *Maternal Thinking,* Sara Ruddick finds preservation and the fostering of growth and social acceptability the key components of maternal work.[24] Charlotte may not nurture growth by providing food, but she nurtures Wilbur's intellectual and social growth. She fosters social acceptability partly by training Wilbur ("chew your food thoroughly") and partly by redefining what makes a pig acceptable to humans. And she certainly preserves.

In this foregrounding of the maternal, *Charlotte's Web* differs importantly from two other books that feature animal adoption and friendship. In Margaret Wise Brown's *The Golden Egg Book,* published five years before *Charlotte's Web,* a bunny plays with an egg from which a duckling hatches, the two become friends, and "No one was ever alone again."[25] There is no imprinting here, no maternal attachment. In Janell Cannon's *Stellaluna,* the most popular of the recent fuzzy adoption books, the adoption does not take. The bat is simply too different from the bird family that has raised her—as she realizes once she meets other bats and is reunited with her birth mother. Stellaluna and her bird siblings remain friends: only friendship can bridge the difference in species. The very popularity of this book probably tells us a good deal about underlying cultural attitudes toward adoption, especially cross-racial adoption. The popular response is to retreat to friendship. White, however, seems to have used friendship as a cover for exploring other kinds of connection.

If we look at the relationship between Charlotte and Wilbur one way, the way endorsed by the narrator, it is friendship. If we look at it another way, in terms of how it functions, it is a mother-child relationship. Or maybe the different relationships are simultaneously present, both/and—a coupling encapsulated in one critic's passing reference to "Charlotte's adoption of Wilbur as her friend."[26] White is indeed celebrating adoption, the social construction of families. He does not use the term *adoption* to describe the relationship between Charlotte and Wilbur, but in creating a maternal spider and a childlike pig, he invokes a metaphorics of adoption.

At the same time, White is invoking a metaphorics of distancing, or more precisely of distancing and connecting. As Perry Nodelman points out, novice "readers need enough distance from this novel to contemplate the unexpected relationships between its characters," a distance gained in part through White's emphasis on "the animal-like nature of his characters."[27] In animal stories more generally, a child is allowed to identify across a comforting distance. Storybooks about animals behaving like humans allow both distance and connection; they both create a buffer and problematize difference, calling difference into question. Storybooks about families that cross species even more pointedly problematize difference as they trope adoption.

Such troping of adoption in literature for young children can open some doors for adoption, to use a metaphor current in adoption circles. It can bridge difference. Yet it does so at some cost. Sometimes, as to some degree in *Char-*

lotte's Web, its bridging is at the expense of biological mothers. Fern's mother and the mothers of other children, White informs us, worry too much: "Mothers for miles around worried about Zuckerman's swing. They feared some child would fall off. But no child ever did. Children almost always hang onto things tighter than their parents think they will" (69). Fern's mother worries about Fern's interest in animals, about her retelling of Charlotte's stories: "Stop inventing these wild tales!" her mother commands (106). Fern's brother, Avery, is not a worry, Mrs. Arable assures the family doctor: "Avery is always fine. Of course, he gets into poison ivy and gets stung by wasps and brings frogs and snakes home and breaks everything he lays his hands on. He's fine" (112). But Fern's interest in animals, rather than boys, at the ripe old age of eight is a matter that requires consultation with a medical expert. So much for the wisdom of biological mothers.[28]

If nevertheless Charlotte represents a kind of ideal mother, White is implying that the ideal mother will sacrifice herself for her family. Maybe Charlotte is not so completely, obliteratingly self-sacrificing as another celebrated cross-species mother figure in twentieth-century children's literature: Shel Silverstein's Giving Tree lops off limbs and even sacrifices her trunk in response to the whims of a demanding boy. Charlotte would seem to preserve some sense of self. She at least demurs about attending the County Fair with Wilbur. But the demurral is in the service of family after all, so that she can devote energy to her eggs; and she ends up going to the fair anyway, because she wants to guarantee Wilbur's life. Furthermore, even if her death is not a direct self-sacrifice for Wilbur, it metaphorically is. "A pig shall be saved," White assured himself as he wrote the story.[29] Yet if White succeeded in saving a pig—as if to compensate for the loss of the pig so movingly described in his 1948 essay "The Death of a Pig"—it would seem to be at the expense of a spider. The poetic logic of the story is that Charlotte dies so that Wilbur can life.

Moreover, even as he celebrates adoptive parenting, White indirectly reinforces a kind of biological mystique. Because the relationship between the adult figure and the child is adoptive, it is easier to allow Mowgli to leave the jungle, to allow Julie to leave the wolves—and, I think, to allow Charlotte to die. Much as the Grimms changed wicked mothers into stepmothers so as not to offend the sensibilities of bourgeois parents, children's authors allow the onstage loss of surrogate parents more readily than that of biological ones. Aunts seem to be particularly vulnerable: I think of the aunts in *James and the Giant Peach*, of how acceptable it is for Tom Sawyer to behave thoughtlessly toward Aunt Polly, and of the humorous but graphic way in which Ted Hughes disposes of an aunt in "My Aunt"—not to mention the way Luke Skywalker's aunt and uncle are so casually disposed of at the beginning of *Star Wars*, clearing the way for Luke's eventual, almost mystical, reunions with his biological father and sister. Charlotte is not figured as an aunt but simply as maternal, yet a similar principle applies. True, her death is central to the plotting of the story—unlike the deaths of Luke Skywalker's aunt and uncle, his adoptive parents—so her death is deeply moving. But it is probably meant to be a somewhat tempered catalyst of loss and grief, somewhat shielding child readers, compared to, say, the death of a main character's biological mother.

The presence of surrogate mothers can, in short, foster independence in child characters, making it easier for them to break free, to be the "rugged individualists" that White envisions his barnyard creatures as being.[30] But the invoking of surrogacy also reinforces the biological mystique to the extent that surrogate parents, unlike biological ones, are disposable in a story for children. For White, an adoptive, surrogate mother may provide better mothering than a biological one, but I think she is also, for him, more disposable. As with other literary celebrants of cross-species adoption, the majority of whom, before the 1990s, have been white men, adoption may be a way of limiting the power of the mother.

Still, White subtly praises the power of adoption even as he attenuates it. Perhaps, in fact, the expectation that adoptive parents are less connected, less smothering, makes the relationship worth celebrating: it frees child characters to find their own ways. If White's portrayal of Charlotte is both/and—she is both friend and mother—then in many ways his portrayal of adoptive parents is both/and as well. An adoptive parent can nurture and protect, like a biological parent, but without perhaps unduly controlling or limiting the child. Adoptive parents are thus, in effect, ideal parents.

Whereas postcolonial and cultural theorists are likely to invoke adoption through direct use of the term, sometimes deploying it to celebrate hybridization and other fruitful connections across racial divides, a children's novelist, such as E. B. White, may invoke it less directly, more metaphorically, but at times to similar effects, anticipating the work of the later theorists. If I might essay a brief allegory, it is not just a maternal role that Charlotte adopts. From a farm animal's perspective, humans are the colonial powers in an all too literal consumer culture. Only when an animal consciously adopts the language of humans, creolizes it telegraphically, puts the language of advertising copy to work in new contexts, and inscribes it in a form that the colonials can read—even as she has adopted the cause of a fellow subaltern—is one of the colonized saved from extermination. Charlotte, like the survivors of the outposts of empire, adopts the colonizers' language to write back.

In *Charlotte's Web,* as in *The Empire Writes Back,* the metaphorics of adoption can be empowering, enabling not imperialist cannibalization but access to a politics of positionality, to an independence that is nonetheless interdependent. Once again, as when Alice blazed the way to the modernist lighthouse, children's literature anticipates serious adult writing, even as critics of literature and other culture for adults continue to condescend to—or ignore (as happens overtly in the Grossberg and Ashcroft volumes)—children and their literature.

NOTES

I am grateful to the members of the child_lit E-mail list, which is archived at <http://www.rci.rutgers.edu/~mjoseph/childlit/about.html>, for stimulating discussion and for generous brainstorming of relevant titles.

1. Pat Johnson recounts: "A 5-year-old girl was 'given' a giraffe by her grandparents through the zoo's adopt-an-animal program. The child was upset to learn that not only could she not take 'her' animal home or care for it directly, but she also could not consider it 'hers' since a different animal would be substituted for 'her' giraffe in the next year's campaign. Another child learned that an acquaintance had been assigned the same animal as had he!" ("The Adopt-A . . . Problem," OURS, March/April 1992, reprinted in The Adoption Rhode Island Newsletter, March–May 1993, 2).

2. George Lakoff and Mark Johnson, Metaphors We Live By (Chicago: University of Chicago Press, 1980), 22.

3. Kobena Mercer, "'1968': Periodizing Politics and Identity," in Cultural Studies, ed. Lawrence Grossberg, Cary Nelson, and Paula A. Treichler (New York: Routledge, 1992), 434.

4. Helena Michie, "Not One of the Family: The Repression of the Other Woman in Feminist Theory," in Discontented Discourses: Feminism/Textual Intervention/Psychoanalysis, ed. Marleen S. Barr and Richard Feldstein (Champaign: University of Illinois Press, 1989), reprinted in Feminisms: An Anthology of Literary Theory and Criticism, ed. Robyn R. Warhol and Diane Price Herndl (New Brunswick: Rutgers University Press, 1991), 58–68.

5. Bill Ashcroft, Gareth Griffiths, and Helen Tiffin, The Empire Writes Back: Theory and Practice in Post-Colonial Literatures (London: Routledge, 1989), 33. Subsequent references to this work are given parenthetically in text.

6. See Beverly Lyon Clark, "Fairy Godmothers or Wicked Stepmothers? The Uneasy Relationship of Feminist Theory and Children's Criticism," Children's Literature Association Quarterly 18 (winter 1993–94): 171–76.

7. Michie, "Not One of the Family," 61.

8. Juliet Dusinberre, Alice to the Lighthouse: Children's Books and Radical Experiments in Art (New York: St. Martin's, 1987).

9. Isabelle Jan, On Children's Literature, translation of La Littérature enfantine (1969), ed. Catherine Storr (1973; reprint, New York: Schocken, 1974), 116.

10. Jerry Griswold, Audacious Kids: Coming of Age in America's Classic Children's Books (New York: Oxford University Press, 1992).

11. By "best" I mean doing the best job of plotting and resolving the adoption story. Artistic kudos would probably go to Molly Bangs for her visually stunning illustrations. The resolutions of most of these stories, however, are unrealistically abrupt.

12. Lynn Reiser, The Surprise Family (New York: Greenwillow, 1994).

13. E. B. White, Charlotte's Web, illustrated by Garth Williams (1952; reprint, New York: Harper, 1973), 27. Subsequent references to this work are given parenthetically in the text.

14. John Griffith, *Charlotte's Web: A Pig's Salvation* (New York: Twayne, 1993), 49.

15. As Janice M. Alberghene also argues, in "Writing in *Charlotte's Web*," *Children's Literature in Education* 16 (spring 1985): 32–44.

16. Eudora Welty, "Life in the Barn Was Very Good," *New York Times Book Review,* October 19, 1952, 49.

17. John Griffith, "*Charlotte's Web:* A Lonely Fantasy of Love," *Children's Literature* 8 (1980): 115.

18. Griffith, *Charlotte's Web: A Pig's Salvation,* 37.

19. Peter Neumeyer, ed., *The Annotated Charlotte's Web* (New York: HarperCollins, 1994), 114 n. 3.

20. I will here forego one such possibility, the possibility of an erotics of friendship, though I note that Joseph Epstein equates Charlotte with White's wife, Katherine, "who was the mainstay of his always shaky life" ("E. B. White, Dark & Lite," *Commentary,* 1986, reprinted in *Partial Payments: Essays on Writers and Their Lives* [New York: Norton, 1989], 318). White has been lauded for shattering a major twentieth-century taboo by courageously portraying death in literature for children and refusing to protect children from the realities of life, but he is nonetheless reticent about the provenance of Charlotte's eggs, how they came to be fertilized, their paternity.

21. This parallel echoes in many other ways as well, as Perry Nodelman so well documents in "Text as Teacher: The Beginning of *Charlotte's Web*," *Children's Literature* 13 (1985): 109–27.

22. As Ashraf H. A. Rushdy also points out, in "'The Miracle of the Web': Community, Desire, and Narrativity in *Charlotte's Web*," *The Lion and the Unicorn* 15 (December, 1991): 52–53.

23. Other critics who read the relationship as primarily maternal include Rosalind Ekman Ladd ("Death and Children's Literature: *Charlotte's Web* and the Dying Child," in *Children and Health Care: Moral and Social Issues,* ed. Loretta M. Kopelman and John C. Moskop [Dordrecht: Kluwer, 1989], 107–20); Lucy Rollin ("The Reproduction of Mothering in *Charlotte's Web*," *Children's Literature* 18 [1990]: 42–52); and Margaret Rustin and Michael Rustin ("The Poetic Power of Ordinary Speech: E. B. White's Children's Stories," in *Narratives of Love and Loss: Studies in Modern Children's Fiction* [London: Verso, 1987], 146–62).

24. Sara Ruddick, *Maternal Thinking: Toward a Politics of Peace* (1989; reprint, New York: Ballantine, 1990).

25. Margaret Wise Brown, *The Golden Egg Book,* illustrated by Leonard Weisgard (1947; reprint, New York: Golden, 1975), n.p.

26. Griffith, *Charlotte's Web: A Pig's Salvation,* 44.

27. Nodelman, "Text as Teacher," 125.

28. Rollin ("Reproduction of Mothering," 48), however, suggests that "the sheer number of different mothers, of varying species, and all circulating around Wilbur, suggests the complexity of the mother image itself: a biological, psychological, spiritual, economic, social, and cultural construct which eludes full description and for which Charlotte's web is the perfect emblem."

29. Cited in Griffith, *Charlotte's Web: A Pig's Salvation,* 36.

30. Letter to Gene Deitch, January 12, [1971], in Neumeyer, *Annotated Charlotte's Web,* 224. Neumeyer notes (57 n. 4) that despite this claim, the interdependence of the animals is nonetheless a frequent theme in the novel.

The Immaculate Deception

Adoption in Albee's Plays

Garry Leonard

I will argue in this essay that much of Albee's work presents the existential absurdity of growing up within the process of the closed-record adoption system. *Within* is the operative word, since Albee seems obsessed with boxes and confined spaces in his plays, and the closed-record adoption system, I will argue, is just such a "closed box" on the existential level. In this vein, Albee has two basic impulses: one is to try to make the audience feel the inherent absurdity of the adoption process by placing them, through the vehicle of the play, in an unpredictable landmine-filled world where affection and hostility erupt in unexpected ways and where presumably inviolable bonds between and among the characters are analyzed to show their basis in need, fear, and dependency. The other impulse is to construct in the play an adoptee figure (Jerry in *Zoo Story* is my primary example) who is apparently unbalanced but who insinuates him or herself into a "normal" situation and begins to destroy it by questioning the truth of situations the characters must believe in if they are to preserve a reality they have always taken for granted. Before I can identify the adoptive experiences as a pervasive influence on Albee's work, I need to defamiliarize adoption itself, because one of the defining features of the experience for Albee is its relative invisibility.

Adoption, especially in the 1940s and 1950s, was viewed as "the same" as having biological parents. The closed-record system had good intentions, perhaps—the woman gets on with her life, the child's upbringing will not be interrupted, and so on—but it also served to inaugurate and protect the myth that once the baby was placed with a family, there was no difference between this placement and a biological birth. Thus, this strategy for legitimating the child, though it has obvious good intentions, is not without problems, for both the adoptive parents and the adopted child, who are both locked into a myth of sameness: for the adoptive parents, this is the child they were unable to conceive; for the child, these are the parents assigned to him or her after his first set abandoned him or her in some way. Once we reproblematize it and view it in a broader historical context, we can see the history of adoption in general and of closed-record adoption in particular as the latest attempt to resolve the essentially unresolvable fact of illegitimacy. The problem of the child born out of wedlock and thus "illegitimate" is always a thorny one from the perspective of social institutions. Compassion dictates that all babies deserve care and protection, but these institutions also rely on notions of "legitimacy" as that which underwrites their own authority to act. Illegitimate events cannot be simply declared legitimate without calling into question what determines the difference between the two, and this, in turn, brings into high profile the constructed nature of authority and even of the law itself. Not surprisingly, then, modern adoption is a court-ordered process that confers a degree of legitimacy on the conception, while keeping track, in sealed records, of the facts of the illegitimate birth.

Before modern adoption, the baby was cared for in some way or another (in Western culture it has always been illegal to murder an illegitimate child), but it was also clearly demarcated as having no natural connection to the social order. In the Poor Law of 1576, for example, one encounters a characterization of the bastard as "an offence against God's lawe and man's lawe."[1] Here we see a moral requirement for the bastard to be stigmatized, but economics is an equally difficult issue: in the absence of a recognizable family connection, who is responsible for the child's welfare? Accordingly, the bastard was *filius nullius,* or "nobody's child," effectively making him a ward of the state and, in 1576, a burden on local taxes. The local tax burden was sure to make the unwed mother the target of financially driven, as well as moral, disdain. Modern adoption also addresses this problem by placing the child with a family willing to pay for the upkeep of the child and willing, in the signing of the adoption papers, to attest to this promise legally. Yet, even in 1576, bastards and unwed mothers, provided they suffered and appeared penitent, were also seen as useful reminders for the general populace about, in the case of the mother, the price of falling away from chastity and, in the case of the child, the permanent handicap of illegitimacy, primarily configured by the impossibility of inheriting land or wealth. Someone might choose to provide for the bastard, but the bastard had no legal right to demand anything more than the basics needed to survive.

From the sixteenth through the nineteenth century, the bastard had to bear some sort of stigma; otherwise, the mother would be insufficiently punished, and the legal system, based on patriarchal blood relations, would be seriously undermined. So the bastard in history has a paradoxical relationship to the law—clearly outside of it and yet, at the same time, helping to maintain its hegemonic force by exemplifying the unenviable fate of defying the law of God and humanity in favor of anarchic passion. As the bastard Edmund in *King Lear* puts it, "thou, nature, art my goddess. To thy law / My services are bound" (1.2.1–2).[2] Born outside the rules, bastards are feared because they seem in a position to make their own rules in defiance of the accepted order. Indeed, they have no choice but to do so, since their connection to the accepted order is highly conditional. The paradox, then, is that illegitimacy must be taken account of and must be subject to socially sanctioned rules, but not in a way that legitimates it.

Jerry in *Zoo Story* seems an oddly modern transformation of the bastard Edmund. Like Edmund, Jerry is an outsider, his origin unclear. Although clearly Jerry is fascinated with the everyday rule of Peter's world, he neither respects these laws as inevitable nor appears subject to them himself. Also like Shakespeare's Edmund, Jerry has a deep envy for Peter's connectedness and at the same time a deep contempt for Peter's thoughtless acceptance of this connectedness as a given. Although Jerry bitterly resents his outsider status, he also, like Edmund, experiences intense emotion at the tremendous freedom it allows him. The bastard, by definition, is one who has "nothing to lose."

What was needed, therefore—understood as early as the Renaissance, but never institutionalized—was some process for reintegrating bastards into the legitimate community as a way of containing their subversive power. The trick would be getting the bastard to accept the very laws that persecuted him. In this way, "society would force the bastard to accept his role as victim. A figure thus brainwashed would consolidate the legitimate hegemony. Texts which speak out in favor of illegitimacy do so with a consciousness of how useful it could be and with the imposition of clear conditions so as to channel its energy in support of the status quo."[3] Certainly Gloucester can be seen, by the careless way he humiliates Edmund in front of Kent, as someone who has complete confidence that the arrangements he has made for Edmund will contain him. But as Edgar neatly summarizes at the end of *King Lear*, for benefit of the dying Edmund, "the dark and vicious place where thee he got / Cost him his eyes" (5.3.162–63).

The problem with Edmund is that, while he may be excluded from the legal order by a law that recognizes him only to the extent it delegitimates him, nonetheless his knowledge of his situation emboldens him to take what he sees in defiance of a law that says, technically, he does not exist. But what if a bastard had no knowledge of his biological origins? What if the people who raised him were, from a biological point of view, strangers; what if they had no knowledge of his origins as well; what if his biological relatives likewise had no knowledge of his present whereabouts; and what if all this information were kept somewhere under lock and key, with all three parties legally barred from having access? Then we would have the process of the closed-record adoption system to which Albee was submitted.

As I suggested at the outset, I have taken this roundabout way to the study of adoption in Albee's plays to offer a brief historical contextualization of closed-record adoption and to highlight it as a procedure with a very long history and an implicit political and social agenda. The adoptive figure in Albee—the legitimated bastard who nonetheless bears the legal stigma of having no knowledge of his biological origins—comes in two basic types: Jerry of *Zoo Story*, the modern day Edmund, torturing and morally maiming the Gloucester-like Peter; or the more subdued, more anonymous boys of *The American Dream*, *The Sandbox*, and *Three Tall Women*, who are the sort of bastard the Renaissance could only dream about—docile, compliant, confused, disoriented, and too preoccupied with the inexplicable absurdities of their situation to offer much of a threat. These Albee adoptee figures comprise a silenced fantasy space that permits others to shore up the illusion of their own presumably innate legitimacy. In *Who's Afraid of Virginia Woolf?* the adopted child has been such an effective fantasy space for Martha and George for so long that they have no memory of an actual child but only a precarious sense of a shared myth about a fantasy child. I take the position that they had an actual child and that Albee's presentation of the way they talk about this child is intended not to suggest they have made it up but to allegorize the way adoptive parents (or at least his adoptive parents) fantasize so much about what a child will mean to the marriage that the actual child "disappears" into their dialogue. In *The American Dream*, Mommy and Daddy cannot remember what they called "the other one"—the first baby, who was systematically mutilated and then died. In *Who's Afraid of Virginia Woolf?* they manipulate "memories" of the child in a way that suggests the actuality of their adopted child never made any impression on them at all; instead, they fight over the right to control the fantasy space such a child represents as they completely incorporate "it" into the fabric of their dysfunctional marriage.

In general, Albee presents the existential reality of the position of the adoptee without explicitly calling attention to the fact of adoption as a social solution for the bastard. The reference to the adopted baby in *The American Dream* as "a bumble of joy" is a subtle exception. If we glance back at the Parliamentary debates that led to the Poor Law Amendment of 1834 in England, an amendment that declared men would no longer be responsible for their illegitimate children and that only the mother would be, we find ourselves in a discourse that seems very Albeesque—one where people of high dignity and self-satisfied moral purpose argue with an apparent reasonableness about what is right and wrong, what is legitimate and illegitimate, and how the distinction might best be maintained. The father must be absolved of financial responsibility, argued one lord in the debate about the bill, or else he is likely to persuade the mother to perform infanticide. Besides, adds another lord, easing the financial burden of bearing a bastard—as the baby is frankly referred to throughout the debate—takes "from the woman every feeling . . . calculated to nourish modesty of thought and delicacy of conduct."[4] The least that can be done for womankind, most of the lords agree, is to show a proper concern for a woman's chastity by doing all that is possible to make sure the bearing of a bastard will inaugurate a period of pain and poverty from which neither the mother nor her illegitimate child will ever recover. Charles Dickens heaps scorn on this Poor Law Amendment at several points in *Oliver Twist*, not least of all in his portrayal of Mr. Bumble, a beadle in charge of a workhouse for orphans, one who colludes with those running the institution to maximize the profits from money given by the state to the workhouse, first, by starving the children, and second, when possible, by selling them as little more than slaves to chimney sweeps, sailors, and anyone else willing to buy them and exploit them in their turn. So, to come full circle, when the adopted baby in *The American Dream* is referred to as "the bumble of joy," we get a hint, rare in its explicitness, that Albee is a student of the history of illegitimacy, and this strengthens my claim that he has thought about the closed-record adoption as the latest arrangement in a five-hundred-year-old legal debate.

There are other connections. One consistent feature of the debates about the Poor Law Amendment is that while a great deal is said about the bastard, the bastard never speaks. Among Albee's characters, this is most true of the young man in Albee's latest play, *Three Tall Women* (if you do not count the purportedly fantastic child of *Who's Afraid of Virginia Woolf?*). *Three Tall Women* is a play Albee has said he could not have written until his adoptive mother was dead. All three versions of the tall woman, who is based on his adoptive mother, fantasize and despise the boy by turns. They even, at various points, recall things he has said, appropriating his voice, and saying them exactly as they remember his saying them. But he himself never speaks. The older of the three tall women, recalls what he said when she said, "I'll have you thrown out of this house." His reply was "*You're* going to fire me?"[5] With this remark, we are back in the world of *Oliver Twist*, though not quite. There is no question that the adoptee in Albee's plays is bought, hired, rented, or sells himself, but he is expected to service the emotional tensions and impasses in a marital relationship, not, as in *Oliver Twist*, to service the chimneys. Nonetheless, the task is equally thankless and leads to an emotional death at a young age, if not, as in the case of chimney sweeps, a literal one.

"I do what I'm paid to do," says the young man in *The American Dream*.[6] He is paid to clean the emotional flue of Mommy and Daddy, which has been smoking rather alarmingly of late, and they can see—Mommy with ill-concealed lust and Daddy with depressed resignation—that he is "a great deal more like it" (124). The "it" would seem to be some unspecified ideal. Albee seems unimpressed by the presumed advances made in the modern practice of closed-record adoption, and he treats it as a rearrangement of the problem of illegitimacy—the most ingenious yet. In this practice, the past of the illegitimate child is sealed; a clean slate is issued in the form of an altered birth certificate; birth mothers are told to forget, adoptive parents are told it does not matter, and the children are not told much, except that they came from somewhere, that the adoptive parents do not know where, that in any event it does not matter, and that even if it did matter, the records are sealed anyway (which does seem to contradict the idea that none of it matters). *But never mind, the children are told. You're just like everyone else, really you are, except other people know their biological origins and are surrounded by people who look like them; but that's really not such a big difference, although we're glad we're not you. But you must accept it; everyone else has.*

"Accept it," the bishop, the lawyer, and the surrogate mother intone to Julian in *Tiny Alice* as they prepare to abandon him forever.[7] In *Who's Afraid of Virginia Woolf?* George tells his guests that birth came easily "once it had been accepted."[8] Easily for whom? "I no longer have the capacity to feel anything," the young man explains to the grandmother in *The American Dream* (115). Compare this with the ferocious energy of the bastard Edmund in *King Lear,* who, unhampered by the closed-record system, rails against his fate but does so with a biological discourse that shows he is exclusively focused on what modern adoption denotes as irrelevant (even as it legally seals it from sight): the biological nature of one's existence from conception to the present.

> Why "bastard"? Wherefore "base",
> When my dimensions are as well compact,
> My mind as generous, and my shape as true
> As honest madam's issue? Why brand they us
> With "base"? . . . (1.2.6–10).

Indeed, Edmund goes further, arguing that the assuredly passionate nature of the illicit coupling that led to his conception marks him as superior.

> Who in the lusty stealth of nature take
> More composition and fierce quality
> Than doth within a dull, stale, tirèd bed,
> Go to th' creating a whole tribe of fops
> Got 'tween asleep and wake? Well then,
> Legitimate Edgar, I must have your land. . . .
> I grow; I prosper.
> Now gods, stand up for bastards! (1.2.11–16, 21–22)

Bastards in touch with their biological inheritance can work themselves up and become highly directed and dangerous adversaries. Just ask Gloucester. But if we turn to Albee, we find little to fear from the biologically decontextualized adoptee, whose body, in the absence of any known—or, rather, any legally knowable—origin, can be chopped until it fits a Procrustean fantasy space, the dimensions of which are shaped by other people's self-delusions. It is not that Edmund is more legitimate than Oliver Twist or the young man in *The American Dream*. He, too, is treated with a fair amount of unconscious contempt: "there was good sport at his making, and the whoreson must be acknowledged" (1.1.26–27), Gloucester remarks when he introduces Edmund to Kent, an introduction that makes up in obtuseness what it lacks in graciousness. He has been away for nine years, Gloucester notes, also in passing, and will away again shortly. But Edmund's frank recognition that he is outside the law and legally incapable of inheritance marks him. Because of this mark, he has a way of making his condition intelligible to himself, a way that Albee's legitimated bastards, primarily as a result of the closed-record system, lack. "My practices ride easy!" says Edmund, "I see the business. / Let me, if not by birth, have lands by wit. / All with me's meet that I can fashion fit" (1.2.159–61). Compare this to the halting, desultory self-alienation of the young man in *The American Dream:* "I don't know what became of . . . the rest of myself . . . except that . . . I have suffered losses . . . that I can't explain" (114). Edmund has suffered losses, too, but at least he can explain them, and finding himself permanently outside the law, he accepts this as a license to operate in any fashion that suits his purpose. What is most consistent about the Albee adoptee is that he has no purpose except what others propose he be to suit their fantasies of completion, security, and purposefulness.

"All legal," says the cardinal to Julian in *Tiny Alice,* when finally it dawns on Julian that all he has been through has, all along, been a plan to abandon him forever (83). When Julian protests he does not want to be left all alone next to a tiny sealed house, with no sense of how to enter it, the cardinal, the lawyer, and his surrogate mother, Alice, all reply in unison: "Accept." "I have done with hallucination," Julian protests. "Then have done with forgery, Julian," the surrogate mother replies, "accept what's real. I am the . . . illusion" (85). "Was I sane then," Julian asks, referring to a time already described earlier in the play, six years spent in a mental asylum. He entered the asylum voluntarily, noting there were no bars on the window because there was really nowhere to run away to. "Those years?" Julian says. "My time in the asylum? Was that when I was rational? Then?" (85). Earlier, he had left the asylum "cured" when he accepted that what he had thought was real there was only hallucination; now the reality that he thought he had made his way back to appears to be hallucination, and his cure— or so he reasons—will consist of going back to the asylum, a place he now calls, with peculiar emphasis, "my asylum. MY! Asylum!" (85). But this will not prove sufficient for the gathered others who have arranged his abandonment; they require he remain suspended, able neither to get back into the sealed tiny house containing tiny Alice nor to be with anyone in their world, which they themselves have described as a replica of this model. So, appropriately enough, the lawyer takes out a gun, one he had secured earlier in case it proved necessary, and shoots Julian, thus assuring the group that they get to move on and that Julian will remain adrift between a reality and hallucination—legitimate according to the contract they have written without his permission or knowledge, yet illegitimate for all that: he is not one of them, not one who knows his biological origins or ever will, and no one who urges him to accept it would be in his place for the world. They thank him for his sacrifice before leaving him alone in the darkness, a darkness Albee describes this way: "the last scene of the play should seem as though [Julian] is in the attic closet, enclosed as a child in the dark, and that no one would come" (32–33).

The history of the bastard, which is crucial to the history of adoption, needs to be understood as a social history as well. One way to attempt this is by noting shifts of what Foucault called an "episteme," a region he describes as "anterior to words, perceptions, and gestures": "in every culture, between the use of what one might call the ordering codes and reflections upon order itself, there is the pure experience of order and its mode of being."[9] The history of dealing with illegitimacy is the history of an ordering code—the Poor Law of 1834, for example, or the founding of the modern adoption agency—that is imposed on the "pure experience of order," so keenly and privately sought after by Edmund in his lust for land by any means, and so disastrously missing in the case of the young man in *The American Dream*. Albee permits this "pure experience of order," taken for granted by those not adopted, to be disrupted by the mere presence of the adopted child. While unsatisfactory attempts have been made by Albee critics to see this as a variant on the theater of the absurd, it might better be viewed as a theater of dislocation. Albee's world is not as pervasively absurd as is the world of Beckett. Rather, his world attempts to consolidate its normalcy, but something keeps dislocating. "You make no allowances for me," the grandmother of *The American Dream* says, suddenly adding: "I want an allowance! I want an allowance!" (70). Here, the word *allowance* is used as a swivel point. It presents one form of order: an elderly person asking for her age to be taken into account before people judge her. Then the same word is used to denote something very different: a child calling for money of her own. This linguistic dislocation is akin to adoption in the closed-record system: the original word *allowance* slips into a different space where, although it is the same word, the context is completely changed, and it is as if the word has split into two separate versions of itself no longer in communication with each other—not unlike the twin pairing of the mutilated baby and the young man.

In *Who's Afraid of Virginia Woolf?* the fantasy child, whose presence through absence underwrites George and Martha's ordering codes, always threatens to disrupt these same codes and dislocate the spurious reality they appear to support. Similarly, most strategies for dealing with illegitimacy that claim to be humane still require that its stigmatized status be maintained. A recent psychological study of what is termed "adoption trauma" offers an unwitting deconstruction of the modern adoption practice. After stressing that closed-record adoptions are better than older systems, such as orphanages—presumably a reference to the horrible world of the original Mr. Bumble—the study describes the key figures in the process of closed-record adoption: "an adoption agent (or agency) which is seldom professional, particularly because of unavailable diagnostic criteria," and "adoptive parents whose profound motivations are unknown, but include 'pregnancy induction,' 'denial of sterility,' and, in a phrase that could be applied directly to *Who's Afraid of Virginia Woolf,* 'triangular mutual sado-masochistic exploitation.'"[10] Despite this frank appraisal of the hidden agendas implicit in this process, the study goes on to detail something called an "adopted child pathology," which includes character disorder, psychotic episodes, delinquency, incest, and homicide. The study concludes by citing the hardly surprising fact that adoptees are two to five times as likely to be referred for psychiatric evaluation as the general population. The reasons that adoptees are often patients include—and this is crucial to understanding adoption in Albee—such factors as "a covert bias against adoption in the general populations," "knowledge of having been relinquished," and "a sense of their rights having been compromised."[11] But because agencies and adoptive parents are not presenting themselves as case studies, it is the adoptee who presents as maladjusted. This is not unlike the way the family in *The American Dream* complain of their first baby. The grandmother details the systematic mutilation of the baby but then records its death as an inexplicable act of selfishness on its part. There is a dislocation in cause and effect, but, Albee shows, to correct this dislocation or even to try to, a "normal" reality will have to be dislocated first.

Such a clinical study on adoption as I have cited, detailing the multiple traumas of adoption, yet focusing on the adoptee as pathological, is directly relevant to an understanding of a character like Julian in *Tiny Alice,* who spent six years in an asylum unable to distinguish reality from hallucination because his faith "abandoned" him. Julian spent the same number of years in the asylum where Albee lived before he was told he was adopted. One study on adoption concludes, "the disclosure of adoption to a young child introduces an ongoing interference with the ability to distinguish between reality and fantasy." But before the disclosure, the child lives under the mistaken assumption that he is the biological child of his parents. Both before and after the disclosure, in different ways, the child experiences difficulty distinguishing hallucination from reality. The further one goes in the clinical literature, the more Albeesque themes seem to proliferate. A 1953 study "clearly described a vicious circle in which the normal instinctuality of an adopted child produces anxiety in adoptive parents who have severely repressed their own instinctual lives."[12] Mommy and Daddy in *The American Dream* are examples: Mommy, we learn, took to sleeping with her own mother until Daddy had an operation and seemed to lose interest in pursuing her; and when the bumble plays with its penis, they cut it off, and when its hands go to the place where its penis used to be, they cut off its hands. How does the adopted child cope? According to this same study, a common coping strategy is to split into twins—one bad, the other malleable to the point of invisibility. This is precisely the case with the split "twins" in *The American Dream:* the mutilated baby and his "twin" who appears later, a vacuous and mercenary young man.

This would seem to be the pathology of the adoptive child, but the study just cited goes on to note, "the child then becomes two different children to the adoptive parents."[13] One is "our" good child, and the other becomes "theirs"— its unknown progenitors' bad child. The study is not sure which comes first— whether the child splits into twins and then the adoptive parents assign bad blood to one and their own idealized fantasies to the other, or whether "parental representations of the child . . . are perceived by the child" and then these representations are followed by a likelihood that "the child will incorporate them into his or her own self representation." "We were separated when we were still very young, my brother, my twin and I . . . inasmuch as you can separate one being," says the young man in *The American Dream* (114). He has a twin, yet he is one being: this is a splitting into twins as a psychological coping mechanism. "You don't know how happy I am to see you!" Mommy says to the malleable twin. "Yes Siree. Listen, that time we had with the other one. I'll tell you all about it some time. . . . Maybe . . . maybe later tonight." "Why, yes," says the young man "that would be very nice" (127). Earlier, when they asked Mrs. Barker what to call this wonderful young man, she said "Call him whatever you like. He's yours. Call him what you called the other one." "Daddy!" Mommy calls out. "What did we call the other one?" (125–26).

In one of the real case studies about adoption, there is a little boy who "drew signs which read 'for sale' and 'sold'" and then told the psychiatrist his adoptive parents had paid two hundred dollars for him when he was a baby. Remarks the psychiatrist, "he had constructed a fantasy that he had been sold to his adoptive parents."[14] Strictly speaking, this may be a fantasy, but the adoptee's sense of having been a commodity in some kind of exchange is very real. Indeed, Albee's fascination with the wrapped box that may or may not be empty is a metaphoric enactment of what it feels like to be a bundle—or a bumble—opened by someone who already knows what they expect to find; if we imagine this box as a person, we need to imagine someone evacuating himself to make room for the other person's idea of who we are. In any event, the grandmother in *The American Dream* stresses at several points that "people very much like Mommy and Daddy" bought the baby. As for feeling sold, we need only remember the young man's frank, but curiously dispassionate, credo: "I'll do anything for money." This is not the motto of an opportunist, or even the battle cry of the amoral Edmund, but the detached voice of a commodity that cannot imagine doing anything except what it is paid to do. Albee's point is that the sense of the modern closed-record adoption process as a commercial transaction, at least on a broader social level, is not a fantasy. Indeed, the distinctive feature of Albee's vision as a playwright is that he is in touch with what is real to a point that is nearly unbearable. In an Albee play, every conceivable form of rationalizing is either isolated, ridiculed, and destroyed, or else left to carry on in a feeble manner, its falsity having been dissected from every angle. In this, Albee himself seems very like the impatient Edmund who brushes aside Gloucester's matterings about astrology as an irresistible force, fatally dictating man's action: "This is the excellent foppery of the world: that when we are sick in fortune—often the surfeits of our own behavior—we make guilty of our disasters the sun, the moon, and stars, as if we were . . . fools by heavenly compulsion. . . . An admirable evasion . . ." (1.2.108–115).

In *Tiny Alice,* Julian is systematically contracted to lifelong abandonment so that enormous amounts of money can change hands, from a surrogate mother, through a lawyer, and then on into the coffers of the church. Here is the Foucauldian triangle of knowledge, power, and desire as it is configured in the ideologically laden process of legitimating the illegitimate in a manner that reinforces the hegemonic status quo, rather than challenging its assumption of authority. Adopted children are commodities in Albee's work, as they are in *Oliver Twist* and are not in the plays of Shakespeare. Cut off from biological orientation and infused with a conflicted and paradoxical ideological orientation, Albee's adoptee figures are able to experience themselves not as agents but only as catalysts for other people's agency.

Yet, for all their compliance, their very "absent" presence seems to deconstruct illusion and self-deception (a central Albeesque theme), perhaps because, as a fantasy space for others, the adoptee's point of view is terrifyingly threatening, since even by having a point of view at all, the adoptee contradicts the illusions and self-deceptions that have been deposited in him by others. Any move toward subjecthood by the adoptee is experienced by these others as an intolerable exposure of illusions they have grown dependent on. In *The American Dream,* any hint that the baby has a center of initiative of its own is met with brutal and systematic mutilation. This is not sadistic from the parents' point of view, because they are, in their own minds, insisting that something fit into the box of their own self-delusions and rationalizations, so they can put a ribbon on it and regard it as something precious—a bumble of joy, or, rather, how they have bumbled their joy, but so nicely wrapped as to not call attention to this fact.

Closed-record adoption needs to be historicized as a relatively recent way of dealing with the very old problem of bastardry and illegitimacy. If, as Foucault claims, the modern asylum grew up in tandem with the success of Cartesian rationalism—that is to say, if the banishment of irrationality from philosophy was mirrored in the social management and institutionalization of mental illness—then the modern adoption agency grew up in tandem with what Foucault calls "bio-power," or a bureaucratized power over life designed to optimize the capabilities of the body, simultaneously enhancing its economic utility while ensuring its political docility. In this light, we can say, nothing is more capable or useful or docile than the bumble of joy in *The American Dream.* Also in this light, the Albee adoptee seems to "pay for himself," or to make other people willing to support him, and thus resolves the issue of who will be willing to take up the economic burden of raising an illegitimate child.

Let me offer another example of what a genealogical analysis—in Foucault's sense of genealogy—would yield about the historical evolution of the concept of illegitimacy from roughly the Renaissance to the modern adoption process to which Albee himself was submitted. The Poor Law Amendment of 1854, already discussed as one of the inspirations for *Oliver Twist*, unwittingly established a legal tie between mother and child, where previously the bastard had been *filius nullius*, "nobody's child." In essence, although this was hardly the point of the amendment, the illegitimate child became legally connected to the mother; this connection could be insisted on by her or relinquished, but she could no longer be left out of the process. This occurred, of course, not because a judge noticed the umbilical cord and deduced a connection but because a pejorative measure designed to save the state money, punish unchaste women, and further stigmatize bastards also happened to establish a legal connection between mother and child. Later plaintiffs were able to cite this connection as precedent.

Significantly, all the early plaintiffs were women who sought to adopt their own illegitimate children, a measure that was viewed with real alarm because it seemed to abolish illegitimacy. Laws were established to lessen the stigmatization of bastardry in order to make children more available to childless couples, not to provide a legal loophole by which a single mother made her bastard legitimate. Adoption, in other words, is intended to shift and obscure the stigma, not eliminate it. Also of special note when assessing the shift from the world of Mr. Bumble in *Oliver Twist* to the "bumble of joy" in Albee, is Foucault's notion that, in the classical episteme, "blood" and "blood relations," as well as attendant systems of power authenticated and authorized by "bloodlines," once were arranged in a particular historical and social configuration that made blood "a reality with a symbolic function." "The new concept of race," however, continues Foucault, "tended to obliterate the aristocratic particularities of blood, retaining only the controllable effects of sex."[15] The shift in emphasis from "blood" as the essence of legitimation to the legal control of sexuality makes modern adoption possible because the child is seen not as morally constructed from his or her bloodline but as an innocent being who needs to be raised properly. The notion that "blood will out" in the moral character of a person, regardless of their environment, so central to the fear of the bastard in Renaissance drama, is replaced by a sense that the same child, once removed from a morally suspect situation, may be expected to respond nicely to an improved moral environment. Of course, while the cultural belief in "blood" as a determining factor in moral character may have no scientific basis, the studies I have cited make it clear that there is still a "commonsense" prejudice against the adopted child, even in the adoptive parents, when negative characteristics of the child get explained as "bad blood" while positive ones are claimed as the result of the adoptive situation. In Albee's plays, the adoptee himself is blank, purchased, cut to size, silenced, fantasized, unheard of, unimagined, and unknown, but the function he serves as this hollowed out symbol, or empty (?) box, is real indeed. Just ask George and Martha in *Who's Afraid of Virginia Woolf?* They struggle to give up this fantasy space in a manner reminiscent of people trying to cure themselves of a drug addiction or a religious delusion or, to use Albee's own metaphor, like people trying to exorcise a demon, one who seduced them once upon a time with a promise to resolve, magically, all the unexamined tensions in their relationships.

Up to the last decade or so, the rebirth of the illegitimate baby into legitimacy has been "sealed," literally and figuratively, by legally confiscating and sealing up the adoptee's biological heritage as it exists in the original birth certificate and issuing a new one, henceforth the "only" one, with the last name of the adoptive family inscribed where the biological mother and/or father's name had been. So the child's illegitimacy is made legitimate, but this makes the child not a legitimate one but rather a *legitimated* one, or one who has been processed so as to appear "natural." Albee, especially in *Tiny Alice,* seems to regard this process as a sacrifice. The adopted child, through this process, is sacrificed by a system that polices the border between illegitimate and legitimate through legal means, even though this is done to preserve the presumably "natural" distinction between the legitimate and illegitimate. The law itself bridges these two terms to seal the connections that would permit a bridge between them. Such a situation, to use Mommy's favorite word from *The American Dream,* would appear to afford "satisfaction." Indeed, this is the final tableau of *The American Dream,* where Grandma hastily draws things to a close by noting everyone is satisfied, only adding (with an ominous note that foreshadows *Who's Afraid of Virginia Woolf?*), "or everybody's got what he thinks he wants."

But it is not so simple. Mommy's allegory of buying a hat is an allegory for deciding to adopt. She went in a hat store and bought a new hat. But another woman observed her with the hat and said, "I always wanted a wheat-colored hat *myself*" (58). Mommy insists it is beige; the woman says, "I know beige from wheat" (59). Mommy says she does, too; but it appears she does not. Where did this hat come from, really? It does not suit her as she expected it to. We might say, "it" does not look like her. So back to the shop she goes, just as Mommy and Daddy went back to the agency when the first baby died. "What do you mean by selling me a hat that you say is beige, when it's wheat all the time?" she asks. Then she adds, "I can tell beige from wheat any day in the week, but not in this artificial light of yours" (60). So the baby seems to be what it is intended to be in the "artificial light" of the agency, but it does not remain a baby: it grows; it looks different. One can continue to call the hat beige, but to other people it is wheat. Mommy reports, "They took my hat into the back, and then they came out again with a hat that looked exactly like it." Mommy says it is wheat; they protest, "It's beige; you go outside and see." "So," says Mommy, "I went outside, and lo and behold, it was beige." Daddy, who rarely offers an unsolicited opinion, ventures to say, "I would imagine that it was the same hat they tried to sell you before." "Well, of course it was," replies Mommy. "You just can't get satisfaction," Daddy says. "Well *I* got satisfaction," says Mommy (61). We see that satisfaction has to do not with the hat/baby but rather with the symbolic system for which the hat/baby is made to stand, the narratives imposed on the hat/baby, which the silence of the hat/baby underwrites.

When the twin of the mutilated baby arrives, he is colorless to himself but has learned to *act* beige, not because it has anything to do with who he is really, but because he has given up the notion of having a self entirely; he no longer affords himself the luxury of feeling, and he has learned, as he puts it, to "accept the syntax around me" (115). The agency, in its artificial light, dictates what is to be regarded as natural in terms of the newly legitimated child. Mrs. Barker, the social worker, mentions she is also the chairwoman of Mommy's club, and Mommy, who has not recognized her, replies, "I would have known you anywhere, except in this artificial light. . . . You have a hat just like the one I bought yesterday." "No, not really," is the reply, "this hat is cream." Mommy tries to do to her what was done to her: "It may look like a cream hat to you, but I can . . ." "You seem to forget who I am," Mrs. Barker interrupts, and the authority of the agency to name shades of color, or of reality, is reaffirmed: "Yes, I do, don't I? Are you sure you're comfortable? Won't you take your dress off?" (78–79). Mrs. Barker's ability to dictate the family reality, as a representative of the agency, means she can invert reality and the others will adjust, so badly do they need what she has to sell: "I don't mind if I do," she replies, and she removes her dress, playing the rest of the scene in her slip.

"It is useless," Albee once remarked, "to attack details on the conscious level. What you must lay siege to is the unconscious."[16] Implicit in this statement is the notion that consciousness can be attacked but never routed. The only way to lay siege to it is by attacking the unconscious. There is an element here of what we might call "adopteestentialism." I'm amending, of course, Sartre's term *existentialism*, but even that term arose from, in part, Sartre's fascination with the experiential world of Jean Genet, another adoptee—a fascination Sartre detailed exhaustively in his biography of Genet, *St. Genet*. Adopteestentialism is a peculiar form of alienation in Albee, though it is traceable to the adoptive experience more generally. It is borne of terror, envy, anger, and contempt at the mundane details of what passes for reality in the world where people know their biological origin. These details, treated thoughtlessly as facts by the biologically grounded individual, as simply "what is," appear in a very different light as reminders of exclusion to an adoptee figure, such as Jerry in *Zoo Story*.

In this play, Jerry wishes to undermine the mundane reality of the unsuspecting Peter, but, like Albee, he has no interest in doing this on any sort of conscious level. He sets out, instead, in accordance with Albee's credo, to do so by laying siege to the unconscious. To pick just one example, Jerry offers details about the objects in his room, but there is one particular detail scattered in among the others: "I have toilet articles, a few clothes, a hot plate, a can opener, . . . a knife, two forks, and two spoons, . . . three plates, a cup, a saucer, a drinking glass, *two picture frames, both empty*, . . ." (23; my emphasis). Jerry, like the clever Edmund who pretends to hide a letter so Gloucester will demand to see it, has situated the item about the picture frames in much the same way, with Gloucester-like obtuseness, Peter plucks it from the pile: "About those two empty picture frames . . . ?" he asks (23). It is significant that Jerry mentions the item, but it is doubly significant that Peter isolates it and then wants to hear more. It is the unconscious Jerry is fishing for, and Peter takes the bait. His plan, quite simply, is to make Peter feel what it can feel like to be adopted, then to observe what this does to Peter's view of himself and his world.

The two picture frames represent the biological imperative to cite one's biological origins—one's parents and/or one's sweetheart (with whom, typically, you intend to become a parent). The empty frames disturb Peter for reasons he cannot know, and his curiosity is directly related to the fact that their emptiness seems "unnatural." He is expecting Jerry to offer a "logical" explanation, but this is just what Jerry wishes to destabilize: "I don't see why they need any explanation at all," he replies, as unhelpfully as possible. "Isn't it clear?" he then adds disingenuously, with that tone of icy simplicity that always accompanies Albeesque contempt, "I don't have pictures of anyone to put in them" (23). Why does he have the frames, then? As an adoptee figure, Jerry exhibits adopteestentialism. As with any humans, he feels a need to place himself within a biological frame, but he has nothing to put there. Getting rid of the frame is not an option. Peter's attempt to supply something to fill the frames—"your parents . . . perhaps"—is reasonable enough and yet not a possible thing for the modern adoptee processed by the closed-record system. Adoptive parents might be another source, of course, but one reason the nonadoptive world places family photos around is to generate the sense of family likeness and to demonstrate, for themselves and others, the biological connectedness for which this likeness is a visual icon. Jerry's flaunting of the detail about the empty frames, and Peter's uncomprehending request for an explanation, can be read as the incomprehension existing between the nonadopted world and the adoptee's interior experience (adopteestentialism).

Peter's prompt about the frames elicits a wild story from Jerry about his dead mother and father. The fantastic implausibility of the story fits in easily with well-documented tendencies among those who are adopted to concoct often grotesque fantasies about the biological progenitors they are told gave them up, about whom they must not be either upset, angry, or even curious, because, as a result of the abandonment (best forgotten), they became special through being chosen by people "very much like Mommy and Daddy" (to quote *The Amer-*

ican Dream). Left to themselves, adoptees concoct a variety of fantasies to illustrate, at least unconsciously, complex feelings of anger. When Peter remarks early in *Zoo Story,* "I thought you lived in the Village," Jerry sees him trying to build up the mundane details that go into his construction of reality—a reality Jerry has felt excluded from all his life—and he moves in immediately with a deconstruction of Peter's methodology for producing knowledge: "What were you trying to do? Make sense out of things? Bring order? The old pigeonhole bit?" Then he subjects Peter to the allegory of Jerry and the Dog, a masterpiece of emotional dislocation where the only goal can be an indifference mutually agreed on. Peter's conscious sensibility breaks down completely: "I . . . I don't understand what . . . I don't think I . . . Why did you tell me all of this? . . . I DON'T UNDERSTAND" (36). The "old pigeonhole bit" breaks down completely, and Jerry has Peter just where he wants him, a place all adoptees encounter—Albee at age six—where one hears, "We're not your biological parents, but it doesn't matter."

Meanwhile, Peter is sitting on his bench in a state of confusion bordering on panic. Suddenly nothing makes sense. "Stop it!" he demands of Jerry. "What's the matter with you?" Then we get to the crux of it, when Jerry says, "I'm crazy, you bastard" (41). This should remind us that at the center of the modern adoption system is the problem of the bastard. In a sort of tag game, Jerry is introducing the increasingly bewildered Peter to the world of the modern adoptee, as if declaring to Peter, "You're it." Peter, like Julian in *Tiny Alice,* panics more and more as the ordered world he took for granted, the "pigeonhole bit," is stripped away until Jerry insists Peter does not even have any innate entitlement to the bench on which he is sitting. The altering of the birth certificate, the sealing of the records, and the approval of church, state, and law all collude to contractualize a social baptism cleansing the illegitimate ones but also requiring that they give up all right to any knowledge of their illegitimate origins. Now Peter is beginning to feel, without understanding—beginning to feel unconsciously, the only medium Albee works in when laying siege—that the world beyond the bench is his hallucination and that only the bench is real. This is akin to the splitting that produces the twin in *The American Dream;* reality and hallucination seem interchangeable when the order by which you make sense of the world is permanently dislocated and yet those gathered around you, who have not suffered the same fate, tell you it does not matter.

Peter's reaction to this existential dislocation echoes Jerry's earlier recitation of everything in his apartment. Peter takes stock of what he has left, what he requires to stay sane, something so basic it cannot be taken away: the bench he is sitting on. He thinks that surely this is a safe assumption: *I sit on this bench, therefore I am.* It is as basic as the assumption that one has been born. But suddenly Jerry is saying, "Get off this bench, Peter; I want it." "I don't care if it makes any sense or not," Peter says, entering the confused world of hallucination and reality where Julian dwells in *Tiny Alice,* "I want this bench to myself" (44). Jerry, suddenly the satanic equivalent of Socrates, is able, finally, to pose questions about Peter's organized world. Is it not enough proof that he exists? Or are his family, his parakeets, and his pigeonhole life built on an assumption of biological connection? "Why?" Jerry responds," "You have everything you want. . . . Is this the thing in the world you fight for? Can you think of anything more absurd?" (44). In effect, Jerry injects adopteestentialism directly into Peter and then watches, fascinated, as it destroys his pigeonhole sense of reality.

Despite his success, Jerry's triumph can only be regarded as temporary at this point. Indeed, when he produces a knife, Peter's orderly world returns to him, allowing him to make sense of this act because it seems to return Jerry to the role of the outsider, the bum, the madman, the illegitimate one: "You are mad! You're stark raving mad! YOU'RE GOING TO KILL ME!" (46). But what Jerry seeks to murder is Peter's too complacent reality in his world where all the picture frames have pictures. He seeks to imprint on Peter's mind a picture of himself within the reframed reality of Peter's world. He tosses the knife on the ground and insults Peter's virility: "You couldn't even get your wife with a male child." This predicament that caused an actual adoption in *The American Dream* and the construction of a fantasy child there—though, in fact, the adoptee is always a fantasy child in Albee—sets an allegorical adoption in motion here; Peter picks up the knife, and Jerry seals the contract by throwing himself on it. In his adoption of death, Jerry's actual identity is born: "And now you know all about what happened at the zoo. And now you know what you'll see in your TV, and the face I told you about . . . you remember . . . the face I told you about . . . my face . . ." (48). But the records must be sealed so that Peter will be left alone with the reality of Jerry's death, abandoned to it, so to speak: "Hurry, you'd better go . . . see?" (49), Jerry says, and the stage directions tell us "Jerry takes a handkerchief and with great effort and pain wipes the knife handle clean of fingerprints." All evidence of the exchange is wiped out. Adoption is here the perfect murder, the immaculate deception. Julian in *Tiny Alice* is shot and Jerry is stabbed, but the big difference is that Jerry did the contract himself, instead of having its effects slowly dawn on him. In this sense, Jerry's actions are re-creations of an original trauma.

The adoptive Jerry is left to die; the only real impression he has made in his life, purchased with his death, is now alive as a nightmare in the mind of Peter. He is Jerry's rock, and upon this rock Jerry has built his church: "I came unto you," Jerry says, "and you have comforted me. Dear Peter." Much has been made of Christian iconography in Albee. The stage directions are explicit that Julian dies in a crucified position in *Tiny Alice,* and a reading that Jerry dies for Peter's sins and to redeem his humdrum life is likewise possible. But the Christ-figure reading and the bastard reading can converge, as even Renaissance theologians knew. Jesus was born to a mother not married to his father. He asked, "My God,

My Father in heaven, why hast thou forsaken me?" The unfathered is not so very different from the fathered by God: in both cases, the father is out of reach, unassailable, gone. *Zoo Story* and *Tiny Alice* are Albee's sacrificial dramas. In *Zoo Story*, we watch Jerry destabilize Peter's constructed sense of certitude so that Peter is reduced to the existential panic Jerry has lived with all his life. With the famously inscrutable *Tiny Alice*, Albee coolly remarked that the meaning was perfectly clear (Jerry's remark about the picture frames, if you recall) and that if the audience merely saw the play through the eyes of Julian, all would fall into place.

To the extent that they do identify with Julian, the audience becomes like Peter, invited to feel what it feels like to be adopted in the closed-record system: the cardinal, the lawyer, and the surrogate mother all act in a manner apparently concerned for Julian's welfare; yet none of them is anxious to be Julian. When Julian embarks on the setup that will result in his abandonment and permanent alienation from his surroundings, the butler shows him a toy house that he is told is a model, of which the castle they are standing in is a replica. "The marvel is . . ." begins the butler. "The workmanship," Julian finishes for him. "That someone would do it," the butler corrects him (18). The butler says of the toy house: "It's sealed. Tight. There is no dust" (19). So his identity will be when the procedure is completed, alone forever, with tiny Alice, who may or may not be there but, in any event, is sealed up and beyond his reach, while the rest go back to their biologically underwritten existence and leave him to his contractually created one. The adoptee is a symbolic construct, brought into existence by language, acts of faith, and legal contracts. "I have now, only my person . . . my body . . . my face . . . ," says the young man in *The American Dream*, adding, "I let people love me. I accept the syntax around me, for while I know I cannot relate, I know I must be related to." As the center of the syntax, the adoptee, as a sort of linguistic fantasy space, permits the sentences of others to form around him in a manner that makes sense to them, but not a sense that includes him. This also approximates the situation of not being related to anyone except by legal fiat.

Albee's adoptee figures have no originating point, so they proceed by tendency and expediency, rather than in a planned or mapped direction. "I've been walking north," Jerry suggests to Peter, who absently agrees. "But not due north," Jerry adds. "We . . . call it north," Peter adds, with a *we* that does not seem to include Jerry, finally adding, "It's northerly" (13). This is a distinction Jerry preserves throughout the rest of the play, even right after being stabbed: "I decided that I would walk North . . . northerly rather . . . until I found you . . . or somebody" (48). An adoptee traveling north is always only traveling northerly, since there is no fixed compass point; and they are always meeting anybody and trying to make them somebody. The point, for Jerry, is not meeting anyone but rather the act of finding someone—anyone—who then becomes representative of the missing reality on the other side of the sealed record. One gets the feeling

Jerry has done this before; there is an element of repetition compulsion to his approach, but this time, he has determined, will be his last time. "Could I have planned all this?" he asks, countering, "No . . . no, I couldn't have. But I think I did." This is the advantage of a lack of orientation. For one who is always lost, finding one's self is a mere act of will with whatever or whoever happens to be around. This suggests the curious status of fate for the adoptee. Strangers, at random, become one's parents, and this impossible to predict combination is then understood as inevitable. It is Peter's misfortune that, for Jerry, anyone not adopted will do, anyone not adopted will fail to understand, and so Peter, whom Jerry could not know was there, turns out to be the person for whom he was looking.

How did the young man in *The American Dream* know to go to the house he did? Did he plan it? He could not have, but he did. He just kept walking— northerly, let us say, but never due north—until he found a group of people who needed someone who could never be found, to take the job of helping them find each other. "This is Mommy," prompts Mrs. Barker from the Bye-Bye Adoption Agency, "Her name is Mommy." "You don't know how happy I am to see you!" the instant mommy replies. Mostly what she sees, right away, is that she does not have to see him, that he is there to be seen as whatever she needs; this is a skill he has perfected, as a response to losses he feels but does not understand. As he explained earlier to the grandmother, "I am but this . . . what you see, and it will always be thus." "Accept," the lawyer, cardinal, and surrogate mother tell Julian in *Tiny Alice*. He asks what he is to accept. "That which is done, and may not be revoked," they say. But if this is done and cannot be revoked, why do they ask for his acceptance? One might glance back at the idea, prevalent in the Renaissance, that the best treatment of bastards is to get them to accept their stigmatization and exclusion outside the law as just and proper and, on this basis, permit them to be legitimated as an endorsement of the (constructed) "nature" of being legitimate.

Turning to the sealed model, Julian protests, "there is nothing there!" The cardinal does not disagree, does not even seem to hear. "All legal," he replies, "all accomplished, all satisfied, that which we believe." But neither the *all* nor the *we* includes Julian, yet the use of pronouns is not ungrammatical. Julian is illegitimate yet contractually created into a facsimile of legitimacy, a replica of a model. The original is sealed, which through exclusionary logic, protects the structure of legitimacy from the destabilizing corruption of illegitimacy. Julian is a pronoun for legitimacy, yet he is cut off from any antecedent. He, too, like the emotionally dead young man in *The American Dream,* is expected to learn to "accept the syntax around him," knowing that this syntax defines him even as it excludes him; indeed, it defines him as the excluded, then includes him on that basis. Syntax is the possible arrangements of words as elements in a sentence to show their relationship. The adoptee exists as a syntactic element that permits other people to understand their relationship with people other than the adoptee. One can see this happening dramatically in Albee's stage directions as everyone prepares to abandon the unsuspecting Julian: "The other characters are away from Julian, unless otherwise specified, they will keep a distance, surrounding him, but more than at arms length" (77). The elements arrange themselves into a sentence around Julian, while sentencing him to an existential death next to the sealed model of their own world. Albee continues: "they will observe him, rather clinically, and while this shift of attitude must be subtle, it must also be evident. Julian will grow to knowledge of it, will aid us, though we will be aware of it before he is" (77).

The young man in *The American Dream* is more successful than Julian, a better adoptee. He has given up trying to reconcile reality and hallucination; he chooses to live in neither an asylum of his own making nor one made for him, instead selling himself to anybody. The part of Julian we watch dying died long ago in the young man: "I don't know what became of my brother . . . the rest of myself . . . except that . . . I have suffered losses . . . that I can't explain." We might be able to explain it better, since we have heard Grandma tell the story of what happened to the first "bumble of joy": it was systematically mutilated each time it showed any sort of interiority—crying out, touching itself, looking at anyone. Any evidence of independent existence on the part of the young man destroys his syntactical function as the fantasy element that permitted other elements in the sentence (the family) to understand one another, to feel satisfied. Put another way, the more real the adoptee is, the more severely challenged is the presumed "reality" of the larger syntactical construct. "It finally up and died," Grandma continues, "and you can imagine how that made them feel, their having paid for it and all. . . . they wanted satisfaction; they wanted their money back." What is clearly not imagined and appears to be unimaginable is how the baby felt.

For people who have grown dependent on a bundle they have converted to a bumble in their effort to manage their disappointment and disillusionment, abandoning the mutilated bumble feels like self-mutilation. After the announced death of the supposed fantasy child, Martha begins again, "I don't suppose, maybe, we could . . ." "No, Martha," George replies. The end of *The American Dream* is an enthusiastic embracing of this refused point in *Who's Afraid of Virginia Woolf?* To say the child in *Who's Afraid of Virginia Woolf?* is a fantasy is to say no more or less than that it is a configuration of the adopted child, never more present than when most absent, and never really there at all except in terms of its effect on how other people regulate their relationships with one another. If we are tempted to read this autobiographically, the adopted child is gone—off to New York City—but the adoptive parents do not notice, because the fantasy so well-established has been decaying for years. It is fitting that the husband should kill it off first when it is finally weak enough to be killed, since the husband in *The American Dream* is the least happy to see it arrive in the first place. "Come see how he is quite the thing, Daddy," the Mommy of *The American Dream* declares. Replies Daddy, "hesitantly," "I can see from here he is quite the thing, Mommy." But what is most chilling about *Who's Afraid of Virginia Woolf?* from the point of view of the adoptee is that when the fantasy evoked by the adopted child dies, there is no sense of there ever having been a real child on which the fantasy has been based. The child of Martha and George dies because George says so; the child dies as he was born, no more than a site for the construction of marital fantasies. When the elements of the sentence slip into their proper arrangement, the syntactical element that permits this disappears as anything except the occasion for other people to make sense of themselves. What was it that sanctioned the illusory syntax that for so long appeared to be grammatical? It was not a bundle, exactly, but more like a bumble. Nobody knows; no one can say, not even the body of the young man of *The American Dream* carved to fit into the box of other people's thwarted ambitions and unrealized expectations. "I have suffered losses," says the young man to the grandmother, "that I can't explain."

NOTES

1. Alison Findlay, *Illegitimate Power: Bastards in Renaissance Drama* (Manchester: Manchester University Press, 1994), 3.

2. William Shakespeare, *The Tragedy of King Lear*, in *The Norton Shakespeare*, gen. ed. Stephen Greenblatt (New York: Norton, 1997). All subsequent references to this work refer to this edition. Here, I use the more accepted spelling *Edmund*.

3. Findlay, *Illegitimate Power*, 41.

4. Charles Dickens, *Oliver Twist*, ed. Fred Kaplan (New York: Norton, 1993). All subsequent references to this work refer to this edition.

5. Edward Albee, *Three Tall Women* (New York: Dramatists Play Service, 1994), 46–47.

6. Edward Albee, *Two Plays by Edward Albee* (New York: New American Library, 1959), 27. All subsequent references to this work refer to this edition.

7. Edward Albee, *Tiny Alice* (New York: Dramatists Play Service, 1965), 83. All subsequent references to this work refer to this edition.

8. Edward Albee, *Who's Afraid of Virginia Woolf?* (New York: Atheneum, 1962), 76. All subsequent references to this work refer to this edition.

9. Michel Foucault, *The Order of Things: An Archeology of the Human Sciences* (New York: Vintage and Random House, 1973), 41.

10. Louis Feder, "Adoption Trauma: Oedipus Myth/Clinical Reality," *International Journal of Psychoanalysis* 55 (1974): 491–93. I thank Dr. Yvonne Parnell for bringing to my attention this article, as well as the articles by Brinich and Schechter cited elsewhere in this essay and that of Jules Glenn, "The Adoption Theme in Edward Albee's *Tiny Alice* and *The American Dream*," *Psychoanalytic Study of the Child* 29 (1974): 413–29.

11. Ibid., 492.

12. Paul M. Brinich, "Some Potential Effects of Adoption on Self and Object Representations," *Psychoanalytic Study of the Child* 35 (1980): 107–34.

13. Ibid., 126.

14. Marshall D. Schechter, "Psychoanalytic Theory as It Relates to Adoption," *Journal of the American Psychoanalytic Association* 15, no. 3 (1967): 695–709.

15. Foucault, *Order of Things*, 37.

16. Remark made by Edward Albee in an address at a conference on adoption in New York City, October 20, 1995.

"I Am Your Mother; She Was a Carrying Case"

Adoption, Class, and Sexual Orientation in Jeanette Winterson's *Oranges Are Not the Only Fruit*

Margot Gayle Backus

You find out who your friends are
some came round, some just let it go
rallies on the Common, people singing
people saying 'no, this is crazy,'
but Scott and Jamie
are still pinballs in a busted machine.[1]

On May 8, 1985, the Metro section of the *Boston Globe* carried an article covering the recent placement of two children in the care of gay foster parents in Roxbury. The article, titled "Some Oppose Foster Placement with Gay Couple," presented as its raison d'être the surprised responses (characterized as "objections" and "wrenching questions") that reporter Kenneth J. Cooper elicited by buttonholing area residents and informing them of this "controversial" placement. The children in question, Scott and Jamie, were removed from the care of their foster parents, Donald Babets and David Jean, hours after the story "hit the streets—and the breakfast tables of members of the Dukakis Administration."[2] Shortly thereafter, the Dukakis administration formalized this controversial call in an administrative policy that "virtually banned homosexuals from becoming foster parents."[3] The new policy mandated "traditional family settings"[4] for all foster children, requiring prospective foster parents to list their sexual preference.[5]

As Kirk and McDaniel have observed in their analysis of adoption policy in North America and Great Britain, adoption can serve "both to mimic certain idealized images of the mainstream family and to prop up the idealization."[6] In the case of Scott and Jamie, a politician's use of the term *traditional family* to identify heterosexual (and preferably married) foster care applicants appealed to and simultaneously reinforced precisely such idealized images. To align his administration with the attractive concept of "proper" middle-class, abuse-free upbringings for orphans, Dukakis found it expedient to stage a public removal

133

of children from an "improper" family. This maneuver and its casual by-product—the institutional stigmatization of gay men and lesbians as unfit to nurture children—exemplify the dynamics that Kirk and McDaniel have found at work in Anglo-American adoption policy. In the well-documented case of Scott and Jamie, moreover, we can also identify an underlying motivation giving rise to a particular child-placement policy that served to "prop up an idealization." In this case, children were publicly removed from a "bad" family and subsequently placed in a "good" family. Scott and Jamie's hasty transfer did not create a literal traditional family: the boys' new primary caregivers consisted of a single woman and an adult son with a prior record of mental illness and sexual molestation.[7] However, imagined in contradistinction to David Babets and Donald Jean's presumed deviance, the boys' new placement did subsidize the creation of a figurative traditional family. Symbolically speaking, Michael Dukakis dismantled an "improper family" to cloak himself in the protective benevolence of a "traditional family" erected at the expense of Scott and Jamie's literal disenfranchisement and endangerment.

The centrality of the virtually meaningless term *traditional* to arguments rationalizing the placement of children in the care of a convicted child molester and further restricting an already overburdened foster care system's alternatives represents a classic example of how, in Eve Sedgwick's words, "obtuseness itself arms the powerful."[8] But precisely what form of arms did Dukakis's insistent ignorance of these children's best interests supply?

The Dukakis administration's uncharacteristic concern for the welfare of children was apparently geared neither to assuage the shocked sensibilities of a handful of Roxbury residents nor even to butch up the governor's image on the eve of an anticipated run for president. Instead, Dukakis's sudden, high-profile move to deprive children of what was, by authoritative accounts, the most loving and secure home they had ever known appears to have represented a public ritual of sorts. As can be extrapolated from a flood of subsequent articles in the *Boston Globe* alleging and citing tragic examples of "a pattern of abuse of children under state care" during this period, child abuse within an increasingly overburdened Department of Social Services system was mounting, threatening the ruination of some hapless politician. Dukakis's public sacrifice of orphans served, paradoxically, to demonstrate the seriousness of his commitment to children and thereby temporarily to exorcise rumors of child abuse hovering like a miasma over the Massachusetts state foster care system.[9]

By defining the "traditional family" as, simply, heterosexual, thereby making heterosexuality synonymous with all other forms of familial normalcy, Dukakis's new policy rhetorically solved the burgeoning problem of abused and abandoned foster children in the state of Massachusetts. Through this policy, the governor officially mandated a healthy, nonaberrant domestic life for all foster children, secured through the simple exclusion of homosexuals from the foster care system. Dukakis's decision to return Scott and Jamie to the "busted pinball machine" of Massachusetts foster care thus used the placement of insecurely affixed children to magically bring into being a new and compelling narrative. By excluding homosexuals from the foster care system, the Dukakis administration symbolically identified foster care families with an idealized middle-class family. Without spending a dime, through this ritual transfer of children the state of Massachusetts conferred a wholly unwarranted air of bourgeois, intergenerational solidity on the state's foster care families.

This significant change in foster care policy mandated by an American governor with his eye on the White House constitutes a helpful point of departure for an exploration of the relationship between class, sexuality, and adoption in *Oranges Are Not the Only Fruit*, a British novel set in the mid-twentieth century. Like the case of Scott and Jamie, Jeanette Winterson's recapitulation of a lesbian adoptee's coming-of-age in a Lancashire mill town affords privileged insight into the specific mechanisms by which "an artificially contrived family form" may prop up an idealized image of the family through the creation of new and compelling narratives.[10] Like *Globe* articles recounting the public events that shaped Scott and Jamie's lives, Winterson's semiautobiographical account of an adoptee's coming-of-age calls attention to displaced children's status as potential sources of moral capital. In both, the movement of children affords opportunities for the constitution of "new knowledges" through the creation of new narratives. Together, these accounts compellingly illustrate how the circulation of disenfranchised children through fosterage or adoption may enact a quasi-magical function, reinforcing heteronormativity and further institutionalizing homophobia as a means by which class designations and the moral authority of individuals and institutions may be reconstituted.

From the outset of Winterson's novel, adoption is identified as a privileged site for the generation of ideological power. Jeanette—Winterson's first-person protagonist—describes her evangelical mother as having brought her in "to join her in a tag match against the Rest of the World."[11] Adoption's power to generate ideological force sufficient to enable Jeanette's mother to take on "the Rest of the World" is quickly revealed to inhere in the radical renegotiation of narrative that adoption makes possible. Jeanette recalls that her mother had "a mysterious attitude toward the begetting of children":

> it wasn't that she couldn't do it, more that she didn't want to do it. She was very bitter about the Virgin Mary getting there first. So she did the next best thing and arranged for a foundling. That was me. (3)

By adopting a foundling, Jeanette suggests, her mother radically reconstituted the narrative of her life. Not only did she evade the most physically painful and dangerous requirement of bourgeois heteronormativity, but in arranging for her own version of the virgin birth, Jeanette's mother also imaginatively positioned herself as a modern-day type of the Virgin Mary. By fashioning herself in the image of Christianity's most prominent figure of female power, Jeanette's mother lends to her life a highly empowering mythic resonance and takes up a position equivalent in its influence and ceremonial power to that of a priest within her small Pentecostal sect.[12]

Jeanette's adoption confirms the sense of middle-class, heterosexual normativity that Jeanette's mother originally sought to establish through her youthful conversion to evangelical Christianity. The role of conversion in establishing her sexual normalcy is first hinted at when Jeanette describes her mother's "very romantic" conversion story as a sort of courtship between her mother and Pastor Spratt, who "looked like Errol Flynn, but holy" (8). Embedded in Jeanette's account of her mother's conversion is an implied narrative concerning her mother's simultaneous adaptation to the requirements of middle-class heteronormativity. The novel hints that Jeanette's mother, whose passive husband— "not one to push himself"—is comically absent from the narrative, is in fact a repressed lesbian who ingeniously manipulated religious and sexual norms to maintain class respectability, preserving her own autonomy in the process by preemptively sacrificing her daughter's.

In describing her mother's conversion process, Jeanette envisions her mother "walk[ing] out one night and [thinking] of her life and [thinking] of what was possible" (8–9). She imagines that her mother, on the cusp of casting her future with the Pentecostals, must have recalled her uncle, a talented actor who once played "a very fine Hamlet" but who died a pauper, and that she must have "thought of the things she couldn't be" (9). Jeanette's mother appears, like the nineteenth-century governesses in Mary Poovey's classic study *Uneven Developments,* to have come from a middle-class family with the resources to educate her but not to support her.[13] Jeanette imagines her reflecting that "she liked to speak French and to play the piano" but wondering "what do these things mean?" (9).

While walking and thinking, on the night when she faces the incommensurability between her talents and interests and her economic prospects, Jeanette's mother "discovered her abiding interest in missionary work" (8). Jeanette imagines:

mother, out walking that night, dreamed a dream and sustained it in daylight. She would get a child, train it, build it, dedicate it to the lord. (10)

Ultimately, Jeanette's mother earmarks Jeanette, rather than herself, to be the missionary in the family, thus enabling her to lay claim to the sacrificial aspirations of a saint without having to sacrifice anything. As Jeanette remarks, the process of rearing a child dedicated to such a holy mission would provide her mother with "a way out now, for years and years to come" (10).

Underlying the ideological power that Jeanette's adoption generates are dynamics similar to those that Rickie Solinger has identified as being in play in the United States during the same period.[14] As Solinger points out, social entitlement has been saliently at issue in the consolidation of adoption practices within the white American middle class. In the years prior to legalized abortion, the symbolically charged practice of taking children from their biological mothers and placing them in the legal custody of unrelated adults, as Solinger shows, enacted a crude morality play entailing the punishment and redemption of unwed white mothers.[15] Through a ritual process of blame, accusation, and diagnosis, familial secrecy and disavowal, childbirth, the surrender of their infants, and a lifetime of enforced silence, these women were reconstituted as respectably marriageable. Through this process, individual white girls and women were cruelly initiated into the values of normative female heterosexuality; if they did not want marriage and the protection of a loving husband before this ordeal, the initiation rites of the home for unwed mothers did their utmost to ensure they would afterward. The ritual shaming to which these women were subjected also served, moreover, as an object lesson to bourgeois white women more generally. For instance, one of Solinger's informants recalls:

When I was growing up in Tulsa, Oklahoma, the local home for unwed mothers was as shrouded in horror and hysteria as an asylum or leper colony. Located outside of town in a field off a rural highway, unmistakably "institutional," it drew my fascination by the lifelessness outside its walls and the miserable types I imagined must dwell within.[16]

As Kirk and McDaniel indicate, adoption in Great Britain prior to reform legislation in 1975 permitting adult adoptees access to their original birth certificates closely resembled adoption in the United States at the same time.[17] In both societies, heterosexual marriage and childbearing within marriage represented the sine qua non of psychological and physiological normalcy. Thus, in both societies, the unwed mother and the nonchildbearing couple started out in similar binds. Within the system of adoption Solinger anatomizes, however, the parallel interests and status of unwed mothers and nonchildbearing married couples are placed in opposition, with the vulnerable position of one being used artificially to bolster the position of the other. In a society in which unwed motherhood is socially stigmatized and economically punished, the coerced removal of a baby from its mother's care enacts the unwed mother's economic and moral inadequacy, while the official bestowal of a child by the state or a private agency institutionally confirms the normative class position and morality of adoptive parents.[18]

Closely paralleling the class dynamics that Solinger identifies in the United States, Jeanette's mother's ongoing struggle to assert her middle-class status in the face of the family's working-class surroundings provides much of *Oranges Are Not the Only Fruit*'s distinctive humor. For instance, one of the novel's funniest scenes occurs when, having kept Jeanette out of school—"a Breeding Ground"—Jeanette's mother folds immediately on receiving papers threatening legal action. Jeanette, intrigued by her mother's unaccustomed acquiescence, points out that St. Paul was always going to prison. Her mother retorts curtly, "I know that, but the neighbors don't" (21).

Jeanette's mother's world is intricately hewn with marks of class insiderness and outsiderness, which are humorously synonymous with her conceptions of righteousness and sinfulness and, above all, sexual normalcy. Jeanette's first consciousness of a world beyond her family is of "Maxi Ball's Catalogue Seconds," a local purveyor of shoddy merchandise at discount prices, about which her mother "filled [her] with a horror" (6). Closely associated with Maxi Ball's in Jeanette's emergent cosmology is "Next Door," a Bunyanesque symbol of class impropriety and sexual deviance, the utter degradation of which is confirmed by its purchase of "everything" from Maxi Ball's (5). Within Jeanette's mother's worldview, which Laura Doan has described as "a philosophy of life of frightening clarity,"[19] sexual sins, especially homosexuality, denote class alterity, while her own capacity to attract and participate in heterosexual romance confirms her middle-class femininity. Jeanette's mother's preoccupation with the class-inflected sins of her neighbors, ranging from their sexual preferences to their shopping habits, account for Jeanette's precocious awareness of specialized aspects of human behavior that normally escape the attention of a preschool-age child. For instance, Jeanette first learns of "Unnatural Passions" (lesbianism)—a mild preoccupation of her mother's all-woman Pentecostal enclave—in the course of a casually denunciatory conversation between her mother and another church member concerning two middle-aged women who run a local paper shop.

Like the documentary record of Scott and Jamie's experiences, *Oranges Are Not the Only Fruit* objectively recounts the means by which the exchange of children can be used to secure an imaginary simultaneity between heterosexuality and middle-class propriety. Unlike the narrative that unfolds through a reading of sequences articles in the *Boston Globe,* however, Winterson's narrative is multilayered, composed of competing narratives and subjectivities. The novel is not *only* the story of a middle-class woman's strategic use of religion, marriage, and adoption to preserve her imperiled class position. Paradoxically, despite the fact that in one important sense Jeanette's mother's "way out" has been established at Jeanette's expense, the novel also registers Jeanette's subjective reaction to her mother's elaborate process of self-reinvention via a series of counternarratives representing Jeanette's own empowering, mythic fantasies. Jeanette's mother's imaginative self-revision, while it cruelly limits Jeanette's access to basic information concerning her own origins and identity, inadvertently provides Jeanette with both motivation and license to herself imaginatively self-create. Shortly af-ter describing her mother's appropriation of Mary's sanctified position as vir-gin mother in the novel's opening pages, for instance, Jeanette produces her own pagan countermythology. In a figure suggesting that from an early age this adoptive daughter had (and required) access to a mythic sphere of vision as a form of self-defense against her mother's all-encompassing personal mythos, Jeanette refigures herself as Athena to her mother's Zeus, describing herself as "[her mother's] flesh, sprung from her head. Her vision" (10).

Jeanette's account of her mother's process of self-recreation is, in fact, com-pletely interrupted by the first of several fairy-tale or nonnarrative reflections that serve as fantasy counterparts to Jeanette's coming-of-age narrative. Through-out the novel, such counternarratives formally interrupt the otherwise seamless unfolding of Jeanette's relationship to her adoptive mother, implicitly calling at-tention to adoption's ritualized aspects. These interpolated fantasy narratives have, of course, been read as symptomatic of Winterson's incipient postmod-ernism. For instance, Laura Doan finds the characteristics of metafiction to be "supremely evident [throughout] Winterson's work."[20] While this is undoubt-edly the case, it is also likely, however, that the fragmentation of narrative in Winterson's first novel reflects practical difficulties in recounting a lesbian adoptee's coming-of-age. It seems reasonable to surmise that Winterson's elec-tion of a postmodernist vocabulary was itself overdetermined not only by her position as a woman and a lesbian but by her position as an adoptee.[21]

In an article that explores similarly fragmented and indirect metafictional strategies in incest narratives by lesbians, Ann Cvetkovich has compared the dis-cursive position of sexual abuse survivors to that of lesbians, arguing that "as with lesbianism, so with incest: 'breaking the silence' is a queer process."[22] Cvetkovich reads Dorothy Allison's *Bastard out of Carolina* and Margaret Ran-dall's *This Is about Incest* as queer "rituals of performance that defy simple no-tions of disclosure."[23] To produce her readings of these texts, Cvetkovich calls attention to the parallel positions of sexual abuse survivors and lesbians, while simultaneously "introduc[ing] the word 'queer' to suggest the unpredictable connections between sexual abuse and its effects."[24] Winterson's novel, with its fantastic interpolations, represents a similarly queer literary performance. Like Allison and Randall, Winterson has crafted a narrative that tells a forbidden story indirectly, via the interpolation of fetishized narrative "objects" (allegori-cal fairy tales) that obliquely express and simultaneously mask an unauthorized account—in this case, the experience of adoption.

Like lesbians and sexual abuse survivors, many adoptees live under a dis-cursive interdiction—a "burden not to tell"—that can "create" . . . its own net-work of psychic wounds [far exceeding] the event itself."[25] Winterson's most ex-plicit reflections on the adoptee's painful position at the center of competing and differently empowered narratives is positioned roughly at the novel's center, in a short, nonnarrative chapter meditating on the mutability and fragility of historical fact, entitled "Deuteronomy." This chapter begins with the observation "Time is a great deadener" (93). In this chapter, the narrator addresses the reader directly, reflecting bleakly: "people have never had a problem disposing of the past when it gets too difficult. Flesh will burn, photos will burn, and memory, what is that?" (94). Jeanette's reflection on the fragility of the past, particularly of human flesh in the face of those with a strong motive to dispose of a past they find "too difficult," corresponds to Eve Sedgwick's assertion that ignorance, far from being "a single Manichaean, aboriginal maw of darkness," could instead best be described as "a plethora of *ignorances*" that are "produced by and correspond to particular knowledges."[26]

Oranges Are Not the Only Fruit bears witness to the ways in which a specific strand of sexual ignorances and knowledges is produced through the circulation of children. As Winterson's novel illustrates, adoptees themselves inevitably become, like adoptive parents and the state, active participants within a traffic in children dedicated to the generation of self-protective narratives. The novel's fantasy sequences correspond to research showing that adoptees frequently have recourse to fantasy as a means of making sense of their unspeakable and incomprehensible situation. For instance, in their study of the psychology of adoptees in the United States, Brodzinsky, Schechter, and Marantz Henig emphasize the significant role of fantasy for adoptive children. Frequently adoptees' fantasies have a particular traumatic onset involving the withholding of information and the assertion of narrative power on the part of a parent; one of their informants recalls:

> My mother told me that she didn't know anything at all about "that woman" but that it really didn't matter because she was really my mother and that was all I needed to know. That was when my fantasy life began.[27]

The first fantasy interlude of *Oranges Are Not the Only Fruit* interrupts the story of Jeanette's mother's simultaneous decision to convert and adopt. The interlude is a simple fairy tale narrating the story of a "brilliant and beautiful princess" whose inordinate sensitivity leaves her (as a gypsy woman also predicts of the child Jeanette) unmarriageable and unable to keep still (7). An aged hunchback who "had in her charge a small village of homely people, to whom she was advisor and friend," asks the princess to take over her position as caretaker of the community. When the princess agrees, she forgets her former life, and the aged steward thanks her and dies immediately (10). This initial narrative intrusion mythologizes Jeanette's adoption as an entry into an enchanted, matriarchal realm and fantasizes her life prior to adoption as a site of discomfort, a place into which she was constitutionally unable to fit.

Jeanette's earliest fantasies thus romanticize Jeanette's adoptive mother.

Later, these serial fantasies, which Doan aptly characterizes as "a 'miniseries' interpolated sporadically within the larger narrative,"[28] reconceptualize the adoptive mother in more complex ways. First portrayed in fantasy as a dying hunchback who recruits a displaced princess to let herself off the hook, Jeanette's mother next takes the more disturbing form of a wounded prince who grows increasingly murderous as he continues to defend his deluded quest for a flawless bride (62–67). She recurs in two brief and moving segments as King Arthur to Jeanette's Perceval, and at last provides the model for the sorcerer who beguiles and tricks the young Winnet, first adopting her and teaching her his magic, then ultimately casting her out in punishment for her normal human desire for a mate (141–48).

Fantasies concerning Jeanette's birth mother are conspicuously absent from all of these episodes. The perfect (but not flawless) woman who tries to teach the idealistic prince the secret of perfect balance seems always to have inhabited her obscure corner of the kingdom. Sir Perceval's earliest memories begin at King Arthur's court, and Winnet comes from nowhere. The glaring absence of origins in the novel's fairy-tale representations of adoption suggests that the fictional Jeanette (and perhaps Winterson herself, who "never traced her genetic parents")[29] derives the gift of vision from the same fertile absence that empowers her mother: the suppression of Jeanette's biological origins.

Ultimately, we learn that Jeanette's mother's "elaborate scheme"[30] to raise a missionary evolved in response to a complex network of transgressions against heterosexual norms committed in her youth. Jeanette's mother's sexual history first begins to surface in response to Jeanette's own sexual maturation. Concerned about the adolescent Jeanette's purported interest in a young man, but probably unconsciously sensing that Jeanette is falling in love with Melanie, a young woman in their congregation, Jeanette's mother tells her a cautionary tale describing a classic heterosexual fall from grace. Dramatically, she reveals to Jeanette that she "nearly came to a bad end" by having sex with a Frenchman with whom she, misguided by the physical symptoms of an ulcer, had imagined herself to be in love (86). Although this story is overtly one of heterosexual excess, her cluelessness concerning her physiological responses to a man represents one of several broad hints in the novel that Jeanette's mother's carefully choreographed heterosexuality, complete with suppressed youthful transgression, is in fact a facade overlaying more deeply hidden strata of affective and erotic history. In addition to her misreading of the "fizzing" in her stomach in response to Pierre—a parodic reversal of fundamentalist homophobia, which mistakes passion for a disease—Jeanette's mother also mixes her codes in other ways. While leafing through her mother's photograph album, for instance, under the heading "Old Flames," Jeanette notices "a yellowy picture of a pretty woman holding a cat" (36). When asked about it, her mother responds evasively, and the next time Jeanette looks, the picture is gone. Most explicitly, in the scene in which Jeanette first learns that there are other lesbians in the world, Miss Jewsbury, a closeted lesbian, comes out to Jeanette and simultaneously chides her for talking unguardedly to her mother, saying "She knows about feelings, especially women's feelings." Jeanette, whose world is falling apart at the moment, reflects, "This wasn't something that I wanted to get into" (106).

Characteristically, Jeanette's mother renarrates the story of her seduction by a Frenchman as that of "disaster narrowly averted," when, from the viewpoint of her fundamentalist faith, disaster was not averted at all, since she did actually commit fornication. Jeanette, whose adoption and cloistered upbringing enabled her mother retroactively to "avert" this and other unspoken transgressions, resultantly has even less comprehension concerning her body and its sexual responses than did her mother. Jeanette's mother at least understood her body's erotic potential, although she misread its responses, mistaking an ailment for romantic passion. Jeanette is completely ignorant concerning sexuality, most particularly the specifics of lesbian sexuality, even though Winterson implies that many of the women in her mother's congregation are lesbians and that lesbian sexuality, or "Unnatural Passion," is a common topic of conversation among them. In the throes of a torrid and newly sexual affair, Jeanette bewilderedly asks her lover whether what they are doing could be "Unnatural Passion," and Melanie assures her: "Doesn't feel like it. According to Pastor Finch, that's awful" (89). Jeanette concludes that Melanie must be right.

Forestalling her own encounter with a material reality that cannot be mythicized away, Jeanette naively loses control of her narrative in a way that her mother was careful never to do. Because Jeanette's mother "knows about . . . women's feelings," she recognizes what Jeanette is describing in her garbled accounts of her relationship with Melanie, with dire results for Jeanette. Ironically, it is owing to Jeanette's mother's own repressed history that she is able to recognize an insurgent outbreak of lesbianism that is once again imperiling her precarious social position. Significantly, this resurgence of the lesbian desire that Jeanette's adoption originally repudiated has the effect of simultaneously disinterring deeply repressed questions concerning Jeanette's adoption and her very identity.

Jeanette and Melanie are first introduced to their identities as lesbians unexpectedly, when the pastor of their fundamentalist sect, at Jeanette's mother's instigation, confronts them before the assembled congregation, announcing that the girls have "fallen under Satan's spell," "fallen foul of their lusts," and are "filled with demons" (108). Significantly, Winterson pointedly juxtaposes this eruption of lesbian sexuality at the center of Jeanette's mother's community with a scene from Jeanette's childhood in which Jeanette's biological origins, in the person of her birth mother, threatened to surface in a similarly unexpected and uncontrolled manner.

Immediately prior to Jeanette's and Melanie's public castigation and immediately following the meditation on the vulnerability of the past to falsification in "Deuteronomy" is an episode in which Jeanette returns unexpectedly from a canceled violin lesson to find the church elders gathered in her house in an odd state of ritual preparation. For only the second time in her life, she reflects, she felt "uncertain." Her thoughts turn spontaneously to her relationship with her lover, Melanie, and she uneasily reviews everything that she has told her mother about the relationship, thinking that she has "told her mother as much as she could, but not everything" (99). She justifies her inability to express certain aspects of the relationship by reflecting that "[her mother] wouldn't really understand," but then she reflects (and this is more to the point) that she herself is not exactly sure what is happening (99–100). The feeling of uncertainty she is experiencing reminds her, in turn, of the "Awful Occasion" on which her biological mother had "come to claim her back" (100).

On this occasion, Jeanette's adoptive mother, who had waved away the adoption papers Jeanette had once found, calling them "formalities" since she "had [Jeanette] from the Lord," confronts Jeanette's birth mother in the parlor while Jeanette uses a wineglass to eavesdrop from the other side of the wall (100). Significantly, the reader is never told what Jeanette hears. As is the case throughout the narrative, even in the novel's fantasy sequences, Jeanette's birth mother is as suppressed as she could possibly be, appearing only indirectly and symptomatically even in the scene to which she is narratively central. Jeanette tells us only that "after five minutes I put the glass away, picked up our dog, and cried and cried and cried" (100). Whatever happens between the two women, Jeanette's birth mother is decisively "vanquished" or, in fact, eradicated as a narrative agent, and the bond between Jeanette and her adoptive mother is symbolically reaffirmed as the sole arbiter of Jeanette's identity. The monolithic authority of the adoptive bond is further asserted in this episode immediately after Jeanette's birth mother has departed. Jeanette's mother slaps Jeanette (the only depiction of corporal punishment in the novel) for uttering the taboo words "She's my mother" and quietly asserts, "I am your mother; she was a carrying case" (101).

In the novel's symbolically backward coming-out episode, the church and family define Jeanette's sexuality before Jeanette has had the opportunity to define it for herself. Winterson's juxtaposition of the episode in which Jeanette hears her birth mother vanquished by her mother and the one in which she is labeled as a lesbian by the congregation at her mother's instigation calls attention to the mutually constitutive relationship that exists within the text between class, sexuality, and adoption. Each of these categories is shown to afford a sensitized locus on which narrative power may be exerted, and each, furthermore, may be used to enhance the vulnerability of the other two loci to narrative pressure. For instance, class and sexual norms undoubtedly play a part in Jeanette's adoptive mother's superior discursive and definitional power relative to Jeanette's birth mother: Jeanette's adoptive mother has symbolically, and, indeed, all but literally, maintained "perfect" sexual continence, while Jeanette's birth mother has demonstrably violated bourgeois norms mandating sexual continence for women prior to marriage. Jeanette's adoption, on the other hand, heightens her mother's symbolic agency in the construction of her own class position. Jeanette's mother uses adoption to reverse the objectification and nullification that, as Solinger has shown, were societally prescribed at this time for the sexually transgressive middle-class white girl. Although she herself engaged in premarital sex, Jeanette's mother's adoption of a daughter on whom she could rigorously enforce moral and sexual norms, along with her own compensatory postmarital chastity, restores the precarious balance that her premarital sexual transgression imperiled.

Winterson's complex interweavings of the master narratives of childbirth and adoption, romance and compulsory heterosexuality, and conversion and religious fundamentalism represent parallel epistemologies relying for their power on the exclusion, negation, and demonization of alternative accounts. As a female child, Jeanette represents a radical solution to what would otherwise constitute, for her mother, an insoluble contradiction between her fundamentalist theology's rabid hatred of the sexual in all of its manifestations and its equally adamant heterosexual mandate. Her adoption symbolically places her adoptive mother in opposition to her "fallen" birth mother and to a potentially corruptible daughter, who must be kept under close surveillance, and whose exposure to the facts concerning sexuality and "the world" must be rigidly policed. Both Jeanette and her birth mother represent female alterities against which Jeanette's mother may reconstitute her own formerly compromised sexuality. This explicit, intentional transformation of Jeanette's mother's life story via the adoption of a child is symbolized in Jeanette's discovery that her mother had changed the ending of *Jane Eyre,* a novel that she had read to her repeatedly as a child. In her mother's version, Jane went off to become a missionary with St. John Rivers. This misleading repetition of a falsified story about an orphan figures the process by which an adoptive parent may, to fulfill his or her own needs, repeatedly reinforce a distorted or misleading narrative in the mind of a child. It also, however, figures the means by which the placement of children offers a means to call on ideologies of class and sexuality to generate new public narratives.

Jeanette's adoption brings her adoptive mother into a productive symbolic opposition to her "fallen" birth mother, against whom Jeanette's adoptive mother's own sexuality is symbolically reconstituted as unimpeachable. Jeanette's adoptive mother's appropriation of the socially laudable position of "mother," with all its spiritual and sentimental capital, is underwritten by the (generally unspoken) punitive demotion of the biological mother, within the adoptive equation, to the position of object, a position into which she "falls" through the contaminatingly bodily sexual intercourse, pregnancy, and labor to which the child she has produced bears witness. In symbolic punishment for her sin of bearing a child outside of wedlock, but also for having a body of sexuality of which cannot be imaginatively reconfigured or repressed, as Jeanette's adoptive mother's body has been through the adoptive bond, Jeanette's adoptive mother metaphorically reduces her birth mother to the position of an object: "a carrying case."

It is important not to miss the significance of Jeanette's memory of an attempt by her birth mother—the bearer of a forbidden and denied narrative—to make contact with her, emerging at a moment when Jeanette senses that her own story, her own right to self-definition, is once again about to be violently undermined. Both moments of dispute over Jeanette's identity exemplify the historical mutability that the speaker in "Deuteronomy" speaks of in more abstract, general terms. Both represent liminal moments of narrative "uncertainty" within which discourses vie for power on an uneven and prejudiced cultural terrain. Winterson's representation of the complexities of the adoptive triangle within a patriarchal and heterosexist culture insists on class, sexuality, and adoption as all equally narrative and interdependent constructs. Not only does Winterson's meditation on the mutability of history, the ease with which bodies and photographs may be burned and memory discounted, point to the sense in which adoption, obviously, represents the triumph of one narrative over another or other possible narratives, but it also refers to the sense in which the narrative of bourgeois heterosexual normalcy has equally come to efface alternate possibilities, as well as to the particular role that adoption has played in maintaining this charade.

Within compulsory heterosexuality, a traffic in displaced children provides raw material for new narratives while simultaneously constituting adoptive parents, as well as larger social collectivities and their leaders, as pure, altruistic, and blameless. Moreover, the use of heterosexuality as a privileged criterion authorizing the formation of adoptive and foster families makes the placement of displaced children into a ritual that perpetually reinforces within the social imaginary an idealized middle-class family to which homosexuals are anathema. In the case of Scott and Jamie, the purportedly benevolent placement of displaced children underwrote, at the formal state level, expulsion of homosexuals from the normative, state-constituted family. In *Oranges Are Not the Only Fruit,* a strategic adoption creates a simulacrum of heteronormative family life powerful enough to obscure, throughout the course of nearly two decades, the nonnormative sexuality of not only Jeanette's mother but nearly every female character in the novel.

Within such a symbolic economy, the adoptive bond and lesbian/gay bonding represent, in effect, end points on a spectrum of human affective bonds, with adoption representing the triumph of structure over content, and with lesbian and gay bonds representing the triumph of affective content over and above the requirement of gendered form. As an adopted child, Jeanette represents a socially produced gendered and raced exchange value who symbolically reconstitutes her mother, both in the ways that all children, in compulsorily heterosexual societies, reconstitute their parents as sexually and social "normal," and in the ways, previously outlined, that a traffic in displaced children may constellate adoptive parents, as well as heteronormative society itself, as particularly benevolent. This primary symbolic function of children, especially adoptive or foster children, becomes spectacularly evident whenever the unabridged and exclusive right of heterosexuals to ownership of and control over all children, but especially orphans, is threatened. The hysteria that invariably erupts when the subject of gay and lesbian foster care and adoption emerges into public discourse, all the rhetoric about the wonderful advantages to children being "chosen" by parents who truly "want" them suddenly notwithstanding, reveals a fundamental hypocrisy underlying a system in which children circulate as a form of culturally confirming capital.

This is not all, however, bad news for the queer adoptee. As Winterson suggests in "Ruth," her novel's final chapter, the adoptee who actively seeks to define her own identity represents a formidable challenge to a heterosexist system in which adoption represents a key site for the reproduction of heterosexist cultural norms. In Jeanette's terms, the adoptee who dares to define herself, or to "choose between the two realities"—like the lesbian who openly breaches the terms of the heterosexual contract—becomes a prophet instead of a priest (160). Although both the priest and the prophet derive power from the irreconcilable schism between two realities that adoption inevitably brings into being, they are polar opposites. The priestly role acquired by Jeanette's mother through her adoption of Jeanette, which she expects Jeanette to carry out, perpetuates a complex cultural network of ignorances by overlaying painful silences with canonical words and stories. The priest has "a book with the words set out. Old words, known words, words of power. Words that are always on the surface. Words for every occasion." For the priest, "The words work. They do what they're supposed to do; comfort and discipline" (161). The prophet, by contrast, confronts the painful discrepancy between irreconcilable narratives, drawing vatic power from the irreparable breach at the core of her identity. The prophet "has no book."

> The prophet is a voice that cries in the wilderness, full of sounds that do not always set into meaning. The prophets cry out because they are troubled by demons. (161)

The analogous position of lesbians and adoptees to which Winterson's novel calls our attention interests me because in teasing out the analogical and causal relations that the novel posits between sexual orientation and adoption, we find not only an explicit critique of compulsory heterosexuality but also an encrypted critique of adoption, expressed via a performative "telling" of a girlhood that is queer in more ways than one. In societies in which children serve as a simple and readily available means for adults to generate falsifying narratives with which to obscure threatening aspects of the past and unpleasant present realities, the struggle for lesbian and gay rights in all spheres, but especially in the spheres of parenting and the nurturing of children, is fundamental to a broader, necessary decommodification of children. Conversely, because the perpetuation of images of an idealized heteronormative family is bound up in specialized ways with the circulation of displaced children, the rights of adoptees and foster children are and will probably remain relevant to the ongoing struggle for gay/lesbian rights.

NOTES

This essay would have been virtually inconceivable to me without the stimulus of Marianne Novy's work on the subject of adoption and literature and without the inspiration of others with whom that work on the subject of adoption and literature brought me into contact, including Tanya Gardiner-Scott, Jill Roberts, and Rickie Solinger. I am especially indebted to Marianne for her copious and helpful feedback in response to several drafts of this essay. The essay also benefited from feedback I received when I delivered a version of it as an invited talk at East Carolina University and from generous and insightful feedback from several of my favorite colleagues: Laura Doan, William H. Harrison, Trevor Hope, Maria Helena Lima, Beth McCoy, Lillian Robinson, and John Roche. I am also indebted to Susan Fanelli, Cheryl Camillo, and Diane Lucas for crucial help and guidance.

1. From the song "Scott and Jamie," words and music by Fred Small, copyright 1988, Pine Barrens Music (BMI); used by permission.

2. Patti Doten, "They Want a Chance to Care; Gay Couple Still Hurts from Decision That Took Away Their Foster Children," *Boston Globe,* September 27, 1990.

3. Ibid.

4. William F. Schultz, "Fostering Prejudice," *Progressive,* January 1987, 15.

5. Peter J. Howe, "Judge Hits Rules on Gay Foster Parents," *Boston Globe,* September 12, 1986.

6. H. David Kirk and Susan A. McDaniel, "Adoption Policy in Great Britain and North America," *Journal of Social Policy* 13, no. 1 (January 1984): 77.

7. These details briefly emerged into public view after one of the boys told a social worker that he had been sexually abused. See Brad Pokorny, "The Foster Care Controversy Resurfaces: Boys Allegedly Abused in New Home," *Boston Globe,* January 9, 1986. A subsequent investigation confirmed that the children had been left with the foster parent's adult son despite his prior record of molestation, but it found no grounds on which to bring charges. See Joan Vennochi, "Two Children Not Abused in Home, Probe Finds," *Boston Globe,* July 29, 1986. Despite the threat this new placement posed to these children, it aroused much less media interest than their earlier placement, and no new policies ensued from it.

8. Eve Kosofsky Sedgwick, *Epistemology of the Closet* (Berkeley: University of California Press, 1990), 7.

9. Cf. Meredith Adams, "Legislator Seeks Roxbury Hearing on State of Foster Care Services," *Boston Globe*, May 25, 1998; Renee Graham, "Child Abuse Action Scored Study: Speed Up Adoption Process," *Boston Globe*, December 6, 1990; Indira A. R. Lakshmanan, "Cases Spur DSS to Review Foster Care," *Boston Globe*, July 24, 1995; Indira A. R. Lakshmanan, "Receivership is Urged for DSS; Lawmaker Alleges a Pattern of Abuse," *Boston Globe*, May 26, 1995; Renee Loth, "Foster Care Improvements Proposed," *Boston Globe*, December 7, 1988; M. E. Malone, "State Panel Blasts DSS Foster Care," *Boston Globe*, October 23, 1990; Adrian Walker, "Demonstrators Rally against Child Abuse; Victims, Activists Cite List of Demands," *Boston Globe*, April 19, 1990; Gregory Witcher, "Budget Increase Sought for Foster Care," *Boston Globe*, March 27, 1987.

10. Kirk and McDaniel, "Adoption Policy in Great Britain," 77.

11. Jeanette Winterson, *Oranges Are Not the Only Fruit* (New York: Atlantic Monthly Press, 1985), 3. Subsequent references to this work are given parenthetically in text.

12. Due to her association with Catholicism, Mary is not frequently chosen as a role model by devout Protestant women. It is important to bear in mind, however, that "far from being still purveyors of conventional Protestantism, Pentecostal Christians are a boisterous crowd given to noisy outpourings of praise and singing" (Fiametta Rocco, "Winterson's Discontent," *Vanity Fair*, February 1995, 149). The Pentecostals as Winterson depicts them seem largely untouched by Protestantism's conventional anti-Catholicism and, in fact, by any stable dogma save a generalized and highly mutable suspicion of all things worldly, with a particular hostility toward sex, especially in the form of "Unnatural Passions."

13. Mary Poovey, *Uneven Developments: The Ideological Work of Gender in Mid-Victorian England* (Chicago: University of Chicago Press, 1988).

14. Rickie Solinger, *Wake Up Little Susie: Single Pregnancy and Race before Roe v. Wade* (New York: Routledge, 1992). Solinger's research demonstrates the tangible ways in which adoption practices can aid in the construction of social discourses that extend in influence well beyond individual children and their adoptive families. Her analysis makes clear the means by which adoption in the United States prior to *Roe v. Wade* compelled pregnant, unmarried white women to serve as vehicles for the creation of displaced children whose placement, in turn, contributed to the construction of a system of differentiated white and black heteronormatives. Within this largely invisible traffic in white babies, the adoptive bond was legitimized through the systematic de-legitimization, pathologization, and erasure of the unwed white birth mother.

15. It is central to Solinger's argument that African American women underwent no such collective sacrificial redemption (African American families typically do not cast out their unwed daughters and their children, and homes for unwed mothers and adoption agencies refused, at any rate, to serve them) and were therefore constituted in the white imagination as incorrigibly prone to promiscuity and "welfare motherhood."

16. Solinger, *Wake Up Little Susie*, 103.

17. Kirk and McDaniel, "Adoption Policy in Great Britain," 77.

18. While the rehabilitation of the adoptive couple may be seen by some community members (and even by adoptive parents themselves) as second-rate, the adoptive mother is, in one respect at least, superior to her counterpart, the biological mother. If the urge to nurture children is in many respects central to sentimental representation of bourgeois womanhood, the adoptive mother represents the apogee of such values: she is a woman with such strong instincts to mother that she transcends even biological ob-

stacles in pursuit of her "natural" drives. Adoptive parents are unquestionably themselves subjected to the harsh scrutiny of compulsory heterosexuality; most have had, or at least feared having, their sexual normalcy held up for public scrutiny in a manner that in certain ways mirrors the institutional and social treatment of unwed mothers. Despite social prejudices against adoption, however, the pervasive and imperious strength of the impulse to obtain and rear children in a form that is in every way identical to biological parenthood remains remarkably resilient and surely to some extent reflects the even greater scrutiny to which the sexuality of the childless may be subjected. The appeal of adoption as perfectly mimicking the "natural" (middle-class) family is evidenced, for instance, in the great difficulty that adoption agencies have traditionally had in persuading adoptive parents to tell their children the truth about their adoption. See Christine Walby and Barbara Symons, *Who Am I? Identity, Adoption, and Human Fertilization* (London: British Agencies for Adoption and Fostering, 1990), 38.

19. Laura Doan, "Jeanette Winterson's Sexing the Postmodern," in *The Lesbian Postmodern,* ed. Laura Doan (New York: Columbia University Press, 1994), 142.

20. Ibid., 139.

21. Fiametta Rocco, exploring connections between Winterson's upbringing and what she depicts as her rebarbative style of self-representation, repeatedly makes assertions that could fruitfully be taken up in a critical exploration of Winterson's writing style. Seemingly exasperated, Rocco concludes ("Winterson's Discontent," 149): "Winterson projects herself as a kind of genetic year zero, with no parents, no gene source, no inheritance of any kind. Her fitness guide advises that you can make yourself any shape you want. All it takes is concentration." Michelle Field, in "Jeanette Winterson: 'I Fear Insincerity,'" *Publisher's Weekly* 242, no. 12 (March 20, 1995): 39, explicitly makes the connection between Winterson's life history and her hermetic writing style implied by Rocco. Commenting on Winterson's reclusive lifestyle, Field writes: "She cut herself off entirely from her parents when she left home for Oxford, declining even to attend her mother's funeral. . . . She has made a principle of detachment. 'What I have tried to do is make my words independent, separate spaces.'"

22. Ann Cvetkovich, "Sexual Trauma/Queer Memory: Incest, Lesbianism, and Therapeutic Culture," *GLQ: A Journal of Lesbian and Gay Studies* 2 no. 4 (1995): 351–77.

23. Ibid., 381.

24. Ibid., 359.

25. Ibid., 380.

26. Sedgwick, *Epistemology of the Closet,* 8.

27. David Brodzinsky, Marshall D. Schechter, and Robin Marantz Henig, *Being Adopted: The Lifelong Search for Self* (New York: Anchor, Doubleday, 1992), 82. The authors also, however, hint that adoption opens up a realm of fantasy for the adoptive parent as well. Adoptive parents may reveal the active role that the absent birth parent plays in their own psychic lives through such charged language as the just quoted informant's mother's use of the phrase "that woman" to describe her daughter's birth mother. Such an imaginative relationship to an adoptee's biological parent, especially the birth mother, allows for far more extensive parental fantasy projections onto children than are possible within birth families.

28. Doan, "Jeanette Winterson's Sexing the Postmodern," 141.

29. Field, "Jeanette Winterson: 'I Fear Insincerity,'" 39.

30. Doan, "Jeanette Winterson's Sexing the Postmodern," 143.

A Junction of Amends

Sandra Mcpherson's Poetics of Adoption

Jan VanStavern

Wildflowers and Earthstars: Accounts of Home

When she talks about meeting her birth parents, the first things Sandra Mcpherson mentions are the wildflowers. When the thirty-seven-year-old poet first approached her birth parents' northern California house, she saw wildflowers and mushrooms spilling across the lawn and began staring at their whorls and shapes, naming them in her head. For her whole life, not knowing her own birth name, Sandra McPherson had been mesmerized by naming things their right names—knowing the name and nature of California poppies, ceanothus, the rangy lupine, waxy-leafed oleander, poisonous to cats and children. Raised by a loving family, the pragmatic and religious McPhersons, she was nevertheless a born pagan, at worship in a field more comfortably than in a nave, and she had always sensed there must be people more like her in the world—the people who had created her and who shared her genes. Now, walking toward the house with her birth sister, Ellayn Evans, who had driven her from the airport, she studied the place she was about to enter and stared at the flowers she knew by heart. When asked now how she felt meeting her birth parents for the first time, she says, "Attentive."

When Joyce and John Todd came out of the house, McPherson immediately saw herself in their faces and their attention to the natural world: before taking her inside, they brushed aside leaves to show her rare mushrooms in the front yard. McPherson wrote a poem describing this meeting of birth-family naturalists, in which Joyce Todd's first act as a mother to her adult child is to introduce her to earthstar mushrooms.

> Geasters. She bent down
> At the dappled base of the tree,
> And among the brown leaves
> Geasters stood up.
>
> Oranges peel like these,
> She said. Rinds bent back.

When it rains, their legs swell up
And walk.

Stranger feet
Than mine
All these years
Outside your door.[1]

McPherson felt as if she had come home—to natural parents, nature-lovers like herself, people who pay witness to life by naming it and studying it carefully.[2] Her love of nature, jazz, and liberalism had made her feel different and sometimes alienated from the McPherson family, who had adopted and raised her; now she was meeting her birth family, whose own impulses toward knowing the land and learning matched her own—Joyce and John were both musicians, as was her sister, Ellayn, who had studied art in college. Long used to the sharp contrasts between her own style and that of her adoptive family and their conservative religious surrounds, McPherson stood outside her birth parents' home as a naturalist and natural daughter, studying what grew outside their door, and thought of her own feet, kept far away: "Stranger feet / Than mine / All these years / Outside your door." Like much of McPherson's writing about her adoption, the scene reveals no bitterness but does include a broad, intimate sense of need and wonder, as well as a faint ambivalence as she approaches the answer to many questions about her own identity. Her life experience with adoption, which is echoed and complicated by poetry she wrote before and after finding these birth parents, reveals a fascination with what the body and genetics gave her, an almost mystical sense of connection with her human roots. In an autobiographical essay, she recalls:

Upon meeting my birth parents, I felt an immediate bond with them and identified with their personalities and quirks. Their house, for instance: it is nestled among wildflowers and wild mushrooms; the trees are full of birds they know all the names of—it seems one can be by heredity a birder.[3]

In this unusually positive birth-family reunion, McPherson located her own unusual hobbies in the family tree, finding that what had seemed her own affinity for naming birds came, as if genetically, from her first family. But this determination that nature rather than culture produced many of her talents is based, as all of McPherson's adoption stories are, in a fertile imagination rather than in scientific fact. Whatever the evidence may present, the most important parts of McPherson's adoption experience stem not from the cold light of science but from the many hued colors of imagination. She was seemingly born, as she used to fantasize as a child, in her own imagination. Longing to understand and re-create the terms of that self-creation flowers everywhere in her poetry. So we have loss, absence, self-transformation, and a joyous and ambivalent wrestling with disappearing figures, be they lovers or mothers, in much of the poetry. McPherson creates a poetry in which the half-light of the imagination is realer than the real world and in which imagined and empty spaces rivet the imagi-nation with their importance: something unseen and very important is there, in the poetry. That something is the presence of her birth parents.

This "hereditary birder's" story of adoption has two important histories: one set in biography and one set in poetry. For McPherson, who did not know her birth parents until she was thirty-seven years old, imagined versions of the birth parents and, more importantly, of the empty space their absence created are constants in the early work. Adoption sets the field for an exploration of self-creation and absence in her poetry; even when it is not explicitly mentioned, it is often hovering just above the surface of the text, giving added resonance and depth to questions of absence and loss. It seems to have inspired her poetic con-nections with an invented imaginary world filled with questions of love, iden-tity, and absence. In this poetic world, McPherson creates a fiercely described invented realm in which the main verbs are those of separation, disappearance, and self-transformation; they tell the story of a poet reinventing herself and thinking through her lost or missing birth parents.

Being adopted seems to have presented McPherson with a rich poetic situ-ation. In her lyrical, semiconfessional early poetry, it required her to forge a very specific relationship with the imaginary, with the invisible and absent. She brings to the page what one adoption theorist calls "the hereditary ghost," a sub-stitute for the developing "genetic ego" that doubles the unknown family and ancestors to an adoptee.[4] In her poetry, this figure is merged with other reject-ing and abandoning characters, especially in work of the 1970s and early 1980s—the time just before McPherson met her birth parents, the Todds. It is as if during that time of intense curiosity and search, absence in her art became almost physically real, as the artist sought to fill and rename it in her own life. Unlike the Lacanian sense of the Imaginary, a prelapsarian, ego-fused world in which the child is unable to distinguish herself from the mother, a "green" world the adult idealizes and longs for as the more real and more special past, this imaginary is an empty room flooded with the grown child's imagination. Iron-ically or beautifully, McPherson claims that that imagination was her biological parents' greatest gift to her. And with it, in the early poetry, she almost creates them in her exuberant forays into the imaginary for lost love. Her poetry delin-eates the space of their continuing absence, but they are never real in it, which poses the question, Does the speaker herself feel unreal, invented?

Psychoanalyst Melanie Klein, a contemporary of Freud's who specialized in child psychology and the influences of childhood experience on adults, saw a deep connection between a child's early loss of a parent and other kinds of loss in adult's lives, an experience that often comes alive in McPherson's poetry.

> We know that the loss of a loved person leads to an impulse in the mourner to reinstate the lost loved object in the ego. . . . In my view, however, he not only takes into himself (re-incorporates) the person whom he has lost, but also reinstates his internalized good objects (ultimately his loved parents), who became part of his inner world from the earliest stages of his development onwards. These too are felt to have gone under, to be destroyed, whenever the loss of a loved person is experienced.[5]

McPherson's poetry implies an adoptee's experience in two crucial ways: it demonstrates an adopted woman's inventive solutions for reinventing the absent parents, especially the mother, in poems written before she met her birth parents, and it later recounts meeting and knowing these birth parents. The poems examined in this essay occur in three books—*Radiation* (1973), *The Year of Our Birth* (1978), and *Patron Happiness* (1982)—the first two published before she met her birth parents, the last published after they met. In the earliest two books, the speaker is preoccupied with lack, the imaginary, and curious double plays on words that reveal a fascination with creating, in intimate detail, a lost and unknown lover, mother, or family. The later poems, found in *Patron Happiness*, describe this reunion and are more narrative than lyric—they appear factually to describe the family reunion. In this final book, the frequent appearance of nature suggests the poet's fascination with her natural and naturalist parents, who share her connection with the wild lands of California. Through her preoccupation with feet in these poems, she also seems to be attempting to locate her own identity through looking at her roots, her feet, her foundations.

McPherson's early books of poetry often examine loss intimately and in unexpected ways; a clear-eyed woman studies winter cardinals, intently remembering her husband's betrayal; an abandoned wife offers her own absence, with childlike sweetness, as a sacramental gift to her unfaithful husband; a female traveler visiting someplace called "the imaginary" thinks of her lover as empty air. Seen as the history of a series of abandonments and losses, the poems in the early books at first appear to tell of a difficult marriage and divorce—McPherson was previously married to poet Henry Carlile—and of the problems of mothering an autistic child.[6] However, when we read these texts through the lens of adoption, we find the emotional intensity of the books to be built on a foundation of earlier loss: the loss of being given up for adoption. This sense of loss is often observed in adopted people, and while many theorists argue that it creates "problems" in grown adoptees, others, such as David M. Brodzinky, claim that adults adopted as infants often experience feelings that are misread as pathogenic but are in fact unrecognized manifestations of adaptive grieving.[7]

In McPherson's case, the poems deal in complex emotional detail with absence and loss—not bitterly, but constantly. Lines about her marriage or her contemporary life can easily be read as statements about the strangeness of being given up for adoption. For instance, she writes:

> Great spaces, I'm thinking of for you—
> as you seem to ask,
> vast intervals.[8]

The speaker in this poem gives her absence to her lover. His withdrawal and rejection of her is met with a gentle, tender gift: she presents him with the gift of "vast intervals" and spaces between them. To a poet preoccupied with creating absence and the absent parents in her work, this is a very tender gift (one she has already practiced making), for imagining the lost loved ones in the invisible also suggests their erasure in real life and your erasure in their own daily lives. McPherson seems to have created her lost parents poetically, not as invented people, but as absence that takes on an almost physical form, a fiercely real presence. All sorts of loss in the poems, as well as all sorts of foundations, origins, and absences, are described with a special wonder and fascination, as if they house someone important, hidden just behind a locked door.

Presence and Absence: At Play with Ancestral Ghosts

In *The Purgatorio,* Virgil, Dante's guide in the afterlife, says to another ghost who has stooped to clasp his feet, "Brother! Refrain, for you are but a shadow, and a shadow is but what you see." The ghost, rising, responds, "Now can you understand the quantity of love that warms me towards you, so that I forget our vanity, and treat the shadows like the solid thing."[9] Sandra McPherson's poetry imagines absence so palpably you can practically swim in it, as she positions it into investigatable realms, mappable regions, and imaginary spaces. Like Dante, she works with such love toward her ghosts that she seems to "treat the shadows like the solid thing." Absent others in her work often seem more real than human characters, bringing to mind a charged, newly realized Elizabeth Bishop, Pablo Neruda, or Denise Levertov—poets whose emotional messages are redolent with visionary descriptions of objects and places.

One of the emotional preoccupations of McPherson's first books is loss, which she studies not as a mourner but as a clear-eyed refugee searching its face to locate her own identity. The subtext of adoption is never better glossed than in the introduction to her second book, *Radiation,* whose epigram claims that our identities are forged by what has rejected us. McPherson quotes Valéry:

The color of a thing is that one which, out of all the colors, it repels and can-not assimilate. High heaven refuses blue, returning azure to the retina. . . . To our senses things offer only their rejections. We know them by their refuse. Perfume is what the flowers throw away.

Perhaps we only know other people by what they eliminate, by what their substance will not accept. If you are good, it is because you retain your evil. If you blaze, hurling off sparkles and lightning, your sorrow, gloom, and stu-pidity keep house within you. They are more you, more yours, than your brilliance. Your genius is everything you are not. Your best deeds are those most foreign to you.[10]

This epigram invites readers to participate in reading the poems both for what they are and for what they are not, a sort of fabric of hidden opposites. Like the poems about adoption, abandonment, and reconnection in *Radiation,* this prose poem concisely burrows between natural experience, the identity of oth-ers, and the poet/adoptee, the "you" who is keeping her emotions housed within. This quote suggests poetic responses to adoption: the sense of being abandoned; the sense that it was done for "the best of all concerned"; the sense that an adoptee's curiosity shifts between the self, the birth parents, and a lost collective we. Valéry shifts pronouns midway through his meditation, so that what is at first an impersonal observation about the sky, perfume, and other inanimate substances becomes next a shared, group experience ("we only know other people . . .") and then an individual, second-person account ("They are more you . . ."). His impersonal naturalist observation—that colors reveal what the object has rejected—becomes a shared metaphor describing others and then intimately describing the self. Whether studied for its direct relation to adoption or its mere obsession with identifying with what is lost, this epigram opens a book of powerful poetry about a woman's emotional and imaginative life. McPherson dedicated it to "My father and mother," Walt and Frances McPherson.

In *Radiation,* two poems midway through the book suggest that McPher-son's visceral relationship with the imaginary is stimulated by a missing link in the family romance. In "Cinderella," the princess's craving for her unnamed lover sounds less like romantic longing than like a desire for parents who "think like" her. The idea that this character seeks not a male other but part of her own identity is suggested in the first line, which evokes Sylvia Plath's violently trans-formative poem "The Mirror."[11] McPherson begins:

When she came to the mirror it was to her
Instrument of change, every scene in it
Total background . . .[12]

The odd jumps of lineation in this strophe suggest that Cinderella studied the mirror not only for her instrument of change, which we read in the entire sentence, but also to find "her." The mirror is somehow supposed to give Cinderella, the classic female orphan, her own self back. As she grew older, McPherson did in fact study her face in mirrors to try to find her own "Total background," looking to see what her parents might look like. In her autobiographical essay, she writes:

> I would occasionally look into the mirror and try to age my face into what I thought my birth father might look like. I scanned my body and tried to imagine my birth mother's figure.[13]

In the poem, she seeks for change and genealogy, her "Total background," which will somehow present herself more honestly than her own mere face. Cinderella's confessional poem takes place in the present but is preoccupied with her past, whatever that might be.

In the next stanza, the womblike connotation of a woman's enchanted room again suggests the adoption subtext; Cinderella misses and invents an enclosed, womblike fantasy space:

> . . . the dream room
> That had been lived in and never opened.
> Everything in it was imagined, the curtains
> The color of Chinese skin, with large printed
> Purple blooms like distant ferris wheels
> At dusk. . . .[14]

This landscape associatively suggests a childhood sensuousness, mixing Ferris wheels with exotic but frightening skin-colored curtains and purple flowers. It intimately details the interior of an unopened and totally imagined space, a womblike box that may represent the imagination or that may symbolize the preverbal memories of a poet's first brief intimate connection to a long-absent birth mother, stretched into visions and similes through the filter of poetic imagination and language.

In another poem in *Radiation*, "Wanting a Mummy," McPherson explicitly refers to a ghostly mother, playfully describing the absent birth mother as a benevolent monster, whom she quizzes. Read through the lens of McPherson's adoption, this poem conflates loss with death, suggesting that she mourns as well as misses her "mummy." As mentioned earlier, several adoption theorists believe that closed adoptions, in which the adopted child has no access to the birth parents, create a subconscious sense of grief, even in infant adoptions where the adopted person has no conscious memory of the absent first parents. David Brodzinsky claims that adopted adults experience a grief similar to that of orphans—but that their grief is given less closure, because there is no body to bury.[15] The grief experienced by adopted adults is in fact similar to a preserved mummy, haunting the imagination, buried with the magical possibility of resurrecting the preserved flesh. Invoking the dead or missing mother in "Wanting a Mummy," McPherson tries to resurrect her seemingly "dead" mother to ask her questions about her own identity and the meaning of life.

This clever poem is not as complex or subtle as many McPherson poems but has a whimsical darkness, like a joyous parade on the Day of the Dead. Its fascination with absent mothers and connection is evident from the poem's title and from its first line:

I've always wanted one,
A connection . . .[16]

The eerie whimsy of wanting a mummy and of double reading the mummified body as a "mommy" or, as the British would pronounce it, "mummy," intersects with adoption issues as soon as McPherson calls her mummy "a connection." Like the "Total background" of "Cinderella," this figure promises a connection to the past and to the self, here with sphinxlike wisdom. Such wisdom is best questioned with a poet's own sphinxlike syntax and circular queries, as the narrator asks:

How do you like the rain?
Are you 3000 years old or still 25? (58)

Referring to the age of a dead mummy and potentially of her own mother at the time of her birth, McPherson links the mythic, user-friendly monster with her lost mother, suggesting the adoptee's sense of anthropology—she is digging into the past, unsure if the lost figure is ancient or stuck in the age at which she "died." Read as an adoptee's poem, there is an interesting take on the death too. The two ages—"Are you 3000 . . . or still 25?"—refer to the two deaths in the adoption triad: the death of the parents in the child's life and the death of the child in theirs. If the "mummy" is "3000," or has aged since being buried in lost memory, she has gone on to have her own life. If she is "still 25," she is frozen in the past, someone not capable of death or change, who can still satisfy the child who lost her by resembling a real mommy—a young mother at the time of birth.

This mathematical conundrum also suggests the identity problem of a child in the adoption triad: adopted people are almost always referred to as adopted children, even when they are thirty-seven years old. An unspoken subtext to her question about the "mummy's" age is a question about her own age; it is as if

McPherson asks, "To you, am I an adult or a child, the child you gave up when you were twenty-five?" This problem of double naming and double lives is most keenly explicated in the poem "Helen Todd: My Birthname."[17] There, speaking to her own double, whom she calls by her birth name, Helen Todd, she ominously says: "I was not born. Only you were." The split self seems more intensely powerful when she knows her birth name and knows that her other life and other self had a distinct title given to her by her birth parents. However, the mystery of the split self, the question of which "half" of her is real, is even keener when she knows that name.

In this poem, as in other poems of the invented absent parents, the figure for her birth parents is quizzed but cannot answer in language: she is "Voluble with symbols / and medallions," much like a poet herself or like the subconscious that constructs her. The poem ends with contrasting images of the speaker's and the "mummy's" hands.

I with my hands like peaches

And my friend all
Shortbread and roots.[18]

The mummy's hands are ginger-and-spice scented, like the traditional cookie of both children's fairy tales and Christmas; she is a homespun heartwarming figure who reminds us of 1950s American kitchens more than Egyptian funerary ritual. The poet associates her with childhood food and with "roots," the "Total background" that creates a sense of stability and a knowledge of the buried past.

The last important sequence of poems that deal with absence and adoption in McPherson's early books is a ten-section poetic sequence called "Studies in the Imaginary," published in her third book, *The Year of Our Birth* (1978), where McPherson refers to herself as two people.[19] Written just before she met her birth parents, this surreal sequence of short lyrics brings to mind Chagall with its brief, crisp imagery and brightly colored landscapes filled with folkloric creatures. Its references to adoption are oblique, but its ability to create a palpable realness, a sensuous presence to the absent, is keen. Its fascinations with absence and being able to invent a world are vivid and closely reflect McPherson's interest in finding the Todds. Reflecting on her lifelong interest in adoption and its influence on the imagination, McPherson says that she enjoyed being adopted as a child because she felt she had "come out of nowhere."

I felt as if I had grown out of the ground or been dropped from a cloud. Having no blood ties, I felt a sense of imaginative freedom and individuality conducive to an aspiring artist. Perhaps this is the reason several poets have told me that as children they pretended they were adopted.[20]

The influence of adoption on the imaginative mind amplifies in "Studies in the Imaginary," suggesting that for an adopted poet who feels she invented herself, the whole world sometimes takes on an unreal, invented quality.

The imaginary zone she created as a person "dropped from a cloud" is both playfully joyous and lonely in the first section of the poem.

> To pray was like living on the road
> that goes on to someone else's house
> even when it is too far to walk.
> Now I'm too far away from hometown streets
> to know any listener, being among strangers
>   approaches
> being among the imaginary.[21]

The imaginative, faith-sustained language of prayer here refers to her parents' Presbyterianism and to the speaker's own sense of reaching, with words, to people who are not there. "Far from hometown streets," she is among strangers, alienated and liberated by the experience of being in disguise, unknown. But rather than reflect on the stranger's notions about her invented reality, she views them as slight fictions—as the imaginary.

The ensuing sections of the poem are delicately and sometimes mysteriously connected but come to form a sort of surreal narrative of an imaginary hotel. By the third section, the narrator has taken a nestlike room (reminiscent of the "dream room" in "Cinderella").

> It is a fine day for a strange place.
> I've taken a room above a bird's nest.
> It is above a pleading noise.
> There are more nests higher up.
> What all these voices want becomes an ingredient
> in a gourmet soup I've never had. (50)

The infant hunger of crying birds, "pleading" for a "gourmet soup" the speaker has "never had," brings to mind her own unsatisfied childhood hungers. Need, hunger, and the blindness of people who seek to see ahead of themselves in this surreal hotel are regularly referred to in the poem.

The problem of being known by name, being identified for what one naturally is, is playfully explored in section 5, when a botany class cannot identify the poet.

> . . . How unlikely they will identify me,
> stop and pronounce the existence of anyone
> moving faster than a locust of colt's foot. . . . (52)

As if she is unknown and unnamable, she threads past the botany class in this scene that reads interestingly next to her meeting her parents and discovering their intense fascination with botany. In a poem about the imaginary, the power and loneliness it holds for the poet speaker, these lines might also suggest a naturalist's craving to be known by her own parents. The narrator sounds more poignant than we might expect when she glances at the class and thinks it "unlikely they will identify me." Her own two-named self, her own unstable footing in the imaginary realm where she can find her lost lover and her birth parents, is not as easy to locate or name as the plants.

The next four sections of the poem introduce romantic absence, which conjures absence so powerfully that it also reads as an emotional gloss to the experience of being adopted. Here, the imaginary takes wings: the speaker cannot tell whether she is imagining her lost loved one or he is imagining her. The first reference to this family romance is in section 6, where she writes:

> There are no longer single rooms:
> any bedroom has an unused bed
> beside my rumpled one.
> I sleep as if beside a corrective mirror
> which relieves the maid. . . .
> Finally I place you in the pane
> you come through like a dove
> and the dove's echo from towns I've just
> passed through: me suggesting you. (53)

The mirror imagery echoes Cinderella's mirror of "True background," and here, the missing lover that could be created in a "corrective mirror" is longed for in bed but fantasized in an "unused bed"—not a romantic fantasy, but a companionable one. Placing this loved one in the "pane," or pain, she concocts him like a bird or its echo, the thing or the imaginary double of the thing. Her best effort at resurrecting the loved one is to create herself ("me suggesting you"). The speaker creates lonely company by invoking not the missing loved one but instead herself as a channel for thinking of him or them.

The idea of knowing the absent one plays in a Neruda-like chain in section 7, suggesting that all this imagining still does not produce a satisfactory person in the darkness of the mind.

> Say I know you shallowly, I know you like
> a firefly following a plane, no better.
> Say it's too early spring for fireflies.
> Say I see you playing on the tennis court,
> running off your fat, drumming out your sweat,
> the art of your oil and water.

like two kinds of painting.
Say I paint you sitting outside full courts
with your one white glove on
as it gets dark and you leave.
It all seems so familiar, the dark,
you'd think somebody would be. (54)

After the incantatory list of ways she might know the absent loved one, a list frequently interrupting itself distractedly to try pinning down the feeling and her
knowledge better, she ends with a cryptic sentence that compares the familiar
darkness with the unknown loved one. The final line of this section has two
meanings: it both pleads for someone's existence, that they simply "be," and calls
the loved one unfamiliar.

After two more sections that focus on the absent one as a lover, McPherson
ends the poem with a wonderfully hermetic prayer that is whimsical and affectionate and unpredictable and mournful: "Dear, I pray you think of me, not as
a tourist / but as an enormous melancholy salesman." Her salesman drops all
his samples into the wild flowering bushes and has "nothing to show you." Her
own face and voice are imaginary, metaphorical, mimicking the "face of a clock"
and the "voice of a cricket," so that she is eventually imaginary. But she also ultimately calls the much invoked, powerfully presented missing one nothing too.

And me suggesting you as one dove
        suggesting
another in another town
believes in the empty air. (57)

The two invented, Chagallian images—dove to dove—are double illusions, and
the empty air between them even has to be believed into existence. She both "believes in the empty air" in that she knows it exists and "believes in the empty air"
as the blank space that is the home from which she is determined to imagine
and believe, despite the empty spaces around her. Charting a path between the
imaginary self and the imaginary, absent loved one is a central crisis and beauty
in McPherson's poetry.

Bay Hikes and a First Name: The Reunion Poems

McPherson has noted:

Because the attorney had not been careful to cover the names of the adopting parents and because the Todds had once been shown a newspaper photo
of me as a child, they knew my adopted name. . . . Long before I contacted

them, they searched for and bought all of my books. When they read, in one, a reference to "the adoption I knew nothing of" ("On Coming Out of Nowhere," in *The Year of Our Birth*), they felt they should do something, but held back partly because of their other daughter, who had not been told.[22]

"On Coming Out of Nowhere," in *The Year of Our Birth*, is the first direct reference to adoption in McPherson's work. Its title is reminiscent of her idea, as a child, that an adopted person was self-invented or "dropped from a cloud." The poem itself is small, dark, and interesting. It is mainly concerned with her adopted father and a trip the family made to the tropics. In the middle of the short poem, the speaker stares at her father's aquarium in winter, remembering the blue crabs in the tropics.

> Your aquarium and the snow rising
> are enough to make me tell you this,
> the adoption I knew nothing about
> but that I want it again and again,
>
> while around your door the new snow makes it hard
> to come and go . . .[23]

The paralyzing snow of her father's house brings up fantasies of continual adoption, which she wants "again and again," but it also reminds her she is trapped in one identity and life now: the new snow holds her still in place, making "it hard to come and go" from this new, second identity.

Several poems in McPherson's next book of poetry, *Patron Happiness*, explicitly tell of meeting her birth parents and of finding her birth name, Helen Todd. These poems tell a story of rebirth or reaffirmation, as the speaker locates parts of herself through language, connection with her birth parents, and their shared knowledge of California's natural wildlands. Most of the poems about herself search through language for knowledge, and most of the poems about her birth parents try to understand and describe them through their language for natural objects—ways they teach their grown naturalist daughter to look at the natural world.

The magical appearance of her own first name had a powerful influence on McPherson. When her newly found birth parents told her what they had briefly planned to name her, one of the questions posed in "Wanting a Mummy" was answered: in that poem, when she had asked if the mummy was still 25 or was 3000 years old, she seemed to wonder if she herself were a child or an adult of adoption. Finding Helen Todd, McPherson seems to have discovered that the adopted child grew up but that the birth child, born under a different name, is still an infant.

Pulitzer Prize–winning poet Donald Justice, McPherson's friend and confidant, wrote a postcard ditty about McPherson's emotional shock on learning her birthname.

Ancient mysteries of the womb—
When you sought a *nom de plume*
Would it not have seemed quite odd
Had you chosen Helen Todd?[24]

Unlike this playful attack on the problems of adoption, biology, destiny, and names, McPherson faced her feelings about the event seriously. She was to imagine her life as the child of these parents, with this birth name, in the poem "Helen Todd: My Birthname."

They did not come to claim you back,
To make me Helen again. Mother
Watched the dry, hot streets in case they came.
This is how she found a tortoise
Crossing between cars and saved it.
It's how she knew roof-rats raised families
In the palmtree heads. But they didn't come—
It's almost forty years.[25]

An eerie fragmentation opens the poem, as the title immediately prepares readers for the speaker's strange angle: she is talking to her birth name or birth self. Split in two, as a person and her lost name, she quietly talks to the child and describes her frightened adopted mother and the dry streets that are empty except for a turtle. Her adopted mother's sense of the natural world, in this poem, comes not from a fascination with nature per se but instead from a fear of the birth mother coming to reclaim this child. She learns of "roof-rats" and turtles while studying the empty road for the birth parents, who "did not come to claim you back." Her adopted mother's desperate gazing out the window is meant to save her child and also teaches this mother all she seems to know about McPherson's keen favorite—nature. The urban nature this woman sees is merely a family of "roof-rats" (suggesting the poverty and humor of this vision), another displaced family, living in the "heads," or imaginative space, of trees. This double family has also relocated its young and lives like the birth parents do for McPherson, in the "head."

Still addressing her imaginary double, McPherson informs her that she found "their" birth parents and, in doing so, found Helen Todd—both the name and the lost history that name once foretold.

I went to them. And now I know
Our name, quiet one. I believe you
Would have stayed in trigonometry and taken up
The harp. Math soothed you; music
Made you bold; and science, completely
Understanding. Wouldn't you have collected,
Curated, in your adolescence, Mother Lode
Pyrites out of pity for their semblance
To gold? And three-leaf clovers to search
For some shy differences between them? (53)

To McPherson, her birth name, Helen Todd, suggests a determined ability with math, a love of the classic swoops of harp music, and a facility with science and geology. These ways of organizing information are almost opposites of McPherson's own: she trades poetry for math, the imaginary for a lineated object. She thinks of the other self she could have been and informs her double of the shy and intimate potential lost when she lost her name.

The final section of the poem ends with a haunting claim and suggests that for the adopted poet, her own existence began not at birth but at renaming.

Knowing you myself at last—it seems you'd cut
Death in half and double everlasting life,
Quiet person named as a formality
At birth. I was not born. Only you were. (53)

The staggered caesuras of the last line give a reluctant, stuttered quality to this final admission, as if it is difficult to say. But McPherson's line breaks suggest that the final line can be read as a single, awful statement: "At birth I was not born. Only you were." The adopted adult reaches to the lost birth name and re-claims it at an emotionally difficult price: by claiming it, she must both admit her existence and admit that adoption killed this person; hence the double, not she, was born in "The Year of Our Birth." Readers unfamiliar with the poem "Helen Todd" may not realize that the title of the collection *The Year of Our Birth* and of the poem by the same name suggests not only a collective we but also a split I. The we who were born that year are not only McPherson's peers but also her double, Helen Todd, whom she claims was born in her place.

From the first weeks of McPherson's reunion with the Todds, they hiked. This immediate connection for the long-separated family appears in all of her poems about them. In her autobiographical essay, she recalls:

My birth father used to take stereo photographs of mushrooms. On this first day united, we went for a walk in the baylands and identified dozens of birds and plants. My birth sister, I discovered, walks along a trail the same way I do—stopping to identify snakes and lizards and wildflowers and shrubs. . . . My birth mother said she felt like sending out birth announcements.[26]

A deep fascination with identity and identification fill all of the poet's accounts of meeting her birth parents, and even though nature walks and knowing the lands and plants and animals around her are a lifelong passion for McPherson, it is interesting how frequently "identity" appears in discussion of meeting the Todds. The poems about their walks together explore the idea of what is natural and namable in the world, studying both the reunited birth family ("natural" family) and the lands they hiked together. Just as Joyce Todd wanted to send out "birth announcements" on meeting McPherson, these poems tell of a rebirth or reaffirmation of being.

The poems about hiking with her birth parents are in the third section of *Patron Happiness.* They include "Earthstar, Birthparents' House," quoted in the first section of this essay, and "Wings and Seeds." In the latter, the intimacy of walking a salt marsh with her birth mother catapults McPherson into an exploration of passion and creation. The lesson her birth mother teaches seems to be: act like the hummingbird, trusting your wings more than your feet. Imagery of ruffles, skirts, and a doll inflects the wild salt marsh of the poem with a girlish double. Even seemingly rejecting "clothing and tea," in the second stanza the two women feminize the landscape with their visions, what they look like and how they see.

We twine hands, we trade heavy binoculars.
The clouds are coming from far out on the sea
Where they'd only fetch a ruffle.[27]

The clouds invade to catch, it seems, more than a ruffle—two nature-loving women hand in hand scanning the world to name it. Later in the poem, feminizing imagery describes terns as "dolled-up stilts in a pool," and the narrator sees godwits as "a thick golden hem on the bay." Rarely does McPherson describe nature in such human and feminine terms, but the presence of her birth mother, in the scene or in the poem, seems to highlight everything with a fascination for the domestic. In this light, the poet explores both her birth as a birth of passion and the passion she had to find these lost parents.

The third stanza and the fifth, final stanza turn from describing nature to describing human nature. In these lines, the women's passion for studying the wilds is reflected in their own wild natures. With the lesson of the hummingbird in mind, McPherson suggests in the third stanza that they have learned to take flight rather than trust their humble feet.

Separately our lives have passed from earthy passion
To wilder highliving creatures with wings.
With our early expectancies
Did we come to think of ourselves as flights of nature? (52)

This stanza can be read as the shift, in two separate, unconnected lives, from childhood passions to adult passions. It can also be read as the story of two women who had children very early in their lives. The difference is that McPherson kept her daughter, Phoebe, and subsequently quit graduate school to raise her, whereas Todd gave up her first daughter, McPherson, to pursue her intellectual pursuits. The "flights of nature" seems to refer to the unexpected course of each woman's life, from the time they were "early expectancies" expecting children, to their growth later to birds of flight.

In one of the most affirming, complex lyric stanzas of her career, McPherson closes the poem by proclaiming understanding and, with understanding, joy.

I was a child of pleasure.
The strong pleasurable seeds of life
Found each other.
And I was created by passion's impatience
For the long wait till our meeting. (52)

Walking a salt marsh with her birth mother, she thinks about their twin flights as unexpected mothers, catapulted by passion into early pregnancy and different kinds of maternal crises: for her mother, giving up a child, for McPherson, raising an autistic child and ending her formal education. The "strong pleasurable seeds of life" found each other not only in McPherson's conception but also when she rediscovered her birth parents. She speaks of her creation in a double way, so that we see her created both by the passion of her young birth parents and by "passion's impatience / For the long wait till our meeting." Passion, she suggests, gave them an urgency to meet, an urgency that grew larger with its own impatience for that meeting. McPherson's linguistically simple and agile stanza suggests all at once the nine or ten different, seemingly contradictory things it means. In its odd geometry, it reveals the equation of love, loss, identity, and discovering that are present in McPherson's reconnection with her birth parents.

Sandra McPherson's most recent books seem to map what are in fact for her colliding, interrelated fascinations: motherhood and nature. Now, she writes of herself as a mother, having collected work from many years of poetry that describe her relation with her daughter, in *The Spaces between Birds* (1996). Since locating her own biological roots, McPherson's writing concentrates on being a mother rather than a daughter and also seems drawn to more stories outside of her own sphere—and to how stories outside ourselves can echo and inform us.

Her poetry books written after her birth-family reunion include extended, collage-like lyrics about quilting and blues music in *Streamers* (1988) and a far-ranging book called *The God of Indeterminacy* (1993). In the acclaimed *Edge Effect* (1997), she explores personal and geographical borders, collapsing the lines between people and definitions in bold new ways to describe human relationships, the arts, and a northern California watershed. Currently, McPherson's home in Davis, California, is crowded with grotesque postcards and antique toys that point toward her next poetry book, *A Visit to Civilization*. She is collecting turn-of-the-century postcards, quilts, children's school materials, games, and wartime propaganda for this poetry book about "extinct objects." The woman who once unearthed a shortbread mummy to locate her lost self now reaches back less far and more locally, to tell stories about the objects that have narrated and influenced other people's lives.

Still gleaning for poetry from the baffling mysteries of things lost and disconnected, she now displays a gift for understanding both the real and the unreal at once. She may partly owe this gift to Helen Todd and to the experiences of imagining and reclaiming her connection to her long absent birth parents. The split self, rejoined, gives McPherson's poetry a vast and expansive vision— one still able to see things intimately and to name the natural world with clarity, but one also able to throw its sight a long way, imagining different cultures and lives with amazing vividness. The force of adoption perhaps presents itself as a lasting trait in McPherson's poetry because of this remnant, this force of imagining the invisible and seeing through two sets of eyes. Whatever the cost and personal importance of this double vision, it gifts us with a poetic philosophy that asks us to join McPherson in simultaneously believing and disbelieving in the invisible with comfort, hardness, and grace. As McPherson puts it in a poem from her collection *The God of Indeterminacy:*

If you spread all your beliefs
crossways to your disbeliefs
the square where they intersect
is holy ground.

Though it is struck from all sides
it is your hearth, your patch, your junction of amends.[28]

Sandra McPherson's poetry details her own journey toward this junction of amends, and her adoption plays a key role in the search for the invisible and in the creative act of crossing the real and the imaginary into one "hearth" and "patch." From playing piano for her adopted parents in her childhood home to her long journey toward her birth parents' front yard, to her own house crammed with postcards of circus freaks and African American quilts, she has crafted a poetry of explorations and boundaries, rich with the voices of transformation and longing.

NOTES

1. Sandra McPherson, "Earthstars, Birthparents' House," in *Patron Happiness* (New York: Ecco, 1982), 51.

2. Sandra McPherson, personal interview with the author, June 1997.

3. Sandra McPherson, "Sandra McPherson," in *Contemporary Authors Autobiography Series* (Detroit: Gale Research, 1984–) 23:228.

4. M. Frisk, cited in Janet L. Hoopes, "Adoption and Identity Formation," in *The Psychology of Adoption*, ed. David M. Brodzinsky and Marshall D. Schechter (New York: Oxford University Press, 1990), 153.

5. Melanie Klein, *The Selected Melanie Klein*, ed. Juliet Mitchell (New York: MacMillan, 1986), 156.

6. McPherson has written many poems about raising her daughter, Phoebe, whose poetic gifts, skill at all things mechanical, and difficulties as an autistic child are explored in *The Space between Birds* (Hanover: Wesleyan, 1996), a volume of poems by the author with quotes from her daughter. Like McPherson, Phoebe seems to have been fascinated with communicating loudly through silent objects—one of her mother's poems describes her recording a compilation tape of singers' breaths before words; another poem recounts how instead of discarding snails from their garden as she had been told to, she wrote "I Love You" with live snails on the side of their house.

7. David M. Brodzinsky, "A Stress and Coping Model of Adoption Adjustment," in Brodzinsky and Schechter, *Psychology of Adoption*, 3–24.

8. Sandra McPherson, "Extract," in *The Year of Our Birth* (New York: Ecco, 1978), 6–7.

9. Dante Aligheri, *Purgatorio*, trans. T. S. Eliot, in T. S. Eliot, *Essays on Poetry and Poets* (London: Faber & Faber, 1957) 219.

10. Paul Valery, cited in Sandra McPherson, *Radiation* (New York: Ecco, 1973), ii; translator unknown.

11. Sylvia Plath, "Mirror," in *The Collected Poems*, ed. Ted Hughes (New York: Harper and Row, 1981), 173. The speaker is a mirror, who, by the second stanza, dwells on the psychological crisis of reflecting a woman honestly.

Now I am a lake. A woman bends over me,
Searching my reaches for what she really is.
Then she turns to those liars, the candles or the moon.
I see her back, and reflect it faithfully.
She rewards me with tears and an agitation of hands.
I am important to her. She comes and goes.
Each morning it is her face that replaces the darkness.
In me she has drowned a young girl, and in me an old woman
Rises toward her day after day, like a terrible fish.

12. McPherson, "Cinderella," in *Radiation*, 32.

13. McPherson, "Sandra McPherson," 227.

14. McPherson, "Cinderella," 32.

15. J. S. Wallerstein's studies are cited in Brodzinsky, "Stress and Coping Model." Wallerstein has examined children of divorce and children who have lost a parent, and Brodzinsky compares these losses to the loss experienced by adopted children who have "lost" the birth parents. He claims that adoptive children, because their grief has no closure or continuing connection to the absent parent, suffer more psychologically from this separation.

16. McPherson, "Wanting a Mummy," in *Radiation*, 58. Subsequent references to this poem appear parenthetically in text.

17. McPherson, "Helen Todd: My Birthname," in *Patron Happiness*, 53.

18. McPherson, "Wanting a Mummy," 58.

19. McPherson, "Studies in the Imaginary," in *The Year of Our Birth*, 48–57.

20. McPherson, "Sandra McPherson," 227.

21. McPherson, "Studies in the Imaginary," 48. Subsequent references to this poem appear parenthetically in text.

22. McPherson, "Sandra McPherson," 228.

23. McPherson, "On Coming Out of Nowhere," in *The Year of Our Birth*, 21.

24. Donald Justice, postcard to Sandra McPherson, cited in McPherson, "Sandra McPherson," 227.

25. McPherson, "Helen Todd: My Birthname," 53. Subsequent references to this poem appear parenthetically in text.

26. McPherson, "Sandra McPherson," 228.

27. McPherson, "Wings and Seeds," in *Patron Happiness*, 52. Subsequent references to this poem appear parenthetically in text.

28. Sandra McPherson, "Ode for the God of Indeterminacy," in *The God of Indeterminacy* (Urbana: University of Illinois Press, 1993), 77.

Adoption, Identity, and Voice

Jackie Kay's Inventions of Self

Nancy K. Gish

Interview with Jackie Kay

Jackie Kay is a Scottish poet. The title poem of her first book, *The Adoption Papers*, draws on her own experience to tell the story of a Black child's adoption by a white working-class couple and experiments with multiple voices—of the birth mother, the adoptive mother, and the adopted child. *The Adoption Papers* won a Scottish Arts Council Book Award, a Saltire First Book of the Year Award, and a Forward Prize. Her other books include *Other Lovers* (1993); *Two's Company* (1992), a book of poetry for children; the biography *Bessie Smith* (1997); her most recent book of poetry, *Off Colour* (1998); and her first novel, *Trumpet* (1988).

The following interview was conducted on September 10, 1997, in Manchester, England, where Jackie Kay now lives.

Q: I'd like to begin by asking you just a couple of facts about when you were writing *The Adoption Papers*. Had you, at the time you wrote the poem, met your biological mother, or was that an entirely constructed voice?

A: No, I hadn't met my birth mother although I was in the process of tracing her, which made me write the book. And tracing made me think about the whole business of identity, all the other selves I've been. During the process, I realized that I had in fact had an imaginary birth mother all my life in different ways; and at various points in my life she had gone through many changes. When I was very young, I used to imagine her to be Shirley Bassey; I saw Shirley Bassey on the television singing "Gold Finger," and I thought, "That's her, that's her!" Then I realized that she was white, and that she was a nurse, so she had to change from Shirley Bassey into somebody else. So I'd always had, and I think all adopted people do have at some level, an imaginative—an imaginary—birth mother that I've carried around with me. I wanted, in my writing, to give birth, if you like, to that birth mother, so that rather than her giving birth to me, this was me giving birth to her. She was my creation rather than me being hers. I wanted to convey that in the style of her voice; her voice is not as real as the adoptive mother's. It's much more ethereal, more wraith-like. She is not meant

171

to be completely a real person: the reader should be aware all the time, as she is listening to or reading these poems, that the birth mother is an imaginary person. She is a mixture of real and unreal. I wanted that to be quite clear in the book.

Q: Just briefly, yes or no, have you met her since then, physically?

A: No, no I haven't.

Q: One other question that came up when you were saying that. Have you seen the film *Secrets and Lies*?

A: Yes, I have.

Q: Did that resonate for you?

A: Oh, yes. I found it very moving. Ultimately it's a very hopeful film because she meets . . . and they're all quite happy in the end to find each other. I found the integrity of the film very moving, and the mother was wonderful. I really think she [Brenda Blethyn] did deserve an Oscar. I was deeply disappointed when she didn't get it. It's incredible how much I identify with other adopted people; adopted people are like a special group, if you like, in society. Whenever I see a film or a book or any mention of adoption, I do very closely identify with the adopted person. There aren't that many adopted people in literature. I mean they appear a lot in soaps, but they always are the kind of people that didn't really know who they were, in *Dallas or Dynasty*, until they found out and then suddenly became transformed and suddenly different. And I don't find that so interesting as the idea that you actually do know who you are when you are adopted; it's just that you are different.

Q: Different in what way?

A: Different in that you always have this knowledge of yourself, and it's very close to yourself, of fate, I suppose, that you could have been somebody else, that you could have led a completely different life, that you could have had a different name, you know, that you could have had different parents, a different house, different religious upbringing, political upbringing. Everything could have been different but for that moment in fate. So you have a sense of difference quite strongly. Or I did.

Q: But it's very interesting because the child in *The Adoption Papers* is very aware of feeling a physical source that's clearly not identifiable with the adopted mother. That is, "She is faceless / She has no nose." To what extent does that sense of difference identify itself with needing roots in body?

A: It would be a different answer depending upon when the question was asked. At any point in our lives when we look at different issues that are central to the whole of our being, if you like, our perspective on them changes depending on what age we are. In *The Adoption Papers*, when it says, "She is faceless / She has no nose," that is really the daughter talking about the birth mother, the birth mother in particular. She is saying that she can't properly imagine her; she can't make her real no matter how hard she tries; she can't make her physically real for her. Whereas her adopted mother is very physically real, very affectionate, warm, earthy, full-blooded, the birth mother is not; she is the opposite of those qualities. But the daughter both knows and doesn't know herself; she also is searching for herself. She is doing both simultaneously in the book. She is searching for herself, and she knows herself, and I think you can do both at the same time.

Q: What I'm hearing, I think, is two slightly different things; you say she knows herself, but she might easily have been someone totally different.

A: That's right.

Q: So could you speak about the notion of "self."

A: Well, I think the whole notion of self is such a complex one for everybody, the whole sense of who you actually are. Who are you really? And I mean the truth is that nobody knows. And the other truth is that some people don't give a damn anyway. And then there are those people, you know, and I'm guilty of this, that are obsessed with this whole question of self, of what is, what you can say is a real identity anyway. I'm just very interested in this because it seems to me that often that very identity that the rest of society calls "real" is false. And the opposite is true as well. So I think that, for instance, adopted people are always thought of like this: "well we don't really know their bloodline, so we don't really know what has gone into them, so we don't know a lot about them." There's a lot of prejudice about adopted people that runs right through our culture and society—bastards that were thrown out, the shame of illegitimacy, what part of your blood in America is Black and what part isn't. There are all sorts of prejudices, and these prejudices lead people to the conclusion that adopted people have a false self, which I think simply isn't true. It is not true that identity for the adopted person is false, but rather that it is different. There is no point in denying that it is different to grow up knowing that your mother is not actually your mother, and that your father is not actually your father, but nonetheless they are your mother and father. Those seeming opposites—how can someone be your mother and not be your mother? how can somebody be real and not be real?—are just at the heart of what it means to be adopted; you have to contain both those supposed opposites together. And if you can manage to combine those, then you can accept that, and you can accept that that is actually a great richness, as Walt Whitman famously put it: "you say I contradict myself? / Very well, I contradict myself, / (I am large, I contain multitudes.)"

The self is multitudes. The self is complex and often contradictory. It's all right for me, for instance, to say I'm Black and I'm Scottish; it's not a contradiction for me, although lots of people regard it as such. That is my experience; I'm Black and I'm Scottish. There is no problem with that at all.

Q: Would you vote for devolition if you were in Scotland?[1]

A: Yes, I would definitely. Definitely.

Q: But you can't because you're living in England.

A: Exactly, that's true.

Q: Many of my friends are Scottish Nationalists, so I'm sure I would too, and I worked on Hugh MacDiarmid,[2] who also loved to quote that Whitman line, "I contradict myself. . . ." Of course, he was both Chris and Hugh. ["Hugh Mac-Diarmid" was the pen name of Christopher Murray Grieve. He used both names.]

A: That's right, and I think, especially as we move into the twenty-first century, we have lots of different ways of people being seeming opposites. We have men that dress as women; we have lots of people who change their sexes from man to woman. We realize the whole fluidity of gender and culture, and it becomes more and more apparent to us as there become more ways of changing yourselves: women taking hormones to grow beards, men changing themselves to make themselves more feminine. We live in a culture in which, gradually, even the most ordinary of people are starting to know about these things and accept these things and think well, "fair enough, if they're more comfortable that way, then they're more comfortable that way." There's still a huge amount of prejudice, but there seems to be a greater knowledge and openness of the very many different ways that people could try and be themselves, be comfortable in being themselves. So I think of identity as being a very fluid thing, and my own identity as being very fluid, as something that changes with culture and with time and with perspective. I think of it as being not at all static and not at all fixed. And I think the adopted person's identity is even more fluid than a person who is not because everything that is behind them is moving. Sometimes we don't even know about it. The past is unknown to them, adopted people; the past is constantly open to dreams, imagination, fantasy, and interpretation. It's something that can be re-invented: the possibilities for the adopted person to constantly re-invent themselves are endless. You could just go on and on and on. As I do. I mean I don't stop writing about adoption because I just find it an interesting subject to write about.

Q: You also write about many different characters, and that seems to me to be partly linked to a Scottish tradition of many voices. Medieval ballads have dia-

logues; there isn't the lyric voice at the center that is somehow fixed and continuous. You say on *The Usual Suspects*[3] that they are you and they are not you,
or it's your voice. Could you comment on what you meant specifically by that?

A: I think when you're a writer, what you choose to write about, even if it's not
directly autobiographical, is linked to your own experience. Of course there is
the imagination, and of course everybody makes things up, but the very fact that
you are drawn to write about certain issues or certain people shows that you
have some sort of affinity or deep, deep empathy with them; otherwise you
wouldn't really attempt to do it. And so all the people that I choose to write
about in the first-person voice I have a deep affinity with to begin with. When I
write about them I also explore different parts of myself. So if I'm writing about
a gay man dying of AIDS, although I am not a gay man dying of AIDS, I will,
when I'm writing that poem, explore my own obsession or fear of death or my
own feelings about illness, or, in the case of a poem that I did write about a gay
man dying of AIDS, "Dance of the Cherry Blossom," it might have been provoked by somebody I knew. A lot of the poems that I write are provoked by either something—somebody that I actually knew—or somebody that I have
heard fleetingly on a bus, some overheard piece of conversation. But at any rate,
it's always people, and voices of people, that inspire me to write what I write. I
am much more influenced by people's voices than I am by, say, landscapes or art
or paintings or music, although music is probably the next thing to voices on
my little list of key influences. But I'm really interested in trying to capture the
human voice at a moment of time that is heightened for them in some way, that
is tense and therefore dramatic, because the drama of people's lives interests me
just as much as their voices, the stories that they tell. So it's like capturing somebody at a moment in time, and in capturing them at that moment in time I hope
to kind of capture myself too, some fear, some paranoia, some joy, whatever. But
I always feel as if I find out something about myself too. So I don't just think,
"Oh I'm creating this person—they're totally separate," at all. They just become
part of this multiplicity I was talking about earlier.

Q: Speaking of that multiplicity, one of the things that fascinates me in many of
the poems is in a poem in *Other Lovers*. "Tough," where you're climbing through
a window, and then your little child comes in and you read aloud from a story,
and it ends up with "I'm right inside your head." Is this multiplicity sometimes
experienced as internal voices, different voices that are not necessarily a single
voice in control?

A: I think actually that I like to explore different kinds of voices depending on
their mental states, if you like. So the voice that says in that poem, "I'm right inside your head," is a voice that is kind of unstable, mentally unstable at that time
and feels as if it has the power to get right inside of people's heads, those people

that are also vulnerable to those kind of mental states of depression or insecurity. But as well as exploring voices, I like to try and explore people, people at different kinds of times in their lives when they will be more or less certain of their own identity, more or less certain of themselves. You have times when people just don't know who they are and feel really quite frightened of that, you know, often when somebody has just died. I'm writing a novel at the moment that has a woman in it whose partner has just died, and that forces her to question her own identity and her whole life in fact. And I think that often at different moments in people's lives they ask themselves very fresh and almost naive, almost absurd, questions all over again, like you've suddenly met yourself again, that you've just got married to yourself, and I think that happens, again and again, if you're open to change.

Q: I guess what I was fascinated by is how you would define multiplicity and fluidity when you're talking about that sense of identity as multiple, fluid, changing. I wonder if you could talk a bit about how you would define those terms.

A: Well, multiplicity is knowing that you can be, that your identity can be, complex, and that you can contain more than one self. I mean I'm not talking about schizophrenia or having different voices. But, for instance, in *The Adoption Papers*, there are three voices; there's the two mothers and there's the daughter. When I was writing *The Adoption Papers*, I found it much easier to write the voices of the two mothers than I did the daughter. The daughter's voice I had real trouble writing. Now the daughter's voice is the voice that is the most closely linked to my experience. I am adopted and was brought up in Scotland, yet I found her very difficult to write. It was as if, when I was writing those voices in that book, that I contained the voices of those two mothers, that within me were both those mothers, and the voices just came very easily, flowing out of me, but the voice that you would expect to be the autobiographical voice, the "real" voice, didn't so much. And I think that that is a strange thing, but that can often happen. When we write, we tap into other selves; we tap into our self at different levels of the conscious mind and the subconscious mind. And I do believe that we do use our subconscious mind to write poetry. I know a lot of people have differences, opinions, but I do believe that, just like dreams I suppose. And so I think that if you write in that way, you will find as you're writing that it is almost as if your self has got many layers, and every person has different layers. Writing is, effectively, scraping the top layer off and going straight to the layer underneath, writing about that and then going to the layer underneath. That process, I suppose, I would describe as multiplicity, finding a way to write about the other selves that we already contain. In a sense, I am my adopted mother, I am my birth mother, I am both these women, and am also myself, and I am also my son. It's like that Sweet Honey in the Rock song; it's just a kind of a sense of continuity, of linking yourself up with the other people that are out-side you, but also the people that are inside you, and I think that we do that. Some people have a great sense of their own past, feel that their grandmother or their great-great-grandmother, or people they never met are part of them be-cause they've heard stories about them and because they've got their eyes, their nose, or whatever, and I suppose I've created for myself that sense of identity from not having those things genetically, but from finding other ways to get those things. So in *The Adoption Papers* the mother says, "Closer than blood. / Thicker than water. Me and my daughter," which is to say you don't need ge-netics or biology to keep close in that very spiritual way in which you can in-habit each other's selves, but you can do it in lots of different ways.

Q: It's interesting that the daughter, the one you say would be most autobio-graphical, speaks broad Glasgow in the opening when she's little, and then it be-comes much more smoothed out. In your own speech I can hear the Glaswe-gian underlying the sort of educated Scots.[4] Is there a reason why you write what you do? On the page it is English, but when I hear your voice, even if only a few words are Scots, like "blether,"[5] "ritual blether," I'm hearing a distinctly Scottish voice, rhythm, pattern, things like that. Is there a reason why you don't phonet-ically transcribe a Glaswegian sound?

A: Is there a reason? What's the question?

Q: I'm thinking of the difference between what you do and someone like Tom Leonard.[6]

A: I suppose that's a conscious choice. I don't think there's anyone who writes quite like Tom Leonard. I think Tom Leonard is Tom Leonard, and I think he is wonderful, and I love the way he writes. I couldn't write in that way. For a start, I don't actually speak that broad Glaswegian. I suppose, for a second, I want my work to be accessible to people who are not Glaswegian, and I want the speech patterns to be Glaswegian, so my speech patterns and rhythms and emphasis are very Glaswegian. So anybody that knows that would recognize that, in terms of the word orders, the structures, the syntax, and the emphasis and the repetition, and the use of repetition; all these things tell you that the work is very Scottish. And some language, as you say, some words do as well. But I don't want that work to be so densely Scottish, so densely packed with Scottish language and writing, that it kind of traps me in, because I think that by being very, very per-sonal, you can also be universal as long as you can find a way to make the lan-guage work for you in terms of how you choose to write. And so lots of Scottish writers these days write in exactly the way that Tom Leonard or Jim Kelman writes, and I think it's great to do that, but I don't feel completely comfortable with writing in that way. Perhaps because I'm Black. And perhaps because, what-ever. But that way of writing just doesn't come naturally to me in the same way.

But I do want to convey a sense of being Scottish. I do want that to be obvious as well in the rhythms.

Q: I can feel the rhythms, but I see a difference between an ordinary audience who can read this and a coterie audience who would pick up the codes, the language play, that sort of thing. A colleague of mine, for example, said this is sentimental, and there is no way a Glaswegian would hear sentimentality. I'm wondering if, to a certain extent, flattening out on the page only could lose the qualities of emotion, rhythm, or whatever that is there.

A: I don't think of it as flattening it out, and I don't think of it as being sentimental either. I wanted the voices to be quite plain so they weren't too overloaded or too invested with things. I agree with Toni Morrison when she said about her characters that she likes creating her characters, but she doesn't quite finish them off. She likes to leave certain things open so the reader can come with their sexuality, their identity, their dreams and put themselves in there. And I remember thinking of that quite a lot when she said that and thinking the best thing anybody could say to you when you are a writer is to read something, to identify with it themselves, and to have put themselves in there. Because that's when books really matter, when you are reading them yourself, when you put yourself in there and literally the book becomes part of your experience. It is your life. I suppose my aim is to try and do that.

Q: I am interested in the fact that you have said, I think on *The Usual Suspects* or maybe in one of your interviews, that you do see what you're doing as political, as a political choice. I'd like to hear you talk about that. Do you regard your work as experimental? And if so, how? And is that related to your political conception of what you're doing?

A: I suppose I think it's not too good—for myself anyway as a writer, and I don't think it's too good for many others either—to be too self-conscious about what they're actually doing when they write. Because I think then that leads to parodying yourself or getting stuck in a rut and finding a style that works and writing the same sort of style over and over again, and I think it becomes very deeply boring. So initially, when I wrote *The Adoption Papers*, which was my first book, I did think of myself as being experimental because I wanted to try and write a kind of novel in poems, and I wanted to write a narrative book; I wanted to arrange it into chapters, and I wanted the three voices to counterpoint and intermingle and upset each other and disturb each other. I wanted one voice to give you more sense of the other and all sorts of different echoes. I did think of that as being quite experimental. But basically, if you're sensible as a writer, you know that there's very little you can do that is completely new. So I suppose what interests me about being experimental, not in a language, is theme. Although there are basically themes that cannot be made different—either love, death, illness, whatever—I think that there are certain voices that we haven't heard much from in our culture due to the dominant cultures. And so that when you write about a Black Scottish woman, you are automatically being political in some way, just because that identity is coming to the fore and you're writing about it, almost irrespective of what you say. Because you're questioning and challenging people's assumptions of what they think of as Black and what they think of as Scottish right away. So I do think of myself as being experimental and challenging in themes. And the themes I write about are largely the same, whether I'm writing about being Black and Scottish, or whether I'm writing about the blues. I'm interested in taking different things from Black culture, different Black cultures around the world, and linking them up to my own identity. In the poems that I've written about Bessie Smith, I make her mine. So the language of the blues and the language in Scotland sort of fuse so you have a mixture, a sort of Celtic blues I suppose you might call it. I'm trying to copy some of the rhythms of the blues, but change them too, and echo some of the rhythms of Scottish folk songs, but change them. So what you end up with is an experiment I suppose, something new or something different: a Black voice that is Scottish and Blue. And that's part of a thematic exploration but also an exploration in style and form that interests me a lot in trying to make language somehow correlate with my own experience, somehow echo my experience in the language itself.

Q: Liz Lochhead said that everybody has many voices and multiple selves but Scots are aware of it; that's the difference,[7] because they're Scottish and they've had to have that division. So there's something in being Scottish that means English, Scottish, Highland, Lowland—all those things. So you've added on other layers, being also Black, being also adopted. Do you think that being adopted has highlighted that for you in a way that those other divisions don't seem to do?

A: Well, it seems to me that those other divisions are perfectly ordinary; that is just part of what it is, being Scottish. Most Scottish people are aware of how England has treated them and how they've suffered like the Irish at the hands of the English and how the English have so many stereotypes of Scottish people. Scottish people, when they move about the world, or come down to England in particular, they will experience that. "Oh, you're from Glasgow"; "Oh Jimmy this" and "Oh Jimmy that,"[8] and all this cajoling and joking that the English do about the Scottish all the time. I think that that's quite a common experience. It is outside in that way, but it's outside in a huge majority, which means along with every other Scottish person. What interests me particularly is the way in which you can be in a society that is cordoned off and oppressed but also be oppressed within that society, or divided within that or not belong to the common group in exactly the same way. I do think that sense of being outside with being inside Scotland—with being very proud of the country and very proud of being Scottish, and also being outside in terms of receiving a lot of racism from other Scottish people—is what fuels my sense of how and what I write. Definitely. It definitely has affected me. I think it's good. I'm not unhappy that any of the things that happened to me have happened. I'm very glad, for instance, that I was adopted. I wouldn't swap my own experience for any other experience. It just makes me more aware of things in a different way.

Jackie Kay's Inventions of Self

"Difference," for the most part, has been contained in categories of race, class, gender, ethnicity, sexuality. Adoption remains outside our seemingly wide and potentially permeable boundaries. Yet for Jackie Kay it is the most fundamental form of difference, a difference "of fate, I suppose, that you could have been somebody else, that you could have led a completely different life." Adoption, both in her own experience and in her conceptualizations of identity and voice, provides a different—and distinct—identity. But unlike traditionally normalizing views of identity construction, in which "difference" is problem or stigma, Kay's "difference" is possibility. For her, adoption can allow "great richness, . . . as Walt Whitman famously put it: "you say I contradict myself? / Very well, I contradict myself, / (I am large, I contain multitudes.)" Adoption means that "the possibilities for the adopted person to constantly re-invent themselves are endless." To study Kay's work is to explore relations of adoption, identity, language, and voice. More particularly, it is to study poetic voices that move outside binaries of self and other to speak as "different" forms of identity, forms in which cultures, languages, and experiences of many and other may coexist, forms of "invention" that challenge both the lyric "I" and the externalized dramatic character. The "I" who speaks may be neither the lyric "I" of the author speaking as a traditional unitary self nor the dramatic "I" of the author's fictional constructions. Rather, it may be both self and other, a voicing of internal multiplicity. To read Kay's poems is to encounter the voices she calls "layers." These "inventions" Kay attributes to the richness of adoption.

What distinguishes the difference of adoption from other forms of difference is, first, its individualized form—an experience that, unlike blackness or Scottishness or homosexuality, is not shared with others. And, second, adoption creates an internal differentiation, an awareness of all the people one theoretically might have been: "the self is multitudes. The self is complex and often contradictory."

Kay's experiments with identity and voice draw from this understanding of identity as fluid and multiple. In writing her first book, *The Adoption Papers,*

Kay saw herself as experimenting primarily with theme, introducing previously unused or marginalized voices and stories:

[S]o that when you write about a Black Scottish woman, you are automatically being political in some way, just because that identity is coming to the fore and you're writing about it, almost irrespective of what you say. Because you're questioning and challenging people's assumptions of what they think of as Black and what they think of as Scottish right away.

While the experimentation Kay calls thematic is the voicing of alternative identities, voices outside dominant culture, she creates not simply many voices, an array of dramatis personae, but rather complex coexistences of voice, voices both herself and other, voices that express the complex "layering" of self that adoption helps her acknowledge and engage. In "The Adoption Papers" itself, she initiates these poetic experiments in an autobiographical narrative form, representing adoption as theme through the three voices of the adoptee, the birth mother, and the adoptive mother. Yet in the later poems, both in "Severe Gale 8" (the second section of the book *The Adoption Papers*) as well as in *Other Lovers* and in *Off Colour*, the distinctive uses of identity and voice developed in her direct treatment of adoption are extended to a greater range and more experimental practices. My interest here is less in the representation of adoption itself than in the experimentation made possible—in Kay's perspective—by the fluidity it allows. Specifically, it becomes a fusion of self-expression and dramatization, a set of language codes that produce what is new and different and challenging of convention: what she calls "a Black voice that is Scottish and Blue."

The specific form of Jackie Kay's adoptive experience frames her choices of theme in ways she has frequently described. The child of a Nigerian father and Highland Scots mother, she was adopted at birth by a white, working-class, communist Glasgow couple. She spent her school years speaking broad Glaswegian (which in Scotland is generally perceived as a low-class or denigrated speech) and never seeing another black face, except for pictures, including one of Angela Davis and the cover of a Bessie Smith album. She began writing as a teenager to "create some images for myself"[9] and addressed one of her first poems to Audre Lorde because she had not known there was another Black lesbian in the world. Yet her relation with her adoptive mother was apparently close, and she grew up to speak in a distinctively Scots voice and to experience herself as Scottish. Though she *looks* like Angela Davis or Audre Lorde or Bessie Smith, she *sounds* like her Glaswegian adoptive mother even through layers of education. Her identity formation is thus complicated—like that of many adoptees—by a sense of physical and cultural "difference" from the "family" who raised her. In Davis, Lorde, and Bessie Smith she found surrogate mother figures to form a Black identity, thus appropriating a connection with another, "different," self she felt herself to be, while retaining the deeply "Scottish" cultural identity she also inherited and experienced. She has described this sense of discovered identity in her book on Bessie Smith: "In my street," she writes, "and in the neighbouring streets to Brackenbrae Avenue, I never saw another black person."[10] And when she imagined Bessie's life, it seemed "inextricably linked with her colour":

> I could not separate them. I could not separate myself. I am the same colour as she is, I thought to myself, electrified. I am the same colour as Bessie Smith. I am not the same colour as my mother, my father, my grandmother, my grandfather, my friends, my doctor, my dentist, my butcher, my teacher, my headmaster, my next door neighbour, my aunt, my uncle, my mother's friends, my father's friends. The shock of not being like everyone else; the shock of my own reflection came with the Blues. My own face in the mirror was not the face I had in my head.[11]

Studies show a sense of being not only different but confused and "out of place" to be common in adoptees, and it can be explicitly represented in racial or ethnic difference.[12] The common need to search for birth origins, then, involves engaging profound cultural contradictions. In Kay's case this demands addressing issues of language central to identity. The languages of Scotland and of American Black speech are both marginalized and dismissed. Yet for Kay they are inseparable from her multiple layers of identity and thus inseparable from the issue of adoption. It is the voices of her mothers (the birthmother's "soft Highland" voice, the adoptive mother's Glaswegian) and of her desired Black ancestral voices in Bessie Smith's songs that coalesce as the "different" self she does know, not a "false" self, as much literature of adoption assumes, but a new and different one. In her most recent book of poems, *Off Colour*, she includes voices from Africa, including imagined ancestors.

It is, of course, true that all of us could have been someone totally different.[13] But precisely because the upbringing and physical inheritance of non-adoptees are seen or assumed to be continuous, they can feel a sense of knowing their own identity since it is continually mirrored back to them in the faces of relatives and behaviors of friends and neighbors. For the adoptee there are no comparable mirrors. And found mirrors may have to be taken from outside the familial and community circle. This gap between self and mirror sets up the sense of "true" and "false" selves or identities. Voice, like body, can mirror: one hears one's mother or father in one's own intonations, vocabulary, rhythms, even laughter. For Kay, voice and body mirror back quite different selves: a black face, a Scottish voice. Music and song, blues and ballads, are for her interconnected oral traditions. This need to join Black and Scottish and blues goes beyond the nonadoptee's potential others; it is, rather, a direct awareness of the other selves one might have lived out and, in fact, does participate in. The distinction is not so much in multiplicity itself as in awareness of and access to that multiplicity or fluidity of identity so easily closed off by the apparent continuities of life.

One way of understanding this complex sense of identity is through current reconceptualizations of the subject. Traditionally framed, "identity," whether individual or national, presumes a relatively fixed and continuous core "self." Social identities, whether based in race, nationality, sexuality, gender, or any other definable category, are predicated of a unitary subject, the "I" who speaks, who may grow and change in limited ways but is nonetheless singular and in some recognizable way "the same." A Black person is black; a gay person is gay; a woman is a woman. Behavior that does not remain within predictable borders is either acting (the creation of personae) or pathological (the fragmentation of what is "normally" one). This traditional unitary "I" who speaks or ostensibly speaks in texts has been for some time under pressure; yet in reconceptualizing this "I," it is not sufficient to displace the "self" entirely in favor of symbolic systems that construct the subject. If we take seriously Jackie Kay's sense of more fluid, multiple identities, we need alternative explanations of the notion of an "I," one that goes beyond recognition of the many socially constructed roles or identities we all assume to acknowledge genuine multiplicity or "layers" of "self."[14]

These "layers" allow for a complex creativity distinct from "self-expression," on the one hand, or simply participation in given discourses, on the other. Like the notion of "I," the relation of subject and text must be reconfigured. A model I find helpful is the concept of a "discursive subject," both because it moves outside the binary of a unitary self or a pathologically fragmented self, and because it acknowledges the inseparability of language and identity. In the case of Jackie Kay, the discourses of American Black culture and of Scotland are inseparable from her own awareness of a voice that is "Scottish and Blue." In "Subjects and Agents: The Question for Feminism," Susan Hekman argues for a "discursive subject both constructing and constructed" that "does not entail reference to a prediscursive 'I' but, instead, entails that subjects find agency within the discursive spaces open to them in their particular historical period."[15] That is, there is no pregiven subject who is essentially Black or Scottish or gay, but neither is there simply a site constituted by social institutions and discursive forces. "Jackie Kay" is thus neither Black in some racially essential way, nor constructed as a Scot despite her skin, nor constructed as both simply by the forces of ballads and blues. Rather, "she" is the result of choices from among those possibilities. "The creativity involved in establishing subjectivity is analogous to the creativity involved in the speaking of a language," Hekman argues. "Language speakers are bound by their language in their efforts to create unique sentences. Yet they do so in distinct and sometimes awesome ways. The creation of subjectivity is much the same: it is bounded by given discourses, but it can and does result in unique creations."[16]

I wish to push this conceptualization somewhat further to address the nature of subjects who both construct and are constructed as plural and neither integrated into a unity nor broken off from it but rather functioning as a coalition, let us say, or a conversation, what Trinh T. Minh-ha calls "multiple presence," where "A critical difference from myself means that I am not i, am within and without i."[17] Like Minh-ha, Kay describes her experience in such terms and her poetry presents such forms of voice and "multiple presence."[18] Her multiple and shifting discourses are more aptly defined by Hekman's model of the discursive subject and by "multiple presence" than by any version of earlier binaries. The distinctiveness of Kay's use of voice is partly the use of adoption as a theme, in her sense of telling an adoptee's tale, being experimental by virtue of foregrounding suppressed identities. But while her awareness of the infrequency of adoption as theme and her multiple-voice representation in *The Adoption Papers* is key to her sense of being "challenging" as well as political, her modes of voice extend far beyond those immediately personal themes. Specifically, she uses the multiple "different" form of identity she attributes to adoption to challenge dominant culture through the fusion of Black and Scottish and Blue. The poems after "The Adoption Papers," while not about adoption, take their forms of voice from the constant re-invention adoption enables.

In a discussion of Kay's reception and the relative popularity of "The Adoption Papers" over "Severe Gale 8," Gabriele Griffin states that "In terms of its content, the first section of *The Adoption Papers* [the title poem] can (which does not mean, 'should,') be read in terms of a politics infused with the back-to-basics ideology: . . . overweening desire for maternity . . . punishment of sex outside of marriage . . ." and the adopted child's "difficulties in coming to terms with her status as adopted."[19] Griffin argues, however, that if one recognizes the continuity of desire from "The Adoption Papers" to "Severe Gale 8," one must acknowledge the subversive exposure and defamiliarization of "what is 'natural'" in the first as well as the second section. But though I would agree that the content "challenges," in Kay's words, in both sections, the continuity, I think, is more significant than a general sense of critiquing normalization.

On *The Usual Suspects*, a BBC interview program,[20] Jackie Kay was questioned about her relation to her characters. "When you encounter a Jackie Kay poem," the interviewer noted, "you do not have a consistent voice; you may encounter someone else." Kay responded that she wanted to create someone else, someone she might not agree with, who might even appall her. But she hoped a reader or listener would also hear something of her poetic voice in it. She is thus speaking as another and as herself in layers of voice not wholly distinct but also not the same. This structuring of difference follows the model she defines (in the interview presented in this essay) for adoption:

There is no point in denying that it is different to grow up knowing that your mother is not actually your mother, and that your father is not actually your father, but nonetheless they are your mother and father. Those seeming opposites . . . are just at the heart of what it means to be adopted; you have to contain both those supposed opposites together.

Kay conceptualizes and writes her way into a form of voice that enacts Minh-ha's "critical difference from myself." Kay's characters are not Kay but they are also not personae, not masks or deliberate fictional selves; they explore experience that is in a sense hers or what might have been hers or what she can imagine as hers in some form, and at the same time they are someone else with whom she might not agree. The coexistence of these voices—the I, not I, or lyric/dramatic, forms Kay's distinctive and experimental language uses. Initiated in "The Adoption Papers" as the three-voiced mother-mother-daughter, the fusion of I/other in voice is extended to tell stories of many kinds of "different" identities.

To be Black and Scottish is a contradiction by traditional definitions; "Scottish" is constructed as white. But to be Scottish in "Britain" is already to be marginalized. The two key sources of identity Kay takes from her "parents," birth parents and adoptive parents, are thus already "different," outside the "norm." Moreover, the speech of both American Blacks and Scots is already denigrated discourse. The language of Glasgow, moreover, is denigrated in Scotland as is the language of the blues in America; and both are linked to stories of struggle and sorrow. Kay's "multitudes" of self are thus drawn from sources presumed to be essentially different from each other and socially marginal in themselves. To be Scottish is, significantly, to be already aware of multiple identities and voices because every Scot is bilingual, trained in school to speak English, yet retaining Scots or Gaelic in varying degrees. They are, moreover, both "British," closely linked to England, and distinctly and self-consciously "Scottish." For Jackie Kay, then, being Scottish already marks her as "different," a difference compounded by her non-Scottish color and extended by adoption. Her notion of thematic and linguistic experimentation, of challenging dominant cultures, is in her own terms "fueled" by the awareness of being different and by the different forms of awareness adoption allows or facilitates. In "The Adoption Papers" the identity "coming to the fore" to question and challenge people's assumptions is the identity of adoption itself. But the linguistic effects of multiple voicing as self and other, overlapping, and fusing, are carried over to poems not directly about Kay herself or adoption.

In "The Adoption Papers," for example, Kay represents the birth mother she has never met as "not as real" as, "more ethereal" than the adoptive mother, and cues the reader to her "soft Highland voice," a sound very different from the adoptive mother's frank and earthy broad Glaswegian. And yet the birth mother is both an imaginative construction of the adopted child and a real person inaccessible but known to be there. In one section that gap or opposition of real and unreal is foregrounded as theme:

> She's lying in bed; I wake her up
> A pinch on her cheek is enough,
> Then I make her think of me for hours.
> The best thing I can steal is sleep.
> I get right under the duvet and murmur
> *You'll never really know your mother.*
> I know who she thinks I am—she's made a blunder.[21]

In this passage the voice would be spoken in Highland accent, but when Kay reads, you also hear her own very distinct Scots sound with rhythms of Glaswegian. In oral presentation the overlapping sounds emerge most distinctly, the layering of another's voice murmuring inside one's head.

In another section, the adoptive mother contemplates the physical connectedness she feels with her child and hears in voice itself:

> I listened to hear her talk,
> and when she did I heard my voice under hers
> and now some of her mannerisms crack me up (23)

When Kay reads, you hear one voice under another. And like voices, images overlap and layer. The adopted child, for example, imagines seeing "mannerisms" in her birth mother if she could meet her:

> Once would be enough,
> just to listen to her voice
> watch the way she moves her hands
> when she talks. (30)

As the child thinks, "I want to know my blood," the adoptive mother thinks, "Closer than blood. / Thicker than water. Me and my daughter," and the birth mother thinks, "Does she imagine me this way? / . . . Does she talk broad Glasgow?" They enter and reenter one another's mind and voice, sound, speech, body even.

"The Adoption Papers" thus establishes—in theme and in oral presentation—a form of character who is both self and other, as Kay explores the "different" awareness of identity as unfixed, potentially quite other than it is. The "subject" of these poems is neither any individual "Kay" nor a set of dramatic characters but the enacting of multiple subjectivity in Hekman's terms: the piecing together of "distinctive combinations, that is, individual subjectivities, from the discursive mix available to them." Such subjectivities are not fixed or final:

> The subject that emerges from this perspective is a heterogeneous subject. It is a subject that is a product of the fluctuating, changing, and often conflictual historical and social influences that impinge on it. This subject is not without an identity, but identity is no longer conceived in even quasi-essentialist terms.[22]

What this heterogeneous subjectivity allows Kay is a structure of identity incorporating and affirming that "difference" adoption does not create but makes apparent—the others within whom one includes or might have been or could be.

The apparently greater experimentation of poems in "Severe Gale 8," in *Other Lovers*, and (more recently) in *Off Colour* is less a thematic shift to more radical content than an extension and complex working out of the structures of voice and identity initiated in "The Adoption Papers." The layering and fusing of identity that seem more easily understandable in mother-daughter relations appear in characters who are someone else, someone she might not agree with, who might even appall her.

In the later work Kay engages in a process of containing, exploring, releasing, participating in the multitudes that constitute and reconstitute any "identity," a process of enacting multiplicity. By "enact" I wish to suggest that process of constant "re-invention" as it becomes poetic voice. While Kay "enacts" voices across an increasingly broad range, I wish to clarify this point by focusing briefly on the fusion she calls "a Black voice that is Scottish and Blue," the contradictions of her adoptive "difference."

Black writers in "Britain,"[23] as in America, are inevitably constructing and constructed by both dominant and marginal languages, discourses, cultures. In the case of Jackie Kay, overlapping layers of Scots dialects and sounds, English, blues rhythms, coded vocabularies, and pronunciations provide the discursive mixes for shifting and complex voices of "I." Because for Kay to "be" Black and Scottish and Blue and yet to be always confronted by assumptions that these are mutually exclusive or contradictory is to speak *as* an "I" for whom there are no or few mirrors, no group identity to "speak for," no individual identity that can be presumed as coherent and "real." Her poetry is, moreover, more polyphonic than print can convey because language that is voiced takes on differentiation not available to print, just as the opposite is true; what appears "English" on the page, if spoken in a Glaswegian voice, becomes something quite different, and a poem performed in specific tones and rhythms is not the same as a poem silently read. It matters that Kay's contradictory sources in Scottish and Black culture both retain powerful oral traditions.

Both pronunciation and rhythm, for example, join with the emotional resonance of blues when she writes of and to Bessie Smith in "The Red Graveyard":

> Why do I remember the blues?
> I am five or six or seven in the back garden;
> The window is wide open;
> her voice is slow motion through the heavy summer air.
> Jelly roll. Kitchen man. Sausage roll. Frying pan.
> Inside the house where I used to be myself,
> her voice claims the rooms. In the best room even,
> Something has changed the shape of my silence.
> Why do I remember her voice and not my own mother's?
> Why do I remember the blues?

Kay reads these lines in an educated, Scots-inflected English with the distinct accent of her adoptive mother's Glasgow voice, yet she describes the poem also as having an echo of a twelve-bar beat, an echo she enhances on the framing lines:

> There are some stones that open in the night like flowers
> Down in the red graveyard where Bessie haunts her lovers.
> There are stones that shake and weep in the heart of night
> Down in the red graveyard where Bessie haunts her lovers.[24]

Rhythm, sounds, voices, double meanings are both persistently used as codes in Kay's work and thematized as ways of involving memory or desire or forms of experience. In the forty poems of *Other Lovers*, her second collection, nineteen include the word "voice." Most of the others refer to speech or sound or to "tongue,"—"our special tongue," "can't tell what. Not even in our tongue." Her sense of doubled or multiplied voice is central to her "obsession" with identity and with inter-enactments of self and other: "So it's like capturing somebody at a moment in time, and in capturing them at that moment in time I hope to kind of capture myself too, some fear, some paranoia, some joy, whatever. But I always feel as if I find out something about myself too." In "The Red Graveyard," many interlinked voices become part of the multiplicity that comprises "Jackie Kay": her own as a child, her own as an adult poet, Bessie Smith's on record in "Kay's" childhood and in adult memory, her father's and her "own mother's," who seems here to be her adoptive mother because she too is evoked: "My mother's voice. What was it like? / A flat stone for skitting. An old rock" (*Other*

Lovers, 13). The concrete specificity of her sounds and echoes of ballad stanza and "The Cherry Tree Carol" link her voice with the "mother" who raised her. In this poem, Black, Scottish, and blues conjoin, and two denigrated discourses—Black blues of the American 1920s and broad Glasgow speech of the 1960s—are both represented primarily in "Standard" English words but in resistance to its rhythms, meanings, assumptions: Scots words, ballad echoes, cues to voices of Bessie Smith and Kay's adoptive parents, to speech rhythms of blues and ballad stanza, and to the lives of "difference" claiming a space for sound—all disrupt any simplistic reading of a lyric of memory or a melange of discrete characters. As "part of this multiplicity," they serve as entrances to "other," "different," but at another level internally "known" lives whose stories it is both a challenge to dominant assumptions and a political choice to tell.

Kay has described singing blues at twelve and thinking a sausage roll was the kind cooked with puff pastry, then learning how the language was full of codes for all kinds of suppressed life: bisexuality, drugs, raunchy sex, violence, wanting to murder someone. The women blues singers, she says, could talk about anything; there was no self-censorship. They talked in the doubled language of their dual identities and dual audiences; to a coterie audience who shared the code word of "jelly roll" as vagina and "kitchen man" as a backdoor lover, one who came in through the kitchen, and to a broader, straight, white audience who thought Bessie Smith's "Kitchen Man" was a song about food. Reading it in the voice of her working-class, communist, white, adoptive parents who taught her "not how to be Black but how not to be grateful,"[25] Kay multiplies potentialities of identity and experience as a Glasgow Scot with black skin, running her hands over the picture of Bessie Smith's face, "her black face / her magnificent black face" (*Other Lovers,* 13).

Who then is the "I" of this poem who shifts ages, voices, cultures, and rhythms and layers Bessie Smith's voice over her mother's voice over "her" current voice in the place where "I" "used to be myself"? Neither here (when the speaker is at least ostensibly Kay) nor in any Kay poem (and many or most are in other voices) is there a fixed or stable unified consciousness. But neither is there simply a construction site. Rather, there is an interplay of discourses, born into, constructed by, chosen as identification, and experienced as layers. Susan Hekman's model of the "discursive subject" in which agency is a product of discourse comparable to language formation more aptly defines Kay's use of multiple and shifting discourses than any version of earlier binaries. But more specifically to her formation of multiple presence or layered "I" in poetry, it defines a model for subjectivity and identity that can accommodate the individual and distinctive "difference" and "re-invention" Kay predicates of adoption.

The courage Kay sees in blues singers, courage to move into all of life, to tell any story, may well demand or at least more often derive from the awareness institutionalized marginalization can provide—the awareness of how one's mirrors fail. American Blacks know it as a "real" and "unreal" sense of being American, citizen, equal. Scots know it as a thought process of trained English speech with an emotional life in another language denied as full or rich speech. But for Kay, the adoptee knows it in a special way, a sustained awareness that the multiple selves one (any/one) may or could or might be are also what one is. Her characters are palimpsests, not as dramatis personae overlaying some "true" self but as layers and layers of the personae that are Kay and that are also others. Among the most significant of these layers and discourses in Kay's history are Scots, Black, Blue, gay, Glaswegian, woman, Highland, Lowland, mother, daughter, lover, poet. But the status of adoptee has meant for her an acute and complex awareness of all co-existing and of all interacting with external selves that resonate within, enter in, become or realize themselves within.

NOTES

1. On September 11, 1997, Scotland—in a historic election—voted for a separate parliament in Edinburgh that assumed many powers previously in the British Parliament in London. In a separate question they voted to grant the Scottish Parliament tax-varying powers. This devolution altered the governmental relations of Scotland and England after nearly three centuries of joint rule. The Act and Treaty of Union took place in 1707.

2. Hugh MacDiarmid was a founding member of the Scottish Nationalist Party, and his poetry was, in part, an instrument for Scottish Nationalism.

3. *The Usual Suspects* is a BBC radio talk show. Jackie Kay was interviewed on the show on September 6, 1996.

4. Scots is a sister language of English that developed from Middle Scots and, earlier, from Northumbrian, the northern version of Anglo-Saxon. In modern Scotland, Scots has many distinct regional dialects. Glaswegian is the dialect spoken in Glasgow. It is generally associated with the working-class urban population. Most Scots words are easily recognizable cognates of English, and most current Scots speech consists of English words in a Scots accent and Scots rhythm. There is, however, an extremely extensive Scots vocabulary not existing in English, including many words, like *blether*, that are in common usage. While Early Scots (1375–1450) and Middle Scots (1450–1700) constituted a national language of law, literature, and politics, the standing of Modern Scots as a distinct language is controversial. Nonetheless, it is increasingly a literary choice.

5. The noun *blether* means "nonsense, foolish talk." The verb *to blether* means "to talk nonsensically, to prattle, to jabber."

6. Tom Leonard and many other contemporary Scottish poets phonetically transcribe Scottish voices to reproduce the sound of Scots speech. They also use Scots words not found in English.

7. Liz Lochhead, interview by Emily B. Todd, *Verse* 8, no. 3, and 9, no. 1 (1992): 90, 93–94.

8. "Jimmy" is a derogatory generic name for a Scot, like "Paddy" for an Irishman.

9. Jackie Kay, "Jackie Kay," interview by Rebecca E. Wilson, in *Sleeping with Monsters*, ed. Gillean Somerville-Arjat and Rebecca E. Wilson (Dublin: Wolfhound, 1990), 121.

10. Jackie Kay, *Bessie Smith* (Bath, England: Absolute, 1997), 9.

11. Ibid., 13.

12. John C. Sonne, "The Psychological Consequences of Ignorance: Adoptees' Right to Know Who Their Biological Parents Are," *Journal for the Psychoanalysis of Culture and Society* 2, no. 1 (1997): 106.

13. I wish to thank Charles Altieri for suggestions that helped me define the following distinctions.

14. This conceptualization of difference is more radical than claims for multiple social identities; it posits internal multiplicity. In *Woman, Native, Other* (Bloomington: Indiana University Press, 1989), 94, Trinh T. Minh-ha defines a layered "self" in similar ways: "'I' is, therefore, not a unified subject, a fixed identity, or that solid mass covered with layers of superficialities one has gradually to peel off before one can see its true face. 'I' is itself *infinite layers.*"

15. Susan Hekman, "Subjects and Agents: The Question for Feminism," in *Provoking Agents,* ed. Judith Kegan Gardiner (Chicago: University of Illinois Press, 1995), 202.

16. Ibid., 204.

17. Trinh T. Minh-ha, *Woman, Native, Other,* 90.

18. In recent years, for example, the phenomenon of "multiple personality" has evoked much debate. That many people experience themselves as internally many is, I believe, unquestionable; the structure and meaning of that experience, and the many ways in which it may manifest itself, are far less certain. Neodissociation Theory, however, posits, in Ernest Hilgard's terms, "multiple cognitive processing systems or structures." According to Hilgard, "These systems interact, but occasionally, under special circumstances, may become somewhat isolated from each other. The concept of a totally unified consciousness is an attractive one, but does not hold up under examination" ("Neodissociation Theory," in *Dissociation,* ed. Steven Jay Lynn and Judith W. Rhue [New York: Guilford, 1994], 38). See also Erik Z. Woody and Kenneth Bowers, "A Frontal Assault on Dissociated Control," in ibid., 52–79. Woody and Bowers argue for the "assumption that some multiplicity of mental process is typical and normal." My point about Jackie Kay is that this "typical and normal" multiplicity is generally suppressed and denied, but that Kay's awareness and use of it are central to her poetics.

19. Gabriele Griffin, "The Adoption Papers," in *Kicking Daffodils: Twentieth-Century Women Poets,* ed. Vicki Bertram (Edinburgh: Edinburgh University Press, 1997), 171.

20. Jackie Kay, interview by Brian Morton, on *The Usual Suspects,* British Broadcasting Corporation, September 6, 1996.

21. Jackie Kay, *The Adoption Papers* (Newcastle upon Tyne: Bloodaxe, 1991), 29–30. All subsequent references to *The Adoption Papers* refer to this text.

22. Hekman, "Subjects and Agents," 201.

23. I place "Britain" in quotation marks because the term, in fact, is indistinguishable in most commentary from "England." The quite distinct cultures, discourses, and literary histories of Scotland, Wales, and Ireland (both the Republic of Ireland and Northern Ireland) are easily subsumed under analyses based on English works alone, and not, therefore, generally applicable. The specific effects of the many dialects of Scots, for example, and more significantly the choice to write in any of them create issues not present for writers of English.

24. Jackie Kay, *Other Lovers* (Newcastle upon Tyne: Bloodaxe, 1993), 13. All subsequent references to poems from *Other Lovers* refer to this text.

25. Kay, interview by Brian Morton.

Genealogy Revised in *Secrets and Lies*

Paris De Soto

For years, I imagined that my birth mother was either a fabulously wealthy and famous actress or a brilliant, eccentric archaeologist. I would look for her any-time I visited crowded, urban areas, such as San Francisco, Los Angeles, and New York. In dreams, we all have access to "a lost otherworld / A world we lose merely by waking up,"[1] and my "lost otherworld" would inevitably include my lost, repressed—or rather, suppressed—maternal origin. I remember a por-tion of a recurring dream I had when I was about eight: Kate Jackson (of the television show *Charlie's Angels*) was my "real" mom, who would drop by my adoptive parents' house unannounced and take me to the roller-skating rink she owned. There we would hang out with her best friends Cher and Farrah Fawcett, and she would allow me to eat unlimited quantities of chocolate ice cream. Sixteen years later, this little fantasy and the whole of my family ro-mance would be undermined by one Pauline Elmensdorp,[2] a secretary work-ing in the basement of a suburban hospital outside of Chicago, born and raised in Dubuque, Iowa.

As disappointing as it has been for me to replace fantasy with very quotid-ian reality, surely the reality check that Pauline Elmensdorp represents in my psychic life is preferable to relying on myths and flights of fancy for the answer to the question "Where did I come from?" Yet the rights of an adoptee to seek out and find her birth parents is at the center of one of the most heated debates in adoption policy, the sealed-records debate. In the United States, adoptees do not have that right unconditionally. Depending on the state, an adoptee may have very limited legal avenues by which to pursue her birth parents, and these limits have angered adoptees who want to search and birth parents who want to be found.

Protests against the sealed-records policy take place with increasing fre-quency on a variety of levels, from national radio and television programs to lo-cal adoption-related events. I encountered the latter last year: when I saw Mike Leigh's film *Secrets and Lies* at the State Theater in New Brunswick, I was ac-costed on my way out by adoptees' rights activists. They were distributing copies of a local newspaper editorial debating the pros and cons of "breaking the seal," that is, the seal to an adoptee's records. These activists insist that an adult adopted as a minor should have the right to access her original birth certificate and medical records, sealed at the time of her adoption. Many of them claim that an adoptee's knowledge of her biological and historical origins is "an integral part of [her] identity formation"[3] and that a lack of such knowledge results in "genealogical bewilderment."[4] Their opponents, however, argue that adoption records should remain sealed to protect the confidentiality of the birth parents and to prevent any disturbance to the adoptive parents once the adoption has been decreed.

Given my own experience as an adoptee who found her birth mother four years ago, it makes sense to assume that I would side with the activists. Of course, I support an adoptee's right to her own records, and I agree that knowledge of her origins may recover an integral part of her identity. From my perspective, I can tell you that an adoptee who finds her birth parents will be able to undo the notion that she is a "fake child," a "synthetic product" who simply "appeared one fine day without having been carried in any known womb."[5] Yet knowing her origins can provide the adoptee with neither a whole identity nor genealogical continuity. Although an adoptee's search for origins may start out as a search for identity, it becomes ultimately a search for narrative: an adoptee's discovery of her origins will enable her to account for certain key facts and events in her life of which she has been ignorant. Knowledge of her birth parents may fill a gap in an adoptee's biography, but it cannot fill a gap in her being.

Most adoptees' rights activists claim that an adoptee's access to her records will reveal not only the "truth" of her origins but also the "truth" of her identity; yet with these truth claims, they resort to fiction themselves. Although I do not agree with the essentialist rhetoric used by most adoptees' rights activists to justify an adoptee's search, I do not mean to suggest that sealed records should remain sealed. Instead, I want to examine some of the terms of the sealed-records debate so that we may acknowledge—as Leigh's film acknowledges—that both identity and genealogy are complicated processes, not stable entities, for adoptees and nonadoptees alike.

When I look at a history book and think of the imaginative effort it has taken to squeeze this oozing world between two boards and a typeset, I am astonished.
    —Jeanette Winterson, *Oranges Are Not the Only Fruit*

The current dominant adoption practices in the United States represent a conscious and legal attempt to change the identity of the adoptee by intervening in her individual history. Adoption is itself a fiction, a story, a narrative governed by a system of conventions that revises the adoptee's genealogy. The court creates a new parent-child relationship between the adoptive parents and the adoptee and simultaneously seals the records that document the transfer of the child from the birth to the adoptive family. To produce a child who "passes" as the "real" offspring of her adoptive parents, it is necessary to cover up the adoptee's birth history and to rewrite her past. The only birth certificate to which the adoptee has access is amended with the claim that she is the biological child of her adoptive parents.

To replace the adoptee's birth identity with her adopted identity involves much more than mere substitution. To rewrite the adoptee's narrative involves extensive bureaucratic efforts—"conventions" of the adoption narrative. The documentation required to produce the adoptee's amended birth certificate includes the relinquishment form that the birth mother must sign; the adoption application and the petition to adopt that the adoptive parents must fill out, along with their medical history and employment and marriage verification forms; and the acknowledgment of the relinquishment, the acknowledgment of the petition, and the decree of adoption that the court must endorse. The impetus behind these bureaucratic efforts to "squeeze this oozing world" of the adoptee's past into a single slip of paper is to "protect the interests" of the adopted child. Replacing the adoptee's original birth certificate with an amended one represents an effort to conceal the stigma of the adoptee's illegitimacy: no one can tell that the adoptee's beginnings are different from anyone else's.[6] By substituting the adoptive parents' names for the names of the birth parents, the amended birth certificate also conceals what is, in most cases, the adoptive parents' infertility. The adoptee's complicated and inauspicious beginnings are thus contained and concealed by a seemingly simple, straightforward piece of paper.

To perpetuate the fiction that the circumstances surrounding the adoptee's birth are no different from anyone else's, the adoption narrative tries to maintain the continuity of the genealogy of both the adopted child and the adoptive family. To maintain the continuity of the adoptive family, however, there has to be a break in the continuity of the adoptee's birth family. As Betty Jean Lifton observes, the adoptee must be "lifted out of her own genetic and historic family line to fix the break in the adoptive parents' narrative."[7] The "genetic and historic family line" in which the adoptee is born is effectively erased and replaced by a new family line. To say "erased" is problematic, however, because the information about the adoptee's birth identity is not really destroyed but sealed and legally restricted from view.

The bureaucratic efforts to conceal the illegitimacy of the child also conceal the "illegitimacy" of the adoption narrative itself. By covering up the "deviant" and "disturbing" narratives of unwed mothers, parentless children, and childless parents, the closed-record adoption system tries to ensure that the adoption narrative is the only narrative. Or, rather, the adoption narrative tries to deny its existence altogether, as proven by the practice of sealing the adoption records.

Once the legal transfer of parental rights from the birth parents to the adoptive parents is accomplished, the adoptive family "passes" as a biological family. Yet designing adoptive families to imitate biological families implies that adoption is, as Elizabeth Bartholet argues, "an inferior and not quite real form of family which can at best aspire to look like the real thing."[8] Because the records of an adoptee's genetic and historic family line are legally inaccessible, not eradicated, there does seem to be an implication that blood ties are too sacred to destroy, that we must only hide them. Although the closed-record adoption system seals the adoption records, the records themselves point to a bureaucratic effort to establish and maintain the adoptee's "real" genealogy, as opposed to the genealogy given to her by the adoption narrative.

Most adoptees' right activists justify an adoptee's efforts to seek out her "real" genealogy in terms of "the morality of truth and authenticity and the inviolability of the blood relation."[9] By prioritizing biology over the social elements of kinship, these activists perpetuate the fiction that the adoptive family is inherently inferior—a fiction that the closed-record adoption narrative perpetuates to justify its efforts to seal the adoptee's records. To argue that the bond of blood is sacred and cannot be severed by the "paper kinship"[10] created by adoption only makes the adoptee's origins more mystified.

Here I want to acknowledge the adoptees' rights activists who concede that while the biological connection is no better than the adoptive one, it should not be denied or suppressed either. To reject the notion of origins completely is also to reject the biological, bodily fact of motherhood (as opposed to paternity, the "legal fiction" that haunts Stephen Dedalus in James Joyce's *Ulysses*). We are all of woman born. Those of us who do not know which woman bore us may have a certain amount of ontological anxiety. Not to know one's origins may in some sense be liberating, but it is also unsettling. As Lifton puts it a bit too dramatically:

> Even though the family romance reveals the universal curiosity and fundamental quest for origins that everyone shares, it is not a *romance* for the adoptee. . . . While adoptees share the fantasy of royal blood along with everyone, they are also having negative fantasies—of whores, rapists, murderers.[11]

Once the child is told that she is adopted, the adoption narrative must compete with the family romance narrative, which gives the adoptee the opportunity to rewrite the narrative assigned to her by adoption. According to Freud, we all imagine ourselves as the offspring of lost, special parents and imagine the parents we now have as "mere impostors, the humble people who brought us up, not the true, royal parents to whom we really belong."[12] Yet because the adoption narrative revises the adoptee's origins, what is a "romance" for everyone else is in some sense "real" for the adoptee, as Lifton points out. The parents to whom the adopted child has been given are, in fact, "impostors" whose names have been grafted onto the adoptee's birth certificate.

So that she may replace the fantasy of her family romance with "reality" and repair her broken narrative, the adoptee may seek out and find her birth parents; at this point, the family romance narrative is superseded by the search-for-origins narrative. In my own case, finding my biological mother has confirmed my suspicions that I am Irish, has helped me to determine that I need to be watchful of breast cancer and adult-onset diabetes, and has given me a "blueprint" of how I will most likely age.

Although knowing that breast cancer runs in the family is important, the rest of what I have learned about my biological origins has been pretty incidental to my identity. Unlike most adoptees' rights activists, I disagree with the claim that "there is no other way an adoptee can acquire a true sense of identity than to have basic questions of origins answered."[13] Given the popular literature on adoption published in the last twenty years—*A Quest for Wholeness* is the subtitle of Betty Jean Lifton's newest book, *The Journey of the Adopted Self*—it is easy to see why an adoptee would believe that the discovery of her birth parents could make complete her own sense of self. But this wholeness is a myth: nonadoptees who have always known their origins can be considered no more complete and whole than adoptees. The sense of missing part of oneself is obviously not unique to adoptees. "Identity" is not a stable entity that can be discovered from one's origins; it is a process that can never be completed.

As I see it, an adoptee who opens up her sealed records, rather than feeling complete and whole, will more likely feel fragmented and confused. Faced with two sets of parents and two genealogies, the adoptee must reconcile the facts of her biological origin with her adoptive upbringing and "re-place"[14] herself in a new biography. She will also be forced to replace her various family romance fantasies with reality. In my experience, discovering that I was biologically related to the Elmensdorp clan from Dubuque, Iowa, when I had spent twenty-four years knowing only about the De Soto family from San Jose, California, was unsettling and, to be quite honest, disappointing. The names *De Soto* and *California* have a sense of romance that *Elmensdorp* and *Iowa* lack, at least by conventional standards of the culturally and geographically exotic.

I do not regret finding Pauline Elmensdorp, despite the disappointment and confusion that this discovery has entailed. We share a common race, class, and even facial features, but psychologically, we are worlds apart, so apart that we have not contacted one another for over four years. I realize now that I had replaced one fantasy, the fantasy that I had to be the offspring of actors and archaeologists, with another, the fantasy that finding my birth mother would reveal to me the "lost ingredient"—to borrow a bit from Anne Sexton—"that would keep [me] calm and prove [me] whole at last."[15] That finding my birth mother would entail a sense of loss seems contradictory, but I have been able to understand this experience in a more resourceful and meaningful way with the help of theory.

I have found Foucault's "Nietzsche, Genealogy, History" particularly useful in helping me to move beyond my somewhat simplistic and unproductive sense of disappointment, to accept a loss of romance in my own origins, and to de-mystify further the fiction of the "truth" and "inviolability" of origins that is per-petuated by most adoptees' rights rhetoric. What I find most striking in his es-say is the way a literal interpretation of Foucault's argument can be used to debunk the belief held by most activists that origins are lofty and sacred. He writes, "What is found at the historical beginning of things is not the inviolable identity of their origins; it is the dissension of other things. It is disparity."[16] Foucault borrows Nietzsche's revised definition of genealogy to emphasize that genealogy is a cultural convention, haphazardly constructed, not essentially de-termined. As Foucault points out, Nietzschean genealogy "does not pretend to go back in time to restore an unbroken continuity"; instead, it reveals to us that what "lie[s] at the root of what we know and what we are" is not Truth or Being but a series of "accidents," "minute deviations," "errors," "false appraisals," and "faulty calculations."[17]

Although I can understand the argument that only someone who has always known his origins (Foucault was not adopted) can play with the idea that ori-gins are neither sacred nor lofty, it seems that the situation of many adoptees, myself included, does indeed resonate with Foucault's theoretical observations. The genealogy of most, if not all, adoptees makes clear the "accidents" and "de-viations" to which Foucault refers. Most adoptees are only too aware that, as the result of unwanted and unplanned pregnancies, theirs is not an unbroken con-tinuity: their beginnings are the result of "errors," "false appraisals," and "faulty calculations," in response to which legal authorities have taken a branch of one family tree and grafted it onto another to establish a pretense of permanence.

Although Foucault may claim that at our roots is the "exteriority of acci-dents," not truth, and that these accidents may be without purpose, they are not without meaning. According to his argument, the search for origins does not entail the "erecting of foundations." Instead, "it disturbs what was previ-ously considered immobile; it fragments what was thought unified; it shows the heterogeneity of what was imagined consistent with itself."[18] Certainly, the adoptee's search disrupts notions of unified foundations, for her search will most likely uncover two sets of parents, a pile of paperwork, and the stigmas of illegitimacy and infertility.[19] Despite the "chosen baby" story that is told to the adoptee to make her feel special, not stigmatized, the adoptee realizes that her origin "lies at a place of inevitable loss,"[20] the loss of her biological parents. The "truth" that is revealed in Foucault's argument involves the understanding that although origins are privileged because we imagine them unspoiled, they are ac-tually awkward and accidental. This is, in part, the truth that is also revealed in Leigh's film.

Secrets and Lies begins with death, the death of the adoptive mother of a young, well-educated black woman from London named Hortense Cumberbatch

(Marianne Jean-Baptiste). As an optometrist, Hortense helps people to see more clearly, and clearer sight is what motivates her search for her birth parents. Discovering that her mother is a white, East End factory worker named Cynthia Purley (Brenda Blethyn) does not discourage Hortense from pursuing a reunion with this woman. The relationship between mother and daughter progresses from wariness to warmth. Cynthia decides to introduce Hortense to the rest of her family, including her brother, Maurice (Timothy Spall), and his wife, Monica (Phyllis Logan), at the birthday party of her second illegitimate daughter, Roxanne (Claire Rushbrook), whom she has raised alone. The already volatile mother-daughter, sister-brother mix and the unconvincing pretense that Hortense is Cynthia's factory mate produce moments of unbearable discomfort and tension—so unbearable that the secrets and lies eventually come spilling out.

It is no secret that Hortense was adopted; she has known that she was a special, "chosen" baby for years. That she is a Cumberbatch by birth is a lie that society has only too willingly accepted—indeed, the lie, the fiction that Hortense's adoption represents, is preferred over the truth that she is the result of an illegitimate affair between a white woman and a black man. The fiction of the adoption narrative in Hortense's case is so powerful that it exorcises not only illegitimacy but miscegenation. Until she goes to the social services agency to pick up her adoption records, the only birth certificate to which Hortense has access is amended with the claim that she is the biological child of the Cumberbatches, a black child "born of" black parents.

Although the film does not resist the search for origins, it does not sentimentalize or naturalize the bond between the adoptee and the birth mother either. Hortense's genealogy is obviously accidental, and it is so awkward that Cynthia throws up in the kitchen sink after Hortense's initial telephone call. Hortense's search puts Nietzschean genealogy into practice by showing how the search-for-origins narrative disrupts the coherency and continuity crafted by the adoption narrative. Hortense's search "fragments what was thought unified"—namely, her own seemingly stable identity as a black professional woman. Her search also "disturbs what was previously considered immobile"—namely, Cynthia's stagnant, unhappy life.

The notion that origins are lofty and inviolable is deflated throughout the film. Although a provision in Britain's Children Act of 1975 allows the adoptee to open her sealed adoption records, the law stipulates that she must first meet with a counselor.[21] Jenny, the social worker handling her case, treats Hortense with an unsettling mixture of well-rehearsed casualness, penetrating interrogation, and not-so-subtle boredom: this day of discovery may be of crucial importance to Hortense, but it is routine for Jenny. Before giving Hortense her heretofore sealed adoption records, the records that will reveal the secret of Hortense's biological beginnings, Jenny offers Hortense a Rolo and makes small talk about eating lunch and needing an eye exam. Hortense makes this discovery in the decidedly uninspiring setting of Jenny's "prison cell" of an office, "bare and institutional,"[22] its pasty walls covered with posters describing various social problems.

These posters appear to suggest that adoption is a social problem as well a solution to one—a social problem that often dramatically alters the birth mother's life for the worse. Adoption may solve the problem of parentless children and childless parents, but what problems does it create for the "childless" birth mother? In Cynthia's case, she seems trapped by her past: neither her name nor her address has changed since she put Hortense up for adoption in 1968, so Hortense has no trouble finding her. Cynthia has cluttered her parents' bedroom with old furniture and cheap artifacts to try to "fill a space" (39), as she says to Maurice—a space, we may guess, that has been created by her relinquishment of Hortense twenty-eight years ago, as well as by the death, disappearance, and disdain of the other members of Cynthia's family: Cynthia's parents are both dead, her brother never calls, and the daughter she did keep scowls at her motherly concern. Thus, one of the lies perpetuated by the adoption narrative, that the birth mother can simply forget about giving her child away and move on with her life, is exposed in the film.[23] Cynthia has not moved on in any sense. Working in a dreary factory and living in a rented house with no car and no social commitments—as she herself complains, "I'm never bloody doing anything" (49)—Cynthia is stuck physically as well as psychologically.

In contrast to Cynthia, Hortense has moved on past the initial trauma of being rejected at birth; thus, the film also dispels the myth that adoptees are more likely to have psychological problems.[24] The most well-adjusted of all the characters in the film, Hortense is mature, responsible, educated, gainfully employed, and independent: she owns both her own flat and her own car. Although she was brought up by her adoptive family "not to pursue things" (31), she confronts conflict and pain directly. We see this early on, when she sorts through her mother's belongings the weekend after the funeral and immediately tracks down Cynthia even though Jenny has advised her to use the "professional service" of the agency (24). Hortense is not satisfied with the blurry or the unresolved, and she is determined to replace the ghosts of her first and lost set of parents with flesh-and-blood people. But because adoption usually involves moving a child from a "disadvantaged" mother to a financially secure couple, Hortense's birth parents are most likely less "royal" than the so-called impostors, her adoptive parents.[25]

If the audience has any unrealistic expectations about Hortense's first and lost set of parents, we are forced to abandon them immediately. The film makes every effort to show that Cynthia is not in the least "royal," as we see from her introduction in the screenplay: "In a bleak box factory, a sad-looking middle-aged woman stands alone, operating a machine that cuts slits in sheets of cardboard. This is Cynthia" (5). Cynthia lives not in a palace but on a street of "small

Victorian terraced houses with no front gardens" (33), with a backyard that is literally a toilet. The assumption that a white mother will have a status superior to her black daughter is troubled immediately by the film's emphasis on class difference—Hortense may be of a "subordinate" race, but Cynthia is clearly of a subordinate social class.

Most adoptees search for their birth parents not only to satisfy their curiosity and to fill in some gaps of their life stories but also to find, finally, someone who looks like them. Because Cynthia is white, however, Hortense knows it is unlikely that there will be any family resemblance. At their first meeting, Hortense does not find a mirror image of herself in Cynthia; in fact, there is an utter alienation between the women on two levels: neither the characters of Hortense and Cynthia nor the actresses who play these characters had ever met before filming the reunion at the underground station.[26] The mirror that is supposed to exist between mother and daughter is distorted by differences in race as well as class. Hortense cannot recognize herself at all in Cynthia; Cynthia is other to Hortense's self—white to Hortense's blackness; working-class to Hortense's educated, middle-class background. If blood relations were really so sacred and inviolable as most activists argue, Hortense and Cynthia would recognize each other instantly.

Outside the station, where Hortense and Cynthia have agreed to meet, they literally cannot even see each other. Twice the screenplay indicates, "Neither notices the other" (51), and the long shot in the film reinforces the distance and the missed connection between the two women. When Hortense introduces herself to Cynthia, Cynthia insists Hortense is mistaken, but Hortense has the papers to prove otherwise and coaxes Cynthia into a cup of tea at a nearby café.

Following this initial meeting is a remarkable eight-minute uncut medium close-up with less than four pages of dialogue. This two-shot of Hortense and Cynthia in a coffee shop demands that they confront the situation head-on, particularly Cynthia, who is literally trapped in a booth between a wall and Hortense. During these eight minutes, long and painful silences are interrupted only by brief question-and-answer periods and Cynthia's sobbing. During this scene, we see most vividly the "proliferation of errors"[27] that make up Hortense's genealogy. Cynthia at first cannot even remember that she had sex with a black man; she was probably drunk at the time.[28] She then realizes that she "got the dates all wrong." She whimpers, "All this time I thought you was born six—six weeks premature, but you wasn't . . . you wasn't" (53). Having slept with this man was apparently so enormous an error that Cynthia has repressed the episode for twenty-eight years and can only offer an agonizing wail when Hortense presses her for information about him.

Once Cynthia accepts the fact that she is Hortense's biological mother, race becomes "almost irrelevant"[29] in their relationship, particularly when compared to the class differences between the two women. The only other reference

Cynthia makes to Hortense's skin is complimentary: "God, you've got beautiful skin!" (68). In fact, Cynthia tries to locate only their similarities, claiming that Hortense looks more like her than Roxanne does, that they have the "same build" (72), to which remark Hortense makes a justifiably puzzled face. Cynthia seems to dote on Hortense, possibly because she has at last found someone who wants to spend time with her, unlike the rest of her family. The film suggests that although the relinquishment of a child leaves the birth mother feeling empty and "lost," a reunion with her child may provide the potential for her to be "found." As Richard Blake argues, "With her education and security, Hortense opens up new layers of dignity in her mother."[30] The "space" that Cynthia has been trying to fill with material objects from the past seems less gaping with Hortense's presence. Hortense's discovery may be seen as a reversal of the Demeter-Persephone myth, where the daughter searches out her mother, who very often has been living in hell. It would be more accurate to ascribe the role of Demeter to Hortense, who brings her "daughter" (Cynthia) back from the dead. Cynthia may be older and white, but Hortense's education and poised professionalism plainly mark her in the position of power, the articulate adult and parent to Cynthia's blubbering baby. J. Hoberman's description of the dynamic between the two women is perhaps even more apt. Hoberman claims, "Like a fairy godmother in a generationally reversed Cinderella, Hortense casts a benignly transformative spell on a slatternly Cynthia."[31] Cynthia's transformation is undeniable. When she is with Roxanne, she looks unhappy and unkempt: she keeps her slovenly dyed hair in a dirty terry-cloth "scrunchie" on top of her head and wears shabby capped-sleeved sweaters and cheap leggings. When she goes out with Hortense, she styles her hair and wears flattering pastel suits and floral dresses, and the two of them have "a jolly time" according to the screenplay (71), laughing and chatting easily.

To discover that her daughter is a professional, well-educated young woman may represent a sort of upward mobility for Cynthia; however, the discovery entails a movement downward, from middle class to working class, for Hortense. Although this movement is downward, Hortense seems secure enough to accept and even appreciate the differences in Cynthia's race, class, and temperament, particularly Cynthia's good-natured, unsophisticated sense of humor. We might see the faces that Hortense constantly makes as a trace of Cynthia, of the Purley heritage peeking through. Certainly she did not "inherit" these antics from her adoptive mother—whom, Hortense suggests, wasn't "a laugh" (68). Hortense also seems to prefer Cynthia's affable honesty to the lies that her adoption has perpetuated. Yet her criticisms of adoption are suggested only by the fact that she has resolved to face the awkward truth of her origins.

If she has any misgivings about her adoptive parents, she is hesitant to articulate these feelings in the film. For Hortense, the family romance is problematic, not only because as an adoptee, the romance is real, but also because she does not seem to feel entitled to express ambivalence toward the parents who "saved" her. Hortense represses this ambivalence to the point that she makes her parentage a product of fate, reversing the "chosen baby" story to a "chosen parent" story. As she says to her friend Dionne, "We choose the parents that can teach us something; so that when we go into the next life, we get it right" (32). Yet when Jenny suggests that Hortense and her family should have discussed the fact that she was adopted, Hortense responds somewhat defensively, "My parents loved me, and that's all that matters." She then adds, hesitantly, "Isn't it?" (22).

Hortense's ambivalence toward her adoptive parents is all the more striking when we examine other parent-child relationships in the film, most notably the relationship between Cynthia and Roxanne—a relationship that the film demystifies to the point of pathology. Roxanne ignores Cynthia's attempts at conversation and rejects Cynthia's gestures of motherly concern. When she is not acting motherly, Cynthia tries to act inconspicuously in an effort to avoid her daughter's bullying and temper, which explodes when Cynthia tells her about Hortense. When Hortense is revealed as her half sister, Roxanne screams at Cynthia: "Don't you touch me or I will smack you, you slag! You fuckin' slag! Ain't it enough you 'ad to 'ave one bastard, you 'ad to 'ave two an' all!" (94). With this rather pathological representation of blood kinship, the film undermines the assumption that adoptive relations are inferior to biological ones.

Although the film relentlessly demystifies the "sacred bond" of blood in birth families, it is much more subtle about demystifying the bond in adoptive families. There are only a few moments where Hortense's adoptive family is seen as having many of the same strengths and weaknesses of any other family. The audience is forced to infer these strengths and weaknesses on the basis of Hortense's comments and expressions alone. We see no interaction between her and her adoptive relatives. Even during the scene when both Hortense and her two adoptive brothers are in their parents' house, where some interaction is expected, they are physically and emotionally separated. As she sorts through her mother's things upstairs, she hears her brother arguing downstairs, and she is described as "both concerned and detached" (8). Because Hortense's adoptive parents are both dead at the start of the film and infrequently discussed, they linger as ghosts in the audience's imagination, much like the ghosts of her birth parents, who have lingered in Hortense's imagination.

Yet absence definitely has a presence in the film, despite Monica's claim that "you can't miss what you never had" (41). When Cynthia discloses the identity of Roxanne's father, her previously stoic, surly daughter shakes with tears. Monica's claim that "you can't miss what you never had" is also clearly false in her own case. She so desperately misses what she never had—children—that she forces herself to endure painful infertility treatments. Having to settle for her new house as a substitute baby, she is determined to leave her mark, to graft her identity onto this "child" by stenciling the walls. For most of her day, she fusses over the house as she would over a child: when she shows off the downstairs bathroom to Cynthia and Jane, she fluffs the curtains and puts down the toilet seat as a mother might comb her child's hair and pull her child's finger out of her nose.

Of course, the most notable absence in the film, the absence of Hortense's birth father, points to the film's suspicions about uncritical claims of authenticity and wholeness: obviously Hortense cannot be made whole in her search for origins, if only because Cynthia refuses to name her father. Yet the film's very title, *Secrets and Lies,* implies that there is some truth to be told. The truth in Leigh's film is that, as he himself says, "there is no unambiguous, fixed truth inherent in the connection" between parent and child,[32] even and especially if the parent and child are biologically related. Blood is not a stronger or more stable bond.

Nor is the bond of blood simple, as Hortense's discovery narrative reveals. For Hortense and Roxanne to tell people that they are half sisters will involve chaos and confusion—"too much explainin' to do," as Hortense says. Yet she then insists that it is "best to tell the truth . . . that way, nobody gets 'urt'" (103). The language of birth relations is not only confusing but also unintentionally confessional. To introduce Cynthia by the seemingly innocuous term *birth mother* discloses a complicated story, a story that reveals that Hortense was the unplanned, unwanted result of an illegitimate, interracial affair. Introducing Hortense as her birth daughter reveals even more about Cynthia: that she lost her virginity at a young age; that the man with whom she got pregnant was black; that she gave away this child, was found by this child, and now has a relationship with this child she once left.

The film seems to find solace in the confusing and confessional, and it implies that facing up to the fact that our identity is a product not of genes or fate or careful construction but of the arbitrary and the accidental is, as Maurice tells Hortense, "very brave" (100). Coming to terms with this reality, however ugly or unglamorous, is redemptive and much preferred to repressing it for the sake of appearances. We see this redemptive quality even in Roxanne, who at the end of the film stands side by side with Hortense, smiling when she has spent most of the film wearing "a face like a slapped arse" (5). Some critics have faulted Leigh for concluding with this fairly optimistic resolution,[33] but the end of the film actually suggests the beginning of a new narrative and a new family—fragmented by racial and class differences, but at least somewhat functional. The high shot of Cynthia, Roxanne, and Hortense as they sit in Cynthia's backyard and "enjoy the afternoon together" suggests that this new family of three is feasible, if awkward and unusual (103). In *Secrets and Lies,* Hortense's discovery of her white, working-class origins does not relieve her genealogical bewilderment; rather, her discovery reveals that genealogy is often bewildering.

NOTES

1. Sylvia Plath, "The Ghost's Leavetaking," in *Collected Poems*, ed. Ted Hughes (New York: Harper and Row, 1981), 90.

2. To protect my birth mother's privacy, I use this pseudonym for her throughout the essay and simply note that her real name sounds similarly unromantic.

3. Arthur D. Sorosky, Annette Baran, and Reuben Pannor, *The Adoption Triangle: The Effects of the Sealed Record on Adoptees, Birth Parents, and Adoptive Parents* (New York: Doubleday, 1978), 219.

4. H. J. Sants, "Genealogical Bewilderment in Children with Substitute Parents," *British Journal of Medical Psychology* 37 (1964): 133–41.

5. Jean-Paul Sartre, *Saint Genet,* cited in Betty Jean Lifton, *Journey of the Adopted Self: A Quest for Wholeness* (New York: Basic, 1994), 88.

6. In many jurisdictions, the birth certificates of illegitimate children were a different color until the 1960s. See E. Cole and K. S. Donley, "History, Values, and Placement Issues in Adoption," in *The Psychology of Adoption,* ed. David M. Brodzinsky and Marshall D. Schechter (Oxford: Oxford University Press, 1990), 284.

7. Betty Jean Lifton, *Journey of the Adopted Self: A Quest for Wholeness* (New York: Basic, 1994), 37.

8. Elizabeth Bartholet, *Family Bonds: Adoption and the Politics of Parenting* (Boston: Houghton Miflin, 1993), 48.

9. Katarina Wegar, *Adoption, Identity, and Kinship: The Debate over Sealed Birth Records* (New Haven, Conn.: Yale University Press, 1997), 84.

10. Judith Modell, *Kinship with Strangers: Adoption and Interpretations of Kinship in American Culture* (Berkeley: University of California Press, 1994) 226.

11. Betty Jean Lifton, *Lost and Found: The Adoption Experience* (New York: Harper and Row, 1988), 28–29.

12. Christopher Badcock, *Essential Freud,* 2d ed. (Oxford: Basil Blackwell, 1992), 154.

13. Barbara Cohen (member of the board of directors of the New Jersey Coalition for Openness in Adoption), editorial, *Home News and Tribune,* March 17, 1996, C9.

14. Erica Haimes, "'Now I Know Who I Really Am': Identity Change and Redefinitions of the Self in Adoption," in *Self and Identity: Perspectives across the Lifespan,* ed. Terry Honess and Krysia Yardley (New York: Routledge and Kegan Paul, 1987), 363.

15. Anne Sexton, "The Lost Ingredient," in *Complete Poems* (Boston: Houghton Mifflin, 1981), 30.

16. Michel Foucault, "Nietzsche, Genealogy, History," in *Language, Counter-Memory, Practice,* ed. Donald F. Bouchard (Ithaca: Cornell University Press, 1977), 142.

17. Ibid., 146.

18. Ibid., 146–47.

19. Here I would like to emphasize "most likely," as not all adoptees are born out of wedlock and not all adoptive parents are infertile.

20. Foucault, "Nietzsche," 143.

21. Because of section 26 in the Children Act of 1975, adoptees in England and Wales are permitted access to their records; see John Triseliotis, "Obtaining Birth Certificates," in *Adoption: Essays in Social Policy, Law, and Sociology,* ed. Philip Bean (London: Tavistock, 1984), 38.

22. Mike Leigh, *Secrets and Lies* (London: Faber and Faber, 1997), 20. Subsequent references to this screenplay are cited parenthetically in text.

23. Sorosky, Baran, and Pannor note (*Adoption Triangle*, 56) "It's quite obvious that birth mothers never really forget the child and that for some, relinquishment results in deep emotional problems, in 'psychological amputation.'"

24. See Janet L. Hoopes, "Adoption and Identity Formation," in Brodzinsky and Schechter, *The Psychology of Adoption*, 149.

25. See Modell, *Kinship*, 130.

26. See Brian D. Johnson, "Lost Child, Lost Souls," *Maclean's* 109, no. 42 (October 14, 1996): 92.

27. Foucault, "Nietzsche," 143.

28. The film does not provide an easy, unambiguous explanation for what happened between Cynthia and Hortense's biological father. In my reading of the film, I have resisted rape as the connection between Hortense's father and Cynthia, because such a reading resorts to simplistic and harmful stereotypes of black manhood and fatherhood that I do not think the film intends to perpetuate.

29. Richard A. Blake, "Visions," *America* 175, no. 14 (November 9, 1996): 22.

30. Ibid., 22.

31. J. Hoberman, "Sweet Mysteries of Life," *Village Voice* 41, no. 40 (October 1, 1996): 64.

32. Leonard Quart, "Raising Questions and Positing Possibilities: An Interview with Mike Leigh," *Cineaste* 22, no. 4 (1997): 53.

33. See, for instance, Richard Porton, "Secrets and Lies," *Cineaste* 22, no. 4 (1997): 51–52.

Natural Bonds, Legal Boundaries

Modes of Persuasion in Adoption Rhetoric

Judith Modell

Adoption in the United States is the permanent transfer of a child from one parent to another parent. At the core of American adoption law are stranger adoptions, in which a child is transferred into a family unknown to her family of birth. Through most of the twentieth century, stranger adoptions laid the foundation not only for adoption law but also for the stereotypes that surround adoption in the United States.[1] In stranger adoptions, birth and adoptive families are not supposed to have contact.

In the mid-1970s, adoptee support groups came into being all over the country. One way or another, these groups are actively engaged in challenging the customs, presumptions, rules, and symbols of American adoption. The effort stems from concern over the terms of conventional adoption as these have existed in the United States since the early twentieth century.[2] Adoptees engaged in searching may claim that they do not know their "real" parents, that they lack their "true" identities, and that they are deprived of the rights and liberties all other adults in American society have. Throughout this movement, vocabulary is significant and words accumulate meanings in context; so, for instance, the term *real* can be used to make a point about the inherent attachment to a birth parent and, in another context, can equally refer to the nurturing and enduring relationship with an adoptive parent.

As the language suggests, adoptee support groups draw on principles that are presumed to be fundamental in American culture. Conjunctive pairs like "rights and freedoms," "nature and culture," refer to core values: adoption discourse elegantly exposes the ambiguities in pairs. At support group meetings, stories that are personal and emotional examine and elaborate the links between historical principles and deeply held values. The narratives accumulate, eventually constituting an argument for change. The argument appears in newsletters, in bulletins sent to television stations and other media, and in petitions presented to state legislatures and the federal government.

This essay analyzes the process by which accounts grounded in "passion" are transformed into arguments characterized by the use of reason, by groups for whom a personal passion remains the motivation for taking a stand in public.[3] Behind the process I describe lie wider efforts to balance consciousness-raising activities with the increased attention to lobbying that has occurred in support groups in post-1960s American society. I suggest that the intersection of tactics of passion with strategies of reason leads to a redefinition of principles held to be self-evident in an American cultural context. Specifically, adoption support groups convert personal narratives about being adopted into a critique of adoption law and judge the "sins" of adoption practice against an ideology of the rights granted all American citizens. The result is a critique of concepts of kinship and identity that occurs in the context of political agenda setting.

I base my interpretation on data from my participation in one adoptee support group. I attended regular meetings of the group for eight years, from 1985 through 1993. The data I gathered at monthly meetings is supplemented by my attendance at support group meetings for birth parents, as well as at several for adoptive parents.[4] Most support groups also distribute newsletters, and such texts both complement and reformulate the oral narratives created at meetings. Moreover, for the past ten years I have been doing research on changes in American adoption practices that involves, besides attending meetings, doing intensive interviews with members of the triad and with professionals who handle adoption, from social workers to local court judges.[5] Over the past decade, too, changes in American adoption have prompted a growing literature on this form of kinship, including deeply personal stories, scholarly analyses, and legislative reports. Much of this material has gradually filtered back into support groups, adding new vocabulary to the one existing among individuals affected by adoption.

Adoptee groups may be local or national; they may pursue their goals independently or join forces with like-minded groups arguing for the reform of American adoption. Patterns of leadership and of organization vary, depending on region, membership, and history. In some instances, a hierarchy develops in which more articulate members control the stories told by participants, channeling distinct narratives into similar forms. Other groups are casually organized and egalitarian; the content of meetings then tends to be digressive and anecdotal, the end result a less integrated view of the adoption experience than in more tightly run groups. In both instances, however, emotional catharsis alternates delicately with the formation of a political agenda.

The group I focus on in this essay was local, not part of a national organization. It did maintain a strong connection with an adoptee group in a large metropolitan area in another part of the state. Karen, the woman who founded the group, led the meetings through all the years I attended. Her accounts of being adopted and her personality pervaded the Sunday afternoon gatherings, which usually lasted between three and four hours. Her vivid presence did not, however, suppress or silence the voices of the adopted people, occasional birth parent, and even more occasional adoptive parent who attended. Karen is not her real name; Throughout the essay, all names have been changed, identifying details altered, and anonymity thoroughly maintained.

Background

I call the group Adoptee Support Group (ASG), a pseudonym to protect the confidentiality of members. The group was founded in 1976, the year Karen decided to search for her birth family. She had begun by calling Jean Paton, an adoptee who established a successful search organization called Orphan Voyage.[6] Paton advised Karen to start her own support group. An advertisement in the local newspaper elicited responses from adoptees who also wanted to search, and five of them agreed to meet one afternoon at Karen's house. Neither Karen's decision nor the response from other adoptees came out of the blue: the mid-1970s saw what historian Wayne Carp describes as the "second adoption reform movement."[7] Out of the previous decade's wars for civil rights, freedom of information, and an end to administrative secrecy and lying came a call for openness in personal and kinship relations. Karen and the original founders of ASG rode the crest of a wave, one that swept through much of the rest of the nation.

On ASG's tenth anniversary, Karen described the occasion of its founding. Her house, she wrote, was being torn apart by workmen, and minutes before everyone was to arrive, her son broke his leg. An emergency hospital trip and four hours later, the meeting of adoptees was at last underway. "Under the circumstances everyone would understand if we cancelled, but it took one year for the five of us to get up the nerve to meet! After all, what we were doing could be against the law, couldn't it?" Tired and trembling, she wrote, they talked of their "need" to locate their roots, find a blood connection, and see an unamended record of having been born (*ASG Newsletter,* October 1986).[8]

The strategy of announcing a dramatic crisis and nearly insurmountable obstacles became a familiar one, for Karen and for the group as a whole. Overcoming odds—like a rush to the hospital and back—conveyed the inevitability and the necessity of a person's decision. Such a narrative device "can also express a psychological commitment that transcends rationality,"[9] which is precisely the function it served for ASG members. The broken-leg emergency fired up the energy of those early founders.

Karen's juxtaposition of a reference to law and an assumption of psychological need is equally typical of ASG rhetoric. The linguistic juxtaposition indicates the oscillation between reason and passion that ultimately structured the public statements made by ASG. The word *law,* in this case, refers as much to a view of the world as to specific legislation: law represented "reason," the rational and objective. As anthropologist Clifford Geertz put it, the "law side of things" is "part of a distinctive manner of imagining the real."[10] When the word did refer to a body of legislation, it had several referents: state laws of adoption; the law of the land (expressed as "the Constitution" or "the Bill of Rights"); the federal acts that serve as guidelines for local practices; the state laws that actually regulate adoption in the United States. In the discourse of birth parents, the word *law* has another referent as well, natural law, often synonymous with divine (or sacred) law. The exact reference of the word was not always clear, but the values presumed by referring to law were unmistakable.

According to anthropologist F. G. Bailey, Western culture recognizes two ways of persuading another person: "The first is the Platonic way, the use of reason. This method is possible when the persuader can find some value that the other person accepts, and that can serve as the premise from which to lead an argument. . . . The other form of persuasion (direct use of the passions) seeks to eliminate the mind and the critical faculties. It provokes feeling rather than thought."[11] Bailey's effort is less to isolate the two ways from one another than to indicate a long tradition in which rational and emotional dimensions intertwine in the presentation of a position. The skill of a rhetorician—the ability to persuade—comes from a cunning or inspired (or both) elicitation of audience response to both the affective and the cognitive aspects of his appeal.

To put it another way (the way appropriate for adoptee support groups), for a value to move an audience to agreement or to action, it must be not only comprehended but also felt. A man is persuaded if "he likes what you promise, fears what you say is imminent, hates what you censure . . . ," wrote Augustine in the capstone of Western modes of persuasion.[12] We return to Bailey, then: the element of passion represents a moment when the heart leads the mind and the audience shares the fear of the orator; for persuasion to work, however, reason must already have added an interpretation.

In developing an argument for open records, adoptee support groups combined the two ways, couching a personal quest for proof of a "real birth" in terms of lawful claims and adult rights. The passion prompted by lacking what others have (knowledge of biological kin) is legitimated in a call to justice: adoptees are treated like second-class citizens. A brochure from the Adoptees Liberty Movement Association (ALMA), one of the largest national adoption support groups, displays the full persuasive force that lies in the yoking of reason and passion: "The denial of an adult human being's right to the truth of his origin creates a scar which is imbedded in his soul forever."[13]

The content as well as the joining of appeals to reason and to passion (law and need) connect adoptee support groups to other special-interest groups in an American context. And though the audience for ASG stories, statements, and testimonies ranges from fellow members of the triad to legislators and social workers, no one who listened would be unfamiliar with the constellation of values, truths, feelings, and emotions adoptee rhetoric utilizes. Grounded in dominant cultural presumptions and interpretations, adoptee reform groups initiate a dialogue in a language that is completely familiar in American society today.

After ASG's first meeting in 1976, as Karen put it, "things evolved so fast" (*ASG Newsletter,* October 1986). The stage was set, and she barely had to request the role of spokesperson for adoptees in her area. Before she knew it, Karen was appearing on radio and television, attending conferences, and speaking for a group of people who called themselves an "oppressed minority." Almost against her will, her self-presentation suggests, Karen carried into the world of media and legislative debate the personal narratives she heard from individuals who attended ASG meetings.[14] Mostly adoptees, these individual arrived with various experiences and assessments of adoption. No one who came on those Sunday afternoons was content with the current state of American adoption, as both their presence at the meetings and the content of their life stories demonstrated.

These stories constituted the resources for a larger argument about adoption, identity, and the rights of a citizen and a human being. At ASG, recognition of shared experiences provided the potential for collective action or at least for shared definition of interests. From the civil rights movement to the abortion controversy, there were clear precedents for bringing highly personal stories to bear on public problems. There were precedents, too, for using emotional responses as the core of a rational argument.

Although concentrated collective action and direct lobbying were not explicit goals for ASG, Karen's statements in the *ASG Newsletter* and on panels revealed her sense that an "ordinary person" could speak out, be heard, and have an impact on national policy. The group she founded exemplified the post-1960s American optimism that voicing concerns in a collective forum actually could shape legislative decisions. In this instance, legislation concerned the transfer of a child from one parent to another and the rights of individuals subject to a sealed and secret kinship.

Reason and Passion

From the beginning, ASG had a cause. The group supported any adoptee who intended to locate a birth parent, whatever explanation he or she gave for the quest. By extension, ASG argued against confidential adoption, the anonymity that kept birth parents invisible to their children and to an adoptive family, and the denial of information about their origins to adopted individuals. The position initially taken by ASG was that an adoptee should have access to all documents pertinent to the adoption and, essentially, to the facts of her or his life.[15]

Eight years after its founding, ASG was forced further into public. In 1984, the state legislature approved a bill that prevented adoptees from seeing their original, preadoption birth certificates.[16] Between 1953 and 1984 seeing the original document had been possible. An adoptee could request a copy of the long (i.e., unamended) form of her birth certificate from the Bureau of Vital Statistics. The long form contained at least the name of the woman who gave birth and sometimes the name of the father. By the mid-1980s, a ground swell of opposition to access had developed, prompted by concern for the privacy of birth parents as well as that of adoptive parents and led by the National Council for Adoption under William Pierce. Legislators spoke of the dangers of opening records, of disturbing the decisions made years earlier, and of violating the terms of a contract made in good faith. A local newspaper talked of a loophole in the adoption law of the state: "The legislation would also close a loophole in the current law which enables people who are adopted to learn the identities of their natural parents simply by getting their [original] birth certificates" (quoted in *ASG Newsletter*, December 1984).

For ASG, this legislation threatened its primary mode of action. Until then, the group had been able to urge adoptees to write for the long form, arguing that it did not hurt to have all available information about oneself and that it might help. Just before the bill became law, Karen advised adoptees and adoptive parents to move fast: "We have to tell adoptees and adoptive parents they still have time" (*ASG Newsletter*, December 1984). The bill became law in February 1985. Publicity was abundant and in fact provided my first awareness of the group, which previously had not had wide attention. The law did allow adoptees to request information, through the court and without endangering the anonymity of the birth parent. Preadoption birth certificates were barred from release. Discussion first of the bill and then of implementation of the law provided ASG not only with a cause but also with a new vocabulary. From then on, arguments in the *ASG Newsletter* and at meetings applied the word "oppressed" explicitly defining adoptees as people whose rights the law denied rather than granted, people who did not have the "ordinary freedoms" guaranteed by a bill of rights.

"The heart of this bill is to take away an existing law to get our original birth certificate," wrote Karen in the *ASG Newsletter*. Adoptees in this state, she continued, "have had this right for 31 years only to have it taken away in 1984." She claimed that the law deprived adoptees in particular of their rights: "I thought our Constitution said that all men are created equal." Then, shifting from an arguing position based on the law of the land to a position based on emotion, Karen concluded her article with a plea to the state: "Wake up, before it is too late for us. Adoptees are *Real People* not *Cabbage Patch Dolls* with no hearts or souls" (*ASG Newsletter*, December 1984). She repeatedly designated the state as unsympathetic and inhumane: "The state does not recognize that adoptees have feelings," she wrote in the October 1986 *ASG Newsletter*.

The yoking of a call for action based on rights with an appeal to the heart—adoptees are human beings—characterized Karen's statements whatever the forum, whether out loud at meetings or printed in the *ASG Newsletter*. The phrases she used in her first protest against the state law established the terms on which an ASG agenda would subsequently be elaborated: a demand for rights based on the American Constitution combined with the passionate conviction that knowing one's biological origins was crucial to an individual's identity and well-being.

These terms determined the transformation of personal narratives into the argument that ASG presented in public. The transformation occurred in individual stories, as narrators honored a kind of master narrative organized around the cultural principles of rights to knowledge, to identity, and to self-determination. Complaints about social workers, lawyers, and adoptive parents abounded, depicting them as villains who upheld laws that were essentially unjust and discriminatory. "It was really frightening," a woman reported. "Like I said, when we started it, we were all just scared, like we shouldn't be doing it because everybody always told you that since you're adopted you just don't have any rights."[17]

As in any classic support group, individuals presented strongly self-referential narratives—autobiographical and often confessional in form. ASG meetings provided a safe and secure place for an exploration of one's past, an outpouring of emotion, or a reflective account of "being adopted." Over the course of an afternoon, and even more obviously over the course of several meetings, biographical details merged into generalizations about the adoptee in the United States. Construction of the status of "being adopted" in late-twentieth-century American society proceeded bit by bit, story by story, person by person.

Karen and other old-timers played a part in the process through which the personal narratives composing a meeting's main activity were transformed. Partly they effected a transformation by retelling their own stories, with the modifications that came from long experience in an adoption reform movement. Partly, old-time members effected a transformation in newer narratives by imposing a search framework on much of the afternoon's autobiographical disquisition. As coordinator and expert, Karen asked lots of questions about access to records, documents, and "facts" about oneself. Did an adoptee have only an amended birth certificate? Had the adoptee checked with the Bureau of Vital Statistics? Had the person been back to the adoption agency, if she or he knew which one it was? What papers did a person have in her or his possession? Questions about the information a person had, as well as about the steps of searching, hung over the afternoon's proceedings—a persuasive formulation of the adoption experience for those who were there.

I never, at any meeting, observed Karen or anyone else silence, correct, or condemn the presentation made by a member of the group. Stories were given relatively free rein, though the issue of confidentiality, secrecy, and hidden facts tended to dominate, especially in the more casual conversation that followed someone's personal narrative. At the end of an afternoon meeting, the impulses for and various shapes of an adoptee search lay before us, a landscape of possibilities. No outcome or conclusion was wrong, and some were triumphant, satisfactory, and exemplary. Yet one principle clearly stood out, especially in the years following the closing of adoptee birth records: redressing the wrong done to adoptees as adult citizens of the United States.

The concept of rights legitimated the insistence on granting an adoptee access to vital documents, above and beyond particular expressions or motives. On the one hand, ASG meetings were thoroughly democratic in that no one was silenced and all stories earned equal hearing; on the other hand, the goal of meeting at all was unmistakably to figure out ways of getting documents, individually and collectively. Interpretations of self-identity and of psychological development that emerged from personal narratives energized and filled out the concept of rights.

In American society today, the adoptee in a conventional stranger adoption is totally cut off from her or his birth family. For many adoptees, that cutoff, which is both actual and symbolic, constitutes the heart of a life story and the flaw in a development of self-identity. At ASG meetings, participants recognized the significance of "not knowing birth" and conveyed the complexity of its meaning. From lacking a connection with those genetically like oneself to being deprived of information all other persons have, the ignorance imposed on an adopted person is profound. When individuals at ASG meetings turned these issues into a social problem, they were phrased in terms of a denial of rights.[18] A reigning metaphor, the denial of rights and their counterpart, access to information, linked the ASG agenda—and adoptees—to a larger American cause. The cause had been acknowledged on a national level by the passage of the Freedom of Information Act in 1975.[19] By the mid-1980s, when I went to ASG, the habit of setting the personal pain of being kept in ignorance or in a less-than-adult status against principles of justice and fairness was in place. The adoption reform movement had had over a decade not only to mature but also to hone its devices and to accentuate its particular relation to American history and tradition. The context prompted an easy (though by no means superficial) reference of adoptee concerns to rights guaranteed by the American Constitution.

At the same time, adoptees at ASG were not willing to relinquish the distinctiveness of their concerns and the discrimination against them. "Everyone else has a family," adoptees told me; anyone else can get medical information, knows how much she weighed at birth, has relatives who look familiar. The distinctiveness of an adoptee experience in turn influenced the meaning of concepts like rights, freedom, and equality in ASG discussions and publications.

Battle Grounds and Enemies

"I thought our Constitution said that all men are created equal," Karen wrote in the *ASG Newsletter* in December 1984. This statement illustrates a mode of persuasion that was to become popular with Karen and members of the ASG: insisting on the minority status of adopted persons in the United States. Taking on minority status, however, contradicts a stereotypical image of the adopted person as fortunate, blessed to be in a new home, better off than she or he would have been: the clichés are well known. Adoptee rhetoric deconstructs this point of view, showing how it serves the interests of those who would keep adopted persons silent and secondary citizens. The purpose of adoptee rhetoric is not to deny the luck in being adopted but to demonstrate the discrimination that under current law and practice accrues to the status of being adopted.

In the late 1980s, Karen had a concrete example of discrimination in the change in the state law regarding adoptee birth certificates. Karen, with ASG as her support, entered a battle in which the enemy was well defined. Local agencies, legislators, lobbyists, and others who insisted on closed records formed the brunt of the opposition. Rhetorically, the creation of an enemy is a crucial tactic of persuasion. How did it work for ASG?

Primarily, the enemy had to be both unproblematic and consistent in position. In the end, Karen's favorite enemy was William Pierce, head of the National Council for Adoption, a powerful pro-adoption lobbying group in Washington. An outspoken opponent of opening adoption, Pierce presented a program and a persona that cast him well as the villain in reform movement rhetoric. Furthermore, Karen had a personal encounter with Pierce that energized the rhetorical purpose he served.

She described the encounter: "As far as he [Pierce] is concerned, adoptees have no rights. Several years ago Mr. Pierce told me that because I needed to know my biological parents I had a mental problem. What I really had was a heartache from 'Genetic Amputation'" (*ASG Newsletter,* May 1986). Here and elsewhere in the *ASG Newsletter,* Karen attributes a mode of persuasion to Pierce: denigrating the position of an adversary by attacking her or his person. In Karen's account of the run-in, Pierce dismissed the adoptee reform position by calling the spokespeople for such a position mentally unstable, irrational, incompetent, and nuts.

Characterization of Pierce and his approach substantiated Karen's own rhetorical tactics. As Bailey has noted, "Assertive rhetoric seems to require the presence, whether openly or implicitly, of the infidel: the person to hate or despise or ridicule, the person who, if not hated, is at least on the outside, the person whose difference from us makes clear the nature of our identity, who we are and for what we stand."[20] William Pierce was openly despised. Ultimately (and cumulatively), Karen portrays Pierce as the devil, his position as evil. In the *ASG Newsletter* in which she confronted Pierce's position, Karen reprinted a letter she had written to a local newspaper: "According to Mr. Pierce, if an adoptee needs to search he has a mental problem, he is ungrateful and he is told he would not search if he loved his parents. He cannot be trusted with his own mother's name.

There are no other groups of people in the world who are kept from their identity except for an adoptee. . . . No, Mr. Pierce, not having the right to our own identity makes us second class citizens. And what does our Constitution say? All men are created equal. Adoptees are not equal until you give us back our heritage" (*ASG Newsletter,* May 1986).

The lines of battle are laid here. Throughout the late 1980s, Karen's criticisms of Pierce passionately defended the adoptee position. The vocabulary was personal, drawn from Pierce's own accusations that searchers were nuts. Exploiting the direct reference to her character (Pierce had called her unstable), Karen extended the point made more generally by searchers: wanting to know is a sign of mental health, not of mental frailty. Counteracting the dismissive argument that searchers are crazy, members of search groups emphasize an American theme: the importance of knowing where you come from and what your biological background is in order to move forward. Statements made at ASG meetings translated a personal need to know one's genetic heritage into a matter of rights granted by the American Constitution and freedoms accorded by the Bill of Rights.

Establishing links to rights and citizenship pushes the adoptee position toward a moral imperative. In the midst of battle, such moral imperatives are indistinguishable from "truth" or fact. "The kind of opinion with which rhetoric deals, in its role of inducement to action, is not opinion as contrasted with truth," Kenneth Burke writes, but opinion that is one with truth.[21] Bailey offers a similar analysis of modes of persuasion. "Assertive rhetoric is intended—one of its tasks—to confer on values the status of facts," writes Bailey, adding, "Values may also be presented as moral or divine imperatives."[22] Repeated references in ASG rhetoric to the Constitution and the Bill of Rights serve the purpose of transforming value into truth (or fact). The value—that a person should have vital information about her or himself—blurs into the Constitutional truth of guaranteed civil and personal rights. Referring to the highest law of the land also transforms the value into a moral imperative: respect for the rights of a citizen and of a human being means granting all people access to vital information about themselves. Within this framework, adoptees deserve equality and freedom of knowledge.

Karen did not have a political lectern. She did have a group of committed individuals, people who shared her values, her interests, and her passions. During the Sunday afternoon meetings, I observed the process by which particular life stories contributed piece by piece to the formulation of general moral imperatives.

Narratives accumulated and changed over time. Meetings drew diverse adoptees, as well as birth parents and adoptive parents, and the state and the nation reconsidered the value of confidentiality and sealed records. Different populations and different public causes shifted the content of meetings. Yet a mode of persuasion persisted: stories moved between the poles of personal desire and public interest, psychological need and cultural value, that braced the discourse of the adoption reform movement as a whole. One word unified these potentially divisive emphases. Used in individual narratives and in the *ASG Newsletter*, the word *bond* carried a heavy rhetorical burden.

Natural Bonds, Legal Boundaries

With its multiple denotations and connotations, the word *bond* conveys the heart of the adoptee argument for opening records, as well as its complexity. In ASG narratives and the newsletter, *bond* had at least three meanings, and with those meanings came different emotional tones. First, *bond* refers to the contract of adoption, the signatures on paper that create an adoption. Second, *bond* refers to the trust and love that develop in an adoptive family—individuals who are permanently bound to one another. Third, *bond* refers to biological ties, the links formed by genealogical connections: blood is thicker than water. By extension, biology merges with the more abstract concept, nature, which itself acquires aspects of the divine or sacred.[23]

Adoption is by American convention a contracted kinship. A legal contract accords the adoptive parent complete and permanent kinship with the child. Legally, in the United States the adoptee is "as if begotten," no different from a biological child born to her adoptive parents. For those who are critical of American adoption, however, a contract represents a "man-made" connection between parent and child that cannot fully replace the natural connection. With genealogy as the prototype of kinship, in the United States a relationship created in court is not considered as inevitably enduring as a relationship created in nature. For some adopted individuals who protest against the terms of conventional American adoption, the bond formed by a legal contract symbolizes a kind of bondage. Sealed records lock the child into one family, denying access to the other family.

"I feel people are sadly unaware and misinformed [about adoption]," wrote an adoptee to the *ASG Newsletter*. "When a hurting child is locked behind bars, something is wrong. When a vulnerable person is told that they're bad and unworthy, something is wrong" (*ASG Newsletter*, October 1993). Her argument, like others I heard at ASG, consists of a passionate plea to be "released" from the "prison" of closed adoption. In these interpretations, the adoptee who is not allowed to "glimpse" anything or anyone outside the adoptive family is bound by a contract signed by others.

"The hard and cruel fact," a thirty-year-old adoptee said to me, "is that the one person who is not consulted in this whole thing is the kid." In his view, birth parents and adoptive parents sign papers that then bind the child to an agreement for life. The word *fact* is significant in the comment. The adoptee here draws on a lesson from American history and a principle of American law: a person cannot be bound by a contract he has not signed. His reference to a "constitutional" "truth we hold to be self-evident," turns his interpretation of an adoptive contract into a "fact." His audience has no choice but to accept the interpretation. As Bailey notes, "In rhetoric, to proclaim something a fact is to tell the audience that they have no alternative than to give their assent, on pain of being excluded as crazy people."[24]

Carried to a logical extreme, the adoptee's reference to contract in his argument for opening records forces an audience to agree with his conclusions—under peril of being considered crazy or nuts. A person who claimed that a contract should hold a nonsigner would be violating the fundamental values of American culture—would, in effect, be supporting "bondage." The contract that exists, creating the adoption, rightly has no constraining force on the adopted person. Of course, as this adoptee added, the adoptee is a baby who cannot sign papers anyway. By teasing his own interpretation, however, he further validates the next point he makes: "And so when the kid becomes of an age where he or she wants to know what their biological roots are, they just, they are then essentially, I hate the word victimized because I think it's overused, but in a sense they are victimized by a system that they had no part in. Yeah, they're bound by a contract that they didn't sign."[25]

ALMA also exploits the significance of contract in American culture to defend searching and to advocate opening adoption records. In a list of ten common fallacies about American adoption, the organization included the following: "#8: *An adoptee is bound to honor the agreement of adoption and to never challenge the wisdom of the sealed records; he has a right only to the information that others are willing to give.* Bound by what? Why should an adoptee be required to honor an agreement he never saw, never read, and never agreed to?" Like the personal narrative I just quoted, this ALMA statement turns a given assumption (in italics) into a fallacy and turns a value (freedom of contract) into a fact, beyond doubt and beyond questioning.

Here the use of reason and the appeal to passion mesh. A contract that binds those who did not sign evokes the specter of slavery and that evocation prompts a predictable emotional response in an American audience. Here adoptees utilize the symbolic meaning of contract to insist on its guarantee of individual rights and personal autonomy; rhetorically, then, *contract* does not represent particular strictures or regulations of a state but freedom of entry into an agreement by autonomous persons. From that perspective, breaking an adoption contract has a particular meaning for the adopted person.

"You know, it's not unethical," said an adoptee about searching. This adoptee continued: "I don't think it's unethical, well, I don't think it's immoral, maybe it's unethical. I definitely don't think it's immoral, it might be unethical. But I don't—. I see it as a legitimate breach of ethics, if there is such a thing."[26] This is one version of a point of view that emerged from the exchanges of stories at ASG: the conviction that law is negotiable and ethics are situational. According to this conviction, there are stronger bonds and higher laws than the secular laws addressed in the first meaning of the term *bond* in adoptee rhetoric. Being convinced means maintaining the terms of a legal contract can be broken without violating the bonds within an adoptive family or the sacred bonds of nature.

"I'm not looking for a family. I'm looking for roots. That's so important," a young adopted woman told me. She explained: "Roots means where we came from, who looks like me. It's completing the circle to have it."[27] The importance of a notion of "roots" to adoptee searches is well documented.[28] The concept also serves a rhetorical function, raising the pursuit of one's origins to a plane higher than curiosity, interest, and even the need for family history. The 1977 presentation of Alex Haley's *Roots* on television dramatized for a vast U.S. audience the idea that ancestry is something sacred and not just secular—something above the law in that sense. After *Roots,* ethnic background was seen as essential to identity—not a package of superficial traits, but absolutely crucial to who a person is. After *Roots,* the arguments made within the adoptee search movement touched the wider American public.

In the rhetoric of the adoptee search movement, knowing one's heritage and ethnicity contributes to the formation of an integrated identity. Information about and connections with those who came before complete the circle of the self—a position that accords with American cultural theories of identity formation. Linking ancestry to identity and self-fulfillment also rearranges cultural interpretations of the bonds of kinship, and this is central to the way a search solidifies an adoptee's ties to "two families."

The theme in adoptee accounts is that a search integrates the self. A search does not disintegrate the bonds within an adoptive family. The emphasis on self-formation and strengthening one's identity takes search stories away from a quest for a "new family" or a search for "other parents." The implication instead is that completing the circle means becoming newly bound to previously known relatives, or, to put it another way, attached to the several roots of one's being.

Karen's narrative about finding her birth mother stressed the good it did her and her adoptive family. Gaining more self-confidence from finding her roots, she told the group, allowed her to attach more closely to her adoptive family. "I think that it [searching] was something that I had to do for me and if it was selfish, I am sorry. It has done me more good than anything else in the whole world." In an *ASG Newsletter* (January 1991), she wrote: "Our adoptive mothers hold our hands and are in our hearts forever. . . . Our birth mothers are always in our hearts so all we really need is to hold their hand for just a little while. There is no competition here because each plays an important role in our lives."

As Karen's story illustrates, an emphasis on self-fulfillment removes the perceived threat that searching poses to an adoptive family. The claim that searching has to do with oneself confronts a powerful objection to releasing adoption records, that when an adoptee meets a birth family she or he will desert the adoptive family. In responding to the critique, adoptee narratives further elaborate the complex meaning that *bond* already has. A concept of roots justified the search for one's own ethnic and ancestral past and for, ultimately, the sources of one's being. What came in the next round referred more closely to heritage as biological. Not precisely defined, "biology" stood for the aspect of one's identity linked to genes and the physical traits one inherits from blood relatives. "I want to see a face that has similar genes to mine." Statements like this deny the intrusion of a search into existing kinship ties; they also connect searching with contemporary articulations of the significance of genetics to who one is and will become.

An adoptee told me she was searching for her birth mother to find out why she looked the way she did—"because of this big hole, and you have to jump over it every single day, cause there's a whole big gap in your life." Another adopted person remarked: "But it just kept eating at me, you know. Mostly all my cousins looked like their sisters and brothers." As the founder of ALMA, Florence Fisher, put it: "Blood. Yes, who you look like and walk like are more than idle curiosity. Blood."[29] Whether phrased in the symbolism of blood or in the recent vocabulary of genetics and DNA, the notion of a biological template connects adoptee search narratives to a modern discourse of identity and of rights—the right not to be denied the knowledge of who you inherently are.

But adoption is a matter of kinship, and references to roots represent the kind of kinship an adopted person uniquely experiences. Search narratives describe a double-rootedness and the enduringly dual attachments that make up an adoptee's life. Rooted to a genealogical ancestry, the adoptee is not less but more tightly bound to her adoptive family. First a botanical term, then a cultural term, *roots* captures the distinctiveness of adoptive kinship, the need continuously to bridge biology and environment, blood and contract. The intertwining was noticeable in the stories told at ASG meetings. There, search narratives presented two forms of genuine kinship, one begun by birth and the other initiated by contract. The former evokes the transcendental law of nature, viewed as mystical and often described as sacred; the latter represents the power of secular law, itself sacralized in references to "the law of the land."

Adoptee narratives effected a reinterpretation of kinship by recognizing different levels of law. If trying to locate a birth parent broke the boundaries of state law, narratives showed the quest did not violate *all* law. In the framework of search rhetoric, adoption is a "man-made" contract of kinship, not the highest law binding on a person. At the same time, adoptees recognized the value of secular law for inscribing and maintaining relationships between individuals. They honored adoption even while insisting on the special, and specially enduring quality of, bonds created in nature. In an extreme example of throwing the mantle of secular law over natural bonds, a birth father adopted the child he had relinquished thirty years earlier.[30] In a newspaper article quoted in the *ASG Newsletter* (March 1987), he was quoted as saying: "I felt that the law had separated us and that there was no way to wipe out the past without the law redeeming us and rejoining us as a family. It needed the significance of the legal action."

In the same newspaper article, the newly adopted daughter described her first meeting with her birth father: "I cried out and we hugged each other. It was incredible. We had an instant, almost cosmic rapport. We talked for 15 hours straight around the clock." Her account resembles a number of reunion stories I heard, sounding a theme that is much more common than the note her father sounded. Adoptees who found members of a birth family relished the overwhelming, awesome, "cosmic" or sacred feelings a reunion prompted.[31] Accounts of these feelings transform the third meaning of *bond* from "biology" to "nature," rhetorically a vast difference.

At meetings and in interviews, members of ASG emphasized the extraordinary impact of meeting a birth parent. As one adoptee described his reunion: "it wasn't an intellectual type of thing; it was this kind of feeling, this is where [I belong]. It was really just a gut feeling of, this is comfortable." The mixture of recognition, attachment, and identification often transformed these meetings into events that seemed destined; biological connection acquired the quality of a mystical bond in a number of reunion accounts I heard.[32] "There's almost some innate understandings among biological parents and siblings [i.e., the children] that is not there among adoptive parents and siblings," an adopted person explained to me, adding, "my temperament is just so different than either my [adoptive] mother or my [adoptive] father."

In other accounts, the mystical quality was expressed in terms of the spiritual dimension of a meeting. Several adoptees referred to the sacredness of bonds between those related by birth. "I know God had planned this," one woman wrote to Karen about her reunion (*ASG Newsletter,* January 1991). Adoptee references to God were more instrumental than those in accounts by birth parents. Birth mothers tended to use words like "blessed" or "God-given" for describing the encounter with a relinquished child, while adoptees shied away from that usage. Instead, adoptees referred to God and the sacred nature of birth bonds to justify a decision to search: "sometimes it takes a long time for the desire of your heart to come true. I must say, I believe God gave me wisdom to do the investigating I did" (*ASG Newsletter,* March 1987). In the end, the subtle rhetorical difference represents notably distinct interpretations of the natural bonds between parent and child by birth parents and by adoptees.

Yet in both instances, the outside-the-law and beyond-the-contract quality of a meeting is unmistakable. Adoptees and birth parents similarly claim a nature above the fray, a divine law that a person obeys even when she or he disobeys the laws made by men. These are assumptions that incorporate the values of the surrounding culture, as well as resonating to political developments of recent decades that condemn the injustice perpetuated by some man-made laws. Karen used such assumptions rhetorically when she wrote, "In this world where many desire 'skeletons in the closet' to remain there, I am reminded of an ancient truth which declares 'You shall know the truth and the truth shall set you free'" (*ASG Newsletter,* October 1986).

Exchanged week after week at the monthly meetings, adoptee narratives establish an effective arsenal of strategies of reason and tactics of passion. Under the informal tutelage of Karen and each other, members of ASG stockpiled a variety of rhetorical devices for describing searches and reunions. Yet with all the armaments, the battle has not been thoroughly won. Adoptee support groups that oppose the permanent sealing of adoption records and the persistence of confidential adoption have not been entirely successful in gaining a public hearing or achieving the changes in policy they demand. Continuing with ASG as my primary case, I suggest the complications of the adoptee position in the next section.

Obstacles to Change

ASG discussions and newsletters oscillate between particular stories and general demands for equal rights. Karen established the tone and the parameters of this discourse, conducting meetings and single-handedly editing the *ASG Newsletter.* In both roles, she created a public persona out of the private person she claimed she was. On ASG's ninth birthday, for instance, she asked members: "Do you have any idea how lucky you are to have a group in this area? It was very difficult for five adult adoptees (Insecure but adult) to even begin ASG. . . . As your coordinator I have now made about 30 such appearances [on TV and radio]. All this from a woman that never recited in school because she was so insecure" (*ASG Newsletters,* October 1985).

In a real way, ASG would not have survived without Karen. Her living room was the editorial office and mailing site for the newsletter; her son taught her how to use a computer and fixed the well-used answering machine; she took care of her husband and her two mothers while coordinating all of ASG's activities.[33] The highly personalized organizational structure had advantages and disadvantages. The advantage lay in the strength of Karen's commitment, which manifested itself in her enthusiastic response to the stories that came pouring out on Sunday afternoons and, she told us, on her answering machine. The arguments Karen took to the media and to the state legislature, couched as they might be in the vocabulary of reason, were grounded in substance in the stories she heard (and had a remarkable memory for, as I observed). The disadvantage was that a pattern developed that cut down on ASG's flexibility in responding to local and national changes in adoption. The result of Karen's monopoly over ASG activities was a stalemate, or, more accurately, a slowdown in the transformation of an effective support group into an influential pressure group.

As the coordinator of a support group, Karen encouraged the production of open-ended, unconstrained narratives; she was generous as a listener and a leader. But this was part of the problem. In efforts not to stymie any person or any version of the adoptive experience, she rarely raised the afternoon's proceeding above the level of sympathy, support, and suggestions for searching. While these were and continue to be very important (as well as faithful to the group's original purpose), they do not transform the intensely personal and necessarily random elements of life stories into a political agenda. Turned inward, reflecting on past experiences and present problems, the stories Karen encouraged were not attuned to the language of legislative debate. The meetings did not produce concrete proposals for reform, either of state law or of agency practice. Favoring a confessional or testimonial mode, ASG meetings tended to seem static and, over the years, repetitious in content.

Still, in public Karen put the material to use. Out of the numerous stories, with similar themes and issues, she built a case for adoptee second-class status and deprivation of rights. An accumulation of detail proved the discrimination against adoptees, particularly apparent in the negative response to requests for information (on birth and background) that all other citizens of the United States possessed. Borrowing the language of civil rights and of the adoption reform movement in general, ASG rhetoric characterized adoptees as an oppressed minority. Yet the language and imagery of civil rights and citizenship did not automatically grant ASG or Karen herself a hearing. The chore of persuading an audience of the adoptee case and of an adopted person's losses goes against the conventions and stereotypes that surround American adoption.

Conventions halt the process of change, especially in areas that are close to the heart, like family and the well-being of children. To an extent, then, the slowdown in ASG also reflected the molasses-like conditions of its external context. The state legislature refused to amend the law ASG had begun protesting in 1984. Other states are more willing to open adoption records.[34] However, the expressed reluctance of lawmakers and social workers to end the confidentiality and anonymity of American adoption keeps groups like ASG in the same arguing position year after year. As long as closed records remain an issue and adult adoptees are deprived of access to the facts of their own lives, Karen's strategies serve a purpose.

Conventions about adoption and stereotypes of the adoptee also contribute to policy makers' lethargic response to adoptee claims. Stereotypically, adoptees are privileged members of the triad, presumed to have gained an advantage by being adopted. The stereotype may be all the stronger since it overlays (or compensates for) a deeper conviction that the adoptee is unlucky: she or he has been severed from genealogical kin in a society that values biological kinship. Searchers challenge the stereotype of the fortunate adoptee, letting the side of adoption that speaks of loss and emptiness appear.

Conclusion

In the end, in an American cultural context, adoptees stand a real chance of effecting reform. The principle of American adoption, "the best interests of the child," gives all adoptees a claim. The moral imperatives in adoptee modes of persuasion extend the meaning of "child" the principle evokes through an emphasis on personhood. Furthermore, a notion of personhood is essential to an argument about contract: in the United States, a person cannot be bound by a contract she or he has not signed. Obedience to the existing legal bonds of adoption, in this view, constrains the ability of the adopted person to thrive, to acquire self-esteem, and to establish an identity. This view is increasingly supported by legal opinions advocating reform of adoption law. Indeed, as this essay approached publication, records opened to adoptees in four more states— Delaware in 1998, Tennessee in 1999, and Alabama and Oregon in 2000.

In many places, it is true, searches are still condemned, and contact between birth and adoptive families is considered dangerous. Although the shibboleths of secrecy have characterized American adoption for less than a century, their symbolic value and their centrality to cultural interpretations of kinship give them great stature in debates about policy and practice.

But clearly support groups for adoptees and birth parents have made a dent on American adoption practice. The activities of searching and of publicizing reunions have prompted adoption professionals into reconsidering the implications of confidentiality and of denial of information to members of the triad. In this essay, I have tried to show the equal importance of the way arguments are presented by support groups that sponsor searches, write to lobbyists, and march to Washington. The presentation exemplifies the modes of persuasion that reign in contemporary American culture: strategies of reason and tactics of passion. References to law, a legal system, the Constitution, and the Bill of Rights jolt the audience into agreement by citing conditions no "reasonable" person can dismiss. The strength of reason comes from a reference to values that have the backing of history, custom, and common understanding.

The complementary mode, a tactical use of passion, appears in the content of the values: human rights, dignity, autonomy, and freedom all elicit emotional responses (empathy) on the part of an audience. Bailey notes, "The appeal to emotion may be designed either to create such a shared value [if none exists] or to provoke a direct connection between feeling and action without the intervention of mind and its capacities for criticism."[35] In her role as coordinator of

ASG, Karen demonstrated her awareness that to be persuasive, reasonable talk about rights, an appeal to the head, had to be grounded in intense life stories, an appeal to the heart. ASG rhetoric exemplified the way a tactical use of passion is crucial to the deployment of weapons of reason.

A goal of my analysis has been to show how passion and reason intertwine in adoption reform rhetoric. It is not that one supersedes the other, even in close sequence, but that one is grounded in the other: an appeal to the heart does not work unless understanding accompanies the message; the heart responds to what the head recognizes as a truth. Similarly, appeals to the "mind" in adoption discourse are rendered moving (i.e., they move an audience) to the extent that cognition taps a root of emotion. The freedom with which adoptees told their stories at ASG, under Karen's loose regime, provided an opportunity—informal and spontaneous—to lock these dimensions together.

An adoptee support group like ASG requires a full and flexible arsenal, inasmuch as the audience toward whom pleas for reform are directed is diverse. Modes of persuasion in the adoption reform movement are directed internally, toward members of the triad, as well as externally, to members of a broad public. Meetings are the location of the former; television, radio, news magazines, and sometimes professional journals are the venue of the latter. Success of the movement depends on persuading individuals who are involved in adoption not only to delineate the terms of their relationships but also to recast personal insights as a social problem. Success also depends on persuading a general public that knowledge of the bonds of biology is not a threat to the solidarity of bonds of contract.

At ASG, members sharpened the tools of passion and of reason through the ongoing exchange of stories. Personal, emotional, and confessional, these stories contain an acute critique of current American adoption custom. While adopted persons, like everyone else, tell stories to themselves about their lives, their decisions to bring their stories into public (even as safe a public as a support group) indicates a perception of the special interests that accrue to being adopted in the United States. In this context, personal stories are de-privatized and diffused into a general movement for change. Although ASG is not formally or legally a lobbying group, its modes and methods offer an example of how such groups work best.

The example is a reminder, too, of how important individuals are to the process of changing adoption custom and, eventually, state adoption law. Positions do not simply occur; they are established by people—an obvious fact often ignored. In the instance I analyze here, people provide the material for a debating position in a series of (sometimes repetitive) autobiographical testimonies). Over the course of an afternoon and over the years of attending meetings, members of ASG explore the parameters of their experiences and, through the telling and retelling of their life stories, move from the particular to the general: narratives of particular experiences begin to reflect and to reiterate the value-laden general concepts of deprivation of rights, discrimination, and second-class citizenship. The emotional energy with which one person reports a blank wall here, a reluctant social worker there, a "wide gaping hole," or a "genetic amputation" fuels the rational content of an argument for opening records when those involved in adoptive kinship request an end to secrecy and confidentiality.[36]

The gist of the argument that emerged from ASG stories, the *ASG Newsletter,* Karen's letters to the editors of local newspapers, and her media appearances was a reconsideration of the meaning of contracted parent-child relationships. Assessing the meaning of the contract that establishes the relationship between an adoptee and her or his adoptive parents, adoptee discourse connects the terms *contract* and *person* to their sources in American history and tradition. Traditionally, in America a contract promises freedom of signature and freedom of revocation. On the one hand, no one ought to be bound by a contract he or she did not sign; on the other hand, a contract pledges ongoing loyalty and obligation between those who agree to its terms. In the adoption reform argument, a person (no longer the "adopted child") cannot be bound by terms to which he or she did not agree. Simultaneously, entered into freely, a contract holds persons together through ties based on trust and shared concerns.

With play on its literal and legal definitions, the term *contract* is used as a symbol in adoptee discourse. As a symbol, *contract* expands the meanings and the implications of adoptive kinship, for the individual and for the culture. With the concept of contract, adoptees argue for the preservation of personhood in adoptive arrangements and for the enduring solidarity of significant relationships.

The adoption reform movement essentially demands that the historical implications of contract be incorporated into the arrangement of adoptive kinship. That may mean opening adoption at the onset—allowing all (adult) parties freedom in drawing up a contract, a freedom that requires the exchange of information and trust.[37] In the framework of the reform movement, a recognition of the full (and fully cultural) meaning of contract logically demands an extension to postadoptive relationships. Adoptive kinship and the identity of the adopted person are ongoing processes, requiring a continual "openness" about the clauses of the contract. As much symbolic as legal, *contract* represents a form of negotiation, done with honesty and dignity and recognizing personal autonomy. Moreover, the concept of contract releases the concept of bond from the connotations of being barred or imprisoned either in a genealogical or in a socially constructed relationship.

The lesson of adoption reform rhetoric extends into a critique of dominant ideologies of kinship in an American cultural context. An emphasis on bonds, rights, and privileges links a concept of the person to an interpretation of being related. This link shifts "being related" away from the assumption of one absolute, impermeable, and fixed (whether by law or by birth) connection between individuals. The language of adoption reform links kinship with self-identity and with the full status of person in an American setting, while not narrowing the meaning of kinship to *either* legal *or* biological, *either* adoptive *or* blood. The language of adoption reform, then, reforms the cultural conceptualization of kinship.

Adoptees who search are not attacking adoption. Rather, the demand for open records and for an end to sealed documents, anonymity, and the mutual invisibility of birth and adoptive families pushes adoption to its best incarnation, where freedom of information does not alienate but attaches *persons* to one another. The demand for contact and communication is a logical extension of contracted kinship, exploiting the potential of a contract to be continually reviewed and renegotiated. Ironically, through the force of their rhetoric and the effectiveness of their modes of persuasion, reform groups comprised of adoptees and birth parents may succeed in radically redefining American kinship even if they fail to repeal specific state laws.

The strategies I have described in this essay would not be necessary if change moved faster in the United States in the realms of child-placement policy and family values, both of which embrace adoption. At the same time, when they do happen, changes in adoption influence all policy focused on children and substantially modify American ideologies of the family.

Whether or not ASG intends a complete reconfiguration of cultural interpretations of kinship, that is the potential result of its Sunday afternoon supportive conversations. As Karen realized in her frequent media appearances, the distance from those Sunday meetings to a national forum was short. Because of groups like ASG, the distance to changing the structure of adoption in the United States will now be shorter.

NOTES

The first version of this essay was drafted quite a while ago; much has changed in the domain of adoption over the past five years. Still, the importance of search groups like ASG cannot be underestimated, and the honors given to persons like Karen testify to the public's recognition of the importance of support groups like the one I attended for so many years. My primary thanks, of course, go to ASG and all its members, with special thanks to Karen for her help, support, and encouragement of my project. Others have read and commented on the essay in its various drafts: Henry Krips, Alan Kennedy, Albrecht Funk, and—with editorial patience—Marianne Novy. My thanks to them and my apologies for ignoring some good suggestions in favor of pursuing my own argument.

1. Adoption law in the United States is state law. Although there are federal guidelines, there are no federal laws regulating adoption.

2. In 1855, Massachusetts passed the first adoption law; other states followed. In

1917, Minnesota passed the first law mandating confidentiality in (stranger) adoptions; other states followed that precedent.

3. The distinction comes from F. G. Bailey's analysis of persuasive rhetoric in *The Tactical Uses of Passion: An Essay on Power, Reason, and Reality* (Ithaca: Cornell University Press, 1983).

4. I was welcomed in all groups as an anthropologist and an adoptive parent, identities I always revealed.

5. The term *triad* refers to birth parents, adoptive parents, and adoptees and replaces the sharper and presumably less humane term *triangle*.

6. Orphan Voyage provides a reunion registry for adoptees and for birth parents who want to locate "lost" kin; contact depends on a successful match of names. Voluntary and mutual, such registries are legal in most states.

7. Wayne Carp, *Family Matters: Secrecy and Disclosure in the History of Adoption* (Cambridge; Harvard University Press, 1998), 142.

8. All adoptees in the United States receive an amended birth certificate, which records the names of adopting parents as if they were the genealogical parents. This convention is a source of controversy in adoption circles; see Judith S. Modell, *Kinship with Strangers: Adoption and Interpretations of Kinship in American Culture* (Berkeley: University of California Press, 1994).

9. See Bailey, *Tactical Uses of Passion*, 29.

10. Clifford Geertz, *Local Knowledge* (New York: Basic Books, 1983), 173.

11. Bailey, *Tactical Uses of Passion*, 22–23.

12. Quoted in Kenneth Burke, *A Rhetoric of Motives* (Berkeley: University of California Press, 1969), 50.

13. From a newsletter of ALMA in the author's possession.

14. Informally, everyone who came was called a member, but there were membership dues. Virtually every issue of the *ASG Newsletter* reminded people to "please pay."

15. Because of its (growing) concern with altering the terms of American adoption in general, ASG welcomes birth parents, adoptive parents, and anyone interested in eliminating the confidentiality and secrecy of traditional American adoption. At the meetings I attended, adoptees were always in the majority.

16. Under the bill (which became law in February 1985), an adoptee could petition the court for his or her birth records. An adoptee could also go back to the agency through which he or she was adopted and request help in finding a birth parent. Several agencies in the county cooperated in such requests, while respecting the privacy of a birth parent.

17. Quoted in Modell, *Kinship with Strangers,* 150.

18. See Joseph Gusfield, *Contested Meanings: The Social Construction of Alcohol Problems* (Madison: University of Wisconsin Press, 1996), on the creation of "social problems" that receive attention from legislators, policy makers, and the media.

19. See Carp, *Family Matters,* chap. 5, for a discussion of the political events influencing the adoption reform movement. In 1975, real teeth were put into the Freedom of Information Act, making it both public and effective.

20. Bailey, *Tactical Uses of Passion*, 134.

21. Burke, *Rhetoric of Motives,* 54.

22. Bailey, 133.

23. The tendency to treat *biology* and *nature* as synonyms is not unique to adoptees

or to the adoption reform movement but in fact occurs in both scholarly and popular writings on family and kinship.

24. Bailey, *Tactical Uses of Passion,* 132.

25. Quoted in Modell, *Kinship with Strangers,* 157.

26. Quoted in ibid., 154.

27. Quoted in ibid., 143.

28. Most recently and thoroughly by Carp, in *Family Matters.*

29. Florence Fisher, *The Search for Anna Fisher* (New York: Arthur Fields, 1973), 112.

30. Evidently the adoptive parents had agreed to dissolve the adoption. I have not seen any reports of their role in the case.

31. I have described this in more detail elsewhere; see, for example, Modell, "'Where Do We Go Next?' Long-Term Reunion Relationships between Adoptees and Birth Parents," *Marriage and Family Review,* 25, no. 1/2 (winter 1997): 43–66.

32. New problems arise when an adoptee and birth parent extend their contact over time.

33. Karen had met her birth mother several years before I joined ASG, and her story of the reunion became a model for other searches; see Modell, *Kinship with Strangers,* especially chap. 7.

34. As of this writing, in late 2000, six states—Kansas, Alaska, Delaware, Tennessee, Alabama, and Oregon—provide adoptees almost completely open access to records, and four others—Montana, Ohio, Colorado, and Vermont—provide access with some further qualifications. Kansas and Alaska never had sealed records; the others have all opened in the past ten years. See Adam Pertman, *Adoption Nation: How the Adoption Revolution is Transforming America* (New York: Basic, 2000), 32, 82.

35. Bailey, *Tactical Uses of Passion,* 23.

36. My impression was that some members thought all adoption should be open and nonconfidential, while others were arguing for the opening of records to those who requested such information and contact. A few of the members I met supported reunion registries, even though those required the consent of both a birth parent and an adoptee.

37. See Modell, "Open Adoption: Extending Families, Exchanging Information," in *New Directions in Kinship,* ed. Linda Stone (London: Routledge, Kegan Paul, 1998).

"File It Under 'L' for Love Child"

Adoptive Policies and Practices in the Erdrich Tetralogy

Jill R. Deans

Who gave to me
The breath of life
My frame of flesh?
Who gave me
The beat of heart
My vision to behold
Who?
     —Ojibway creation story[1]

Louise Erdrich is a creator in more ways than one. In a cosmological sense, she is the *manitou*, or spirit voice, of a dynamic fictional world.[2] She is also a mother. Language and birth appear lovingly entangled in Erdrich's prose as she develops ways to consider both the construction and the conception of identity in her work and life. A successful contemporary literary voice, drawing the attention of both scholars and popular readers, she challenges us through interconnected novels that inform each other as they narrate separate incidents and threads of existence. She invites us to inhabit her texts diachronically, to probe not just the history of events but also the genealogy of a community, the intricate relativity of time, place, and circumstance.

Adoption weaves its ways throughout her first four novels: *Love Medicine* (1984, 1993), *The Beet Queen* (1986), *Tracks* (1988), and *The Bingo Palace* (1994).[3] It occurs to locate and root stray individuals. It occurs also to demonstrate how elusive identity can be, especially when an adoption is informal, contested, or just unsuccessful. Part of Erdrich's strategy in this regard is to juxtapose the public record, however messy or inaccurate, to the living characters inscribed therein. In this way, adoption as a practice can be subversive, if it eludes or contradicts policy. It can also serve to restrict or seal one's fate, once an identity is written or claimed. It serves most of all to complicate the genealogy of Erdrich's shifting cultural landscape, a terrain fraught with tension between the written and the oral, between the official and the unofficial, between *constructed* identities and *natural* ones.

Three of the novels unfold on Chippewa reservation land, while *The Beet*

Queen explores Erdrich's German-American ties in a fictional town called Argus. There is constant interaction between the Native American and white populations and across class and gender divisions. June Kashpaw (of *Tracks* and *Love Medicine*) is raped and enacts her revenge at the Kozkas' butcher shop in Argus (the setting for *The Beet Queen*); Dot Adare (title character of *The Beet Queen*) appears as Gerry Nanapush's partner in *Love Medicine*; and so forth. Characters that are peripheral in one novel loom large in others, demonstrating basic principles of perspective as well as complicated social relations. My analysis of these interactions is likewise patterned on an intricate and jagged weave, as I isolate moments from across the four novels in no particular chronology but in terms of the thematic impact of records on adoptive identities.

Erdrich's own family appears as complicated as her fictional families. When this essay was first conceived, Erdrich was still married to, though separated from, writer Michael Dorris. At forty-one, she was the mother of five children, three by birth and two by adoption. A third adoptive child, Abel, had been killed tragically in a car accident in 1992 at the age of twenty-three. Dorris had adopted Abel years before Erdrich or the other children entered the picture, when single-father adoptions were virtually unheard of and placements of "hard-to-place" Native American children were increasingly controversial.[4] Bringing Abel *home* signified both domestic and political boundary crossings for Dorris, who himself identified as part–Modoc Indian. In *The Broken Cord* (1989), he describes his commitment to maintaining his "nontraditional" family despite these and other obstacles, which would lead him on a journey to recover Abel's obvious behavioral and mental difficulties, ultimately diagnosed as Fetal Alcohol Syndrome (FAS), the result of his birth mother's alcoholism. Erdrich reacts pointedly to the drama of her husband's household in the foreword of his book: "I never intended to be the mother of a child with problems. . . . it simply happened" (xii).[5] It happened through adoption, a legal procedure that binds their family and Erdrich's fate with Abel's "problems."

Since then, Erdrich has been confronted with other serious family problems. In 1997, Dorris committed suicide, having struggled with depression and allegations of abuse leveled by his remaining adoptive children, Madeline and Sava. Erdrich has had to cope not only with an investigation but also with the aftermath for her three biological daughters. Eric Konigsberg's story on the family in *New York Magazine* reveals perspectives and data regarding the "scandal" that appear to challenge Erdrich's sensitivity to adopted children. For example, Sava Dorris, who once "had a violent tantrum and beat Erdrich up with a piece of wood," makes the painful accusation that Erdrich knew about the abuse committed by Dorris against the adopted children but did nothing to stop it.[6] Konigsberg reports Sava as saying: "She had to know that her own blood was being hurt before she did anything."[7] Whether or not such allegations are true, the fact that Sava felt that the adopted children were not as valuable to their mother as her "natural" children could be significant as we examine the uprooted or dispossessed in Erdrich's fiction.

My analysis, however, reveals in the author a remarkable, if complicated, sensitivity to adoptees and individuals who may have fallen between the cracks of conventional family structures. This need not preclude Sava's suffering now as an adoptive adult who (a) may indeed have suffered serious abuse and (b) may have otherwise struggled with his identity and sense of place(ment). Konigsberg reports further that Sava, having moved to Denver at the age of nineteen, began a romantic relationship with Eileen Kalim, a forty-two-year-old woman who claims "their relationship was in many ways like that between a mother and a son."[8] Clearly, Sava is searching for answers—an activity familiar to adoptees. He was arrested for beating Kalim, now the second mother figure he has attacked, and we can speculate that Sava's violence is in part connected to the fact that he is adopted. The question of whether or not Erdrich failed to protect her adoptive children is complicated not only by the strictures that may have been placed on her, living in an allegedly abusive household and caring for children with FAS, but also by facets of adoption and its problems that Erdrich may have faced everyday in her life and her writing.

Adoption is an institution difficult to describe in overview. Laws still operate state by state, with little uniformity and plenty of risk involved for all members of the triad (birthparents/adoptive parents/adoptees). While some feel empowered by the act of choosing a safe, productive environment for children, others approach adoption fraught with feelings of inadequacy for their inability to conceive or keep a child. Adoptees rarely have agency in the process, despite the unifying sentiment that all placements should consider the "best interests of the child." Adoption now includes private, public, and open adoptions, all rallying around this credo.

At the time of the Dorris adoptions, however, most "formal" adoptions were "closed," regulated by public agencies that sealed records to protect the privacy of all parties and minimize confusion regarding the nuclear makeup of the adoptive household. Historian E. Wayne Carp explores the evolution of sealed-record adoption in his book *Family Matters: Secrecy and Disclosure in the History of Adoption* (1998), noting particularly that confidentiality was not intended, initially, to prevent "parties of interest" (i.e., adoptees, birth parents, or adoptive parents) from viewing court records and birth certificates.[9] Gradually, through the professionalization of social workers, the impact of psychoanalysis, shifting demographics in postwar adoption, and a desire for confidentiality, adoption records were locked away at the discretion of the courts. In this process, however, the hidden documents gained an elusive power reflected today in the impassioned searches and activism by adoptees who remain confused about their identities and feel entitled to identifying information, including medical records and genealogies.

Although Carp contends that the privacy of birth parents was (and still is) a factor in the sealing of otherwise public documents, he emphasizes that the stigma attributed to the out-of-wedlock parent conflicts with a general romanticizing of biological ties in our society. Given the privileging of the biological as a model for relatedness, some birth and adoptive parents are now questioning the logic behind the secrecy of adoption. How, they ask, have their identities as parents and individuals been violated by such practices? After all, closed adoptions rely on the fiction that birth parents, for all intents and purposes, do not exist. This fiction enables adoptive families to operate "as-if-genealogical," as anthropologist Judith Modell puts it, discrediting nontraditional families that appear other than nuclear.[10] How such fictions work and break down is of significant interest to me as I read Erdrich and negotiate the interdependency between narrative and identity.

Michael Dorris was forced to challenge the primacy of biology, as he discovered that adoptive families should be *as good* (as nonadoptive families) on their own terms and that to pretend that the adoptive child is a biological child could have damaging consequences. In *The Broken Cord*, Abel is renamed "Adam" to protect the young man's privacy—an act that reenacts the rewriting of subjectivity that occurs in the adoption process. Ironically, while the author hides Adam's true identity, he is frustrated by a system that has similarly "sealed" Adam's past, including his medical history. While he admits that initially, "[c]onfidentiality suited me fine" (77), he later craves information that could help to establish equilibrium in a child who is haunted physically by poor prenatal care: "The less I knew about Adam's natural family, the less they knew about me. Unfortunately, as I was to reluctantly discover, the less I knew about them, the less I knew about Adam" (77). Avoiding the fray of the adoption rights movement (which advocates for open records), Dorris appeals primarily for increased education and funding for prenatal care in the Native American community. Common sense and compassion regarding the accessibility of Adam's "history" is a practical necessity, in his view. He sets out to crack the code of Adam's genealogy like a researcher or mathematician in search of *x*. History and records have in this case a specific healing property that can serve as a metaphor for the function of history in Erdrich's writing. History isn't identity per se (as many adoptees who search discover) but serves an adhesive function to bind individual and communal subjectivity.

Poised amid the paucity and inadequacy of Adam's history in *The Broken Cord,* we find Erdrich herself, written about as a participant in the coded regulation of Dorris's family. With Erdrich in the picture, Dorris resorts to some naturalizing tendencies to conceive his family. He explores the art of rendering a family, at the pivotal moment when he, Erdrich, and his three adoptive children become a legal kinship unit.

I listened as Adam's, then Sava's, then Madeline's name was read, heard them say yes, and watched as each child in turn was embraced by Louise. As she and they signed their names to papers that formalized the pact we had already begun to live, my eyes followed the line of ornate woodwork that bordered every wall of the room. The surface gleamed with wax, and the corner joints were fitted together so seamlessly that the carved pattern appeared unbroken, as if it had been crafted from an enormous tree. (127)

Dorris's narrative captures the convergence of the adoptive and the biological. He conjoins obvious juridical aspects of identity formation (the voice of a judge, signing papers, the formality of chambers) with very traditional naturalistic imagery (the enduring, seamless wood carvings, the presence of some great organic continuum). The family tree or totem, here carved but unbroken (symbolizing biological kinship as likewise inscribed but appearing adhesive), contrasts with the "broken cord" that separated Adam from his alcoholic birth mother. With the judge's ruling, Dorris effectively affirms a consensual agreement, based on love and care, "that they had already begun to live," thus naturalizing an "unnatural" relationship, and thus validating the restorative bond between Dorris, Erdrich, and their children.

This blend of constructed and "natural" imagery that surrounds identity formation should be familiar to Erdrich's readers as well, especially in light of her book *The Blue Jay's Dance* (1995), which describes her experiences with childbirth and motherhood.[11] It is very possible to accuse Erdrich of romanticizing the "natural" mother and child union in these pages, of inferring a more authentic connection to her "natural" daughters. She makes it clear in the "Dedication and Household Map" that this book is for and about her birth children. Although she writes, "We raised our children as equally as we could," the "older adoptive children" fall off the map once she enters her birthing narrative (x, 4). The book is not, however, without sensitivity to these children or for adoption in general. Erdrich reveals that her paternal grandmother, Mary Erdrich Korll, adopted Erdrich's father and his three brothers (200). Erdrich's maternal grandmother, Mary Lefavor, is also an adoptive mother. By mentioning this grandmother's affection for "other women's children," Erdrich reveals a careful awareness of adoptive kinship (139). If adoption were truly *as if* biological, why note it? Clearly, for Erdrich it is not quite the same, though she demonstrates throughout that motherhood requires both biological and adoptive impulses.

An infant's attachment to the birth mother seems to be a vital component to Erdrich's understanding of motherhood. The book is filled with naturalistic imagery, metaphors of nest building and planting, conception and harvest. "I'm an instinctive mother," she writes, "not a book-read one, and my feeling is that a baby must be weaned slowly from its other body—mine" (64). Her "instincts" are sometimes perilously close to the Victorian concept of Mother Consciousness, which served in the nineteenth century to define woman's domain under patriarchy as house- and child-bound. In her essay "Social Construction of Mothering," Evelyn Nakano Glenn provides a useful summary of this ideology.

> Mothering in Western cuture has been defined in terms of binary oppositions between male-female, mind-body, nature-culture, reason-emotion, public-private, and labor-love. Mothering has been assigned to the subordinate poles of these oppositions: thus it is viewed as flowing from "natural" female attributes, located only in the private sphere of family and involving strong emotional attachment and altruistic motives.[12]

Although traditional Ojibway culture does not "subordinate" mothering, it maintains a similar binary, notes Basil Johnson: "For men the vision was necessary for self-fulfillment; for women a vision was not essential. By giving life through the first mother, women were fulfilled."[13] Erdrich's romance of the birth process more likely stems from this latter sense of fulfillment, the ability to "create" life through the body, rather than from Victorian ideals that limit women to their instincts, their bodies and "nature."

Like her Ojibway male counterparts, Erdrich is a writer with plenty of "vision." In *The Blue Jay's Dance*, she demonstrates her physical fulfillment through language, through metaphors and analogies of gestation and birth, such as the fertile images of her family garden or her cat heavy with kittens (28, 40). She is thus both physically and intellectually (pro)creative. In opposition to traditional gender binaries, Sara Ruddick's essay "Thinking Mothers/Conceiving Birth" explores how the balance between "birthgiving" and "maternal thinking"—the bodily and the discursive—is jointly emblematic of women's experience.

> In these maternal conversations mothers represent to themselves and to the world their maternal commitment. Often, in these efforts of self-(re)presentation, they find themselves invoking the promise of birth: *this* body counts; each birthgiver's bodily labor, each new body she creates, is a testament of hope.[14]

The constructed and the innate mingle, and motherhood is qualified as something that is written about (if not written itself), that can be engaged from without. Elaine Tuttle Hansen, in her analysis of the "mother without child" in Erdrich's fiction, makes the important point that motherhood in Native American traditions is often jointly understood as both physical and thought-based. Furthermore, Hansen draws from Paula Gunn Allen to explain how nonmothers could participate in the important status of the mother through assisted child-rearing practices (or informal adoption): "the link [in these traditions] between biological procreation and mothering was looser," she writes.[15]

As both a birth and adoptive parent, Erdrich celebrates unabashedly her fertility of both body and mind in her maternal conversations in *The Blue Jay's Dance*. She equates such cultivation with her own migration from North Dakota to New England (where she and Dorris lived at the time of the book's gestation).

> Perhaps if we water these peonies, these clumps of red sedum, these pensees, these tiny bleeding hearts, maybe if I water my asparagus bed with tears, I'll grow real roots, I think, caught up in the abject melodrama of the exile. Maybe if I dig and fertilize I'll flourish, I'll belong where I am. (94)

She demonstrates that identities, like plants, *take* roots rather than *have* roots. Later, she compares her children to weeds that sprout willy-nilly, their seeds blown by the wind, to root almost randomly. "We cannot choose who our children are, or what they will be," she remarks (105). Although referring to her biological daughters, this statement recalls vividly her difficult relationships with her adopted sons, Abel and Sava.

Even while Erdrich clings to her bodily connectedness with her daughters, she infuses that biological relationship with written kinship markers. Words and bodies dance furiously in this book, like the spastic blue jay in her title. The blue jay's dance, she explains, is both the insistence of life and, curiously, a suicidal act, as the bird performs frantically before a hungry hawk. In this image, Erdrich captures the ceaseless birth and death of embodied meaning and equates it with her own fragile existence.

> If . . . my body survives by uttering itself over and over again. . . . If I am one word, so are my daughters, so are all of us in strings and loops. Each life is one short word slowly uttered. . . . Body, what is the meaning of this absurd and complicated story? What word will be erased with me? . . . Who will read this female body? (192)

Sounding like a philosophical linguist, Erdrich invites critics to deconstruct "this female body," to claim her identity as a "series of utterances" or "citations."[16] She balances script and body in her meditations, not without questions and complications, just as her novels more elaborately do. In this essay, I will identify the words-as-bodies that signify the adoptive identity in various examples throughout Erdrich's tetralogy. Erdrich reveals a very contemporary sense of adoption, one that wants both the potency of the biological and the certainty of the written but succumbs ultimately to a relativistic blur of social relations.

Fictional Families: Charting the Disjunctures in the Erdrich Genealogy

The story comes around, pushing at our brains, and soon we are trying to ravel back to the beginning, trying to put families into order and make sense of things. But we start with one person, and soon another and another follows, and still another, until we are lost in the connections. . . . (*BP,* 5)

In *The Bingo Palace,* Lyman Lamartine may run the economics of the tribe, but it's Zelda Kashpaw "who has the record and whereabouts of everyone's ancestors and secret relatives handy to herself" (*BP,* 127). Keeping track of genealogy in Erdrich's fiction is, indeed, a full-time job, although Zelda finds plenty of time to manipulate relationships as she attempts to recast the family not through the warm, lusty example of her adulterous parents' generation but in her own cold image. Zelda is not unredeemable. In fact, her heart literally explodes with passion and regret in the end, when she suffers a coronary in her resolve to rekindle a lost love. Until then, however, she carries on a legacy of maintenance and control that stretches back matrilineally and sometimes fanatically to her grandmothers, Margaret Kashpaw/Rushes Bear and Pauline Puyat/Sister Leopolda in *Tracks* and *Love Medicine.*

Erdrich demonstrates throughout her tetralogy that inheritance is sometimes genetic, sometimes spiritual, sometimes material, and sometimes political, but always messy. It is often contested, frequently lost, and occasionally recovered, like Adelaide's jewelry, Nector's pipe, June's bingo book, Lipsha's "medicine," and Zelda's passion. Erdrich venerates the messiness of inheritance and belonging, constructing characters who indulge like mischievous switchboard operators in plugging, unplugging, and replugging her subjects into a system of relations. Operators, like Zelda, help channel the flow of energy, despite blackouts and breakers and the occasional plug that just won't fit. Some characters, like Lipsha Morrisey, Mary Adare, and Lulu Lamartine, are adopted (formally or informally) but claim an inheritance to their biological origins. Others, like Lyman Lamartine and Nanapush, are not literal adoptees but adopt legal identities to register a claim for themselves or their community. Claims in each case mediate the characters' roles in a society that is always in the process of redefinition. This analysis, in other words, will focus on adoptive policies and practices in a domestic and political landscape that is constantly shifting, a place where redrawing the boundaries of a community is both literal and figurative and is characterized by both strict maintenance and reckless abandon.

Hertha Wong alludes to these conditions in her useful essay "Adoptive Mothers and Thrown-Away Children in the Novels of Louise Erdrich" (at the time, Erdrich's novels included the first edition of *Love Medicine, Tracks,* and *The Beet Queen*). Wong's piece begins by evoking Chodorow's theories of motherhood and the potential for "ego-boundary" confusion in the process of separation. Her point is to establish accepted patterns of developmental confusion that can occur when a child, particularly a girl, is forced to distinguish herself from mother. Ultimately, however, Wong recognizes that Erdrich's Chippewa community expresses a culturally specific definition of motherhood and nurturing.[17] In this context, Wong concludes: "Mothering can indeed be a painful process of separation. . . . But mothering can also be a communal responsibility for creating and maintaining personal identity."[18] Wong explains furthermore how a Native American sense of motherhood reorganizes the role as broadly connective and sustaining: "mothering is not merely an activity but an orientation to the world."[19] In this way, fractured families, particularly rifts between mothers and their children, are not just domestic issues but symptoms of a cultural state of emergency.

Erdrich's novels are full of markers and *tracks,* places where social forces declare or imprint a specific subject identity for a specific purpose. Parent/child separation and connection are thus subsumed under the broader auspices of social regulatory practices. Despite Wong's notation that Erdrich's characters are adoptive "by choice or circumstance rather than by law,"[20] informal adoptions that occur in less obvious moments throughout the novels are no less potent or inscribed than, say, the legalistic example that Dorris provides for us in *The Broken Cord.* Erdrich does mark the shifts in identity that occur, but like Dorris, she laces her transactions with the presence of naturalizing forces and connective elements, shared stories, memories, healing powers, tokens, and other traces of inheritance that don't necessarily have legal status but nonetheless declare an individual's place in the genealogy.

Unwritten transactions dot the narrative, either to seal and/or to break apart a communal or individual sense of self. Erdrich often plants documents or policies in her novels for the sole purpose of mocking their "official" ways. This undermining of the formality of records allows some of Erdrich's characters to resist formal designations and leaves others lost between the cracks of communal recognition. Stephen Greenblatt, in his seminal contribution to new historicism, "Towards a Poetics of Culture," calls for a kind of critical attention relevant to Erdrich: "We need to develop terms to describe the ways in which material—here official documents, private papers, newspaper clippings, and so forth—is transferred from one discursive sphere to another and becomes aesthetic property."[21] Erdrich uses both official and unofficial records as "aesthetic property" in the art of rendering an identity. Her characters craft legends, heroes, and villains from the data they gather. Whereas Wong concentrates on the psychological, my goal is more new historicist, as I discuss the signifying role of records and narrative to define and redefine the public image of the adoptive identity.

Hence, in reading all four novels and trying to plot carefully each biological link, each adoptive moment, each connection and disjuncture, I found myself beholden to a persistent, though often unreliable, paper trail. While I knew that

Erdrich and Dorris had a "kinship chart for our characters in our minds," I also became sure that others were keeping track as well, Zelda being the most obvious.[22] Who keeps records and why? And how does the presence and absence of the recorded identity reflect the mechanism of identity formation in a given society, especially a society facing deep changes—in landscape, economy, technology, and values? How does adoption, furthermore, both typify and belie the recorded identity?

Tracks (which recalls an earlier history of upheaval in Erdrich's native landscape, at the turn of the century) opens with the informal adoption of the young orphaned Fleur, who had only "raw power, and the names of the dead that filled her" (*T*, 7), by Nanapush, who is able to speak those names of the past, "Old Pillager, Ogimaakwe, Boss Woman" (*T*, 7). Their joint birthlike emergence from a diseased aphasic stupor links them, but the older Nanapush retains vivid memories of the past and keeps physical tokens of them stored carefully in a trunk. The first tribal archivist, he can speak and provide evidence, and thus he becomes the guardian not only of Fleur but also of the ghostly remnants of a severely diminished tribe.

Encountering Fleur's brother half-dead with fever, Nanapush "spoke a cure for him, gave him a new name [Moses] to fool death, a white name . . . learned from the Jesuits" (*T*, 35). This moment evokes the adoption of the Judaic Moses, so named because he was "drawn out" of the water by the pharaoh's daughter. In *Tracks,* Moses is kept by his parents, who are instructed to "pretend that the small boy who lived was someone else" (*T*, 36). In both cases, the endangered child finds safety in the identity of the dominant culture, but also in both cases, Moses remains committed to the traditional views of his people—the bestowed identity thus competing with an original. Annette Van Dyke examines "the power of spiritual legacies" in her essay "Questions of the Spirit: Bloodlines in Louise Erdrich's Chippewa Landscape," to illustrate the resources available to Chippewa characters whose cultural footing is beginning to slide out from under them.[23] Most of these legacies are established in *Tracks,* which historicizes the basis for the "Pillager Curse," Lulu's "secret ways," and the secret of those "no good Morriseys"—elusive forms of inheritance that serve to identify various "descendants" throughout the tetralogy.

The legacy passed down from Nanapush to his adoptive daughter, Fleur, and his granddaughter, Lulu, is especially charged with the old man's love and healing, and each woman serves at some point to rectify personal and tribal losses. But unlike Fleur, whose past still haunts and holds her, Lulu is offered a new tangible form of inheritance and a place in a government-sanctioned tribal structure, when Nanapush names her in the church rolls. Is this recorded legacy as productive or powerful as traditional endowments that are orally administered? Critic James Flavin contends:

> The paper trail that has replaced the oral tradition of Nanapush threatens
> the existence of Nanapush's culture. . . . Removed from tribal traditions, his
> tribe . . . may become as paper to trees, weak, neatly filed, easily burned and
> destroyed.[24]

Despite its fragility, this system of records endures throughout the tetralogy, even as the forest is felled, ultimately, for the Bingo Palace, the dream project of Lulu's son, Lyman. The chronology of the series reflects, loosely, a chronology of Native American assimilation and of the threat to Native American mythology. By the end of *Tracks*, Nanapush confesses his role in this emerging reality: "To become a bureaucrat myself was the only way that I could wade through the letters, the reports, the only place where I could find a ledge to kneel on, to reach through the loophole and draw you home. . . . I produced papers from the church records to prove I was your father" (*T*, 225). Nanapush found a way to turn records into "aesthetic property," to create an intelligible narrative of paternity and relatedness.

Of course, Nanapush is not Lulu's biological father, but he rescues her from the government school with this recorded lie. He takes on the *form* of her father within a sanctioned discursive realm. The act is tricky but characteristic of his Ojibway namesake, Nanabush.[25] This healer, like Nanapush, emerges from a plague to teach the people how to survive. Johnson recalls the myth of how Nanabush's mother died after his spirit father abandoned them. The son seeks vengeance on the father, and after doing battle, they make peace with a sacred pipe, which the father then bestows onto the son. (This is, no doubt, the same sacred pipe that is Nanapush's legacy to Lipsha in the tetralogy.) Most curious, however, is Nanabush's ability to change form (a trait he inherited from his spirit father): "It was the only way that Nanabush could accomplish his purpose. As pure incorporeal being he would be neither accepted, nor understood."[26] He would take the shape of rocks and trees and men; no wonder Erdrich's Nanapush conforms so easily to the role of father for Lulu. Now they can both be "accepted" (more or less adopted) by the church and, subsequently, the U.S. government.

Erdrich is subtle with records. They are the receipts for lost political battles, promising land allotments, subsidies, quotas, and other forms of so-called restitution, receipts that even Fleur cashes in eventually. But the author is careful not to center her narrative here and thus limit her world only to that of politics, where she could not probe the intimacy of her characters. In *Love Medicine*, for example, tribal leader Nector Kashpaw demonstrates the personal implications of policy the day the butter subsidy comes in: "Butter. That's right. Seventeen tons of surplus butter on the hottest day in '52," he explains, "That is what it takes to get me together with Lulu" (*LM*, 128). Luckily the reader is not caught up in red tape and can follow Nector and Lulu on their buttery escapades. After the deliveries and the infidelity, Nector again juxtaposes the public with the private by describing his wife Marie's ability to handle a more illicit "surplus": "Marie kept taking in babies right along. Like the butter, there was a surplus of babies on the reservation, and we seemed to get unexpected shipments from time to time" (*LM*, 134–135). Through such examples, Erdrich undermines the value of political receipts by mocking the system that depends on them for order. When Nanapush falsely gives Lulu his name in remembrance of his dead daughter, Father Damien "completes the records" and the adoptive identity becomes official (*T*, 61).

Damien, like Zelda, is a keeper of records, and also like Zelda he had little influence in his quest to legitimize the stray members of his errant flock. Again and again, the church is a place where Erdrich can challenge the record, the self sanctioned not by God, as we see, but by an institution, like the U.S. government, caught up in its own perversions. The ordination of Jude Miller in *The Beet Queen* is a perfect test case. Biological cousin Sita Kozka listens with a kind of raw fascination as the priest threatens excommunication to those "who may perchance be irregular . . . , or under interdict, or suspended, *illegitimate*, infamous" (*BQ*, 93; my italics). Jude was abandoned as an infant at the Orphans' Picnic (appropriately), then effectually kidnapped by the Millers, who become his adoptive parents. Thus, Jude does not know he is the "bastard" son of Adelaide Adare and Mr. Ober—neither does the priest.

Jude slips through the cracks and is ordained by the Catholic Church. His deception is inadvertent, however, unlike that of Pauline Puyat/Sister Leopolda, who denies her background not only to the church but to herself. Leopolda's denial of agency corrupts her power, which weakens dramatically every time she encounters her daughter, Marie, who had since been adopted by the Lazarres. Though they maintain a tortured bond, their mother/daughter status remains unknown in *Love Medicine*. This pathology is explained in *Tracks* by Leopolda's fierce insistence that the conception was at first immaculate, then never happened at all. It is no wonder Marie seems like the devil incarnate to a woman unable to accept the girl's human origins. Of course, Leopolda's own ancestry leaves her little to cling to; she is "an unknown mixture of ingredients. . . . We never knew what to call her, or where she fit." (*T*, 39). The church becomes a refuge for her and a place where her identity, no matter how inaccurate, can be codified. Not so for her daughter, however. Even though Marie is drawn almost instinctually to Leopolda's side, she senses an evil, the poisonous manifestations of her mother's denial. Marie compensates by becoming the mother to several displaced children; she signifies where her own mother is lacking.

Lulu's son Lyman Lamartine, though not an adoptee, demonstrates a more comic and profitable adoptive practice by using the U.S. government to "adopt" an identity that does not belong to him. Unlike Leopolda, however, Lyman confesses his subterfuge to the reader.

> Once I filed, I knew I was on my way back. I was gathering myself. Identity was taking shape. I was becoming legitimate, rising from the heap. The ironic thing was that when I finally got around to the 1099 I saw that someone had typed my box number onto a form that belonged to someone else. . . .
>
> Out of a typo I was formed. Out of papers I came to be. (*LM*, 301)

Lyman capitalizes on the error, signing off on huge financial risks, knowing that his "personal limbo" will only become further mired in the great bureaucratic machinery of Washington (*LM*, 302). Like the church, the government is an unreliable record keeper and manager, leaving room in each case for creative agents like Lyman, aspiring martyrs like Leopolda, and blind followers like Jude to adopt sanctioned identities.

In her essay "Chance in Louise Erdrich's *The Beet Queen:* New Ways to Find a Family," Pauline Woodward explores how comedy is necessarily accompanied by adaptability. She takes her cue from Gerald Vizenor's "spirit of trickster" that resides comfortably in the interstices of the postmodern narrative.[27] Basically, humor is a coping mechanism for tragic displacements, and we laugh at characters who struggle to fit in by seizing opportunities and making them work. Woodward notes that Mary Adare, for example (like Lyman, Jude, and Leopolda), "inhabits the border between belonging and not quite belonging, that space where comic freedom prevails, where, Vizenor tells us, trickster is alive in narrative."[28] When Mary's mother flies off with The Great Omar at the start of *The Beet Queen*, Mary feels "satisfaction" and forges ahead to conquer new family units (*BQ*, 13). Woodward describes Mary's comic power to adapt to her Aunt Fritzie's butcher-shop world and the fatherless home of Celestine and Wallacette (whom Mary brazenly renames "Dot"). But Mary's impulse to respond to her lost mother's feeble concern with a cruel, anonymous note ("All three of your children starved dead") signals a more serious defense mechanism at work to thwart the pain of abandonment (*BQ*, 58).

This defense leads to developmental paralysis and the inability to forge meaningful connections to her new chosen family: "In putting her hands over her ears," writes Woodward, "Mary has effectively cut off the past and therefore cannot ground her future in anything solid."[29] Toward the end of the novel, Mary appears more tragic than comic, impotent as a "father Aunt" figure to Dot, and insensitive to Celestine's wishes for her daughter. As with Sister Leopolda, the pain of her own legacy leaves Mary empty. She clings to her mother Adelaide's jewelry box, hoping to cash in on her only precious possessions, but finds the gems replaced with worthless trinkets. Woodward equates Mary's condition with Didier Coste's notion of "orphanhood as a technique of liberation in narrative."[30] It is important to remember, however, that none of the characters who are called orphans in this novel—Mary, Karl, or Jude—are really orphaned. And Mary may appear liberated for a time, but she can never really escape the tragedy of her past.

Like Mary, Lipsha, a main character from *Love Medicine* and *The Bingo Palace*, is a comic/tragic figure haunted by his abandonment. Unlike Mary, however, he is far less assertive in his quest to be inscribed in the social order. With his mother, June Morrisey, dead and his father, Gordie Kashpaw, in and out of prison, Lipsha was raised by the charitable Marie, his "adoption" always clouded by the specter of his infamous biological parents. A lovable misfit, Lipsha demonstrates how recorded identity sometimes misses the mark and how true selfhood is much more difficult to validate, especially when tribal structures and those who establish them are unable or unwilling to recognize the "illegitimate," the "Love Child," whose inheritance is not only devalued, like Mary's, but unrecognized. "I am waiting for a [tribal] band card," he explains in *The Bingo Palace*, "trying out of boredom to prove who I am—the useless son of a criminal father and a mother who died with her hands full of snow—but in trying to prove myself to the authorities, I am having no luck, for Zelda is a solid force to reckon with" (*BP*, 128).

When Zelda withholds Lipsha's tribal status through her influence, she seethes with bureaucratic perversity. For Lipsha, the result is persistent nonstatus. Elsewhere, however, Zelda works to determine the custody and name of another "illegitimate" child, Redford. With the chilling pronouncement "We have *papers*," she wrenches Redford away from his biological aunts to force a union between his biological parents, Shawnee Ray and Lyman (*BP*, 174). This custody battle is the corrupted counterpart to Nanapush's restoration of Lulu, illustrating how the value of an adoptive identity depends on the forces that create it. In Nanapush's case, Lulu's recorded identity works to preserve tribal unity; in Zelda's case, Redford's custody battle and Lipsha's nonstatus work more to serve Zelda's personal vision.

Once in love with Shawnee Ray's uncle Xavier Toose, Zelda never gave in to her desires, as her father, Nector Kashpaw, did with the lusty Lulu Lamartine (producing Lyman, who now feeds that desire to Shawnee Ray, and so on). She "adopts" Shawnee Ray and Redford, informally but with the intention of formalizing their roles in the tribe, thus glorifying her self-appointed position as tribal matriarch. A marriage between Shawnee Ray and Lyman seems the next basic step: "After all, he's Redford's natural father," she explains to her biological daughter, Albertine (*BP*, 212). A tired, young medical student, Albertine weakly urges her mother to consider Shawnee Ray's aspirations as a designer and possible feelings for the hapless Lipsha. But such freedoms are impossible to Zelda, who claims Shawnee Ray as her charge—the daughter that she and Xavier Toose never had.

Though he is bound by guilt and obligation to Zelda, who "sav[ed] him from the slough" where his birth mother, June, tossed him, Lipsha remains unmarked and unclaimed. Despite—or perhaps because of—his history, Lipsha resides outside the official social script. Taken in "like any old stray" by Marie, he is raised side by side with June's "legitimate" son, King, who taunts him cruelly for his obscure identity: "You little orphant. . . . Who said *you* get a pork chop for dinner? That's for the *real* children" (*LM*, 32, 342). It is significant that both Lipsha and his mother, June, are adopted by Marie under mysterious circumstances. When she took in June, orphaned in the woods, Marie was shocked that there was "no mark on her," no scar to attest to her parentage or experience (*LM*, 87). This detail is significant in light of June's ability to mark others, to make deep impressions to the extent that she is, as critic Robert Silberman claims, the invisible character who drives *Love Medicine*: "June's presence, that is, her absence, haunts the book."[31] Her demise in a blizzard characterizes both the chilling power and the sheer blankness that surrounds her.

Likewise, Zelda cannot fathom how Lipsha survived his ordeal in the slough without visible ramifications. His only "mark" may be the "medicine" he sometimes possesses, inherited from the Nanapush side of the family. When this fails him, however, he loses his identity: "My hands are shocked out, useless. I am again no more than the simple nothing that I always was before" (*BP*, 66). He struggles to avoid imposed markings, like the time he almost had the state of Montana forcibly tattooed to his behind. Instead, he opts for a symbolic falling star emblazoned on his fickle palm. The mark renders visible his remote connection to his birth parents: "[Gordie] and my mother, June, have always been inside me, dark and shining, their absence about the size of a coin," reflects Lipsha after helping his father escape from prison (*BP*, 259).

This thought is accompanied by the bizarre presence of an anonymous infant "heavier than a shrunk down star," who just happens to be in Lipsha's and Gordie's stolen getaway car (*BP*, 255). "Here is one child who was never left behind," notes Lipsha wryly (*BP*, 259). Together Lipsha and the infant form a perfect pair, both without direction or name: "There is no trace where we were. Nor any arrows pointing to the place we're headed. We are the trackless beat, the invisible light, the thought without a word to speak. . . . Before the nothing, we are the moment" (*BP*, 259). Erdrich uses the existential quandary of Lipsha to illustrate how identity is a constant negotiation in the face of moments that either cannot be recorded or fail to exist in tangible ways. The snowstorm scene resonates with June's chilling death, but it also produces an important image: a blanket of fresh snow superimposed on the sublime innocence of the baby. Tracks will form on both over time, but the original moment has no record beyond Lipsha's memory, his sense of abandon and abandonment.

There is the residue of the modern, even the romantic, in the fallen stars scattered throughout Erdrich's texts. Eventually, however, the poetry of these stars is crudely burned into Lipsha's flesh as he identifies with his lost parents. A more postmodern sensibility takes over as the body becomes inscribed to be identified, as loss becomes a defining category. In *The Postmodern Condition*, Lyotard recognizes the slippage that characterizes il/legitimacy in terms of a tension between "the legitimacy of science" and "the legitimacy of the legislator," which identify knowledge in terms of "what is true" and "what is just," respectively. He argues that "knowledge and power are simply two sides of the same question: who decides what knowledge is, and who knows what needs to be decided?"[32] Neither scientists nor legislators can accommodate all forms of knowledge that characterize individuals in a diverse society. The result, as we enter an age of increasing technology, Lyotard notes, is utter atomization, splinter knowledges, and increased relativity.

Lipsha's identification with loss expresses, furthermore, what Susan Pérez Castillo refers to as an "ontological instability," the alienation of the Native American community from white, Western consciousness.[33] In this landscape, a proliferation of border inhabitants straddle competing knowledges. Many of Erdrich's characters—with the exception of June and Adelaide—manage to ride out their displacements. The formal "knowledges" that account for identity—written records—smudge and blur under these circumstances into less precise traces or measures that may be recognized immediately by one group of people and not at all by another. Take, for example, the pipe that Lipsha inherits from Nanapush. A symbol of recognition in the tribe, a token that defines Lipsha's presence there, it is desecrated by white police officers at the Canadian border (*BP*, 31–35). They fail to see its significance, its "legitimacy," and suspect instead drug trafficking (an illegitimacy). Lipsha must be rescued by Lyman, who can discourse in both communities and explain the symbols of his people to the white policemen. Lyman then borrows the pipe, loses it, and almost loses his role in the tribe as a result. Signs, records, and markings are relative here, just as relatives become more and more unstable as the tetralogy progresses.

Lipsha expresses the universal dilemma that individuals cannot reclaim their origins but must reconcile their place in society with scraps of evidence and historical traces. Ultimately filed "under 'L' for Love Child," Lipsha must operate within the system of relations that accepts or rejects him, no matter how strange or hybrid these relations may become (*BP*, 128). As in Dorris's description of the adoptive moment in the judge's chambers, more fluid relations can substitute for "seamless," "natural" bonds. Wong concludes that: "Having had their totem/family identities destroyed by Euroamerican domination, these characters must reformulate notions of self, family, and community."[34] Adoption can easily become a metaphor for tribal absorption by dominant U.S. policy. It also can become a metaphor for those characters on the fringes of a community, like the Adares and the Kozkas of *The Beet Queen,* who adopt, adapt, or go insane with alarming frequency.

To hold people together, Erdrich employs the spider web as a symbol of connection when connection seems least likely. It is an appropriate image when describing adoption, for the web is both constructed and spun from the biology of the spider. Writes Woodward of the web imagery in *The Beet Queen,*

> Vibrating strings create links that form a structure, matching Erdrich's method of orchestrating voices to shape a story that emphasizes both the fragility and the mutability of community, particularly the family, and the transience of human relationships, such as those between parents and children.[35]

In an interview with Nan Nowick, Erdrich commented, "Informal adoption is common in Native American cultures and being temporary parents can be very painful," adding tension to the delicate web of relations.[36]

However we might label the disjunctures—in both Erdrich's writing and her life—it is my task to read how resultant adoptions are coded, to ascertain the function of scripted kinship. There remains in these narratives a desire to connect innately, as if biological ties, too, can be *written.* In the work of Erdrich, we can almost believe it is possible, since here genealogies live and grow and are recognizable in their complexity. She has, in a sense, written biology, as creator of her fictional world, demonstrating how all kinship is scripted on some level. While in real life, perhaps, the balance of relations cannot be so deftly penned, Erdrich expresses, nonetheless, an earnest struggle for stasis, for family on its own terms. While adoption as a practice should not be viewed as a universal metaphor for identity formation, it can inform the way we read other social relations and the regulatory mechanisms, policies, and practices that allow us, as individuals and a society, to recognize and connect with one another.

NOTES

1. Basil Johnson, *Ojibway Heritage* (Toronto: McClelland, 1976), 11.

2. Manitous (native spirits) are part of the Plains Ojibway or Anishnabe tradition with which Erdrich identifies. German-American on her father's side and Turtle Mountain Band Chippewa on her mother's, Erdrich explores her "mixed-blood" identity through her writing. See Louise Erdrich, "An Interview with Louise Erdrich," interview by Nancy Feyl Chavkin and Allan Chavkin, in *Conversations with Louise Erdrich and Michael Dorris,* ed. Nancy Feyl Chavkin and Allan Chavkin (Jackson: University Press of Mississippi, 1994), 220–53.

3. Quotations from the novels are taken from the following editions and cited in the text with the abbreviations *LM* for *Love Medicine,* rev. ed. (New York: HarperPerennial, 1993); *BQ* for *The Beet Queen* (New York: Bantam, 1989; *T* for *Tracks* (New York: HarperPerennial, 1989); and *BP* for *The Bingo Palace* (New York: HarperPerennial, 1995).

4. Native American children were still considered "hard to place" at this time because of their ethnicity. However, David Fanshel's study of the Indian Adoption Project (1958–68) in *Far from the Reservation: The Transracial Adoption of American Indian Children* (Metuchen, N.J.: Scarecrow, 1972), indicates that adoption of Native American children was never "hard" and has been hotly debated for nearly a century due to its imperialist implications. While many Native communities also have a history of intratribal or informal adoption, Dorris adopted Abel from a tribe other than his own via formal, legal channels.

5. Quotations of this work cited in text are taken from Michael Dorris, *The Broken Cord* (New York: HarperPerennial, 1990).

6. Eric Konigsberg, "Michael Dorris's Troubled Sleep," *New York*, June 16, 1997, 35. Supporters of Dorris find fault with Konigsberg's article, which aggressively seeks evidence of abuse. See, for example, Ned Hayes, "An Elegy: Believing in Michael Dorris," *hot ink*, July 29, 1997, <http://www.hotink.com/72997.html>.

7. Konigsberg, "Dorris's Troubled Sleep," 70.

8. Ibid., 35.

9. E. Wayne Carp, *Family Matters: Secrecy and Disclosure in the History of Adoption* (Cambridge: Harvard University Press, 1998), 41–57.

10. Judith Modell, *Kinship with Strangers: Adoption and Interpretations of Kinship in American Culture* (Berkeley: University of California Press, 1994), 2.

11. Quotations of this work cited in text are taken from Louise Erdrich, *The Blue Jay's Dance* (New York: HarperPerennial, 1996).

12. Evelyn Nakano Glenn, "Social Construction of Mothering: A Thematic Overview," in *Mothering: Ideology, Experience, and Agency,* ed. Evelyn Nakano Glenn, Grace Chang, and Linda Rennie Forcey (New York: Routledge, 1994), 13.

13. Johnson, *Ojibway Heritage,* 15.

14. Sara Ruddick, "Thinking Mothers/Conceiving Birth," in *Representations of Motherhood,* ed. Donna Bassin, Margaret Honey, and Meryle Mahrer Kaplan (New Haven: Yale University Press, 1994), 44.

15. Elaine Tuttle Hansen, *Mother without Child: Contemporary Fiction and the Crisis of Motherhood* (Berkeley: University of California Press, 1997), 117.

16. See Judith Butler, *Bodies That Matter: On the Discursive Limits of "Sex"* (New York: Routledge, 1993), 12–15.

17. For a summary of Chippewa or Ojibway understanding of motherhood, see Johnson, *Ojibway Heritage,* 23–26.

18. Hertha D. Wong, "Adoptive Mothers and Thrown-Away Children in the Novels of Louise Erdrich," in *Narrating Mothers,* ed. Brenda O. Daly and Maureen T. Reddy (Knoxville: University of Tennessee Press, 1991), 191.

19. Ibid., 190.

20. Ibid., 180.

21. Stephen Greenblatt, "Toward a Poetics of Culture," in *The New Historicism,* ed. H. Aram Veeser (New York: Routledge, 1989), 11.

22. See Louise Erdrich and Michael Dorris, "Marriage for Better or Words," interview by Charles Trueheart, in Chavkin and Chavkin, *Conservations with Louise Erdrich and Michael Dorris,* 119. The Danish publisher of *Love Medicine* also felt the need to draw up a genealogical chart, which American publishers later used and embellished for distribution among reviewers only.

23. Annette Van Dyke, "Questions of the Spirit: Bloodlines in Louise Erdrich's Chippewa Landscape," *Studies in American Indian Literature* 4, no. 1 (1992): 15–27.

24. James Flavin, "The Novel as Performance: Communication in Louise Erdrich's *Tracks*," *Studies in American Indian Literature* 3, no. 4 (1991): 11.

25. In Erdrich, "An Interview with Louise Erdrich," Chavkin and Chavkin refer to this mythological figure as "Nanabozho," and Erdrich confirms that he was the inspiration for Nanapush (252).

26. Johnson, *Ojibway Heritage*, 20.

27. Woodward draws particularly from Gerald Vizenor, "Trickster Discourse: Comic Holotropes and Language Games," in *Narrative Chance: Postmodern Discourse on Native American Indian Literatures,* ed. Gerald Vizenor (Albuquerque: University of Mexico Press, 1989), 189–96.

28. Pauline G. Woodward, "Chance in Louise Erdrich's *The Beet Queen:* New Ways to Find a Family," *ARIEL* 26, no. 2 (1995): 115.

29. Ibid., 116.

30. Ibid., 115. Woodward's phrase summarizes her understanding of Didier Coste's description of the orphan in *Narrative as Communication,* vol. 64 of *Theory and History of Literature* (Minneapolis: University of Minnesota Press, 1989), 320.

31. Robert Silberman, "Opening the Text: *Love Medicine* and the Return of the Native American Woman," in Vizenor, *Narrative Chance,* 104.

32. Jean-François Lyotard, *The Postmodern Condition: A Report on Knowledge,* trans. Geoff Bennington and Brian Massumi, vol. 10 of *Theory and History of Literature* (Minneapolis: University of Minnesota Press, 1984), 8–9.

33. Susan Pérez Castillo, "Postmodernism, Native American Literature and the Real: The Silko-Erdrich Controversy," *Massachusetts Review* 32, no. 2 (1991): 285–94.

34. Wong, "Adoptive Mothers," 177.

35. Woodward, "Chance," 110.

36. Louise Erdrich, "*Belles Lettres* Interview: Louise Erdrich," interview by Nan Nowick, in Chavkin and Chavkin, *Conversations with Louise Erdrich and Michael Dorris,* 73.

Adoption as National Fantasy in Barbara Kingsolver's *Pigs in Heaven* and Margaret Laurence's *The Diviners*

Kristina Fagan

Pigs in Heaven, by American novelist Barbara Kingsolver, and *The Diviners,* by Canadian novelist Margaret Laurence, are nationalistic fantasies. The novels allegorically reflect the authors' dreams for racial and cultural reconciliation in the United States and Canada, respectively. These fantasies revolve around orphaned characters who achieve, through literal or metaphorical adoptions, cross-cultural identities that include both Native and white cultures. *Pigs in Heaven* is the sequel to *The Bean Trees,* in which a three-year-old Cherokee orphan is anonymously given to a white woman, who then adopts the child and names her "Turtle."[1] *Pigs in Heaven* is set three years later, when a lawyer from the Cherokee Nation finds out about the adoption and tries to have the girl returned to the tribe. In a resolution that manages to keep everyone happy, Turtle ends up with an extended family that peacefully mingles Native American and white cultures. In *The Diviners,* Morag Gunn is a white orphan who knows next to nothing about her birth family. During her childhood, Morag acquires a cultural identity from her adoptive father's invented tales of her Scottish heritage. Later, she has a child with a Métis man, connecting her identity and her daughter's to that of Native people.[2]

These two novels strike a deep and perhaps unconscious chord in European settlers and their descendants, because they enact the desire for a nation that combines and reconciles white and Native peoples. In the settler imagination, Native people represent an authentic North American identity. The fantasy of becoming indigenous, or "going Indian," reflects a longing to be confidently at home on the North American continent. Indigenization also offers a definite break from the Old World.[3] One of the most powerful ways to "go Indian" is to be adopted by Native people. This adoption theme has been played out in the writings of Thoreau, in the art of Charles Russell, in the historical figures of Hawkeye and Long Lance, and in innumerable films and novels.[4] A popular example of this adoption narrative is the 1990 film *Dances with Wolves.*[5]

But while the desire for adoption by Native people is a powerful theme in settler art and literature, the adoption of native children by whites has been a common real-life occurrence. Once again, this practice fulfilled settler desires:

251

pragmatically, it filled a demand for adoptable children; politically, it responded to white society's desire to control Native people. Kingsolver and Laurence are two white writers who draw on settler fantasies of both being adopted by and adopting Natives. I use the term *adoption* in a broad sense, to refer to both adult-adult and parent-child relationships where the adoptee is taken in and given a home and an identity. *Pigs in Heaven* is about the literal adoption of a native orphan by a white family, but it is resolved by the "adoption" of that family by a native community. In *The Diviners*, Morag experiences a lifelong desire for a familial, cultural, and national sense of belonging. This search began with her adoption at three years old, and she repeats this adoptive pattern, looking to each man with whom she is involved for a source of identity. Through her métis daughter, she finally finds a family as well as a connection to indigenous people and hence to an "authentically" Canadian identity. Both orphans, Turtle and Morag, finally become the sites of unions between white and native people. Yet these novels privilege the settlers' point of view. The adoptees are the distillations of and the solutions to national dilemmas, appealing to the hopes and desires of their largely white audiences. The Native is an essential part of that audience's fantasy. However, while the transracial nationalism celebrated by Kingsolver and Laurence helps build the settlers' identity, it does not help and may even hurt Native identity.

Novels have often played a role in building the ideal of national unity and harmony. D. H. Lawrence wrote that the friendship of Chingachgook and Natty Bumpo in *The Last of the Mohicans* represented the dream of "a new society" and "a new world epoch."[6] Huck Finn and Jim were another attempt, in Leslie Fiedler's words, at a "dream of reconciliation."[7] Such narratives allow readers to imagine their country as they wish it to be. Benedict Anderson argues that nations are always the products of such wishful thinking, that they are imaginary constructs, dependent on our belief in them. The *idea* of nationhood brings together a large anonymous group and transforms them, in their own minds, into a community. Novels, Anderson adds, play an essential role in building belief in the nation. The composite form of the novel combines a variety of places, people, and styles into a single national vision.[8] *Pigs in Heaven* and *The Diviners* bring together Native and settler cultures, thus offering their readers an imagined, multicultural nation.

Kingsolver and Laurence are writing in and against a long tradition of nationalistic orphan narratives. In the settler imagination, North America itself is an orphan—a young society, cut off from its European parents and searching for an identity. Orphanhood is "an inherent part of the romance of America, of the myth of eternal fresh starts. . . . [It] is a clean slate, self-reliance and often enchanted solitude."[9] In Laurence's and Kingsolver's novels, the orphans' initial losses of community provide that mythical fresh start and make way for a new and ideal national identity. Though neither Turtle nor Morag can clearly remember their preadoptive lives, they both remember the deaths of their birth parents (*Diviners*, 27; *Pigs in Heaven*, 294). The loss of those parents, who might have given the children solid connections to an existing community and mythology, allows for a new myth created by the novels. Morag turns her birth parents into "totally invented memories" (18) that serve her current needs. Even Morag's family name appears to be without history. When she looks it up in *The Clans and Tartans of Scotland*, she finds that the Gunns have no arms or motto (58). But this lack of history gives Morag's adoptive father free rein to invent an ancestor for Morag: the larger-than-life Piper Gunn. The adult Morag recognizes the way that absence leads to a fixation with identity: "I don't know why names are so important to me. Yes, I guess I do know. My own name and feeling I'd come from nowhere" (311). Many believe that this fear of being without a history or identity is Canada's greatest anxiety. In a comparison that is particularly apt to this discussion, Northrop Frye writes that Canada "developed with the bewilderment of a neglected child, preoccupied with trying to define its own identity."[10] It is this sense of an absence, both in a child and in a country, to which *The Diviners* responds.

Turtle cannot be a blank slate in the way that Morag is. In other people's eyes, her native appearance immediately defines her. Whiteness can act as a non-identity, but people of color do not have that option. Turtle also carries with her the sexual and physical abuse she suffered before she was adopted by Taylor. With her adoption by Taylor, Turtle begins to heal. But to heal fully, she must remember her past. This remembering begins when she is reunited with her birth grandfather (321). Within the framework of Kingsolver's national allegory, Turtle's situation symbolizes the need for Native people to heal from the individual and collective traumas that they have suffered. While to settlers the North American continent may represent a new beginning, to Natives it is a place of long memory and, recently, of horrific experiences. But, while Turtle's and Morag's preadoptive pasts differ, for both of them adoption signals the beginning of new identities—identities with symbolic, national significance.

The new national communities that Kingsolver and Laurence imagine are written against the standard stories of identity that have formed Canada and the United States. In particular, both of these novels are set in the West and reexamine the powerful myths of that region. In the States, the traditional myth of the West is symbolized by cowboys and Indians, the wild frontier, and the empty horizon. These images are accompanied by a philosophy of individualism, self-reliance, progress, and adventure. The American dream relies heavily on the images of the Wild West. Precisely these images, Wallace Stegner argues, make it difficult for westerners to find a sense of a "personal and *possessed* past." Westerners do not feel, Stegner explains, "any continuity between the real western past which has been mythologized out of recognizability and a real western present that seems as cut-off and pointless as a ride on a merry-go-round that can't be stopped."[11] The cowboy-and-Indian myth is particularly useless for Western women and indigenous peoples. Barbara Kingsolver has said that she wants to rewrite the present-day West to include those who never appeared in the old story. The traditional myths, she explains, are not helpful today: "I think the stories that got us westward ho have ceased to become true."[12] She feels that the American dream of the conquering individual must be balanced by other forces.

> I think everything I write is about the idea of community and the special challenge in the United States of balancing our idealization of the individual, our glorification of . . . personal freedom and the individual with the importance of community.[13]

In *Pigs in Heaven,* the conflict between individualism and community is explicitly equated with the conflict between white American and Cherokee philosophies.

Pigs in Heaven draws on the legal, historical, and ethical conflicts over the adoption of Native North American children, an issue with a long and painful history. For many years, culturally biased and paternalistic judges and social workers removed Native children from their families and communities en masse.[14] A 1969 study found that 25 to 35 percent of Native American children had been separated from their birth families, up to nineteen times the rate for nonnative children.[15] The vast majority of those children were adopted by white families and had their native identity wiped out.[16] Many grew up with an inability to deal with a racist society, with confusion about their identity, and with low self-esteem. In *Pigs in Heaven,* Annawake Fourkiller's brother Gabriel, who was adopted out of the Cherokee community as a child and ends up in jail, is a typical example of the results of such interracial adoptions. Knowing this history, Native communities almost unanimously oppose adoption of native children by non-Natives.[17] In the United States, the 1978 Indian Child Welfare Act required that tribes participate in and consent to decisions about foster care for and adoption of native children. While this legislation resolved many problems, it created another. Many native children spend a great deal of time in foster care while social workers search for a native adoptive family. This delay in finding a stable home and family can cause severe emotional harm to the child.

Adoption issues are usually discussed in terms of the child's best interests. However, "best interests" is not an objectively measurable quality. It may mean very different things to native and white communities. Many Americans measure a child's interests in terms of the values of individuality and equality. According to them, native children should have the same rights as white children to quick placement in a family. Furthermore, they argue that the child's individual emotional needs are more important than the needs of the native community.[18] Native communities, however, argue that the child needs the community to develop a strong identity. Furthermore, the community needs to rear and educate their own children if they are to preserve their culture. Annawake, the Cherokee lawyer in Kingsolver's novel, is an articulate spokesperson for the community-based position: "We consider that the child is part of something larger, a tribe. Like a hand that belongs to the body. Before we cut it off, we have to ask how the body will take care of itself without that hand" (338).

Pigs in Heaven presents both of these positions with great sympathy. Alice and Taylor Greer are lovable representatives of a fierce individualism, subverting gender norms by taking on this traditionally male-gendered personality trait. The novel's first words are "Women on their own run in Alice's family. This dawns on her with the unkindness of a heart attack" (3). Alice realizes that once her daughter, Taylor, left Kentucky, there was "nothing to hold" Alice there (5). Alice has no connection to her home, extended family, or community. She passed that sense of independence on to her daughter. Taylor left Kentucky to go West (the classic American individualistic journey), with her main goal "to not get pregnant" (52). Acquiring Turtle was unexpected, but Taylor latched onto the child with all the love that her mother had given her. Otherwise, though, she continued to assert her independence from all, including her boyfriend, Jax. When the Cherokee Nation challenges her claim to Turtle, Taylor immediately leaves Jax and their home to set up a life for her and Turtle alone, trusting in the American capitalist promise: "I should be able to keep a roof over my head if I work at it" (246). She brushes Jax off when he tells her that that promise is "just a story" (246). Taylor is so immersed in the American myth of individualism that she cannot recognize it as a powerful fiction.

Taylor and Alice do have a deep love for their daughters. But that extremely focused love is insufficient, especially when it comes to raising Turtle. The novel's first incident, where Turtle sees a man fall off the Hoover Dam and no one but Taylor will believe her, establishes the close attachment between this mother and daughter. Taylor finally recognizes that her cultural myth has weaknesses when she sees that it is harming Turtle. However, this realization comes slowly. Even, for instance, when unable to pay for good food or electricity, Taylor refuses to give in and return to Jax and her friends. She also refuses to ask for help in the special challenges of raising a child of another race. She is not racist, but she is not race-aware either. Taylor espouses a kind of equality-based, color-blind, "race doesn't matter" attitude that is the ideal of many Americans. But this attitude is not enough to help Turtle deal with her native identity. The way that Taylor forces Turtle to drink milk, not knowing that most Cherokee are lactose intolerant, is a small example of how Taylor may not be able to deal with Turtle's particular needs, needs that will become more complex as she gets older. When the Cherokee child-welfare officer asks Turtle to tell him about her family, Turtle answers, "I don't have one" (324). This is the moment when Taylor realizes that Turtle needs a community.

Of course, Taylor is not a typical white American. Her devoted independence is on the far end of the spectrum. The Cherokee town of Heaven, Oklahoma, is on the other end. In Heaven, everybody knows and is related to everybody else, children are cared for collectively (186–87), and even crazy Boma Mellowbug is loved by all. Sugar Hornbuckle calls the town an "endless family reunion" (186). The novel briefly gestures to the town's unemployment, suicide, and drinking problems, but, overall, Heaven is presented in an extremely flattering light. When Alice goes to Heaven to discuss Turtle's adoption, she is welcomed unquestioningly by the town. Her experience of the stomp dance is a tribute to the power of the communal spirit.

> For the first time she can remember, Alice feels completely included. . . . For a while she tries to keep tabs on where Cash is, but then she forgets to think about it, because she can't quite locate *herself* in this group either. She only knows she is inside of it. . . . Alice's life and aloneness and the things that have brought her here all drop away, as she feels herself overtaken by uncountable things. (271–72)

Alice is without home or roots. She is "adopted" by the whole Cherokee community, given a home, a family, and even a new cultural identity.

Kingsolver ensures that no one will miss her careful embodiments of individualism and community. The characters discuss those terms quite explicitly. For instance, Annawake tells Jax the story of the "pigs in heaven," where six boys who would not work are turned into pigs by the spirits. Annawake says, "I had a hundred and one childhood stories and they all added up more or less to 'Do right by your people.' Is that so bad?" Jax responds with the guiding myth with which he grew up: "I heard the usual American thing. If you're industrious and have clean thoughts you will grow up to be vice president of Motorola" (88). These are the two options with which *Pigs in Heaven* struggles.

At the center of this struggle is Turtle. She has begun to heal under Taylor's love and care. She clings to her mother like a snapping turtle, hence her name. To remove Turtle from her mother would shatter her emotionally. But the warmth with which Kingsolver paints the community of Heaven leaves no doubt as to what Turtle is missing in her solitary relationship with her mother. Furthermore, as Annawake reminds us, Turtle's skin color does not give her "the option of whiteness" (279). She will always be influenced by her race, and Taylor cannot teach her how to deal with that. But this is a novel with no villains. We sympathize with all the characters, and so the first time that I read this book, I was full of anxiety because I could not see the possibility for a truly happy ending. As Jax says, there "is no point of intersection in this dialogue" (89). Janet Farrell Smith, drawing on the terminology of Bernard Williams and Martha Nussbaum, refers to the issue of interracial adoption as "not resolvable without remainder."[19] Indeed, both Taylor's and Annawake's positions are morally sound, and choosing either one would have a negative "remainder" for Turtle. Furthermore, if we expand this conflict, we can also see that the ideals of community and individuality cannot easily coexist in a national myth. To truly act for the maximum benefit of all members of the American national community (if such an entity can be imagined) would inevitably mean taking away some individual rights (and vice versa). This ethical dilemma is at the center of many issues, such as gun control and affirmative action. These issues are also "not resolvable without remainder."

In Canada, the European settlement of the West took place later and was more orderly than in the States. The Mounties and the railroad arrived before most of the settlers. There were no "Indian Wars," except for the Métis uprisings of 1869 and 1885.[20] The land was taken from the Natives through a series of promises and broken promises. And Canada had no revolution to definitively cut itself off from the identity of the British. Western Canadians have defined their story as *not* American, but they have never agreed on what their story *is.* To Laurence, the problem is that Canada is still colonial; Canadians have not grasped a distinctive mythology that would distinguish their country from the old world and establish a closer relationship with their land and history. In *The Diviners,* Morag creates a story that will establish her as definitively Canadian. It is a story of the search for roots, but those roots are acknowledged as largely fictional. Morag knows that time is like the river that "flowed both ways," that we create the past as much as it creates us (11). Robert Kroetsch, another prairie writer, has commented wryly that Canadians "contrive authentic origins."[21] But even though national myths may be fictional, Laurence sees them as necessary fictions. In particular, she has argued, we must find stories that will somehow join settler and aboriginal cultures.

> Will we ever reach a point where it is no longer necessary to say Them and Us? I believe we must reach that point or perish. Canadians who, like myself, are the descendants of various settlers, many of whom came to this country as oppressed or dispossessed peoples, must hear native peoples' voices and ultimately become part of them, for they speak not only of soulsearing injustices done to them but also of their rediscovered sense of self-worth and their ability to tell and teach the things needed to be known.[22]

Here, Laurence explicitly states the need that Canadians feel to appropriate native identity. Canadian settlers have long used Native people as symbols of Canadianness, finding in them a sense of national identity. This appropriation, however, has rarely been accompanied by real action to improve the lives of Native people. Laurence's novel, while it is sympathetic and sensitive toward its native characters, uses them as symbols of Morag's Canadian identity.

Morag is, like Turtle, an orphan and the imaginative center of a national dilemma. And like Turtle's, her story is one of irreconcilable mythologies and philosophies. But we see Morag grow up. She is not only the object of a dilemma; she is also an active subject who can decide for herself what path she will take. Over the course of her life, Morag rejects English imperialism and the appeal of the Scottish Old World. In images repeated many times in the novel, she learns instead to "divine" and "scavenge" her identity from the materials of her own land and home. Morag's life mirrors Canada's movement toward its own national identity.

Morag's adoptive father, Christie, is the first influence in her development of an identity. Since the Gunns have no known history, Christie invents for the young Morag heroic ancestors named Piper and Morag Gunn. Piper Gunn, Christie tells Morag, was one of many who were dispossessed of their land in Scotland and came to Canada. The Gunns had the "strength of conviction" (61), performed superhuman feats, lived for a biblical length of time, and led the settlers against the Métis rebellion. These stories give Morag her own "strength of conviction," helping her live in a class-ridden town that shames her for being the daughter of the garbage collector. This Scottish identity is entirely arbitrary, with no relation to Morag's real ancestors, but it is also necessary. The stories of Piper Gunn embody the theme of settler "survival," which Margaret Atwood has argued is the overriding theme in Canadian literature.[23] But while Morag relies on Christie's stories, she does not consider him and Prin to be her parents. So she continues to search for an "adoption" that will satisfy her.

As she gets older, Morag becomes ashamed of Christie and the smallness and provincialism of Manawaka. She goes away to university and marries her English professor, Brooke Skelton. In this national allegory, Brooke is the imperialist who wants to possess and control the "empty" new world. Brooke is British and grew up in imperial India. He perceives Morag's Canadian identity as simple and quaint: "I like your idiomatic expressions," he tells her (209). Morag knows that Brooke's perception is inaccurate, but rather than contradict him, she tells Brooke that she feels she has no past: "As though it were more or less blank" (211). This lack of identity appeals to Brooke; it means that he can shape her however he pleases. And for several years, Morag is content to be shaped. Brooke calls her his "child" and his "good girl" (243, 264). This marriage is Morag's second "adoption." Her acceptance of Brooke's control represents the colonial attitude that has long haunted Canada, the belief that its identity must lie elsewhere.

Morag does finally leave this unequal marriage. Her divorce, however, does not end her belief that she can find a more authentic identity in the Old World. A few years later, she moves to London, believing it to be the site of literary tradition. Once there, however, she realizes that "publisher's parties in London are no more appealing to her and no less parochial than they were in Canada" (383).

Having discovered that her fantasy of London was false, Morag sets her sights on a Scottish painter, Dan McRaith. When Morag visits Dan at his home in Scotland, she is expecting to also return to her genealogical roots. Yet, once in Scotland, Morag realizes that the place is strange to her and that she cannot find her identity there. She sees that her home is in "Christie's real country"—Canada (415). She can only construct a fulfilling identity from the stories, people, and landscape with which she grew up. The adult Morag knows that Piper Gunn and her Scottish heritage are myths, but she also finally realizes that her roots are grounded in those stories and in the story maker—her father, Christie.

Morag's and Turtle's dilemmas have broad national significance, but they are resolved on an individualized level. Racial and national harmony is achieved within the limits of romantic love and the family. The reader is drawn into the resolutions, which seem to occur inevitably, naturally, even biologically. For both Alice and Morag, a Native man represents an alternative to the confines of their previous lives and their previous men. The new interracial families that they form become symbols for the nation. Neil ten Kortenaar explains, in his essay on *The Diviners*, that this focus on the family is characteristic of national allegories: "The national allegory implicitly and inevitably grounds the imagined nation in the family. It commands the assent of readers to an imagined community by appropriating the forms of a 'natural' community."[24]

Pigs in Heaven ends happily. The resolution reassures us that a little love is all America needs to resolve native-settler disagreements. It is tempting to accept this comfortable thought. But the plot takes some contrived turns to get to that point. Neither Taylor nor Cash (Turtle's birth grandfather) loses Turtle; they are given joint custody. But the joint custody does not divide Turtle, because a union has already occurred between the adoptive and birth families. The grandparents form a bicultural family that will presumably continue into Taylor and Turtle's generations. Furthermore, this cross-cultural mix is found to have already existed in the past. Alice Greer begins to take seriously the fact that she is part-Cherokee herself, through her maternal grandmother. Her cousin, Sugar, explains to her that such mixed-bloods are the norm in the Cherokee Nation: "It don't have to be no more than a drop [of Native blood]. We're all so watered down here, anyway. . . . Being Cherokee is more or less a mindset" (275). This opens the door for Alice and Taylor to both become part of that "mindset" and thus to become part of the Native community. But their acceptance by the community is sealed through the whirlwind courtship and future marriage of Alice Greer, Turtle's adoptive grandmother, and Cash Stillwater, Turtle's birth grandfather. The story of their love is touching, but it also serves an obvious purpose within the narrative. The Greers and the Stillwaters will become one extended family. Turtle will not move from one family to another but will be passed around among relatives, a practice that is common among Native people.[25] The characters form a new interracial and inclusive community. As

Alice says, in the last words of the novel: "The family of women is about to open its doors to men. Men, children, cowboys and Indians. It's all over now but the shouting" (343).

This ending, while very appealing, is also too perfect. It is not that an interracial family is improbable. But Kingsolver posits the Stillwater-Greer family as a solution to a problem that is much greater than one family. The ending is a kind of writerly sleight of hand, a sidestepping of the complications of native-settler relations. By individualizing this utopian racial harmony, Kingsolver avoids the task of imagining how Native people and settlers can learn to live together as large communities. This is a challenge that will need to be met on a much larger scale—involving the settlement of land claims, changes to the educational and legal systems, constitutional changes, and other daunting tasks. Of course, the novel as we know it does not usually deal with such issues.[26] The novelistic form, as has been argued many times, was born out of the importance of the individual. I am not saying that Kingsolver should have written a book that deals with these larger issues. Rather, I want to show that a big part of the appeal of this novel comes from the way in which it sidesteps these big issues by working them out in a way that is apparently natural. The reader is reassured that all the ethical and cultural conflicts that the book lays out can be solved by individual acts of love. There is a contradiction at the heart of Kingsolver's national allegory: despite its emphasis on the importance of community, the novel is resolved by individualization. Its resolution is so unusual and so particular that it does not offer a feasible approach to either interracial adoption or the broader issue of community versus individual interests.

In *The Diviners*, the solution to the national dilemma is also achieved through a sexual union between a white woman and a Native man. Morag has a lifelong relationship with Jules Tonnerre, a Métis from her hometown of Manawaka, and he is the father of her daughter, Pique. Morag and Jules never stay together for long, but they inevitably return to one another. Jules tells Morag stories that show her the other side of the founding of Canada. His stories are of his mythical métis ancestor Rider Tonnerre, who fought with Louis Riel at the Red River Rebellion (159–64). Rider Tonnerre would have fought Piper Gunn, and putting the stories of the two heroes together gives Morag a more balanced Canadian myth, one which sees both the indigenous and the settler points of view. This cross-cultural myth is a powerful alternative to the dry history that Morag learns in school and to the blankness that her British husband saw. The union of Morag and Jules offers a reconciliation to the battles of their ancestors.

The sexual relationship between Morag and Jules, between the Celt and the Métis, is what finally gives her an alternative to her "imperial" marriage. Morag explains the failure of her marriage to Brooke, saying, "we were living each others' fantasy, somehow" (292). But her relationship with Jules is also based on a cultural fantasy. Morag the orphan has finally found an "authentic" identity to replace her own lack of a past. She joins with Jules not for the sake of sex but for larger, mythical reasons.

> In her present state of mind, she doesn't expect to be aroused, and does not even care if she isn't, as though this joining is being done for other reasons, some debt or answer to the past, and some severing of inner chains which have kept her bound and separated from part of herself. (292)

Jules represents the missing part of Laurence's—and Morag's—national myth. After they have made love, he says to her, "I'm the *shaman*, eh?" (294). His "magic" gives Morag, symbolically, an indigenous connection to Canada.

Morag decides to have a child with Jules. Pique, the child of this union, is visibly métis and obviously not Brooke's child, giving Morag an irrevocable end to her marriage. Morag names her after Jules's sister, Piquette, whom the people of Manawaka had marginalized and ignored. Piquette's life and death are a continual source of guilt for Morag and the rest of the town.[27] Through Pique, Morag tries to redeem and replace that racist past. Pique represents a new national future. Like Turtle, she is the child of a bicultural family, and Morag passes on to her stories of Piper and Rider, Christie and Jules. Through her daughter, Morag retroactively relates herself to Canada's Native people. She finds an interracial identity not through her parents but through her child. Neil ten Kortenaar argues that Pique will not struggle for identity in the way that Morag has.[28] Unlike Morag the orphan, Pique has always known about her roots, and her travels are movements back to those roots—to Manawaka and to her métis relatives on Galloping Mountain. Pique's identity is grounded in the Canadian landscape. She sings, "the mountain and the valley hold my name" (490). However, ten Kortenaar does not consider Pique's pain as she struggles with the mixed identity her mother gives her.

Both Laurence and Kingsolver consider the possibility of a unified and balanced nation. Heaven, Oklahoma, is aptly named, since it is only in that little paradise that the ending of Kingsolver's *Pigs in Heaven* could happen. In *The Diviners*, Laurence also tries to imagine a new and ideal nation, but she is more self-conscious about whether such a paradise can ever exist. Morag sees Pique's struggles with her mixed heritage and thinks:

> *How to spare one's children at least some kind of pain? No way. Where in the Bible does it speak of a new heaven and a new earth? That's what we need all right. Lord, but it looks to be a long time in coming.* (447)

I explained earlier in this essay that interracial adoption is an issue "not resolvable without remainder." I would say that the same is true of these two novels.

They, too, are not resolvable without remainder. While both novelists manage to draw their novels together into happy endings, the books still will not settle. In the case of *Pigs in Heaven*, the remainder is in the reader's discomfort with the too comfortable ending. The issues that the novel raises spill over the confines of that ending, raising questions that the novel cannot answer.

The Diviners is a more self-reflexive novel. It acknowledges the fictionality of and the weaknesses in its own national myth. First of all, Morag acknowledges that her memories are largely inventions and that her identity is based on myths with little historical accuracy. She tells Dan: "The myths are my reality. Something like that." (415). Yet the book's emotional impact depends on our believing, like Morag, in those myths and in the idea of Canada that she builds.[29] Second, *The Diviners* examines its own weakness through the voice of Pique. Her difficulties in coping with her mixed heritage remind Morag and the reader that the union of two people does not guarantee a united identity. Pique, like Turtle, does not have "the option of whiteness." Unlike Morag, she cannot freely choose her identity, since her skin color defines her in the eyes of the world. She regularly faces racism—from the teens who call her a "dirty halfbreed" (446), from the businessmen who throw beer bottles at her, and from the police officers who arrest her for being cut by one of those bottles (119–20). Pique deals with a world that Morag's carefully constructed Canadian identity cannot account for or fix.

Pique's sporadic anger toward her mother is also anger toward Laurence's national dream of reconciliation. Since Morag is seemingly the "author" of the "autobiographical" *The Diviners*, Pique's challenges to Morag also apply to the novel itself. When she forces Morag to justify her decision to have a child with Jules, she is also asking Laurence (Laurence is asking herself) to justify her creation of Pique the character. "Why did you *have* me?" Pique demands.

> "I wanted you," Morag said, stunned.
> "For your own satisfaction, yes. You never thought of him [Jules], or of me." (254)

Laurence here reveals the self-serving nature of the national myth that she/ Morag has constructed. The novel is told from a white point of view and speaks to a white audience. Jules and Pique are included because they represent a satisfying redemption for the white settler, an indigenizing that will make the settler authentically Canadian. The novel is concerned only superficially with Native identity. Pique speaks here as a Native, telling her mother that this national myth of interracial unity does not serve her, her father, or any Native people. Interracial and intercultural mixing is a fact of life for Native people, not a fantasy or an idealized identity. They know that such mixing is not enough to create cultural harmony. Pique tells Morag that such harmony cannot be found on the level of family inheritance: "I don't want to be split. I want to be together. But I'm not. I don't know where I belong." Morag's response reveals her (and the novel's) hope for interracial harmony: "Does it have to be either/or?" But Pique answers: "I don't guess you would know how it feels. Yes, maybe it does have to be either/or" (373). Pique is looking for her métis identity, and a cross-cultural ideal can be destructive to that identity.[30] Pique's voice is a challenge to the emotional appeal of Laurence's national dream. Would Turtle end up feeling the same resentment as Pique? This is an unanswerable question but a telling one. A mixed-race identity is not negative or impossible; it is just very difficult.

The Diviners, like *Pigs in Heaven*, has, at its core, a contradiction between individualism and community. Morag is a strong individualist. She is, like Taylor, a single mother moving constantly from place to place, and at the novel's end she lives alone. Most of the significant events in Morag's life have been attempts to connect herself to various communities in search of a Canadian identity. But these connections have been largely symbolic, achieved through relationships with individual men. Despite her (rare) contact with Jules, she has no real connection to any Native community. She cuts all her ties (except imaginative ones) to Manawaka and even leaves the West to live in Ontario. She severs the connections that might have made Pique more at ease in her identity. It is only within this individualized sphere that Laurence can construct her ideal Canadian identity. Examining the country on a larger scale brings contradictions and demands to such an ideal. Perhaps Canada does not and cannot have a national identity because it is too large, too complex, and too diverse for any one story to be sufficient. To create a Canadian myth, Laurence has to put her protagonist alone in a log cabin. While the image of the cabin may be a resonant symbol of Canada, the real challenges of racism, multiculturalism, and finding an identity must be worked out on reserves, in towns, and in cities. In comparison to the problems found in such communities, Morag's identity problems are "too obvious, concrete, and solvable."[31]

Moving outside the world of fiction sheds light on how the myths of Kingsolver and Laurence sidestep the realities of native-settler relations. These authors build on the figure of the adopted orphan a utopian cross-cultural identity. But real Native children adopted by white families do not become the site for an ideal creolized identity, though sometimes they work out a hybrid identity in more realistic terms.[32] Many of them must work through confusion, alienation, and the feeling that they have no identity at all. No matter how loving the individual adoptive family is, it is not a solution to the racism and to the racial/cultural divisions in North American society. Native writers, such as Eden Robinson, Drew Hayden Taylor, and Richard Wagamese, have written of such adoptions and the deep conflicts that they create in Native children.[33] Their works offer very different perspectives on interracial adoption and cross-cultural identity than those offered in the novels of Kingsolver and Laurence.

Perhaps it seems unfair to compare fictional worlds to the real one. And one could argue that since all national communities are imagined, it is useless to speak of those imaginative visions as more or less real. But I bring up these alternative adoption stories to resist the temptations that these novels offer. The issue is not that *Pigs in Heaven* and *The Diviners* should be more real but that they have real effects on their readers. Both of these novels are well loved and extremely popular. I suggest that their popularity arises in part out of the reassurances that they offer their largely white audiences. The adoption narratives make the books' fantasies appear real and natural. But the differences between real interracial adoptions and those in *The Diviners* and *Pigs in Heaven* reveal complexities that overflow the confines of the novels' national visions. Kingsolver and Laurence attempt to create less oppressive and more authentic identities for their countries. But the novelists *use* Native people as a piece of that more authentic identity, privileging settler identity over native identity. The peaceful reconciliation of settlers and Natives on the North American continent should be a goal for all of us. But when reading these novels by Kingsolver and Laurence, we must ask whom these particular fantasies of racial and cultural union serve.

NOTES

1. Barbara Kingsolver, *The Bean Trees* (New York: HarperCollins, 1988).

2. Quotations are cited parenthetically in text from Margaret Laurence, *The Diviners* (Toronto: McClelland and Stewart, 1974) and Barbara Kingsolver, *Pigs in Heaven* (New York: HarperCollins, 1993).

3. Terry Goldie, *Fear and Temptation: The Image of the Indigene in Canadian, Australian, and New Zealand Literatures* (Kingston, Montreal, and London: McGill-Queen's University Press, 1989), 13.

4. See many examples of this adoption narrative in popular culture in Robert Baird, "Going Indian: Discovery, Adoption, and Renaming Toward a 'True American,' from *Deerslayer* to *Dances with Wolves,*" in *Dressing in Feathers: The Construction of the Indian in American Popular Culture,* ed. S. Elizabeth Bird (New York: Westview, 1996), 195–209. Two highly acclaimed novels that use the adoption fantasy and the interracial family in national allegories are Salman Rushdie, *Midnight's Children* (New York: Penguin, 1980), and Keri Hulme, *the bone people* (New York: Penguin, 1983).

5. *Dances with Wolves,* screenplay by Michael Blake, film directed by Kevin Costner (TIG Productions, 1990).

6. Quoted in Hana Wirth-Nesher, "The Literary Orphan as National Hero: Huck and Pip," in *Dickens Studies Annual: Essays on Victorian Fiction,* eds. Michael Timko, Fred Kaplan, and Edward Guiliano, vol. 15 (New York: AMS, 1986), 263.

7. Ibid., 263.

8. Benedict Anderson, *Imagined Communities: Reflections on the Origin and Spread of Nationalism* (London: Verso, 1983), 14–16.

9. Wirth-Nesher, "Literary Orphan," 260–61.

10. Northrop Frye, "Conclusion to the *Literary History of Canada* (First Edition)," in *An Anthology of Canadian Literature in English,* eds. Russell Brown and Donna Bennett, vol. 1 (Toronto: Oxford University Press, 1983), 542.

11. Wallace Stegner, "History, Myth, and the Western Writer," in *The Sound of Mountain Water* (New York: Doubleday, 1969), 199.

12. Barbara Kingsolver, interview by David Gergen, *U.S. News and World Report,* <http.//www.pbs.org/newshour/gergen/kingsolver.html>. Nov 24, 1995. Accessed May 31, 2000

13. Ibid.

14. Ann E. MacEachron, Nora S. Gustavsson, Suzanne Cross, and Allison Lewis, "The Effectiveness of the Indian Child Welfare Act of 1978," *Social Services Review* 70, no. 3 (September 1996): 453–54.

15. Marc Mannes, "Factors and Events Leading to the Passage of the Indian Child Welfare Act," *Child Welfare* 74, no. 1 (January/February 1995): 267–68.

16. Lou Matheson, "The Politics of the Indian Child Welfare Act," *Social Work: Journal of the National Association of Social Workers* 41, no. 2 (1996): 233.

17. Janet Farrell Smith, "Analyzing Ethical Conflict in the Transracial Adoption Debate: Three Conflicts Involving Community," *Hypatia* 11, no. 2 (spring 1996): 25 n. 9.

18. Ibid., 12, 18.

19. Ibid., 2. See B. A. O. Williams, "Moral Luck," *Proceedings of the Aristotelian Society Supplement* 50 (1976): 115–51; Martha Craven Nussbaum, *The Fragility of Goodness: Luck and Ethics in Greek Tragedy and Philosophy* (Cambridge: Cambridge University Press, 1986).

20. Arnold E. Davidson, *Coyote Country: Fictions of the Canadian West* (Durham and London: Duke University Press, 1994), 6.

21. Robert Kroetsch, "The Fear of Women in Prairie Fiction: An Erotics of Space," in *Essays on Saskatchewan Writing,* ed. E. F. Dyck (Regina: Saskatchewan Writers Guild, 1986), 107.

22. Margaret Laurence, "Man of Our People," in *Heart of a Stranger* (Toronto: McClelland and Stewart, 1976), 211.

23. Margaret Atwood, *Survival: A Thematic Guide to Canadian Literature* (Toronto: Anansi, 1972).

24. Neil ten Kortenaar, "The Trick of Divining a Postcolonial Canadian Identity: Margaret Laurence between Race and Nation," *Canadian Literature* 149 (summer 1996): 24–25.

25. Geoffrey York, *The Dispossessed: Life and Death in Native Canada* (London: Vintage U.K., 1990), 217.

26. Toni Morrison's *Tar Baby* (New York: Knopf, 1981) is an example of an adoption narrative that deals with the issues of racial, individual, and communal identities and resists the individualized and romantic resolution seen in Laurence's and Kingsolver's novels.

27. Laurence's short story "The Loons" (in *A Bird in the House: Stories by Margaret Laurence* [Toronto and Montreal: McClelland and Stewart, 1970], 114–27) describes how the MacLeods, a well-off Manawaka family, fostered Piquette for a summer. But Piquette resented the gesture. She refused to be assimilated and remained "a reproach and a mystery" to the family (122). In *The Fire-Dwellers* (Toronto and Montreal: McClelland and Stewart, 1969), 263–69, Stacey Cameron runs into Piquette's sister Valentine in Van-

couver and thinks, after she is told of Piquette's death, "Even her [Valentine's] presence is a reproach to me" (265).

28. ten Kortenaar, "Trick of Divining," 28.

29. Neil ten Kortenaar examines this contradiction in *The Diviners* at length. He concludes that the novel's construction of the nation in terms of inheritance, sexuality, and family creates an appearance of authenticity that overrides the fictionality of Morag's stories; he writes ("Trick of Divining," 25): "The nation, however much of a cultural construct it may be, in the end relies on the same notion of inherited identity as race does."

30. In this society, settler culture is so much more privileged than Native culture that it is difficult for one person to combine those cultures and maintain a sense of balance. Native culture may need, at times, to be protected from the powerful homogenizing force of mainstream society. I am not promoting cultural purity, which would be an impossible and destructive goal. Rather, I want to point out that a cross-cultural identity is an ambiguous thing for Native people and is not necessarily an ideal.

31. Krista Comer, "Sidestepping Environmental Justice: 'Natural' Landscapes and the Wilderness Plot," in *Breaking Boundaries: New Perspectives on Women's Regional Writing,* ed. Sherrie Inness and Diana Roger (Iowa City: University of Iowa Press, 1997), 229.

32. The opposite situation, white children being adopted by native families, is virtually nonexistent.

33. Eden Robinson, "Traplines," in *Traplines* (New York: Henry Holt, 1996), 1–35; Richard Wagamese, *Keeper n'Me* (Toronto: Doubleday Canada, 1994); Drew Hayden Taylor, *Someday: a play* (Saskatoon: Fifth House, 1993).

Should Whites Adopt African American Children?

One Family's Phenomenological Response

Martha Satz

In 1997, after an extended stint abroad as a naval officer, my son entered law school. During the school's orientation week, a professor described her work as lead attorney on the Baby Jessica case, which, as we remember, concerned a couple who took a baby girl into their home, nurtured her as their daughter for two and half years with the intention of adopting her, but eventually were compelled to relinquish her. "Can you imagine," the child-advocacy attorney inquired of the assembled law students, "what it would be like to be two and a half years old and wrenched from the only home you had ever known by people whom you had never seen before?" My son, Michael, raised his hand to offer: "Yes, I can. It happened to me."

I heard this account from my son sandwiched among other enthusiastic stories about the first days of law school as he phoned that first week. At the same time, he mentioned that child-advocacy law attracted him, that indeed eventually he wanted to work with this professor to protect children from experiencing the same trauma he had undergone. Hearing this, I gasped. The moment exquisitely distilled my experience. My son's making this revelation in his new community and desiring to work for children in the future affirmed our life together. It also augured well for my daughter, Miriam, then ten years old, whom I adopted when Michael was eighteen. For Michael, my now adult child, the one I had adopted twenty-seven years ago amid controversies concerning transracial adoption, had joined me in publicly speaking of the complex entanglements of adoption.

That all this had occurred in connection with the Baby Jessica case resonated with me. When the case had reached its climax and the news played and replayed the video of the two-and-a-half-year-old little girl shrieking and kicking as she was removed from her home, I sank into despair. As psychologists and commentators on television shook their heads pondering whether a child could ever overcome such a trauma emotionally, I grieved for my son, who had experienced that very same blow. Most intensely, I relived my own villainy, for I had been the one wresting him from his home, inflicting the pain. But I had never discussed my reaction to the Baby Jessica case with Michael. Thus, it was shocking, but on reflection unsurprising, to discover that we had both responded the same way. The Baby Jessica story was emotionally our own, even though factually it differed radically from our experience.

When I ventured to discuss my horrified reaction to the Baby Jessica story with friends, they thought that they understood my response. The cultural stereotype pits adoptive parents against biological ones. Thus, they assumed that the Baby Jessica story must evoke in me the atavistic fear that one day, the biological parents, the "real" parents, the ones who according to some cultural paradigms have a superior claim, would come and take my children away.

But in my case, experience trumped categories. I had taken my son, aged two years and eight months, away from the only home he had ever known, away from mommy, daddy, sister, brother Dan-Dan, and, for all I knew, a dog named Spot. I had taken him to a motel room where he had tried to get away, crying desperately, "Mommy, mommy." He had made hysterical lunges toward the door. I had barred the way. I had experienced myself as kidnapper.

The story of my son and me interweaves adoption, race, and the politically conservative environment of Texas. In the late 1960s I came to Dallas as a Northeastern, white, Jewish, single woman with an Ivy League education and an almost completed Ph.D. in academic philosophy, to teach in a historically black college. I lived in an apartment on campus, one of a few white people on an all-black campus in an all-black community. I learned a good deal inside the classroom and out about African American culture and life and about myself as well.

I also came to realize that there was something I wanted. I watched myself buying and collecting books and toys for neighborhood children. Their artwork decorated every inch of my walls. I missed them when they went home. Clearly, I desired a child of my own. I did not know whether I would marry, but it did not matter—I wanted a child. At just about that time, I began to read about the phenomenon of single-parent adoptions. I learned that although they had been legal in Texas for a year or so, none had actually occurred. In completing my application with the public agency, I expressed my openness to adopting a minority-race or biracial child. Living in the environment that I did, such a decision seemed natural.

However, in my first meeting with the social worker, she explained that transracial adoption was illegal as the law currently stood in Texas. She asked whether I would be willing to test the law. "Yes," I replied, and I proceeded to talk glibly about the blatant unconstitutionality of the law and the ACLU as resource. I wince recalling this response of my much younger self, who had no notion of what even the threat of losing a child might mean.

A week before Thanksgiving, two months after I had undertaken investigating the adoption process in Texas, I heard news of my son. He was a healthy little boy, whom the examining pediatrician had pronounced "bright." Although he had been available for adoption since infancy, because of his mixed racial heritage—black and white—no one in two and three-quarter years had expressed an interest in adopting him. He had lived continually in one foster home in Amarillo with white parents. They loved him and had expressed an interest in adopting him themselves, but they could not reconcile themselves with his racial background. Because he was light-skinned, they considered telling the world that he was of Mexican heritage. Because of these attitudes, adoption authorities thought it best that his foster parents not adopt him.

The year was 1970, the year before transracial adoptions reached their peak at 2,574 in 1971, having risen gradually from 733 in 1968, the year of Michael's birth—a demographic perspective on the dramatic personal events in our life.[1] The following year, the adamant opposition of the National Association of Black Social Workers (NABSW) to transracial adoptions would cause the number of such adoptions to plunge, reaching 831 in 1975, the last year in which such statistics were systematically generated.

But the statistic that mattered vitally to me at the time was the growth of my family from one to two. In a two-day shopping whirlwind, I assembled a room for a two year old—bed, books, toys. But when I arrived in Amarillo, it was to upsetting news. On learning of my imminent arrival, the foster parents had become emotionally unglued. The foster father entertained the idea of running away with Michael. The foster mother, who had another foster child living in the house at the time, made the authorities come and get her. And Michael was out too. Instead of the gradual getting-acquainted process standard in adoptions with children of Michael's age, Michael's change of homes and lives was abrupt. The foster parents had said that they could say goodbye only once. The adoption worker informed me that Michael was mine from that moment forward.

After his parting from his foster parents, I encountered Michael for the first time, a silent, frightened child. Wordlessly, I handed him a yellow racing car with an orange stripe. In silence, we played for a while, rolling the car back and forth between us. The agency had told me how verbal this child was, but as we continued to play and he remained mute, I began to doubt their truthfulness. Then, at one point, when a hubcap fell off the wheel of the car, Michael sidled up to me, car and hubcap in hand, and uttered his first words to me: "Fix it."

Soon after, we left the adoption agency and went to the motel, where, as I described earlier, I imprisoned Michael. After he realized that it was futile to make his escape, he cried inconsolably, refusing to allow me to touch or comfort him. That night, he fell asleep on the floor, clutching the racing car. I did not move him to the bed, afraid that I would wake him and revive in him the terror of his situation. It was a dark night. I thought the foster parents' inability to accept his heritage a thin reason to separate them. He was distraught. They were distraught. He loved them. They loved him. Who was I to intervene? Ideas about upholding racial identity seemed bloodless abstractions next to this wounded child. As I mused in this way, the telephone rang. "How is the place-ment going? Do you think you want to keep this child?" the social worker in-quired. I had no attachment to him—I had barely touched him—but in a leap of faith, I said yes.

Now, as I write this essay, I have once again been dramatically drawn into those times, with an even more poignant understanding of my son's experience. Suellyn Scarnnechia, the professor who addressed Michael at his law school ori-entation, recently sent me the audiotape of an address in which she had em-ployed Michael's experience as an emotional analogue of Baby Jessica's and of all other children torn away from their psychological families. Listening, I felt the unparalleled pain of a mother hearing the detailed account of her child's an-guish, anguish she herself had induced. Here are her devastating words.

A few years ago I was lecturing to a group of law students using the Baby Jessica case. . . . About halfway through my presentation, a young man in the front row said very quietly, "That happened to me." And of course I was *very* anxious to talk to him. And this is what he remembers. He said that he can remember that he must have known that he was going to be moved from one family to the other . . . because he spent the morning trying to hide. He can remember his foster brother and his foster sister, the two children in the family, trying to help him hide. . . . He can remember the social worker com-ing into the bedroom where he was and taking him. And he can literally re-member having his foster brother and sister hold one arm and the social worker hold the other arm as she pulled him out of the house. He can re-member being pulled out of the bedroom into the living room and seeing his foster parents sitting on the couch crying. And his brother and sister are still hanging on to his arm, and he is still crying and screaming and kicking. And he can remember being put into the backseat of the social worker's yel-low VW bug. And he can remember driving to the adoption agency. He can remember that the walls were blue cinder-block walls. So I said to him, "Why do you think you can remember this?" Of course, I'm one of those people who would really like to believe, for instance, that Jessica might not re-member that day that this all happened. And even though I'm told that of course she might remember all of the details, I was kind of hoping she wouldn't. He said: "Some people forget traumatic experiences. And some people can't forget traumatic experiences—like me." And so I tell you that because I think we all still walk around not knowing for sure whether kids will remember, what they'll know, and certainly it's a story that struck me as compelling. He said that he wants to find his foster parents. And I asked, "Why?" And he said, "I heard that my foster father wanted to run away with me when he heard I was going to be removed and that he wanted to hide me and run away. And so they must have really cared about me. And I want to go back and tell them that I am okay. And of course he *is* okay. He is a marvelous, talented, smart young man who is in Michigan Law School and who has a great future ahead of him. But clearly this was a moment in his life that was very traumatic and difficult.[2]

Emotionally paralyzed by hearing these words, I rediscovered how difficult it is to make oneself understood through the binaries that control the perception of adoption dramas. Some of my friends could not understand why I was so upset—did I not believe I had done the right thing? Their responses adapted the story to the poles of the opposing duality, rightful versus wrongful parent. But adoption, anomalous by its very nature, often reveals its irregularity with a residue of pain. As a phenomenon, it may be akin to what Bernard Williams and Martha Nussbaum have termed moral conflicts irresolvable without remainder.[3] Although the results of Michael's adoption have been, in his own words, "outstanding," the process had nevertheless remaindered pain that no reasoning can either assuage or dissolve. I suffer in knowing that I, however benevolently intentioned, have been an agent in that process.

When I returned in 1970 to the college where I worked, no one believed I had adopted Michael. They thought I had given birth to him and kept him in hiding with some relative until I was ready to acknowledge him. As I learned, adopting Michael had altered my status in society. From then until the present day, when I am with one of my children, at times I receive fixed, hostile stares, for I am perceived as a white woman who has slept with a black man. Several years ago, driving across country with my then six-year-old daughter, we left the main highway in Arkansas and ventured into a small-town café. When we entered, I thought I had fallen into a 1950s movie. Everyone paused in midbite and stared at us with murderous looks. Without consciously intending to do so, in my fear and haste to leave, I poked a man standing at the cash register between the legs with my umbrella. I had been startled by the scene because, living in a large city and a university community, I confront overt racism only intermittently. Often I traverse the world without my children. Thus, undoubtedly lulled by my customary white privilege, I had entered that small-town Arkansas café without thinking about all the consequences. Certainly no black family would ever "forget" the problematic nature of such a place. Among other arguments, critics of transracial adoptions charge that black children placed in white homes will not be taught strategies to deal with racism, certainly a just criticism of me that day in Arkansas.[4]

Prior to such criticisms having been formally advanced by the NABSW, I thought, having become self-conscious about issues of racism by living and working in a black community, that I was both fulfilling my desires and secondarily fighting racism by adopting Michael. So, on the request of social workers, I consented to an interview for the local paper. In September 1971, an article appeared in the *Dallas Times Herald* with the banner headline "Half Black, Half White."[5] The article displayed a picture of me, sitting under the mural in my son's room, storybook in hand, and Michael peering skeptically into the camera. The story begins:

> Martha Satz, 28, is as proud of her three-year-old son as any mother could be of the beautiful, curly-haired, bright-as-a-button boy.
> The fact that Miss Satz is white and single, while her adopted son is of mixed black and white parentage, she regards as "no big deal."
> It sets her teeth on edge "when people tell me what a great, noble thing I've done." She protests, "That's just silly, and it's wrong. I adopted Michael for selfish reasons, because I wanted him."

The article later quotes me as saying:

> I do think he's growing up in a privileged position. A stereotype image of blacks and whites will be impossible for Michael. . . . He may have a strongly black identification, and that would be fine, but I don't believe he would ever become anti-white.

It turns out that I was prescient. Michael has negotiated his complex identities wonderfully well. In college, he simultaneously held offices in the Black Student Association and the Jewish Student Association. In the navy, he proved a strong voice in representing the racial inequities on his first ship, and as a consequence, his captain appointed him Equal Employment Opportunity Officer. In law school, during minority orientation, he listened to informal talk tinged with anti-Semitism among African American students and responded in a conversation-stopping moment, "As an African American and a Jew . . ." In like manner, at the Jewish Law Student Association meeting, he provided counterarguments to their strong anti–affirmative action sentiment. But as a little boy, that headline "Half Black, Half White" confused him, presenting as it does the image of a zebra or a harlequin figure. When I read it to him, he examined his arm, searching for the stripes. Indeed, Michael has turned out to be all of a piece but culturally situated to see diverse perspectives.

It is hard for me to separate Michael's strong sense of identity from the life we have led together. When I eventually left the predominantly black college where I taught when I adopted Michael, I taught African American literature and culture in a predominantly white institution. My rearing of Michael always emphasized cultural issues. I bought him black dolls and action figures. Books became a major tool for me to deal with racism and oppression; I read Greek, Norse, and African myths and legends to him, and I soon read books explicitly concerned with oppression and liberation. When my six-year-old son, in the season of Passover, explained to me why a book jacket referred to Harriet Tubman as the Moses of her people, I rejoiced.

When he entered school, I made sure he attended one that was integrated; in fact, by court order his school was 50 percent black and 50 percent white. Michael explained this fact in a striking way. "My school is half black and half white," he said, "and I," he added, making the shape of a triangle with his hands, "am at the top." The school, however, presented problems for him. Some of the black boys teased and punched him, and some of the white boys called him "nigger." But Michael, a boy with a mind and a tongue, formulated his retort for a number of days and then delivered it: "You can't call me nigger because I'm a honky too, so you'd have to call me 'nigronky' and you can't pronounce that so you'd just better shut up."

He found his circle of friends in school—a mixture of black and white. His best friend Ruben, a bookish African American boy, remained his friend throughout high school. With Ruben and his family, Michael entered black society unaccompanied by his white mother, attending church functions and holiday celebrations. To this day, Michael credits his elementary school experience with his comfort in bicultural situations.

In fact, our entire family has become bicultural. I believe we embody what philosopher Lawrence Blum has articulated as one ideal of interracial community, "the sense, not necessarily explicit or articulated, that one possesses human bonds with other races and ethnicities."[6] Elizabeth Bartholet, legal scholar and adoptive mother, strongly argues for this ideal, opposing the notion that "parent-child relationships can only work, or at least . . . work best, between biologically similar people."[7] Bartholet views the interracial family as a vanguard of interracial relations.

Indeed, I have employed my position in the racial nexus for pedagogical purposes. Lecturing on Toni Morrison's *The Bluest Eye* to politically conservative women uncomfortable with conversations about race, I have talked about my daughter, Miriam, her struggles with her hair, and my own anguish in watching those struggles, as a way of conveying the torment of Morrison's character. Pecola Breedlove, feeling herself ugly because she is black, desires the most quintessentially white attribute—blue eyes. In my talk, I asserted the authority of experience. I, as a white woman, have had the unusual experience of feeling racism directly in a way that my audience would recognize as valid—by living it through my daughter. I talked about hair—their hair, my hair, and Miriam's hair. After the lecture, several women approached me confidentially, talking about conversations with their maids or black children that puzzled them. Suddenly I had made a realm of experience accessible and a sensitive topic possible to discuss.

But in such a performance, was I not exploiting Miriam and aggrandizing myself, arrogantly suggesting that I, a "privileged" white person who had experienced racism through my child, could bridge the chasm between the races? For I fully appreciate the criticisms of black feminists who rail against white feminists who presume to speak for them, a view honed to a devastatingly ironic point in Gloria Joseph's remark "[I]t takes whiteness to give even Blackness validity."[8] Yet for all its complexity and entanglements, I embrace my situation and that of my family.

Nevertheless, conscious of my apparent hypocrisy, I worry about the effects of the Adoption Reform Law passed by Congress in 1999. The law in part states: "A person or government that is involved in adoption or foster care placements may not—delay or deny the placement of a child for adoption or into foster care, on the basis of the race, color, or national origin of the adoptive or foster parent, or the child, involved."[9] In effect, this law forbids any racial preference in placing black children for adoption. Those who favor such a position cite empirical studies that indicate that transracial adoptees do not suffer in self-esteem or positive attitudes about black identity. Bartholet, for example, suggests that transracial adoption may even be advantageous to children because "whites are in the best position to teach black children how to maneuver in the white worlds of power and privilege."[10] I find her view to be a reinscription of racism. Moreover, I am concerned that the Adoption Law Reform will multiply such views. I fear that as the Adoption Law Reform makes adoption of children of color a more feasible option for a greater pool of white families, many will be unaware of the consequences of such an adoption. They will be less sensitive to the radical alteration their family must undergo and the strong demands that responding to racism will require of themselves and their children. For this, I *do* have the authority of experience. However, the law is designed to shorten the time that children languish in foster care, to prevent painful experiences like those which Michael endured, the pain of which I also know from experience. Yet, another approach to this dilemma might take seriously the suggestion of Ruth-Arlene Howe that a more effective means to speed the adoption process of black and biracial children would be to support the black family and find innovative ways to recruit black families to adopt.[11]

Popular culture has treated this dilemma in the 1995 movie *Losing Isaiah*. The plot pits a rehabilitated, formerly crack-addicted, African American mother against a highly educated, affluent, white family in a custody battle for an African American boy of preschool age, Isaiah.

Unfortunately, the movie draws the contrasts between the adversaries in stark terms emphasizing racial difference. In the beginning of the movie, the African American mother appears in the most primitive of circumstances, inadvertently abandoning her baby in the trash during a Chicago winter, an early shot portraying her as a kind of native Madonna. In contrast, the white family, although loving and well-intentioned, completely neglects the African American heritage of their child. The little boy emerges as an alien in their gentrified urban white community, not only because of his race, but also because of his behavioral problems stemming from his mother's addiction. In one striking scene, the two women confront each other in a ladies' room, contending over who is the rightful mother. The African American woman, gesturing to her reflection in the mirror, says, "God says I'm his mother."

When I watched the movie, this image wounded me because of the telling point it conveys, a truth that eluded me until it was made palpable by my daughter. While my son seemingly never suffered from the differences between us, accepting my verbal explanations and storytelling, my daughter experienced things on a much more intuitive level. Seemingly, she directly took in the way the world perceived us as importantly different from each other, and she suffered from that divisive regard. She mourned that we had different-colored skin and different hair and that her friends asked her about her "real mother," assuming that mother was black. She felt our bond, I know, but she grieved over the separations others created.

Losing Isaiah ends with reconciliation rather than division. It heals the rift between the races and between nature and nurture. The court rules in the African American mother's favor. But when Isaiah is inconsolable in his grief for his family, the African American woman, echoing the actions of the biblical mother in the dispute settled by Solomon, returns the boy to the white family, insisting, however, that he attend a school in the African American community. As the credits roll, the viewer understands that, however improbable it seems, the two women will share the child. The movie reconciles the dilemma without remainder. The two mothers, as well as the child, will be satisfied.

In life, however, such solutions are not feasible. As Michael and I recalled in a discussion of the movie, the debate over transracial adoption today is framed in the same oppositional terms as it was in 1972 when *Sepia,* a black magazine with a format similar to that of *Life,* featured an article entitled "Should Whites Adopt Black Babies?"[12] The *Sepia* article as well as *Losing Isaiah* refer to the NABSW's position.[13] In framing the argument against the NABSW, the article remarks, "One tiny voice which would dissent would be that of Michael Satz, who, although only four, already has a sharp little mind."[14] There, in a photo accompanying the article, sit Michael and I, poster children for transracial adoption.

In connection with the present essay, I recently took out that article, and Miriam, reading the headline, "Should Whites Adopt Black Babies?" responded in inimitable eleven-year-old fashion, "Yes, duh." This affirmation, if less eloquent, is as ringing as Michael's endorsement in law school. But my present response to the question posed in the headline would not be as univocal as Miriam's now or my own at the time of the *Sepia* article. I would respond as the women in Carol Gilligan's *In a Different Voice* did: "Well, it all depends."[15] If whites do adopt minority children, they must be prepared for their comfortable worldviews of dualities and certainties to unravel and to take up residence in a realm where the boundaries always shift and where sticky residue always remains.

NOTES

1. Reported by Elizabeth Bartholet, "Where Do Black Children Belong? The Politics of Race Matching in Adoption," *Reconstruction* 1, no. 4 (1992): 29.

2. Suellyn Scarnecchia, keynote address, Hear My Voice Conference, Ann Arbor, Michigan, October 1998.

3. B. A. O. Williams, "Moral Luck," *Proceedings of the Aristotelian Society Supplement* 50 (1976): 115–51; Martha Craven Nussbaum, *The Fragility of Goodness: Luck and Ethics in Greek Tragedy and Philosophy* (Cambridge: Cambridge University Press, 1986).

4. Twila L. Perry, "The Transracial Adoption Controversy: An Analysis of Discourse and Subordination," *New York University Review of Law and Social Change* 21 (1993–94): 33–108; Andrew Billingsley and Jeanne M. Giovanni, *Children of the Storm: Black Children and American Welfare* (New York: Harcourt Brace, 1972).

5. Nadeane Walker, "Half White, Half Black," *Dallas Times Herald,* September 24, 1971, sec. B. pp. 1–2.

6. Lawrence Blum, "Anti-racism, Multiculturalism, and Interracial Community: Three Values for a Multi-cultural Society," Distinguished Lecture Series, University of Massachusetts at Boston, 1991, quoted in Janet Farrell Smith, "Analyzing Ethical Conflict in the Transracial Adoption Debate: The Conflicts Involving Community," *Hypatia* 11, no. 2 (1996): 1–33.

7. Elizabeth Bartholet, "Where Do Black Children Belong? The Politics of Race Matching in Adoption," *Reconstruction* 1, no. 4 (1992): 28.

8. Quoted in bell hooks, *Feminist Theory from Margin to Center* (Boston: South End, 1984), 51.

9. 42 U.S.C. § 1996b (1999).

10. Bartholet, "Where Do Black Children Belong," 34.

11. Ruth-Arlene Howe, "Re-defining the Transracial Adoption Controversy," *Duke Journal of Gender Law and Policy* 59 (1995): 164.

12. Harold Preece, "Should Whites Adopt Black Babies?" *Sepia* 21, no. 7 (July 1972): 16–23.

13. "Position Statement on Transracial Adoption" (Nashville, Tenn., 1972, mimeographed) and "Position Statement: Preserving African-American Families" (Detroit, Mich., 1994, mimeographed).

14. Preece, "Should Whites Adopt," 16.

15. Carol Gilligan, *In a Different Voice: Psychological Theory and Women's Development* (Cambridge, Mass.: Harvard University Press, 1993).

Incorporating the Transnational Adoptee

Claudia Castañeda

Race and reproduction have historically played a significant and even deter-mining role in U.S. adoption policy and practice. To the extent that a child's be-longing in a family is assumed to be the product of biological reproduction and blood ties, adoption remains a less valued, unnatural or at least unfamiliar way of generating family ties between children and adults. To put it in less norma-tive and more inclusive terms, the tie between a child and its parents is not as easily assumed in the case of families generated through adoption as it is in the case of biological reproduction. And the means by which a child is united with adults through adoption includes not only adoption policy and practice but also cultural dimensions that include ways of conceiving those ties.

Contemporary adoption policy and practice is explicitly organized around the idea that adoption must serve the "best interests of the child," a common phrase in the formulation of children's rights (e.g., at the 1989 UN Convention on the Rights of the Child). These "interests" have become a significant channel through which adults articulate their desires for children. Debates about adop-tion policy and practice organized around the child's "interests," furthermore, are certainly about current realities, with all their material and institutional con-straints, but they are also about possible futures. In this essay, I read adoption debates with regard to the visions of the future that they offer, paying close at-tention in particular to the ways that the child adoptee is variously mobilized in these debates, and suggesting that the child adoptee becomes the terrain on which the adoption debate is carried out and so too the terrain through which possible futures are imagined. Transracial adoption emerges as a key issue in this debate, such that the visions projected through the adoptee are also variously racial futures. Because transnational adoptions have been undertaken at least since World War II and in significant numbers since the 1970s and 1980s, these futures may also be global. How, then, are these futures articulated and materi-alized in relation to the child in adoption debates?

Adoption as a Reproductive Technology: An Overview

For the purposes of this discussion, I understand adoption as a reproductive technology, to call on a series of associations between technology and repro-duction that bring together human reproduction, the reproduction of bodies in

277

many different material forms, and the generation of cultural meanings. This set of associations has been made in recent feminist work in anthropology, cultural studies, and science studies.[1] Here, nature has been brought into cultural analysis. It has been denaturalized and deconstructed. No longer the assumed substratum of culture, nature has become a question rather than a grounding for feminist cultural studies. Reproduction, from this perspective, belongs neither to culture nor to nature but requires the inextricable mix of the two. The body generated through reproductive technologies, accordingly, is never simply a body but is generated through technologies of embodiment that render its very materiality as well as its meanings. The reproductive technologies identified as significant in the generation of bodies in contemporary analyses include not only new reproductive technologies, such as in vitro fertilization (IVF), abortion, and artificial insemination, but also visual, legal, and textual technologies as disparate as ultrasound, photography, and advertising. The images, texts, and metaphors of the body generated by these technologies are as significant as the body's more strictly biological incarnations. They, too, replicate, modify, and transform the bodies that we live and know. Indeed, these technologies are inextricably implicated in generating natural facts about bodies, such that the two cannot be easily dissociated. Feminist science studies has observed not only that "every technology is a reproductive technology"[2] but also that every body is reproduced by many different kinds of technologies.[3]

Adoption figures among the technologies conjoined in the generation of families and is itself arguably a form of assisted reproduction. In this essay, I focus on adoption not only as a reproductive technology but, even more specifically, as a reproductive technology of race. Race has historically been naturalized in the biological sciences, at least since the nineteenth century, as a property of the body that, along with other naturalized attributes, such as sex, intelligence, sanity, and sexuality, constitutes the human. Just as a body is generated by means of various technologies, the body's race does not simply exist; the body is racialized. Furthermore, a historically informed analysis of race suggests that this critical signifier changes over time; it must be continually reconstituted. It would be a mistake, then, to assume that we know in advance not only how race is being reimagined through the child body but also what kinds of child bodies and related meanings are generated through the continual rematerialization of race. The emphasis on generation and embodiment offered by the concept of adoption as a new reproductive technology makes it a useful tool for considering how the adoptee is racialized in U.S. debates about adoption—what kind of difference a given version of racialization makes and for whom.

Transracial adoption has been a matter of both implicit and explicit attention in the history of U.S. adoption and in turn features powerfully within current debates on transnational adoption. The United States is presently the largest consumer in the transnational adoption market, such that U.S. adoption has become globalized. While the number of transnational adoptions remains quite small relative to the number of births in the country as a whole, the importance of transnational adoption in relation to adoption more generally extends beyond the actual practice, as the following discussion attempts to show. In the wake of World War II and then the Korean War, various charitable U.S.-based organizations were started for the purpose of facilitating transnational adoptions of children orphaned in war.[4] As a result, European and then Korean children began to be adopted into largely white, middle- and upper-class homes.[5] The establishment of formal (i.e., legalized) transnational adoption procedures and institutions that began at this time expanded in subsequent years; the numbers of transnational adoptions rose to an all-time high in the 1980s with 10,097 adoptions by U.S. adults, leveling off in the 1990s to numbers in the nine thousands.[6] The racialization of the adoptee in contemporary debates takes place in a local global United States that is different even from that of the 1980s, because the countries with which transnational adoptions have been transacted have changed even in the last ten years. As some countries have temporarily and even permanently shut down their adoption systems due to charges of corruption, baby selling, and even baby farming, other countries have allowed transnational adoptions. At present, the largest number of adoptees come from Asia, Russia, and Latin America.[7]

Making Race

This inquiry into adoption as a technology of racial reproduction begins, more specifically, in the domestic United States, amid the pages of *Reconstruction*. Described by its editors as "particularly concerned with providing a forum for uninhibited commentary on African-American politics, society, and culture," this journal recently issued a special report on the long-debated politics of transracial adoption within the United States. The report consists of a lead article titled "Where Do Black Children Belong? The Politics of Race Matching in Adoption," written by Elizabeth Bartholet, a prominent adoption advocate and Harvard Law School professor. The article is followed by a series of shorter responses from key figures in the adoption world that represent a range of opinions on Bartholet's specific arguments for transracial adoption and on the issue more generally. Contributors to the special report include Anita Allen, Georgetown University Law Center professor and author of *Uneasy Access: Privacy for Women in a Free Society;* Ezra E. Griffith, professor at Yale University in the Medical School and the Department of Afro-American Studies; Joan Heifetz Hollinger, editor and principal author of *Adoption Law and Practice,* a reporter for the proposed Uniform Adoption Act of the Commission on Uniform State Laws, and professor at the University of Detroit Law School; Lillian B. Lansberry, vice president of the Adoption Exchange Association and president of the Black Adoption Recruitment Network; William L. Pierce, president of the National Committee for Adoption, editor of *The Adoption Factbook*, and coauthor of *The Encyclopedia of Adoption*; and Rita J. Simon, university professor at American University and author/coauthor of *Transracial Adoption* and *Transracial Adoptees and Their Families*.

By no means representative of the national debate as a whole, *Reconstruction*'s report is read here as a staged debate on transracial adoption, in which specific modes of racialization are variously employed. To the extent that the contributors to *Reconstruction* are also important actors in the adoption world, the modes of racialization they use in formulating their positions may have implications for future adoption policy and practice. Their significance for my purposes here, however, is limited to their cultural significance as visions of future forms of relatedness and to the kinds of raciality on which they depend, as well as those they refuse.

Elizabeth Bartholet's article in *Reconstruction* is adapted from a chapter in *Family Bonds: Adoption and the Politics of Parenting* (1993).[8] In this more popular venue, as well as in her more scholarly work, Bartholet situates the national debate on transracial adoption in a broad framework of reproductive choices that includes IVF and transnational adoption. For reasons that will become apparent, Bartholet projects a future in which adoption will take place primarily on a transnational and therefore transracial basis. This brings the domestic debate on transracial adoption into a transnational domain not addressed directly by *Reconstruction*.

To consider the problem of race in U.S. domestic as well as transnational adoption, I turn to some additional technologies of racialized reproduction available in the media. I use their visual representations to mark a shift between prior modes of racialization and new ones that seem to be emerging not only in Bartholet's writings but also in other cultural domains. I have argued elsewhere that the incorporation of transnational adoptees into U.S. families has depended not only on adoption policies, practices, and institutions but also on the transformation of the foreign adoptee into a familiar family member, a son or daughter. Whereas this transformation was formerly organized largely in terms of homogenization or assimilation, the current mode, particularly with regard to race, seems to be oriented toward a multiculturalist valorization of racial diversity. Here, I use both *Time* magazine's special issue on immigration and the clothing manufacturer Benetton's *COLORS* magazine devoted to race as visualizing tools that help to specify the particular mode of racialization that I find in Bartholet's work. Locating Bartholet's work in this wider domain of late-twentieth-century global culture makes it possible to describe a mode of racialization that is simultaneously a way of imagining global humanity and global family relations.

Family Bonding

Among the many actors in the adoption debate, Bartholet is one of the few who can draw on both her legal authority and her experience as an adoptive parent. Bartholet is a former civil rights lawyer now specializing in family law, the adoptive single parent of two boys born in Peru, and one of many women for whom adoption was a last resort following IVF failure.[9] Her *Family Bonds*, with its well-crafted mix of autobiographical narrative and legal-style reasoning, is arguably among the most widely influential recent popular U.S. publications on the topic of adoption. Bartholet's work addresses a wide range of audiences, appearing in diverse publications, from the *Pennsylvania Law Review*[10] to the California Center for the Future of Children's newsletter[11] and *Adoption Law and Practice*,[12] a sociologically oriented anthology on adoption practice and the law.

Throughout her writings, Bartholet advocates abolishing all legal measures and adoption agency policies that would require a racial match between a child and its adoptive parents. In "Where Do Black Children Belong?" she argues this position explicitly in relation to a history of race in U.S. adoption. For Bartholet, this history begins with a brief period in which transracial adoption was allowed during the 1960s. While racial matching had been a de facto and largely unquestioned practice in adoption until the mid–twentieth century, the civil rights movement of the 1960s was the most important among the multiple forces that raised public awareness of minority children previously neglected by the adoption system. Due in part to its integrationist principles, the civil rights movement helped to change adoption policy as well as adoptive parents' desires, ushering in a brief but important era of relative openness regarding transracial placements. This was followed, according to Bartholet, by the near-total elimination of transracial adoption.

For Bartholet, the members of the National Association of Black Social Workers (NABSW) were and continue to be the strongest proponents of racial matching and the moving force behind the translation of racial matching as a concept into long-standing and widely instituted state adoption policies. For Bartholet, the following quote by the NABSW exemplifies the standard argument against transracial adoption:

> Black children should be placed only with Black families whether in foster care or for adoption. Black children belong, physically, psychologically and culturally in Black families in order that they receive the total sense of themselves and develop a sound projection of their future. Human beings are

products of their environment and develop their sense of values, attitudes, and self concept within their family structures. Black children in white homes are cut off from the healthy development of themselves as Black people.[13]

According to Bartholet, the NABSW's historical success in translating this position into policy and practice was largely due to the "threat" of "black power" that was "exercised directly or through the workers' professional peers."[14] Since previously unspoken agency rules were codified in the 1970s (and only temporarily lifted in favor of transracial adoption in the 1960s), U.S. adoption has been organized around racial matching policies both codified and unspoken. These matching policies continue to be upheld in present adoption practice and law, Bartholet argues, despite the fact that so many children wait to be adopted because of the racial mismatch between available children and prospective parents.

Against this historical backdrop, Bartholet argues that in prioritizing the racial match between parents and children, adoption policies promote separatism through families. They constitute a kind of antimiscegenation tactic that reroots biological notions of race in the adoptive family. The NABSW's argument that transracial adoption is a form of genocide is the strongest statement among many that root children in their community by imagining both race and culture as inhering in the child. Opponents of transracial (and transnational) adoption, argues Bartholet, invoke children as a natural—that is, racial—resource that must be protected, while at the same time ignoring the child's actual interests, above all their need for a home.

In place of racial matching policies, Bartholet offers an invitation to a different kind of world, in which racial meanings have changed. In *Family Bonds,* she articulates a differently racializing version—a reconception—of the child within the family, which becomes a model of "common humanity."[15]

We can celebrate a child's racial identity without insisting that anyone who is born with a particular racial makeup must live within a prescribed racial community. We can recognize that individual members of various racial groups choose to define their identities and to define themselves in relationship to racial and other groups in an endless variety of ways. We can believe that people are fully capable of loving those who are not biologically and racially similar but are "other" and that it is important for more people to learn to do so. We can regard the elimination of racial hostilities as more important than the promotion of cultural difference.

From this perspective, which I share, transracial adoptive families constitute an interesting model of how we might better learn to live with one another in this society. These families can work only if their members have an appreciation of racial difference and love that transcends such difference. And the evidence indicates that these families do work.[16]

From this vantage point, the transnational adoptee is constituted in terms of a very particular form of race, relatedness, and family. Unlike the NABSW's formulation, which attaches the child to its community by virtue of its shared raciality, the child's inborn racial makeup here does not in any way link that child to a given community. The child, with its racial makeup, is entirely movable, allowing the child to travel from one racial community to another. When a white family adopts a black child, it imports a child that is racially other, because the child carries with it a given racial makeup. But this makeup quite specifically and insistently has no cultural content. Racial difference here cannot and in fact must not be associated with cultural difference. And while the child may have a racial identity, that identity is entirely individualized, a matter of choice, such that the child is, in a sense, self-racializing. Yet within this matrix of choice, a clear form of racialization can be discerned. Once individualized and detached from a community and a shared identity, the child can be loved as an other that is, it seems, no longer racially hostile or culturally different. It could be said that in this formulation, the child is constituted in terms of a racial difference that is utterly surface, a racial makeup, a color, to which no cultural difference or community belonging is necessarily attached. It must be purely racial and purely individual.

In frustration at the tenacity of arguments against transracial adoption that appeal to the rootedness of the child through race and nation, Bartholet adds another benefit to her vision of the adoptive family as a model of racial harmony: "Maybe it is too threatening to think what might happen if people were *not* understood to belong to their racial, national, or other groups of origin, if they were free to merge across group lines, if they were free *not* to reproduce more of the group's 'own.'"[17] What the child and its adoptive parents stand to gain from a revamped adoption system in Bartholet's vision is the freedom to merge and to reproduce something other than the group's own. This benefit is offered in part as a means of supporting Bartholet's central contention that the best interests of black children should be defined above all as the need for a home. Her advocacy of transracial adoption is based, in part, on the contention that black children are being used in an "essentially adult agenda of promoting racial separation," rather than insuring that these children's interests are served. Anticipating the concern that black families have not been adequately recruited to adopt black children, Bartholet offers the following assessment:

> It is true that more could be done to find black families. More substantial subsidies could be provided and more resources could be devoted to recruitment. But it is extremely unlikely that our society will anytime soon de-

vote more than lip service and limited resources to putting blacks in a social and economic position where they are capable of providing good homes for all the waiting black children. It will always be far easier to get white society to agree on the goal of placing black children in black homes than to get an allocation of financial resources that will make that goal workable. The danger in using black children to pry the money loose is that white society will not see these lives as warranting much in the way of ransom.[18]

Bartholet's program for facilitating transracial adoption suggests both that racism will prevent black families from becoming adoptive parents and that white families who adopt black children constitute a model of racial harmony.

Alongside the implicit suggestion that most black families are not capable of providing good homes due to their social and economic status, Bartholet identifies benefits that accrue to black children if they are given the "freedom to merge." Among these is the possibility (offered by Bartholet as a counter to the claim that black children need skills for living in a racist society that only black parents can transmit) that whites "are in the best position to teach black children how to maneuver in the white worlds of power and privilege." In addition, Bartholet argues that black children gain "a range of material advantages associated with having white parents and living in the largely white and relatively privileged world that such parents tend to frequent."[19] What does it mean, given Bartholet's description of current U.S. white society as one that does not value black children's lives, that she advocates placing them in the midst of that very society? As William L. Pierce put it in his otherwise favorable response to Bartholet, this "comes perilously close to recommending, as a sort of utopian policy, trans-racial adoption over same-race adoption."[20]

Bartholet is certainly correct in posing adoption as a potential threat to naturalized racial, ethnic, and national belonging.[21] Adoption can deconstruct compulsory reproductive heterosexuality as the basis of relationality, because it separates biological procreation from nurture. Adoption makes families from persons who are not related through biological procreation (and this includes intrakin adoptions, like the adoption of children by their aunts and uncles, their grandparents, and so on). It can also deconstruct naturalized versions of national, racial, and cultural belonging, because it refuses such naturalized ties as barriers to the placement of children. But the possibility of not reproducing more of the group's own is not guaranteed by the freedom to merge. Where power is involved, as in the relations between children and adults or between different racial and national groups, merging might mean anything from a kind of mutual mutation to erasure or assimilation. I argue, in fact, that in the absence of some kind of belonging prior to adoption, the adoptee produced through uninhibited merging (if such a thing is possible) is precisely a reproduction of the group's own, an image made in an economy of the same.

In Bartholet's vision of future adoption practices free of racial matching, the dissociation of race from biology or destiny, its dislocation from a discursive matrix in which race rooted the body in racial and national communities or groupings, is accompanied by a relocation of race in a discourse of choice, freedom, and movement, offered as an invitation to a seemingly antiracist future. The value of choice, freedom, and movement are assumed in this invitation, but what is being offered along with the vision of racial harmony is greater freedom of choice for prospective (white) parents who are consumers in the adoption market. Included in this choice is the choice of racial difference, which is extended to the child in the form of the benefits already named, once that child has been adopted. The following section considers the relationship between racialization, choice, and the dream of racial harmony by switching to a different new technology of racial reproduction and a new cultural domain: *Time* magazine's morphing of a newly hybrid nation.[22]

Morphing the Global U.S. Family

The head-and-shoulders shot of a smiling woman on the cover of a fall 1993 issue of *Time* is set against a background grid of tiny versions of the same image. "Take a good look at this woman," the caption beckons, "She was created from a mix of several races. What you see is a remarkable preview of . . . The New Face of America." The subtitle reads, "How Immigrants are Shaping the World's First Multicultural Society." The face on *Time's* cover was created as part of a larger project intended to "dramatize the impact of interethnic marriage" caused, say the editors, by recent U.S. immigration. Yet the key shaping agent for this cover girl, named the "new Eve" by *Time*, is not immigration but morphing.[23]

Morphing is the same technology that created Michael Jackson's "Black or White" video and *Terminator II*. *Time* used it for the "cybergenesis" of an immigrant nation, represented as a grid of faces. Along the top row of this grid, seven head-and-shoulder photographs of female models are arranged under seven headings: "Chinese," "African," "Anglo-Saxon," "Middle Eastern," "Italian," "Vietnamese," and "Hispanic." Photographs of seven male models labeled with the same seven headings are arranged along the left-hand column. These two series of images are used to generate the offspring that would result from pairing each photograph in the top row with each one in the left-hand column. The remaining forty-nine cells of the grid are filled with computerized images representing these offspring. They were generated by running each pair of photographs through a software program called Morph 2.0.

Note that the seven categories mixed together to generate these images are not immediately recognizable as racial categories. They include what might otherwise be considered national (Vietnamese, Chinese, Italian), regional or continental (Middle Eastern, African), or other geographically specific terms (Anglo-Saxon, Hispanic). These categories are nevertheless quite clearly racialized categories: what is being mixed here—or, more accurately, morphed—are purely physical and surface characteristics. The categories are evacuated of the complicated histories and politics of culture, geography, and nation that they might otherwise signify. This is made clearer by *Time*'s description of the morphing process, in which specific parts of the face are identitied as distinguishing features and then coded as electronic dots. Among the key features chosen were "head size, skin color, hair color and texture, eyebrows, the contours of the lips, nose and eyes, [and] even laugh lines around the mouth." The resulting grid of progeny are naked, pristine, and untouched potentialities made by human and computer. As *Time* pointed out, the ratio of inputs from each of the photographs was up to the programmer. The fifty-fifty ratio of input from the two coupled images used for *Time*'s grid generated, in one case, "a distinctly female face—sitting atop a muscular neck and hairy chest." Even morphing produces unexpected results, but the undesirable offspring reproduced by the morphing process were simply remorphed according to taste.

Donna Haraway has read this grid as a matrix that provides for a kind of race mixing without miscegenation and all of the history that term implies: "All the bloody history caught by the ugly word 'miscegenation' is missing in the sanitized term 'morphing.' Multiculturalism and racial mixing in *Time* magazine are less achievements against the odds of so much pain than a recipe for being innocently raptured out of mundane into redeemed time."[24] This form of racialization does not consist, then, in the establishment of a hierarchy for domination based on biologized or even culturalized racial difference. Its violence— its racism—consists instead in the evacuation of histories of domination and resistance (and of all those events and ways of living that cannot be captured in those two terms), accomplished through morphing as a specific kind of technological (and heterosexual) reproduction.

In the case of transnational adoption, the writing of history entails the writing of the adoptee and the adoptive family. While it is certainly true that the practice of sealing adoption records, as Bartholet points out, serves to cut off the prior history of the child, the writing of history with or without that information is never simply given. I want to suggest here that adoption imagined as the "freedom to merge" is a kind of morphing in that it proceeds by a similar process of evacuation, selection, erasure, and reinscription. Morphing is an example of this process, but more importantly, for my purposes here, it can be used as an interpretive tool; that is, it elucidates a mode of reracializing reproduction that does not obey the rules of historical or biological logics. Given that morphing affords the programmer the possibility of regenerating undesirable images (in this case, offspring) morphing as a means of evacuating history is joined by its capacity for reproduction by replacement, or reinscription. It offers a choice of final outcomes, erasing both distant and much more recent histories, and replacing them by its particular mode of reproduction with an always renewable fund of images. What the evacuation of history does for what *Time* calls the "re-birthing of the nation" as well as for the adoptive family is to produce a space behind the surface, an empty body, on which to write a story. In both cases, that story is reinscribed as the merging of the global into a local U.S. hybridity that is quite precisely not about maintaining racial purity and sociopolitical segregation. The power of morphed reproduction both in adoption and in *Time's* re-birthing of the nation is, paradoxically, not the power to reproduce in the traditional sense of passing on characteristics, heritage, or even genes. It is, rather, the power to reproduce not only without the constraint of history but without historical contingency.

While this power is largely symbolic and therefore not equivalent to actually changing the salience of racialized categories, remaking the nation, or changing adoption policy, it is important to remember that the symbolic has material consequences. Even the virtual reproduction of cybergenesis had such consequences, if desire can be considered a material effect: several of *Time's* staff members are reported to have fallen in unrequited love with their Eve.[25] And while *Time's* morphing produced unfulfillable desires, transnational adoption most directly fulfills adult desires for adoptive children. In Bartholet's version, this fulfillment is accomplished through the evacuation and reinscription of the adoptee, particularly with regard to race. The practice of renaming adoptive children is one small example of the reinscription to which adoptive parents are entitled in the adoption process. As a metaphorical practice of racialization, morphing creates both the opportunity of reinscription and the responsibility of writing a history.

History as a Technology of Racialized Reproduction: Responses to Bartholet

In responding to Bartholet's call for a total elimination of racial matching policies in the "best interests of the child," contributors to *Reconstruction* working in the field of adoption law and practice both contest and applaud her position, and in so doing they offer their own conceptions of race with regard to the adoptee and the adoptive family. Ezra E. Griffith, a professor in the Medical School and the Department of Afro-American Studies at Yale University, argues that the "race-matching concept" is more culturally powerful than Bartholet wishes to admit. While he completely supports her conclusions, Griffith maintains that no amount of legal transformation will change the fact that "[f]amilies built on sameness are the core of nations!"

Of the remaining five respondents, all support some form of what Professor Anita Allen of the Georgetown University Law Center calls "particularized determinations" with regard to race,[26] rather than Bartholet's proposal for a total elimination of any agency-directed or judicially directed stipulations regarding transracial placement. These caveats range from a test that would determine potential parents' "capacity for racial 'sensitivity,'"[27] to the observation that Bartholet seems to ignore the "unmet need for healthy newborns among black prospective adoptive parents,"[28] to Anita Allen's suggestion that there are valid reasons for birth parents', adoption agencies', and adoptive parents' racial preferences. Allen, for example, cites parental desires linking "culturally meaningful tasks" to "racial characteristics," such as a black woman's wish to cornrow an adoptive daughter's hair and "lotion away her 'ash.'"[29]

Not all of these responses are equally compelling, and many of them seem to succumb to a fairly narrow definition of blackness and of familial relatedness. Among the responses published in *Reconstruction*, Lillian Lansberry's stands out as an alternative to Bartholet's historical account of transracial adoption within the United States. In presenting another history, Lansberry's response also reaches a different conclusion regarding adoption policy: she neither reverts to narrow definitions of blackness nor ignores the way that histories of racial inequality are embedded in the history of transracial adoption.

Lansberry is a licensed social worker, president of the Black Adoption Recruitment Network, and vice president of the Adoption Exchange Association. Her alternative account begins with a description of pre-1960s adoption services. Before the 1960s, according to Lansberry, the availability of white, healthy infants converged with adoption policies, in which a desirable infant was defined as just such a healthy, white infant from a "good" family, who could also pass as the biological offspring of the adoptive family. Similarly, adoption services were provided to white, middle-class (and presumably heterosexual) couples who owned their own homes. Proof of inability to conceive a child was frequently required, as was the guarantee that the woman intended to be a full-time homemaker. In an adoption economy dominated by white adults seeking healthy white children (among other variables), and in the absence of any concerted efforts to recruit nonwhite adults as potentially adoptive parents, adoption policies effectively denied children of color—as well as disabled children, older children, and sibling groups—a place in the pool of adoptable children.[30]

The makeup of this pool shifted in the 1960s due to a confluence of factors. Most important among these for Lansberry were the advent of the contraceptive pill, the legalization of abortion, greater acceptance of pregnancy and motherhood for unmarried women, and the attention focused on black, poor, and disabled children by the civil rights movement and the war on poverty. This is an important turning point for Lansberry's account, not so much because transracial adoption became possible (as in Bartholet's version of this history), but because "[t]he means by which adoption agencies refocused their services is at the very heart of the trans-racial adoption debate."[31] According to this account, racial matching policies and practices were overturned both to augment the numbers of children available to the same constituency of adoptive parents serviced by agencies in previous decades and to facilitate the adoption of children previously disqualified from adoption.

For Lansberry, this shift translated into transracial adoption for quite specific groups of children and adults. While the pool of "adoptable" children was expanded to include children of color, especially "mixed-race" children,[32] the providers of adoption services and the clientele they served remained essentially the same. Though some attempts to recruit families of color were made at this time, the *trans-* in *transracial* generally referred to the transfer of children of color into white families only. As Lansberry puts it, adoption agencies "unaccustomed to working with families of color" were "more comfortable trying to fit the existing children into the families of their adoptive applicants than they were in learning how to work with a new group of families."[33] Lansberry does not support racial matching policies per se. But for her, the history of transracial adoption and its continued use in some private adoption agencies indexes the unwillingness on the part of traditional agencies to recruit families of color. High fees bar these disproportionately poorer families from adopting the healthy children of color that are available through these agencies. Thus, "transracial" adoption continues to signify a one-way transfer of children of color into white families. Lansberry's criticism of adoption policy with regard to race (as well as disability and other categories traditionally deemed less desirable in a child) is directed at the ways in which adoption policies and practices constitute adoptive families through their selection of "adoptable" children and available, eligible adoptive parents. It is not so much that transracial adoption should be illegal, then, as that it exists in the absence of concerted efforts to recruit and provide services to families of color, who, among other reasons for deserving equal treatment, possess historically devalued and extremely important skills for surviving racial discrimination. In conclusion, Lansberry neither advocates nor deplores transracial adoption. She advocates, instead, selecting for children of color adoptive parents "who can ensure that [the children's] daily lives include a variety of healthy adult role models of their same racial/cultural background."[34] While Lansberry stresses issues relating to the availability of children and parents for adoption, her account also suggests that desirability—what is a desirable child? for recruiters, what makes an adult desirable as a potential parent?—is so closely tied to availability as to make it nearly impossible to separate the two.

In both Bartholet's and Lansberry's accounts, the availability and desirability of children as well as parents in U.S. adoption emerge at the intersection of shifting adoption policies, political agendas, social conditions, and moral values, in which race and racism work alongside other significant factors. At issue in the debate about transracial adoption in the United States is the power to define the "best interests" of children, where children "belong," and what kinds of laws and policies will best achieve these ends. But Lansberry's history suggests that these issues can be defined and articulated in different terms. Her contribution to the transracial adoption debate questions the terms in which that debate has been set, rather than accepting them and so simply taking up a position for or against racial matching. This shift in terms also suggests a way of reading Bartholet's racialization of the adoptee, her vision of freedom as merging: Lansberry's account suggests that this "freedom" should perhaps be constrained by a clearer historical understanding of who is "free," combined with a sharp attention to whose freedom is assumed to be at stake and to who or what is being merged and to what effect.

Bartholet's program for facilitating transracial adoption claims that racism will prevent black families from becoming adoptive parents. Lansberry is not opposed to transracial adoption per se. But her response refuses to accept the inequalities that support the devaluation of black families and black children on which Bartholet's argument partially rests. Rather than a vision of the adoptive white parent/black child family as a model of racial harmony, she holds out the vision of an adoption system that would redress the inequalities by which black families have been denied equal access to children and that would ensure the significant presence of black adults in the lives of adopted black children.

The responses to Bartholet in *Reconstruction*, including Lansberry's historically informed alternative formulation of the key issues, contribute to the national U.S. debate about transracial adoption with regard to black children and white prospective parents. Limited in that it has tended to address only black-to-white adoption, this debate is also limited in its strictly national scope. While *Reconstruction* frames transracial adoption as a nationally relevant issue, adoption practices, choices, and politics have been significantly altered since the 1980s with the advent of transnational adoption. As I have already mentioned, Bartholet's *Reconstruction* article appears in a slightly altered form in *Family Bonds*, where it forms part of a wider discussion on transnational adoption. Bartholet's *Family Bonds* therefore situates the national debate addressed by her "Where Do Black Children Belong?" in a larger framework of adoption at a transnational level, where notions of racial belonging evident in the national arena are joined to national belonging as a critical nexus of contention.

Indeed, for Bartholet in *Family Bonds*, the special salience of transnational adoption lies in the fact that no matter how domestic policies change, the future of adoption lies in transnational, rather than intranational, adoption. For her, "the world divides into essentially two parts for adoption purposes, one consisting of countries with low birth rates and small numbers of children in need of homes and the other consisting of countries with high birth rates and huge numbers of such children." Bartholet repeats this global mapping with regard to potentially adoptive parents, but in inverse proportion. She notes that in Western industrialized countries, there are large numbers of such parents, while in the "poorer countries of the world there are very few prospective adopters, in comparison with the vast numbers of children in need of homes."[35]

This map of available parents and children is neatly captured by legal language in references to "sending" and "receiving" countries, language borrowed elsewhere in Bartholet's description of the current demographics of transnational adoption, where "sending" countries are those with a surplus of children and "receiving" countries are those with a surplus of prospective parents.[36] Given the current importance of transnational adoption both as an aspect of an increasingly globalized United States and in Bartholet's work, it is important to consider Bartholet's racialization of the adoptee in global terms as well as in the strictly national terms set out in *Reconstruction*. Furthermore, the assumed values of freedom, movement, and choice offered in Bartholet's vision of transracial adoption are linked, in the transnational domain, to an economy of supply (of "available" children), on one hand, and demand (on the part of prospective parents), reproduction, and consumption, on the other. This economy corresponds to the relation of poorer "sending" and richer "receiving" countries of the world. The following section considers again Bartholet's racialization of the adoptee, this time in a global frame, by shifting to another technology of racial reproduction. Benetton is a multinational clothing company that offers its own invitation to a racially harmonious future world. Liberalism, racialization, and consumption, all on a transnational scale, converge in Benetton's promotional magazine *COLORS*, whose 1993 spring/summer issue is devoted to race. Like *Time*'s morphing of a hybrid nation, Benetton's *COLORS* magazine works here primarily as an interpretive tool, useful for detailing a specific mode of racialization.

United Colors

A collage of photographic images depicting racial violence frames the *COLORS* race issue's table of contents. In keeping with the overall design of the magazine, in which the editorial "we" speaks to the reader, these images are accompanied by the following description:

> What are these people doing? We usually don't dwell on the bad news. And racial violence is definitely bad news. But this issue of COLORS is about how race affects our lives and how racism can take many forms, not all as obvious as those we've presented here. These pictures are our way of showing the problem quickly and bluntly. It will take us longer to show you the solutions.

In the remaining pages of the *COLORS* issue on race, photography is employed in a number of ways to depict race and racism, along with a playful use of color, language, and typography. Marked by the liberal use of mixed fonts and letter sizes, bold typefaces, exclamation points, and question marks, the copy comes in two languages, English and Italian. This bilingualism is just one of the many devices that promote Benetton as a global enterprise capable of representing race in all of its forms.

Photography and printing are the principal technologies used in Benetton's reproduction of race. In the manner of fashion magazines, the copy in COLORS appears primarily as an adjunct to large and often compelling photographic images. In this issue of the magazine, these images are thematically arranged according to a series of different treatments of race. Reminiscent of nineteenth-century racial typologies in their use of individual shots of heads and other isolated body parts to represent different racial types,[37] many sections in the series are devoted to an examination of race as a matter of physical difference registered on the surface of the body.

A strategy of racial reproduction runs through this dizzying assortment of visually laden pages: race is evacuated as a signifier of specific histories linked to contemporary social, political, and cultural worlds. For example, while every head in the taxonomy of racial epithets is accompanied by a particular "who" (the group to which it belongs), "from" (its national and regional location), and "by" (the group that uses the epithet), the historical and contemporary specificity of ethnic groups and their relation to one another are absent. This contingency is displaced by the juxtaposition of heads from all over the world, such that each specific relation is simultaneously decontextualized and recontextualized in relation to other similarly decontextualized ethnic or racial relations. Reference to "you," the reader, signifies the leveling of differences by this means, the evacuation of specific histories and significations, since the "you" holds a place for anyone and everyone, without the need to know about the reader in advance.

If there is a thematic unity in this issue of COLORS, it is not simply race but race as a mutable feature that can be altered by choice. Just as skin color can be tinged with orange by the overingestion of foods rich in beta-carotene, so other surface racial characteristics can be altered by other means. One section of the magazine depicts various methods of surgical and topical racial transformation, from eye surgery to widen eyes and fatten lips, to skin-whitening creams and tanning lotions. The arbitrariness of race-as-color-by-choice is useful for thinking about Bartholet's racialization of the adoptee, which suggests a similar shift of race from an essential quality to one that can be chosen. In Bartholet's version of adoption, race is as mutable as color, a medium of difference easily transferred and transformed by choice—the choice of families to adopt a child transnationally, as well as the child's choice of racial identity. Race-as-color-by-choice in Bartholet's version of adoption is what makes the "other" child available for adoption, in contrast to modes of racialization that would root the child to a particular place and community.

This version of race also grounds Bartholet's vision of the transnational adoptive family as a model of racial harmony. The value of transracial and transnational adoption as such a model in Bartholet's new world of adoption is rendered in significant part through bodies made available by the reproduction of race as an individual choice, a palette of mix-and-match colors. In particular, the child's race is imagined as a surface quality that can be detached, chosen, and rearranged in a different palette of colors. Against arguments that link a child to a given community, the adoptee here is racially mobilized, made "available" for adoption and for a broader vision of racial harmony.

Race-as-color is a medium of change and diversity that, perhaps most significantly, is also a medium of ownership: Benetton attempts to actually *own* diversity through its advertising campaigns by establishing and changing the available palette of colors.[38] In Bartholet's vision, similarly, the transracial and transnational adoptee is claimed as the (white) adoptive family's "own" on the basis of the adoptee's racial mutability. While Benetton is concerned with the reproduction of race alone, adoption intertwines the reproduction of race with the generation of families. In Bartholet's vision of adoption, transnational adoption becomes a new reproductive technology of family relations that is also a new reproductive technology of race. Indeed, the mixing and matching of colors generates new relational ties, just as the formation of these ties through transracial transnational adoption generates a new mixing and matching of colors.

Incorporations

Adoption, morphing, and global marketing are not the same kinds of practices, nor do they produce the same material effects. I have used morphing and photography here as visual tools that help both to elucidate the printed text and to describe the constitutive effects of adoption as a racializing technology that reproduces the adoptee. The affinities between these three technologies become more important in attempting to specify how transnational adoption debates are implicated in adoption as a transnational materializing practice. Just as adoption debates project imagined futures, so *Time*'s hybrid nation and Benetton's color-as-choice can be viewed as projections in time, visions of a reracialized global future.

I gloss the affinities between these visions as *incorporation*. From the Latin *incorporare,* or "the union in or into one body," the term *incorporation* signifies both the process by which bodies are constituted as such (the union *in* one body) and the process by which a body is made from two or more separate entities (the union *into* one body).[39] In contemporary terms, this second kind of union includes a more specific process by which economic enterprises gain a particular legal status. While the corporation is hardly new, in the late twentieth century it took on a particular global form: the multinational corporation.

The term *incorporation*, then, signifies three different kinds of processes: embodiment, inclusion, and enterprise. These processes, in turn, are associated here with three kinds of globalized bodies: the racialized human body; the local global U.S. nation, or (trans)national body; and the corporation. Both of the technologies considered here in relation to adoption share with it a racialized embodiment that becomes the basis for inclusion in a larger global body (the family, the nation, the world), enabled in part by a transnational economic enterprise (transnational adoption fees; Time, Inc.; Benetton).

The three kinds of incorporations considered here—Benetton's panhumanity, *Time*'s immigrant nation, and Bartholet's adoptee and its racially harmonious family—all rely on unlimited, individual, and historically unburdened choice. In what might be called the new cultures of consumption, choice is linked not only to desire but to the commodification or economization of culture. Consumer choice is one of the hallmarks of this commodification. But consumer choice, as anthropologist Marilyn Strathern has argued, is severely constrained. The freedom of free enterprise for the consumer only constitutes choice within a limited range of options. Because procreation, she argues, "can now be thought about as subject to personal preference and choice" (she maintains, "the child is literally—and in many cases joyfully—the embodiment of the act of choice"), procreation, too, becomes subject to the limits of consumerism.[40] The liberalization of adoption advocated by Bartholet may be a way of serving the "best interests of the child," then, but it is also a means of increasing consumer choice in adoption—especially transnational adoption—which is at the moment a highly bureaucratic, confusing, and cumbersome procedure.

The notion of race-as-choice offered as a part of this argument implies that the goal of adoption policy liberalization is to make the child's race an aspect of the embodiment of the act of choice. In Bartholet's formulation, this choice entails a form of racialization that will "promote the elimination of racial hostilities over the promotion of cultural difference."[41] I argue, however, that this is a difference "chosen" to make no difference. The child "freed" for adoption is racialized as a body or space left open for the writing of a history, such that this writing, too, becomes an instance of "free" choice. Incorporation, here, works as a process of denaturalization, rather than naturalization, with regard to the racialized body. It disarticulates race as a natural fact—as something that means beneath the skin—but at the same time refuses it any historical or cultural significance. This is a relativizing, liberal mode of racialization, in which race is both empty and innocent. According to this multivalent signification, then, incorporation becomes a process of racialization working across the three technologies.

Finally, Bartholet's vision of transnational adoption employs a specific mode of racialization that is not unique either to Bartholet or to transnational adoption debates. Other, quite different technologies are used to generate a similar mode of racialization in quite different cultural domains. This mode exists, currently, alongside virulent reassertions of race in utterly immutable, hierarchized terms. An adequate response to these divergent but equally problematic versions of race requires attention to the multivalent and contradictory ways that race is being generated and mobilized as the basis of various kinds of inequality and injustice.

The Child as the Embodiment of Racial Harmony

Of the three technologies considered in this essay, transnational adoption is alone in generating a vision of the child per se. At stake in the debate is the power to define the kind of body and person that the child will become. In this child, the potential, the possibility, the hope at the heart of the adoption debate is embodied. I have argued that a very specific version of the child as a mutably racial body is generated when adoption is imagined as a site not only of family making but of racial and global harmony as well. The child, more than the parents, is reracialized in order to accomplish this harmony. Historically configured as a body-in-process, the child has been rendered newly available as the possible embodiment of parental (adult) desire by means of this reracialization. Not only does race take on a newly valued flexibility across the three technologies I have named, then, but with regard to transnational adoption in particular, this transnationally transracially flexible body is the body of the child. Like *Time*'s hybrid but still adult offspring, the child is constituted through the incorporation of global differences and embodies harmonious global relatedness: the child becomes the global.

bell hooks has argued that desire for relatedness with an Other—for my purposes the desire of U.S. adoptive parents for the foreign child—can "act as a critical intervention challenging and subverting racist domination, inviting and enabling critical resistance." This, she adds, "is an unrealized political possibility."[42] It will remain unrealized, I argue, both within transnational adoption and outside of it, as long as visions of global relatedness maintain their innocence, continuing to evacuate history from race. These histories are not simply "available" for reappropriation, and children are not simply "available" for incorporation. The ways in which global relatedness is imagined and sustained should be accountable to history or, to be more specific, to histories of racial domination and resistance. When global relatedness is envisioned through the child, this vision should also be accountable to the child and to the history of adult uses of the child.

I have suggested that Lillian Lansberry's alternative history of transracial adoption provides one example of such a vision. It takes into account the history of racial inequalities by which children of color were made available to mostly white adults for adoption. In addition to Lansberry's alternative, the recent history of what Kathleen Biddick has called "distributive maternity" among whites and blacks troubles the simple mapping of available children and desiring adults.[43] "Distributive maternity" refers to how reproductive technologies (including sterilization) locate reproductive labor among women disproportionately by race and class—and, I would add, by location in transnational circuits of exchange. Poor women of color in the United States and poor women of many ethnic and racialized groups in the Third World have been subjected to forced sterilization and suffer higher rates of infertility and infant mortality. At the same time, scientific resources and public investment in maternity are distributed in favor of the comparatively fewer middle- and upper-class heterosexual women of the dominant races with infertility problems, especially white women in industrialized countries.[44] The problems related to maternity among the first group of women are largely ignored, partly due to the representation of these women as the cause of overpopulation and as unable to care for the children they produce. Thus, we have the notion of "sending" countries, sources for a steady supply of children. How would notions of children's availability for adoption change if such issues were taken into account?

So far, I have concentrated on racialization as a focal point in this aspect of the adoption debate and on the relation between race, histories of racial inequality, and their manifestation in terms of how children are made "available" for transracial and transnational adoption. It is equally important to emphasize, again, that racialization is only a small part of how children are made available for transnational adoption. Missing from my own account, for example, is any mention of the extent to which the practice of transnational adoption itself actually produces available children. Many questions remain to be asked about transnational adoption, but I will pose only one final set here, about the child in particular: What kind of Other is a child? an adoptee? a foreign child? What kind of "race"—or gender, or sexuality, or any one of so many other social categories—"belongs" to a child? What kind of history "belongs" to a child? And how can we answer these questions in a transnational domain, when these questions may be answered differently in different cultural communities? To the problem of imagining forms of global relatedness that work against inequalities as they are being generated now, in global cultural forms, can be added the problem of the child as a body-in-process. This problem is posed not just for adoption policy but for other social practices and for cultural theory as well. The mutability of the child figured as a body-in-process makes it eminently appropriable; not yet fully formed, it has no prior being that must be displaced and then replaced. It only has to become, according to taste. Perhaps this is not the familiar, liberal individualism that it might at first appear to be. Perhaps the new world order poses new forms of inequality that do not work in terms of immutable, "natural" attributes. Perhaps they work, instead, through change, through the power to change an other according to taste or to become an other by appropriation. If so, perhaps we must imagine a different kind of incorporation, one that resists both naturalization and those forms of denaturalization—or deracination—that refuse relevant histories, one that resists the simple "availability" of children for adult visions of the future.

NOTES

A version of this essay will also appear in Claudia Castañeda, *Worlds in the Making: Child, Body, Globe* (Durham: Duke University Press, forthcoming).

1. See, for example, Ludmilla Jordanova, ed., *Languages of Nature* (London: Free Association Books, 1986); Donna Haraway, *Simians, Cyborgs, and Women: The Reinvention of Nature* (New York: Routledge, 1991) and *Primate Visions: Gender, Race, and Nature in the World of Modern Science* (New York: Routledge, 1989); Emily Martin, *The Woman in the Body: A Cultural Account of Reproduction* (Boston: Beacon, 1987) and *Flexible Bodies: Tracking Immunity in American Culture* (Boston: 1994); and Barbara Stafford, *Body Criticism: Imagining the Unseen in Enlightenment Art and Medicine* (Cambridge: MIT Press, 1991).

2. Zoe Sofia, "Exterminating Fetuses: Abortion, Semiotics, and the Sexo-Semiotics of Extraterrestrialism," *Diacritics* 14, no. 2 (1984): 47–59.

3. See Monica Caspar, "Fetal Cyborgs and Technomoms on the Reproductive Frontier," in *The Cyborg Handbook,* ed. Heidi J. Figuerow-Sarriera, Chris Hables Gray and Steven Mentors (New York: Routledge, 1995); Lisa Cartwright, *Screening the Body: Tracing Medical Visual Culture* (Minneapolis: University of Minnesota Press, 1995); Sarah Franklin, *Embodied Progress* (New York: Routledge, 1996); Valerie Hartouni, "Reproductive Technologies and the Negotiation of Public Meanings: The Case of Baby M," in *Provoking Agents: Theorizing Gender and Agency,* ed. Judith Kegan Gardiner (Urbana: University of Illinois Press, 1992); Rosalind Petchesky, "Fetal Images: The Power of Visual Culture in the Politics of Reproduction," *in Reproductive Technologies: Gender, Motherhood, and Medicine,* ed. Michelle Stanworth (London: Polity Press, 1987); Janelle S. Taylor, "The Public Fetus and the Family Car: From Abortion Politics to a Volvo Advertisement," *Public Culture* 4, no. 2 (1992): 67–80; Carol Stabile, "Shooting the Mother: Fetal Photography and the Politics of Disappearance," *Camera Obscura* 28 (1992): 1789–806.

4. Everett M. Ressler et al., *Unaccompanied Children: Care and Protection in Wars, Natural Disasters, and Refugee Movements* (New York: Oxford University Press, 1988).

5. Rita J. Alstein and Howard Simon, *Intercountry Adoption: A Multinational Perspective* (New York: Praeger, 1991).

6. National Committee for Adoption, *1992 Factbook* (Washington, D.C.: NCA, 1992).

7. Of the visas for adoptive children issued between October 1993 and September 1994, for example, the highest number was for Korea (1795), followed by Russia (1530), China (787), Paraguay (483), Guatemala (433), India (412), Colombia (351), and the Philippines (314). These statistics are listed in U.S. Department of State Bureau of Consular Affairs, *International Adoptions* (Washington, D.C., October 1995).

8. Elizabeth Bartholet, *Family Bonds: Adoption and the Politics of Parenting* (Boston: Houghton Mifflin, 1993). Elizabeth Bartholet, "'Where Do Black Children Belong?'" *Reconstruction* 1, no. 4 (1992): 22–43.

9. The promise of IVF far exceeds its actual results. Bartholet's frustration with the amount of money spent on this and other reproductive technologies relative to that spent on encouraging adoption as a valid way of making a family is an important part of her argument, but not one that I consider here. For a wide-ranging discussion regarding women's experience of the failure of IVF in contrast to its representation and implementation as a valid treatment for infertility, see Sarah Franklin's *Embodied Progress* (London and New York: Routledge, 1997).

10. Elizabeth Bartholet, "Where Do Black Children Belong? Politics of Race Matching in Adoption," *Pennsylvania Law Review* 139 (1991): 1163, 1198–99. This is the original version of the *Reconstruction* article and the treatment in *Family Bonds*.

11. Elizabeth Bartholet, "International Adoption," *The Future of Children* 5, 1992.

12. Elizabeth Bartholet, "International Adoption: Overview," in *Adoption Law and Practice* ed. Joan Hollinger (New York: Times Mirror, 1992).

13. Uncited study quoted in Bartholet, "Where Do Black Children Belong? The Politics of Race Matching in Adoption," *Reconstruction* 1, no. 4 (1992): 28.

14. Bartholet, "Where Do Black Children Belong?" (1992), 28.

15. Bartholet, *Family Bonds*, 143.

16. Ibid., 112.

17. Ibid., 43.

18. Ibid., 43.

19. Ibid., 36.

20. William Pierce, in "Responses to 'Where Do Black Children Belong?'" *Reconstruction* 1, no. 4 (1992): 58.

21. See also Judith Modell, *Kinship with Strangers: Adoption in American Culture* (Berkeley: University of California Press, 1994).

22. The following section was written in conversation and through the exchange of writing between myself and Donna Haraway. Her writing on the subject can be found in Donna Haraway, "Universal Donors in Vampire Culture: It's All in the Family: Biological Kinship Categories in the Twentieth-Century United States," in *Uncommon Ground: Toward Reinventing Nature,* ed. William Cronin (New York, London: W. W. Norton, 1995), 321–66.

23. The quotes from *Time* in this paragraph and subsequent paragraphs are from "Rebirth of A Nation," in *The New Face of America*, special issue of *Time*, fall 1993, 66–67.

24. Haraway, "Universal Donors," 365.

25. Commenting on this phenomenon, Haraway focuses on the gendered aspects of the scenario, or what feminists have called "masculinist birthing." She writes ("Universal Donors," 339): "The curious erotics of single-parent masculine, technophilic reproduction cannot be missed. SimEve is like Zeus's Athena, child only of the seminal mind—of a man and of a computer program."

26. Anita Allen in "Responses to 'Where Do Black Children Belong?'" *Reconstruction* 1, no. 4 (1992): 27.

27. Joan Heifetz Hollinger, in "Responses to 'Where Do Black Children Belong?'" *Reconstruction* 1, no. 4 (1992): 49.

28. William Pierce in "Responses to 'Where Do Black Children Belong?'" 54.

29. Allen in "Responses to 'Where Do Black Children Belong?'" 27.

30. Lillian Lansberry in "Responses to 'Where Do Black Children Belong?'" 52–53.

31. Ibid., 52.

32. So-called mixed-race children have been particularly ill served by strict racial matching systems because they cannot be matched to a distinct racial group, according to the logic of matching. With the decrease in available healthy white infants, writes Lansberry (ibid., 52), adoption agencies began to place these mixed children in white families if the children were "half-White."

The debate on transracial adoption in this essay is organized around the binary of black and white, a binary through which so many debates about race tend to revolve in U.S. public arenas. Among the other racialized groups that have emerged in the debates on transracial adoption are Native Americans. The Indian Child Welfare Act of 1978, established due to pressure from Native American groups out of concern for tribal survival, requires that Native American children be placed in Native American homes. See U.S. Administration for Native Americans, *The Indian Child Welfare Act of 1978: Questions and Answers*, (Washington, D.C.: Washington Health, Education, and Welfare, Office of Human Development Services, Administration for Native Americans, 1979). See also U.S. government hearings (Senate and House of Representatives Select Committees on Indian Affairs) on the Indian Child Welfare Act, held subsequent to its passage in 1978 through 1988. It should be noted, furthermore, that the transracial adoption of Native American children is also transnational adoption, given the status of Indian tribes in relation to the U.S. government (Joanne Barker, personal communication with the author).

33. Lansberry in "Responses to 'Where Do Black Children Belong?'" 52–53.

34. Ibid.

35. Bartholet, *Family Bonds*, 141.

36. Ibid., 146.

37. See Fatimah Rony, "Those Who Sit and Those Who Squat—the Iconography of Race in the 1895 Films of Regnault, Felix, Louis." *Camera Obscura* 28 (1992): 263–89; Nancy Lays Stepan, *The Idea of Race in Science* (London: MacMillan, 1982).

38. Celia Lury, "United Colors of Diversity: Benetton's Advertising Campaign and the New Universalisms of Global Culture, A Feminist Analysis" (paper presented at University of California, Santa Cruz, January 7, 1994).

39. See also Jonathan Crary and Sanford Kwinter, eds., *Incorporations*, Zone Books Series, no. 6 (Cambridge: MIT Press, 1992).

40. Marilyn Strathern, *Reproducing the Future: Anthropology, Kinship, and the New Reproductive Technologies* (New York and London: Routledge, 1992).

41. Bartholet, *Family Bonds*, 112.

42. bell hooks, *Black Looks: Race and Representation* (Boston: South End, 1992), 22.

43. Kathleen Biddick, "Stranded Histories: Feminist Allegories of Artificial Life," *Research in Philosophy and Technology* 13 (1993): 162–82.

44. See Angela Davis, *Women, Race, and Class* (New York: Vintage, 1982); Patricia Williams, *the Alchemy of Race and Rights* (Cambridge: Harvard University Press, 1991).

Select Bibliography

Alstein, Rita J., and Howard Simon. *Intercountry Adoption: A Multinational Perspective.* New York: Praeger, 1991.

Anderson, Benedict. *Imagined Communities: Reflections on the Origin and Spread of Nationalism.* London: Verso, 1983.

Bagnell, Kenneth. *The Little Immigrants: The Orphans Who Came to Canada,* Toronto: MacMillan of Canada, 1980.

Bartholet, Elizabeth. *Family Bonds: Adoption and the Politics of Parenting.* New York: Houghton Mifflin, 1993.

Bean, Philip, ed. *Adoption: Essays in Social Policy, Law, and Sociology.* London: Tavistock, 1984.

Behlmer, George K. *Friends of the Family: The English Home and Its Guardians.* Stanford: Stanford University Press, 1998.

Boswell, John. *The Kindness of Strangers: The Abandonment of Children in Western Europe from Late Antiquity to the Renaissance.* New York: Pantheon, 1988.

Brodzinsky, David, and Marshall D. Schechter, eds. *The Psychology of Adoption.* New York: Oxford University Press, 1990.

Brodzinsky, David, Marshall D. Schechter, and Robin Marantz Henig. *Being Adopted: The Lifelong Search for Self.* New York: Anchor Doubleday, 1992.

Carp, Wayne. *Family Matters: Secrecy and Disclosure in the History of Adoption.* Cambridge, Mass.: Harvard University Press, 1998.

Daly, Brenda O., and Maureen T. Reddy, eds. *Narrating Mothers.* Knoxville: University of Tennessee Press, 1991.

Dever, Carolyn. *Death and the Mother from Dickens to Freud: Victorian Fiction and the Anxiety of Origins.* Cambridge: Cambridge University Press, 1998.

Dubrow, Heather. *Shakespeare and Domestic Loss: Forms of Deprivation, Mourning, and Recuperation.* Cambridge: Cambridge University Press, 1999.

Estrin, Barbara. *The Raven and the Lark: Lost Children in Literature of the English Renaissance.* Lewisburg: Bucknell University Press, 1985.

Fanshel, David. *Far From the Reservation: The Transracial Adoption of American Indian Children.* Metuchen, N.J.: Scarecrow, 1972.

Fildes, Valerie. *Wet Nursing: A History from Antiquity to the Present.* New York: Basil Blackwell, 1988.

Findlay, Alison. *Illegitimate Power: Bastards in Renaissance Drama.* Manchester: Manchester University Press, 1994.

Foucault, Michel. *Discipline and Punish.* Trans. Alan Sheridan. New York: Vintage, 1977.

———. *Language, Counter-Memory, Practice,* Ed. Donald F. Bouchard. Ithaca: Cornell University Press, 1977.

Gager, Kristin. *Blood Ties and Fictive Ties: Adoption and Family Life in Early Modern France.* Princeton: Princeton University Press, 1996.

Golden, Mark. *Children and Childhood in Classical Athens.* Baltimore: Johns Hopkins University Press, 1990.

Goody, Jack. *The Development of the Family and Marriage in Europe.* Cambridge: Cambridge University Press, 1983.

Grossberg, Michael. *Governing the Hearth.* Chapel Hill: University of North Carolina Press, 1985.

Hacsi, Timothy. *Second Home: Orphan Asylums and Poor Families in America.* Cambridge: Harvard University Press, 1977.

Hansen, Elaine Tuttle. *Mother without Child: Contemporary Fiction and the Crisis of Motherhood.* Berkeley: University of California Press, 1997.

Harrison, Phyllis. *The Home Children: Their Personal Stories.* Winnipeg, Manitoba: Watson and Dwyer, 1979.

Holt, Marilyn Irvin. *The Orphan Trains: Placing Out in America.* London: University of Nebraska Press, 1992.

Ito, Susan and Tina Cervin, eds. *A Ghost at Heart's Edge.* Berkeley: North Atlantic, 1999.

Kirk, H. David. *Shared Fate: A Theory of Adoption and Mental Health.* 1964. Reprint, New York: Free Press, 1974.

Laslett, Peter, Karen Oosterveen, and Richard M. Smith, eds. *Bastardy and Its Comparative History.* London: Edward Arnold, 1980.

Lifton, Betty Jean. *Journey of the Adopted Self: A Quest for Wholeness.* New York: Basic, 1994.

———. *Lost and Found: The Adoption Experience.* 1979. Reprint, New York: Harper and Row, 1988.

———. *Twice Born: Memoirs of an Adopted Daughter.* 1975. Reprint, New York: St. Martins, 1998.

Marsh, Margaret, and Wanda Ronner. *The Empty Cradle: Infertility in America from Colonial Times to the Present.* Baltimore: Johns Hopkins University Press, 1996.

May, Elaine Tyler. *Barren in the Promised Land.* New York: Basic, 1995.

McClure, Ruth K. *Coram's Children: The London Foundling Hospital in the Eighteenth Century.* New Haven: Yale University Press, 1981.

Modell, Judith. *Kinship with Strangers: Adoption and Interpretations of Kinship in American Culture.* Berkeley: University of California Press, 1994.

Nussbaum, Martha Craven. *The Fragility of Goodness: Luck and Ethics in Greek Tragedy and Philosophy.* Cambridge: Cambridge University Press, 1986.

Omi, Richard, and Howard Winant. *Racial Formations in the United States, from the 1960s to the 1980s.* New York: Routledge and Kegan Paul, 1986.

Paster, Gail Kern. *The Body Embarrassed: Drama and the Disciplines of Shame in Early Modern England.* Ithaca: Cornell University Press, 1993.

Paton, Jean [Ruthena Hill Kittson, pseud.]. *Orphan Voyage.* 1968. Reprint, Cedaredge, Colo.: Country, 1980.

Pertman, Adam. *Adoption Nation: How the Adoption Revolution Is Transforming America.* New York: Basic, 2000.

Pinchbeck, Ivy, and Margaret Hewitt. *Children in English Society.* 2 vols. London: Routledge and Kegan Paul, 1973.

Ruddick, Sara. *Maternal Thinking: Toward a Politics of Peace.* Boston: Beacon, 1989.

Sedgwick, Eve Kosofsky. *Epistemology of the Closet.* Berkeley: University of California Press, 1990.

Shell, Marc. *Children of the Earth: Literature, Politics, and Nationhood.* New York: Oxford University Press, 1993.

Simpson, Eileen. *Orphans: Real and Imaginary*. New York: Weidenfeld and Nicolson, 1987.

Solinger, Rickie. *Wake Up Little Susie: Single Pregnancy and Race Before Roe v. Wade*. New York: Routledge, 1992.

Sorosky, Arthur D., Annette Baran, and Reuben Pannor. *The Adoption Triangle: The Effects of the Sealed Record on Adoptees, Birth Parents, and Adoptive Parents*. New York: Doubleday, 1978.

Stepan, Nancy Lays. *The Idea of Race in Science*. London: Macmillan, 1982.

Wadia-Ellis, Susan. *The Adoption Reader: Birth Mothers, Adoptive Mothers, and Adopted Daughters Tell Their Stories*. Seattle: Seal, 1995.

Walby, Christine, and Barbara Symons. *Who Am I? Identity, Adoption, and Human Fertilization*. London: British Agencies for Adoption and Fostering, 1990.

Wegar, Katarina. *Adoption, Identity, and Kinship: The Debate over Sealed Birth Records*. New Haven: Yale University Press, 1997.

Young, Robert J. C. *Colonial Desire: Hybridity in Theory, Culture, and Race*. London: Routledge, 1995.

Zelizer, Vivian. *Pricing the Priceless Child: The Changing Social Value of Children*. New York: Basic, 1985.

Contributors

Margot Gayle Backus is an assistant professor of English at the University of Houston. Her articles have appeared in *Tulsa Studies in Women's Literature, American Imago*, the *Canadian Review of Comparative Literature, Cultural Critique*, the *Journal of Homosexuality*, and *Signs*. She is also the author of *The Gothic Family Romance: Compulsory Heterosexuality and the Anglo-Irish Settler Colonial Order* (Duke University Press, 1999).

Julie Berebitsky is a visiting professor of history and the director of women's studies at the University of the South in Sewanee, Tennessee. She is the author of *Like Our Very Own: Adoption and the Changing Culture of Motherhood, 1851–1950* (University Press of Kansas, 2000).

Claudia Castañeda is a Lecturer at the Centre for Science Studies and the Institute for Women's Studies, Lancaster University, U.K. Her work lies at the intersection of postcolonial, feminist, and science and technology studies. She is the author of *Worlds in the Making* (Duke University Press, forthcoming), which considers embodied figurations of the child in transnational circuits of exchange.

Beverly Lyon Clark teaches English at Wheaton College in Massachusetts. Her previous work includes *Talking about Writing* (University of Michigan Press, 1985), *Lewis Carroll* (Starmont, 1990), and *Regendering the School Story* (Garland, 1996), and she coedited *"Little Women" and the Feminist Imagination* (Garland, 1999), and *Girls, Boys, Books, Toys* (Johns Hopkins University Press, 1999). She is currently completing *Kiddie Lit*, a book on the cultural construction of children's literature in the United States.

Beverly Crockett is a lecturer in English and Interdisciplinary Studies at Northwestern University. The essay in this volume developed out of research on her Ph.D. dissertation in English from the State University of New York at Buffalo.

Jill R. Deans is an assistant professor of English at Kansas State University, where she teaches twentieth-century American literature, ethnic literature, women's literature, and film. Having completed her Ph.D. dissertation (at the University of Massachusetts, Amherst) on adoption and the rhetoric of illegitimacy, she has since published several articles on adoption in late-twentieth-century American cultural texts.

305

Paris De Soto is an English teacher at Los Gatos High School in California. She is working toward her Ph.D. in English from Rutgers University, New Brunswick. The essay in this volume is part of her dissertation.

Kristina Fagan is a doctoral student in English at the University of Toronto. Her dissertation is entitled "Laughing to Survive: The Comic Spirit in Contemporary Canadian Native Literature."

Nancy K. Gish is a professor of English and women's studies at the University of Southern Maine. She is the author of *Time in the Poetry of T. S. Eliot* (Macmillan, 1981), *Hugh MacDiarmid: The Man and His Work* (Macmillan, 1984), *The Waste Land: A Poem of Memory and Desire* (Twayne, 1988), and *Hugh MacDiarmid: Man and Poet* (National Poetry Foundation and Edinburgh University Press, 1992), as well as articles on Marianne Moore, Denise Levertov, and contemporary Scottish women poets. She is currently coediting an anthology on gender, sexuality, and desire in T. S. Eliot.

Garry Leonard is an associate professor of English at the University of Toronto. He is the author of *Rereading Dubliners: A Lacanian Perspective* (Syracuse University Press, 1993) and *Advertising and Commodity Culture in Joyce* (University Presses of Florida, 1998), as well as numerous articles on modernism, cinema, and popular culture, published in such journals as *Modern Fiction Studies, Novel, American Imago*, and *College Literature*. He is currently writing a book called *Making it New: Technology and Subjectivity in Modernism and Modernity*.

Judith Modell received her Ph.D. in anthropology from the University of Minnesota in 1978. She is currently a professor of anthropology, history, and art at Carnegie Mellon University, where she has been teaching since 1984. Her publications include *Ruth Benedict* (University of Pennsylvania Press, 1983); *Kinship with Strangers* (University of California Press, 1994); *A Town Without Steel: Envisioning Homestead* (University of Pittsburgh Press, 1998); and *A Sealed and Secret Kinship* (Berghahn Press, forthcoming March 2001), which deals with changes in American adoption and the way those changes come about.

Marianne Novy is a professor of English and women's studies at the University of Pittsburgh. She has published *Love's Argument: Gender Relations in Shakespeare* (University of North Carolina Press, 1984) and *Engaging with Shakespeare: Responses of George Eliot and Other Women Novelists* (University of Georgia Press, 1994; rpt. University of Iowa Press, 1998) and has edited three anthologies on women's responses to Shakespeare: *Women's Re-Visions of Shakespeare* (University of Illinois Press, 1990), *Cross-Cultural Performances* (University of Illinois Press, 1993), and *Transforming Shakespeare* (St. Martin's, 1999). She is currently writing a book on literary representations of adoption.

Tess O'Toole is an associate professor of English at McGill University. She is the author of *Genealogy and Fiction in Hardy: Family Lineage and Narrative Lines* (St. Martin's, 1997) and several articles on nineteenth-century fiction. She is currently completing a manuscript on adoption in Victorian literature.

Martha Satz is an assistant professor of English at Southern Methodist University. She has exploited her dual academic background in philosophy and literature to publish essays on such diverse topics as Jane Austen, Mary Wilkins Freeman, Kafka, Thomas Mann, Richard Wright, the Holocaust, and issues of gender and race in children's readings. The first single woman in Texas to adopt a child, she is currently at work on a book on adoption, race, culture, and literature.

Jan VanStavern is an assistant professor of English at Dominican University of California, where she teaches poetry, women's literature, and creative writing. Her poetry and criticism focus on the ways that identity articulates itself in lives and literature, as she explores the implications of adoption, gender, and race. While studying at the University of California at Davis, she worked with fellow poet and adoptee Sandra McPherson, who inspired her to consider more deeply how poetry and adoption inform one another.

Index

Abortion, 7, 137, 278, 288

Adoptee rights activists: and claims about searching, 193–94, 198; dismissed as irrational, 215, 216; international, 5; and search movement, 5, 6, 8, 193–94, 209. *See also* Adoption; Identity

Adoptees: and absence, 125, 153–55, 159, 161, 162, 220, 224, 253; and attachment to adoptive family, after search, 219; curiosity of, 40, 156, 219; docile, 114, 116–17, 124; and double family, 3, 220; as fake children, 194; as fantasy space, 114, 115, 116, 121, 123, 127, 128, 130, 131; as fortunate, 215, 216; and gender, 9, 51–52; as group, 6, 172, 223; ignorance imposed on, 214; and imagination, 9, 11, 43, 57–58, 71, 125, 126, 138–41, 152–54, 157, 159, 160, 161, 162, 171, 174, 253; mature and responsible, 200; as mothers, 167–68, 242; mutilated, 121, 130, 215, 226, 243–44; and names, 151, 160–61, 163–65, 240, 253, 287; and need for community, 46, 47, 52, 254–56; as oppressed minority, 223; as outsiders, 2, 3, 51–52, 113, 117, 124–25, 126, 128–29, 152, 160, 244–45, 252, 274–75; pathological, 3, 119, 139; as perpetual children, 6, 37, 158–59, 163, 214; and reality/fantasy problem, 119, 126; and religion, 46, 136, 160, 221, 242; and self-invention, 160, 163, 174, 180, 257, 262; and self-knowledge, 172–73; and sense of difference, 1, 11, 41, 172–73, 180, 181, 185, 275; and sexuality, 141–44; silenced, 5, 115; splitting, 118, 120, 159, 164, 165, 168; violent, 113, 223; without rights, 213, 215

Adoptees' Liberty Movement Association, 9, 210, 218, 220

"Adopteestentialism," 124, 125, 127

Adoptee support groups, 207–27; international, 5; rhetoric of (personal narratives), 209–26; search framework of, 213, 214; structure of, 208

Adoption: as absurd, 111; and American values, 4, 7–8, 20, 86, 207, 224, 252; and denial of difference, 111, 115, 116, 126, 195, 234, 280, 284; and acculturation, 7–8, 22, 52, 86, 99, 241, 246, 252, 254; ancient Roman, 4, 19; as beneficial, 9, 24, 50, 84, 86–89, 146, 156, 203, 244–45; changes in twentieth-century American, 4–5, 86, 207, 219, 223–24, 279, 288; in children's literature, 100–108; and choice, 26–27, 30, 84, 89, 90, 92, 98, 146, 196, 198, 203, 239, 285, 291, 294; as connection, 10, 23, 29, 247; as "contract" murder, 127; crosscultural, 40, 47–50, 52–53, 171, 181–82, 185, 187, 251–57, 259–60, 263, 267–76, 277–97; cross-species, 100–107; and deconstruction of naturalized belonging, 284, 294; in dictionary, 98; as disastrous to family, 1, 2, 18; English and American attitudes toward, compared, 4, 20, 92, 137; and erasing/rewriting history, 8, 10, 135, 144–45, 194, 195, 234, 258, 286–87, 294; as fiction/construction, 1, 10–11, 12n. 2, 17–18, 98, 105, 194, 199, 202; and fostering independence, 100, 102, 107, 159, 244, 291; in French Revolution, 4; and friendship, 102–5; function of, in literature, 2–3, 7, 18, 35; and gender, 3, 9–10, 22, 50–52; ideological power generated by, 135, 137, 143–44; informal (de facto), 4, 17–18, 61, 231–59; and inheritance, 19–31, 52, 238, 239, 240, 241, 243, 245, 246; international,

309

Adoption (*continued*)
5, 7–8, 277, 278–79, 280, 283, 286, 290– 97; as irresolvable without remainder, 256–57, 261–63, 271, 276; and language, 6; and legal contract, 4, 217, 218–20; as metaphor, 7, 18, 95–108, 242–43, 246, 251–52, 258; and mobility, 18, 25–26, 243, 291; and morphing (freedom to merge), 283–84, 285–87, 290; as natural, 36, 235, 268; as inferior bond, 85, 92, 97, 195, 232, 277; in nineteenth-century England, 4, 17–19; open, 5, 226; and plot, 1–2, 3, 17–19, 21, 22, 24, 30, 36, 40; racial matching in, 281, 282, 287, 288, 289; as recruitment, 25, 135; as repressive/commodifying, 9, 24, 69–70, 71, 115, 120, 121; and reproductive technology, 277–78; as restrictive and subversive, 231; revitalizing family, 18; ritual aspects of, 139; and sexuality, 10, 28, 43; single-parent, 29, 86, 255, 268; sixteenth-century French, 4; statistics on, 7, 269, 279; stigma of, 5, 20, 37, 92–93, 119, 122, 173; and structure over content, 145; as term, in fund-raising, 97; as transitory, 97, 217; transracial, 5, 8, 9, 101, 105, 171, 181–82, 188–89, 256–57, 260, 261, 262, 263, 264, 267–76, 277–97; as trauma/loss, 5, 41, 118–19, 127, 154–56, 157–58, 167, 168, 198, 245–46, 253, 267, 270

Adoption Act (Britain, 1926), 19
Adoption agencies, 118, 119, 121, 123, 124, 129, 270, 281, 282, 288, 289
Adoption records, 231–46; closed, 4, 5, 10, 111, 113, 115–18, 120–21, 123, 125–29, 193, 194–95, 214, 217, 222, 223, 233, 234, 244, 286; open, 4, 5, 10, 11, 193, 194–95, 199, 210
Adoption Reform Law (United States, 1999), 274
Adoption triangle: and community formation, 5, 6; and identity, 9, 145; and risk, 233
Adoptive fathers, 9, 163; distant/hostile, 130–31; and invention of heritage stories, 251, 253, 258, 259; nurturing, 25, 36–39, 47–48, 70; socially integrated, by adoption, 23, 46. *See also* Nurture
Adoptive mothers, 9, 75, 242; absent, 50; death of, 106–7, 198; and difference/stigma, 85, 87, 89, 91–93, 113–14; difficulties of, 87, 89; and emphasis on choice, 89–93; exploitative, 115, 238, 244–45, 273; frightened, 164, 268; identifying of daughter with, 176–77, 186, 187, 215, 219, 273; identifying with Virgin Mary, 136, 139; limited power of, 107; nurturing, 25, 73, 104, 173, 235, 256; as "real" mothers, 83–84, 173; as rescuers, 86–88, 242, 245; romanticized, in fantasy, 140; self-portrayal of, in writing, 87, 89; and sexuality, 141; stereotyped, 87; voice of, 188–89. *See also* Nurture
Adoptive parents, 1, 2, 9; and anxiety, 119; attachment to, after search, 219, 220; death of, 106–7, 203; fantasies of, about child, 114; as ideal parents, 107; as "real" parents, 1, 207; splitting child, 120; stereotyped, 2–3, 50, 87
African Americans, 4, 5, 101, 173, 181–82, 188–90, 268–276, 279, 281–85, 287–90, 295–96. *See also* Adoption, transracial; Identity
Albee, Edward, 5, 8, 10, 111–31; *American Dream,* 113–31; *Sandbox,* 113–14; *Three Tall Women,* 113–14, 115; *Tiny Alice,* 116, 117, 119, 121, 127, 128, 129, 130; *Who's Afraid of Virginia Woolf,* 114, 118, 119, 123, 130, 131; *Zoo Story,* 111, 113, 124, 126–29
Allen, Anita, 279, 287, 288
Allen, Paula Gunn, 237
Allison, Dorothy, 139
American Adoption Congress, 6, 9
American constitution as basis for adoptee rights, 212–17, 224
Andersen, Hans Christian: "Ugly Duckling," 38, 102
Anderson, Benedict, 48, 252
Artificial insemination, 7, 278
Arthur, King, 21, 57, 71, 141

Atwood, Margaret, 258
Aunts, 106–7, 243, 284
Austen, Jane: *Mansfield Park,* 19, 22, 25, 27

Backus, Margot, 5, 9, 10
Bagnell, Kenneth, 62, 76
Bailey, F. G., 126, 210, 218, 224
Baker, S. Josephine, 85
Barnardo, Thomas, 59, 62
Bartholet, Elizabeth, 9, 12n. 5, 195, 272–94
Bastard Nation, 13n. 9, 15n. 30, 56n. 37
Bastardy. *See* Illegitimacy
Beer, Gillian, 49, 50
Benetton, 280, 291–94
Berebitsky, Julie, 9, 10
"Best interests of the child," 6, 224, 233, 254, 277, 283, 289
Bicultural families, 259, 261, 271, 273, 282–83
Biddick, Kathleen, 296
Birth fathers, 9, 37, 42, 46, 47; absent, 204; absolved from financial burden, 114; and adoption of relinquished child, 220; identity of, discovered, 203, as "real" fathers, 37. *See also* Reunion
Birth mothers: absent, 50–51, 113; and adoption of relinquished child; 122; concerns of, rejected, 243; and confidentiality, 2, 6, 7, 194, 233, 234; and denial, 242; dying, 106, 245; exiled, 24–25, 39–40, 42–46; identifying of daughter with, 9, 176, 187, 219; imagined, 8, 157, 171–72, 173, 176, 186, 193, 196, 197; maternal impulses of, 39–40; nurturing, 1; privacy rights of, 2, 9; punishment of, 42, 114, 137, 144–45; as "real" mothers, 83, 193, 275; search for, 3, 171, 197, 199; searching, 9; suppressed, 143, 144–45, 193; trapped by past, 200. *See also* Reunion
Birth parents, 6, 8, 11; and connection with adoptee, 245–46; death of, remembered, 253; as ghosts, 153, 155, 157, 200, 244; as invented memories, 11, 253; and pressure to marry, 244; as

"real" parents, 1, 8, 15n. 27, 107, 108; search for, 3, 5, 9, 151–53, 197–98, 199, 211, 213–14, 219–20; sources on, 15n. 27; as term, 6. *See also* Reunion
Blake, Richard, 202
Blood: concept of, 13n. 8, 20, 21, 26, 27, 28, 29, 36, 62, 85, 87, 92, 122; importance of, in nineteenth century, 47; and "sacred bond," affirmed, 220; and "sacred bond," critiqued, 196, 201, 203; stigma of, 173, *See also* Genetics
Blood Brothers (musical), 3
Bloom, Harold, 100
Blum, Lawrence, 273
Bodenheimer, Rosemarie, 36, 37, 45, 48, 54n. 3
Bonding: and adoption contract, 217, 218, 220, 225, 235; and love in adoptive family, 217, 235, 275; and natural/biological ties, 217, 220, 221, 225
Boston Globe, 133, 138
Boswell, John, 4
Brace, Charles Loring, 63
Brodzinsky, David, 154–55, 158; and Marshall D. Schechter and Robin Marantz Henig, 140
Brontë, Charlotte: *Jane Eyre,* 144
Brontë, Emily: *Wuthering Heights,* 3, 17, 19, 32n. 20
Brown, Margaret Wise, 105
Burke, Kenneth, 216

Cannon, Janell: *Stellaluna,* 105
Carp, Wayne, 4, 209, 233–34
Castañeda, Claudia, 8, 9, 10
Century Magazine, 91
Child abuse, 62, 134, 139, 232–33, 253
Children Act (Britain, 1975), 199
Children's literature, 56–58, 68–76, 100–108
Chodorow, Nancy, 238
Cinderella, 156–57, 202
Civil rights movement, 209, 223, 281, 288
Clark, Beverly Lyon, 9, 10
Class, 3, 4, 24–27, 28, 30, 32n. 16, 40, 46, 59, 61, 137, 138, 201, 202, 258
Cohen, Susan R., 18

Colonization/decolonization, 5, 8, 257–58
COLORS (magazine), 280, 291–94
Confidentiality, 2, 6, 7, 194, 233, 234
Contract, 127, 218, 224, 226
Cooper, James Fenimore, 251, 252
Coste, Didier, 244
Craik, Dinah: King Arthur, 4, 18, 19–22
Crockett, Beverly, 10
Cultural diversity/multiculturalism, 8, 49, 53, 252, 257, 259, 262–63, 280, 286
Cultural Studies, 98
Cvetkovich, Ann, 139

Dahl, Roald: James and the Giant Peach, 106
Dallas Times Herald, 272
Dances with Wolves (film), 251
Dante Alighieri, 155
Davis, Angela, 181
Deans, Jill, 8, 10
Demeter-Persephone myth, 202
De Soto, Paris, 8, 10
Dickens: Bleak House, 17; Great Expectations, 17; Oliver Twist, 1, 3, 114–15, 121, 122
Disability, 6, 7, 289
Discursive subject, 183, 187
Disraeli, Isaac, 48–49
Doan, Laura, 138, 139
Dorris, Michael, 232, 239, 240, 246
Doyle, Andrew, 62
Duckworth, Alistair, 19
Dukakis, Michael, 133–35
Dusinberre, Juliet, 100

Eliot, George, 8, 35–53; as stepmother, 35–36, 43. Works: Adam Bede, 44; Daniel Deronda, 3, 8, 9, 16n. 29, 17, 32n. 22, 35; Felix Holt, 17, 19, 29, 35; Mill on the Floss, 35; Romola, 36, 54n. 5; Silas Marner, 1, 3, 9, 30, 35, 36, 46–47, 50; Spanish Gypsy, 35
Erdrich, Louise, 8, 10, 231–47; Beet Queen, 231, 232, 242, 243, 247; Bingo Palace, 238, 244, 245, 246; Bluejay's

Dance, 235–37; Love Medicine, 232, 238, 241, 242, 243, 244, 245; Tracks, 238, 240, 241, 242
Estrin, Barbara, 77n. 5
Ethnicity/ancestry, 3, 4, 5, 6–7, 10, 30, 40, 46, 47, 49, 50, 52–53; diversity of, in England, 48; as essential to identity, 219. See also Blood; Genetics/heredity; Identity; Race
Exposure of children, 4, 71, 245

Fagan, Kristina, 8, 9, 10
Family, 2, 10, 11; bicultural, 259, 261, 271, 273, 282–83; in national allegory, 251, 259, 260; "traditional," 133–34; in Victorian fiction, 17–18
Family romance, 2, 40, 159, 161, 193, 196; critiqued, 200, 202
Father: defined, 36–37, 53; as legal fiction, 196. See also Adoptive fathers; Birth fathers
Fertility, 237; impact of race and class on, 296; stereotypes of, 2–3, 10
Fetal Alcohol Syndrome, 232, 233
Fiedler, Leslie, 252
Flavin, James, 240
Fostering/foster care, 4, 32n. 115, 36, 48, 50, 58, 61, 64–67, 254, 269, 270, 274. See also Adoption, informal
Foucault, Michel, 59, 118, 121, 122, 197–98
Foundlings, 58, 59, 67, 135
Freedom of Information Act, 214
Free Willy (film), 102
Freud, Sigmund, 2, 40, 196
Frye, Northrop, 40, 253

Gager, Kristin, 4
Gale, Zona, 88
Gates, Henry Louis, 8, 16n. 35
Gays/lesbians, 136, 138, 139, 141–43, 145, 146, 147, 157, 175; and affective bonding, contrasted to adoption, 146; and analogies to adoptees, 145, 146; excluded from fostering or adopting children, 133–35, 136, 145. See also Identity

Geertz, Clifford, 209
Genealogical bewilderment, 104, 204
Genet, Jean, 98, 124
Genetics/heredity, 2, 5, 6, 8, 27, 28, 36, 38, 41–42, 47, 48, 51, 52, 53, 59, 73, 202, 238; imagery of, 50; imagined, 152; as motive for search, 220; resemblance combined with opposition of values, 44; romanticization of, 234; and "home children," 59, 62, 66, 73; valorization of, treated critically, 37, 38. *See also* Blood; Ethnicity/ancestry
Gilligan, Carol, 275
Girard, Linda Walvoord: *We Adopted You, Benjamin Koo,* 101
Gish, Nancy, 1, 8, 10
Globalization, 277–96
Good Housekeeping, 87, 88
Greenblatt, Stephen, 239
Griffin, Gabriele, 184
Griffith, Ezra E., 279, 287
Griffith, John, 103–4
Grimm, Jacob and Wilhelm, 106
Griswold, Jerry, 100

Hacsi, Timothy, 59
Hamilton, Virginia: *The Planet of Junior Brown,* 101
Hansen, Elaine Tuttle, 236
Harrison, Phyllis, 63
Hekman, Susan, 183–84, 187, 189
Heterosexuality: as criterion for adoptive and foster parents, 10, 133–35, 145–46; deconstructed by adoption, 10, 284
Hoberman, J., 202
Hollinger, Joan Heifetz, 279
"Home children," 59; nurturing of, 63, 66; physical abuse of, 62, 64, 65, 67; seen as workers, 65; sexual abuse of, 65–66, 67; and stigma, 62, 66, 69
Homosexuals. *See* Gays/lesbians; Identity
hooks, bell, 295
Howe, Ruth-Arlene, 274
Hughes, Ted, 106
Hybrids/hybridity, 49, 55n. 26, 98, 100, 107, 246, 261, 262, 263, 268–69, 287, 293. *See also* Identity, multiplicity of

Identity, 1, 6, 8, 9, 243, 245; of adoptee, 8, 30, 40, 46, 47, 48–49, 50, 52–53, 142, 145, 146, 152, 153, 156, 158, 163, 166, 167, 171, 173, 174, 176, 183, 194, 197, 204, 214, 219, 231, 234, 235, 237, 239, 240, 244, 245, 259, 263; of adoptive mother, 83, 86; of birth mother, 242; black, 171–90; 272–73; black/Scottish, 179; Canadian, 252, 257, 258, 260, 261, 263, 289; ethnicity as central to, 219; gay, 183; interracial, 251, 261, 262, 263; Jewish, 35, 43–53, 272; and language, 176, 183, 185, 189; lesbian, 142–47, 181; multiplicity of, 174–90, 272; national, 252, 264; Native/Metis, 252, 254, 262, 263, 264; racial, 5, 183, 269, 274, 282–87, 292–94; Scottish, 174, 177–80, 181, 182, 258, 259; search integrates, 219–20
Illegitimacy, 3, 23, 24, 25, 26, 41, 52, 66, 111–23, 126–29; and economics, 114–15; greater acceptance of, 7, 288; in Lyotard, 246; and silence, 115; stigma of, 10, 11, 26, 59, 112, 122, 137, 173, 195, 198, 199, 234, 242, 244. *See also* Bastard Nation
Immigrants/immigrant children, 59, 60, 62, 63–67, 72, 74–76, 86, 285; and analogy to adoption, 7
Incorporation, 293–94, 297
Indian Child Welfare Act (1978), 254
Indians. *See* Identity, Native/Metis; Native Americans
Individualism, 296; as American myth, 255, 256, 257
Infertility, 198, 203–4; blamed on women, 86, 195; impact of race and class on, 296; stereotypes of, 2–3, 10, stigmatized, 87, 111
International adoption. *See* Adoption, international
Interracial adoption. *See* Adoption, transracial
In vitro fertilization (IVF), 278, 280, 281

Jan, Isabelle, 100
Jarrell, Randall, 102

Jesus, 127–28
Jewishness, 35, 43–53, 272
Joseph, Gloria, 274
Joyce, James, 196
Justice, Donald, 164

Kay, Jackie, 1, 6, 8, 9, 10, 171–90; *Adoption Papers,* 171–90; *Off Colour,* 182; *Other Lovers,* 186–89
Kincaid, James, 25
Kingsolver, Barbara, 8, 9; *Bean Trees,*1, 52, 251; *Pigs in Heaven,* 52–53, 251–64
Kinship, 11, 50, 224, 226–27, 234, 235, 237, 240, 247; contracted, in adoption, 217; double, in adoption, 220
Kipling, Rudyard, 106
Kirk, David, and Susan McDaniel, 134
Klein, Melanie, 153–54
Konigsberg, Eric, 232
Kroetsch, Robert, 257

Lacan, Jacques, 153
Ladies' Home Journal, 85, 89, 90
Lakoff, George, and Mark Johnson, 98
Lansberry, Lillian, 280, 288, 289, 290, 295
Laurence, Margaret, 8; *Diviners,* 251–53, 257–64
Law: natural, 210, 212, 219, 220, 221; state, 4, 5, 211–12, 215, 220, 221–22, 223, 268
Lawrence, D. H., 31, 252
Legitimacy, 112, 123, 129, 246
Leigh, Mike, 204. See also *Secrets and Lies*
Leonard, Garry, 5, 10
Leonard, Tom, 177
Lesbians. See Gays/lesbians; Identity, lesbian
Lewes, Charles, 35–36
Lewes, G. H., 35, 45
Lewes, Thornton, 45
Lifton, Betty Jean, 3, 6, 55n. 35, 195, 196, 197
Living Age, 92
Lorde, Audre, 181
Losing Isaiah (film), 274–75
Lyotard, Jean-Francois, 246

MacDiarmid, Hugh (Christopher Murray Grieve), 174
Marshall, David, 50
Maternal education, 90–91
Maternal instinct, 10, 51, 106; of adoptive mothers, 84, 85, 88; idea of, critiqued, 40; sufficiency of, questioned, 89, 90–91
Maternal work, 11, 105. See also Adoptive mothers; Nurture
McPherson, Sandra, 6, 8, 9, 10, 151–69; *God of Indeterminacy,* 168; *Patron Happiness,* 155, 163–67; *Radiation,* 154, 155–58; *Year of Our Birth,* 154, 155, 159–63
Mercer, Kobena, 98
Michie, Helena, 98
Minh-ha, Trinh T., 184, 185
Mirrors/mirroring, 44, 156–57, 161, 182, 184, 187, 189–90, 201, 275
Mitchell, Sally, 20, 21–22
Modell, Judith, 8, 10, 11, 50, 234
Montgomery, L. M.: *Anne of Green Gables,* 1, 19, 57–58, 68–76; *Anne of the Island,* 69
Morphing compared to adoption, 285–87
Morrison, Toni, 178; *Bluest Eye,* 273
Moses, 48, 49, 51, 240, 273
Motherhood: biological and adoptive, 235, 236; and biological bond, 85, 196, 237; defined, 83–84, 90–92; and nineteenth-century sense of importance to society, 84–85; physical and mental, 236; romanticized, 235–36; scientific, 89–90; as separation, 238–40; spiritual, not physical, 84, 88, 177; sustaining, 239. See also Adoptive mothers; Birth mothers; Maternal instinct; Maternal work

National Association of Black Social Workers, 269, 271, 275, 281–82
National Council for Adoption, 212
National myth, 253–54, 255, 256, 262
Nation/nationalism, 7, 47, 48, 50, 52, 53, 251–52; and imagination, 252

Native Americans, 231–47, 251–57, 259; Cherokee, 52, 251, 254, 255, 256, 259; Chippewa, 232–40; Modoc, 232; Ojibway, 236, 271

Native/Metis, 251–65

Natural as kinship term, 6, 36, 42, 152, 166, 235, 244, 246

Nature, concept of, 36, 41–42, 44, 53, 151–67, 184, 217, 220, 221, 235, 236, 237, 278

Neruda, Pablo, 155, 161

Neumeyer, Peter, 104

Nodelman, Perry, 105

Norris, Kathleen, 89–90

Novel: and idea of nation, 252, 259; and individualism, 260; and preoccupation with family in Victorian period, 17–19

Nurture, 2, 6, 8, 11, 21, 27, 39, 48, 50–51, 90, 105, 107; by adoptive father, 25, 36–37, 42, 47; by adoptive mother, 21, 22, 87–90, 105; by birth mother, 1. *See also* Adoptive mothers; Maternal work

Nurture Assumption, 2

Nussbaum, Martha, 256, 271

Oedipus, 1, 2, 45, 48

Orphanages/orphan asylums, 59, 114, 118

Orphans, 11, 13n. 9, 17, 57–59, 61, 66, 67, 68, 70, 72, 77n. 5, 157, 251–52; contrasted with adoptees, 11, 158, 244; as metaphor for North America, 252; and stigma, 57–59, 69, 71, 74, 113, 133–34, 144, 245

Orphan Voyage, 209

O'Toole, Tess, 9, 10

Oxford English Dictionary, 98

Parenthood, defined, 1, 11

Paton, Jean, 3, 14n. 20, 14n. 24, 209

Pauper apprenticeships, 60–63

Paxton, Nancy, 40

Pennsylvania Law Review, 281

Pérez Castillo, Susan, 246

Pierce, William, 212, 280, 284

Poor Law Amendment (1834), 114, 115, 122

Poor Laws (1576), 60, 112

Poovey, Mary, 136

Postcolonial criticism, 98–100, 107–8

Postmodernism, 139, 243, 246

Queer. *See* Gay/lesbian.

Race, 3, 4–5, 6–7, 98, 101, 122, 173, 183, 199, 201, 251, 255, 262, 264, 268–76, 278–97; as choice, 292, 293, 294; and race suicide, 86; and relation to culture, 47, 283. *See also* Adoption, transracial; African Americans; Ethnicity; Identity

Ragtime (musical), 3

Randall, Margaret, 139

Ragussis, Michael, 48

Reconstruction (journal), 279, 287, 288, 290

Reiser, Lynn, 101

Reunion, 2, 10, 36, 37, 43–46, 151–52, 163–67, 172, 197, 199, 201–2; and mystical language, in describing, 221

Richardson, Samuel: *Pamela,* 22

Robinson, Eden, 263

Roe v. Wade, 7

Roots, as concept/term/image, 41–42, 219, 237, 257, 259, 261, 282, 283. *See also* Blood; Ethnicity; Genetics

Roots (television show), 219

Rothman, Barbara Katz, 12n. 6, 13n. 8

Ruddick, Sara, 11, 15n. 33, 105, 236

Russell, Charles, 251

Rye, Maria, 62

Sanger, Margaret, 90

Sartre, Jean-Paul, 124

Satz, Martha, 10, 272

Satz, Michael, 267–75

Scarnnechia, Suellyn, 267, 270–71

Scott, Sir Walter, 48

Scottish identity, 49, 174, 177–80, 181, 182, 258, 259

Secrecy, 41, 44, 45, 46, 213, 224. *See also* Adoption records, closed

Secrets and Lies (film), 3, 6, 8, 172, 193, 194, 198–204

Sedgwick, Eve, 134, 140
Semmel, Bernard, 35
Seneca the Elder, 19
Sepia (magazine), 275
Seuss, Dr. (Theodor S. Geisel): *Horton Hatches a Who*, 102
Sexton, Anne, 197
Shakespeare, William, 46; *King Lear*, 70, 112, 113, 116, 117, 120–21, 125; *Winter's Tale*, 1, 15n. 29, 15–16n. 34, 42–43, 46
Silverstein, Shel, 106
Simon, Rita J., 280
Simpson, Eileen, 77n. 6
Skin color, 183, 185, 253, 256, 262, 269, 275, 283, 292
Smith, Bessie, 179, 181, 188, 189
Smith, Janet Farrell, 256
Solinger, Rickie, 4–5, 137, 144
Soyinka, Wole, 49
Star Wars (film), 106
Stegner, Wallace, 253
Stepmother, 35–36, 43, 92, 106
Stevenson, Robert Louis: *Treasure Island*, 101
Strathern, Marilyn, 294
Sweet Honey in the Rock, 176

Taylor, Drew Hayden, 263
Ten Kortenaar, Neil, 259
Thackeray, William: *Henry Esmond*, 32
Time, 280, 285, 286, 287
Transracial adoption. *See* Adoption, transracial
Trollope, Anthony, 9; *Cousin Henry*, 33n.

24; *Doctor Thorne*, 17, 22–31; *Ralph the Heir*, 31n. 14
Twain, Mark: *Huckleberry Finn*, 101, 252; *Tom Sawyer*, 106

United Nations Convention on the Rights of the Child (1989), 277
Usual Suspects (television show), 184

Valery, Paul, 156–57
Van Dyke, Annette, 240
VanStavern, Jan, 19
Vizenor, Gerald, 243
Voice, 171–90

Wagamese, Richard, 263
Wegar, Katarina, 3
Welty, Eudora, 103
White, E. B.: *Charlotte's Web*, 10, 102–7; "Death of a Pig," 106; *Elements of Style*, 103; *Stuart Little*, 112
Whiteness, 137, 256, 271, 273–74
Whitman, Walt, 173, 174, 180
Wild West, myth of, 253–54
Williams, Brad, 256, 271
Willsie, Honore, 91–92
Winterson, Jeanette, 5, 8, 9, 184; *Oranges Are Not the Only Fruit*, 135–47
Women's Day, 92
Wong, Hertha, 238, 239, 246
Woodward, Pauline, 243

Yonge, Charlotte, 19
Young, Robert J. C., 55n. 18